NIGHTSONG

Performance, Power, and Practice in South Africa

Veit Erlmann

With an Introduction by **Joseph Shabalala**

The University of Chicago Press

Chicago and London

VEIT ERLMANN is currently the Heisenberg Fellow in the Department of Social Anthropology of the Freie Universität Berlin. He is the author of several books and monographs, including *African Stars,* published by the University of Chicago Press in 1991.

The University of Chicago Press, Chicago 60637
The University of Chicago Press, Ltd., London

© 1996 by The University of Chicago
All rights reserved. Published 1996
Printed in the United States of America

05 04 03 02 01 00 99 98 97 96   1 2 3 4 5

ISBN 0-226-21720-5 (cloth)
      0-226-21721-3 (paper)

Library of Congress Cataloging-in-Publication Data

Erlmann, Veit.
    Nightsong : performance, power, and practice in South Africa /
Veit Erlmann ; with an introduction by Joseph Shabalala.
        p.   cm. — (Chicago studies in ethnomusicology)
    Includes bibliographical references, discography (p.   ), and
index.
    Isicathamiya—History and criticism.   2. Zulu (African people)—
South Africa—Music—History and criticism.   3. Folk music—South
Africa—History and criticism.   4. Folk songs, Zulu—South Africa—
History and criticism.   I. Title.   II. Series.
ML3760.E76   1996
782.42162'963986068—dc20   94-24977
                                                          CIP
                                                          MN

Portions of Chapter 3 appeared earlier as "Migration and Performance: Zulu Migrant
Workers' Isicathamiya Performance in South Africa, 1890–1950," in *Ethnomusicology*
34, no. 2 (Spring-Summer 1990): 199–220. © Society for Ethnomusicology, Inc.
The Chapter 11 interview with Joseph Shabalala appeared earlier as "A Conversation
with Joseph Shabalala of Ladysmith Black Mambazo. Aspects of African Performers'
Lifestories," in *World of Music* 31, no. 1: 31–58.

∞ The paper used in this publication meets the minimum requirements of the
American National Standard for Information Sciences—Permanence of Paper for
Printed Library Materials, ANSI Z39.48-1984.

It is just not possible to live that way.

Nadine Gordimer and David Goldblatt, *Lifetimes: Under Apartheid*

And then, thought Krug, on top of everything, I am a slave of images. We speak of one thing being like some other thing when what we are really craving to do is to describe something that is like nothing on earth.

Vladimir Nabokov, *Bend Sinister*

Contents

Video Contents

A sixty-minute VHS-format video tape, order number 0-226-21719-1, is also available. To order please contact:

The University of Chicago Press
11030 South Langley Avenue
Chicago, Illinois 60628
U.S.A.

P R A K T H I S A

Kings Boys [1'10]

Jabula Home Defenders [5'09]

Cup and Saucer
  "Akhasangibaleli" [9'53]

Durban City Boys [11'51]

Jabula Home Defenders
  "Somebody Is Calling My Name" [14'37]

Natal Universal [21'21]

Harding Boys [24'20]

New Home Brothers [27'42]

K O M P I T H I

Natal Universal [35'40]

Note: Numbers in brackets indicate location in time of the song on the tape.

Figures and Musical Examples

FIGURES

MUSICAL EXAMPLES

Note on Orthography and Translation

Unless otherwise noted, all translations from isiZulu and German are my own. English words in original isiZulu song lyrics appear in italics. No attempt has been made to standardize the different systems of Zulu orthography that have been in use in South Africa.

All direct quotations without a source indicated are from my personal interviews with the performers.

Song titles appear in quotation marks, album titles in italics. Most of the spelling on record labels prior to the 1960s differs from current practice and—even where incorrect—was left unaltered for the sake of documentary accuracy.

Preface

Book titles are sensitive matters. The title of this book— *Nightsong*— is a particularly precarious one. Problematic perhaps as the nature of ethnographic knowledge itself, *Nightsong* is a delicately condensed account of two related and highly ambiguous processes: ethnographic writing and performance. The name *Nightsong* is a slightly (and purposely) disfigured version of "song of the night," a translation of the no less ambiguous isiZulu term *ingoma ebusuku*. It was thus that a generation of performers during the 1950s and 1960s named a performance tradition that is nowadays better known under the name *isicathamiya* (from *catham–*, to walk like a cat). Like marabi, jazz, and *mbaqanga*, this rich body of competitive song and dance is an expression of the creativity of black South Africans. Performed by male a cappella choirs, isicathamiya performance is also located at the core of black, isiZulu-speaking migrants' social practice. Although over the past few years isicathamiya attracted a great deal of international attention, the culture and consciousness of South Africa's migrant labor army—the performances, leisure activities of miners, domestic servants, and so on—remain largely unknown.

This book is an attempt to translate, to rewrite one fragment, one set of practices from this world of migrant labor. But this endeavor, as the title *Nightsong* indicates, throws into sharp relief some of anthropology's most vexed problems. For the translation of the images of one cultural domain into those of another, as Michel de Certeau has pointed out, was an operation that only acquired the role of an "economy," a "hermeneutics of the Other" with the "discovery" and the subsequent writing of the savage. This "economy of translation," as de Certeau calls it, replaced the "being-there of a beginning with a transformation which unravels on the surface of languages, which makes a single meaning pass from tongue to tongue" (de Certeau 1988, 223). This transformation makes the being "come from the foreign place itself, where it is the gold mine hidden under an exotic exteriority, the truth to be discerned beneath primitive babble" (224). In the end, de Certeau concludes, the point of departure for this operation, the writing of the Other, "becomes a place for *truth*, since here the *discourse which comprehends the world* is in use" (225).

In an earlier critique of the economy of translation and while searching for a more self-reflective role of the translator, Walter Benjamin wrote that to "grasp the genuine relationship between an original and a translation, requires an investigation analogous to the argumentation by which a critique of cognition would have to prove the impossibility of an image theory. There it is a matter of showing that in cognition there could be no objectivity . . . if it dealt with images of reality; here it can be demonstrated that no translation would be possible if in its ultimate essence it strove for likeness to the original." Translation, Benjamin concludes, does not produce copies but an echo of the original. It is a "provisional way of coming to terms with the foreignness of languages" (Benjamin 1968, 73). In analogy to this, anthropology, ethnomusicology, performance studies, and other related fields could be seen as the study of the way in which societies recognize themselves through their projections of foreignness.

Nobody could have been more alert to the ambiguity and multilayeredness of translation than Joseph Shabalala, leader of the highly acclaimed Durban-based choir Ladysmith Black Mambazo, one of the finest representatives of this tradition today. "When you say in English 'nightsong,' it is good, it is perfect," Shabalala commented on my choice of title. "But when you come to isiZulu, *ingoma ebusuku*, they'll say 'hmm.'" Shabalala, an experienced "translator," mediator, and traveler between many worlds, seemed to be aware of the disjunction and fragmentation that occurs when different cultural realities converse with each other, translate each other, come to terms with each other's foreignness. *Nightsong* was acceptable as an English title, he seemed to imply, because it did not pretend to translate the foreign into the familiar, to render, as Stephen Tyler has written, "the meanings of another folk in terms already known to us" (Tyler 1986, 137).[1] From Shabalala's perspective, *Nightsong* was as good, bad, or foreign as any other English word.

But Shabalala, a master of deep isiZulu and suave rhetoric, also knew of the profound ambiguity of metaphor. For *ingoma ebusuku* is anything but an unequivocal term in isiZulu, either. He continued, "The name *ingoma ebusuku* was not well received by the people, because it just cursed them. They said, oh, those *ingoma ebusuku*, making noise every time. Because they thought the sound is not good." Among speakers of isiZulu, then, the term *ingoma ebusuku* translates quite diverse perspectives. Township residents, for instance, used the term in a pejorative sense to refer to the "uncivilized" habit of singing at night, when "regular," educated townspeople and their families stay indoors and sleep. For isicathamiya practitioners, on the other hand, the term contains a hidden, more positive meaning. The night has, of course, never been an ideal time for black South

Africans—township residents and hostel dwellers alike—when the insecurity that characterizes their lives during daytime is heightened by crime, curfews, and police raids. And thus the practice of staging isicathamiya competitions on Saturday nights not only takes account of the timing of industrial labor but in part at least is also conditioned by curfew regulations and unsafe streets. No one can leave the venue before the early Sunday morning hours, but no one—or few (such as police and gangsters)—can enter, either. The night, in order words, sets isicathamiya apart from the flow of ordinary events during daytime, determined as it mostly is by forces outside migrants' control: train schedules, clocking in and out at work, pass laws that determine when they are allowed to be in a certain place and for how long, and so on. The nightsongs, then, create, in James Boon's phrase, "privileged operational zones," which temporarily protect their practitioners from outside intervention by the hegemonic order.

There can be no doubt, then, that Shabalala's interpretation (and critique) of the term *ingoma ebusuku* alludes to one of the central predicaments in the ethnographic discourse. Not only is something always lost when an expression travels from one language to another. Like Benjamin's translator, the ethnographer is never just dealing with a given text encapsulating an unmediated, authentic meaning which he only needs to translate into his own language. Understanding, as Mikhail Bakhtin has written, cannot be understood as a "translation from the other's language into one's own language" (Bakhtin 1986, 141). The ethnographer lives "in a world of others' words" (143). In this sense, the title of this book belongs to no single cultural reality as such. By choosing *Nightsong* as the title of this book I seek to disclose the disfigurement inherent in translation, to break down and reshape our language by transporting the ambiguity of the isiZulu term into an unfamiliar, synthetic term. I want to produce—as J. Hollander has suggested—"transformed instances of the original, not authoritative textual representations of it" (Hollander 1959, 23). Instead of anglicizing an isiZulu term, the word *Nightsong* "zuluizes" the English language.

Clearly, then, ambiguity lies at the very heart of the ethnographic process. Like Nabokov's Professor Adam Krug, ethnographers are slaves of images. Condemned to tell stories we cannot control, we nevertheless constantly rebel against the necessity to "speak of one thing being like some other thing." For in ethnographic writing, or, at any rate in the more innovative texts produced within the genre, the relation of fact to allegory is an intensely contested domain (Clifford 1986, 119). At the same time, for a more self-consciously critical anthropology, this strange configuration between empirical description and allegorical narrative has served as a reminder of the old promise of the Enlightenment for a progressive understanding of the world.

What thus in ethnography reflects a troubled and uncertain moment in the history of anthropological thought, in performance is inscribed in its own, innermost constitution. Here images and ambiguity are of the very essence. To say how the things are, performers cannot but express themselves in images of what these things are not. At first glance, though, the nightsongs—beneath all the stark expression of grief and despair—often remain remarkably laconic and unambiguous:

> *Nisibona nje, nisibona silapha siphuma kude siphuma le ebunzimeni.*
>   As you see us here, we come from afar.
> *Sihamba nje sizulazula senziwa yindaba zokuhlupheka.*
>   We are roaming around because of suffering.
> *Sashiya abazali nezihlobo zethu.*
>   We left our parents and family.
> *Thina sihamba sifuna imali.*
>   We travel in search of money.
> *Ngihlupheka, ngihlupheka, ngihlupheka.*
>   I suffer, I suffer, I suffer.
>
>   Greytown Evening Birds
>
> *Namhlanje kimi, kukude emuva, kukude phambili.*
>   Today, for me, the past is far and the future is far.
>
>   Empangeni Home Tigers

Sparse and plainspoken words about travel, home, places, and distances. Deepsongs, sorrow songs, as W. E. B. DuBois once called a sister genre, the African American spiritual. However, far from being a case of impoverished, detraditionalized poetry, these song texts deliberately shun a rich, metaphoric vocabulary. Like countless other songs, these verses by the Greytown Evening Birds and the Empangeni Home Tigers speak of the unreconcilable alienation of migrant life, of the given and now, the iron law that forces the individual and the present together in an arbitrary and abstract logic ("today, for me"). In fact, nightsongs are condensates of experience, compact, matter-of-fact descriptions of an amorphous "here," of a void, an in-between that does not have a space. The locus of these nocturnal performances is the nowhere of "roaming," their affective condition one of "suffering."

But to say how the things are, is always a condition for imagining another order of things, in much the same way as to "imagine another kind of world is always a judgment about this one" (Beidelman 1986, 204). And thus, the nightsongs seem to be marked by an opposition between verbal descriptions of the naturalness of the today and its deprivation and unspoken, embodied imaginings of the past and the future. What can be remembered and what is imaginable may perhaps not be cast in words, but the yesterday and the tomorrow are inscribed in movement, texture, and color—beyond the grasp of the today, protected from its immediacy by their evasiveness. The truth of movement, sound, and color cannot be reduced to the tradition that produced them; nor can it be called into question because the site of these symbols is fantasy.

The performers of the nightsongs know this. Their practice is animated by the knowledge that the ambiguity of symbolic action, the incompleteness of a known completion, as the literary critic Charles Morgan might say, is both a source of power and the cause of a deep dilemma. Power (*amandla*), a key concept in Zulu thought, is essential for the continuation of life and the things that happen in it (Berglund 1976; 247). The ability to shape and continually re-create the world inheres in all things material, in the forces of the supernatural world and in human action. Performers, like diviners and healers, by virtue of their ability to direct the flow of power through special channels of words, music, and bodily movement, are privileged in handling power. This is why performance, unlike ethnographic description, potentially transforms individuals into persons in control of their own destiny.

But if, on the other hand, it is "just not possible to live that way"—and all migrant performers seem to agree on that point—and if, as Vladimir Nabokov suggests, we are all slaves of the images, why perform at all? Why write stories and ethnographies? Why sing songs and dance dances? Do all these things really make us slaves? Certainly, there is a good deal in the evidence which this study hopes to present to suggest that isicathamiya is an attempt to mediate between powerful and seemingly insurmountable dividing lines between center and periphery, "here" and "home," and that the engrossing, invigorating power of this mediation derives from the sensory, embodied configurations of an imagined social order beyond the here and now. In the final analysis, however, isicathamiya seems to be marked by a deep tension it cannot resolve between the impossibility "to live that way" and the ultimate impotency of images to materialize in real terms an alternative way of living.

Ultimately, this tension is the result of a dialectic that characterizes all performance and especially, all music. Music everywhere says yes and no at the same time. The ideological nature of music, its affirmative element, as Theodor W. Adorno once wrote, does not, unlike the other arts, consist in its specific content or even in the harmonious functioning of its form. It resides in the fact that it only commences, that it *is* music in the first place.

> The language of music per se is magic, and the entry into its isolated sphere a priori has something of enchantment. The suspension of empirical reality and the constitution of a second one sui generis says, almost beforehand: it is well. In its origin, the tone is consolatory and bound up with this original moment. At the same time, this does not precisely denote music's place as truth. One might say that, as totality, music is under the spell of the appearance in a more immediate and complete way. But it embraces this a priori from the outside, as it were, in some kind of general condition, whereas in its innermost dynamic music is more free than other arts because of the lack of objective and unambiguous referentiality. Its distance from reality endows reality with a redempting sparkle, but in return this distance also keeps music clean from obeying reality. (Adorno 1993, 25 ff.)

How, then, to live with this aporia—Professor Krug's dilemma—is what isicathamiya performance is about. At least, so it seemed between 1981 and 1987, when I lived in South Africa. And like any other society whose seemingly immutable status quo not only produced convincing evidence of willing complicity on the part of those living under its sway, but also its own symbolic mode of interrogation, South Africa was then bubbling with discourses and practices that not only questioned the legitimacy of this order but also provided the imaginable with a form. Like any serious study of these traditions, *Nightsong* perforce had to be a quest for the spiritual, intellectual, and creative wellsprings of another order. If, I asked myself, the ultimate downfall of the forces of racism, oppression, and apartheid was but a matter of the objective course of history, what are the subjective resources of the new South Africa? How will South Africans, to use the words of poet Wally Serote, "completely clean the streets and alleys of the townships" in which they "killed each other, raped each other, abandoned our children to a merciless future"?

Such questions are, of course, not novel in South African cultural studies and have been used in probing many a musical, theatrical, and literary tradition. But the controversies to which these questions gave rise time and again have nowhere been surrounded by more confusion and often downright ridiculous comment than in the debates about such forms of migrant expressive culture as isicathamiya. Some authors commenting, for example, on the songs of Ladysmith Black Mambazo and Abafana Baseqhudeni, have objected to the "disgustingly sexist" lyrics and have wondered "whether tribal issues, religion, and cattle are issues worth singing about in 1980" (Andersson, 1981, 127 ff.). Others, echoing widespread Western resentment against Paul Simon's album *Graceland* and Ladysmith Black Mambazo, have found it "difficult to imagine that either the group or its music will have any positive impact on the black struggle for liberation" (Hamm 1989, 300). The African National Congress's (ANC) cultural officer Barbara Masekela, on the other hand, has "reclaimed" isicathamiya as an "authentic South African people's art form" that had simply been "buried by the notorious Gallo and other institutionalized capitalist-oriented recording companies." It was only through the "development of the struggle," she argues that isicathamiya had gained a "rightful place in our people's culture" (Campschreur and Divendal 1989, 255).

In reality, of course, there is nothing about the nightsongs that needed to be retrieved or instrumentalized for the "struggle." Isicathamiya performance itself is—and always has been—a form of struggle. Tribal issues, religion, and cattle are the topics of so many isicathamiya songs, not because, as Muff Andersson has claimed, most choirs have "absorbed the attitudes the state wants of them" (Andersson 1981, 128), but because these are precisely some of the problems that are on the minds of South African migrants. The songs and dances express the concerns—patriarchal as they may be—of a great many migrant laborers and South African men who more than ever worry about domestic cohesion and parental authority. However, unlike the more visible manifestations of black dissent and opposition such as strikes, street barricades, and political rallies, isicathamiya performance is rarely written about in the press. In contrast to mass demonstrations and street rioting it has never become the subject of academic seminars, and its performers—differing here again from the more conspicuous actors on South Africa's public stage—have seldom stood in front of TV cameras. Thus, instead of gaining a place, of becoming a particle in a predefined whole, isicathamiya is itself a place-maker. Rather than being authenticated by a totality, the nightsongs authenticate and author individual selves; instead of an art form of the people, isicathamiya is an art form of people.

However, like all popular practice, the symbolic construction of a world beyond the here and now is a Janus-faced process involving both accom-

modation and resistance. Every established order, including the most re-
pressive system of minority rule, tends to naturalize its own arbitrariness
(Bourdieu 1977, 164). But such orders also frequently exhibit willing
complicity on the part of the powerless. Thus, when isicathamiya competitions generate images of power, home-oriented fraternity, and solidarity
based on "home-boy" networks, they clearly evoke a particular gendered
order of things, an order marked by parental authority and male-centered
gender relations. The performances become part of the hegemonic construction of asymmetrical gender and family relations. (And it is because
isicathamiya, after all, emphasizes the "family at home," that the genre
received generous support from the apartheid media during the 1950s and
1960s.)

On the other hand, hegemonic power relations sometimes also generate
their own peculiar mode of interrogation. While performance may not occupy the privileged place among the subversive practices of the powerless
that some authors have attributed to it, it may, as recent ethnographies of
performance indicate, assume a key role in the dialectic between structure,
as the givenness of the world, and agency. Even where this performative
mode of interrogation does not query the legitimacy of social inequity per
se, it does at times generate alternative power relations. Resistance, as
James Scott points out, does not engender powerless realms of social interaction. The power relations generated among subordinate groups are often
the only countervailing power to the hegemonic force. The "hidden transcript" of subordinate groups "reacts back on the public transcript . . . by
opposing its own variant form of social domination against that of the
dominant elite. Both are realms of power and interests" (Scott 1990, 27).

Scott's discussion of the dialectic of power and resistance is a strong
challenge to students of performance not to seek easy, either/or answers
to the problems raised by counterhegemonic social practice in oppressive
societies. Collective resistance, although it may provide direction and im-
petus to the action of the powerless, does not necessarily create integrated,
consensual communities. I therefore hesitate to see isicathamiya choirs as
what Greil Marcus, somewhere, has called "images of community." Instead, *Nightsong* portrays isicathamiya performance as a force field of conflicting and intersecting interests, aesthetics, and ideologies.

Thus, in embodying and giving form to the structural dispositions and
discrepancies of South African society, migrant performers are neither reactionary, obsolete or revolutionary. Through isicathamiya migrant laborers have acted and reflected upon their experience in a multitude of ways,

using a vast spectrum of aesthetic forms and ideologies. At the very least, isicathamiya is an attempt to return to the world some coherence and tractability, to mend a fabric of social relations that has been torn apart by forces beyond the grasp of its practitioners. And as such, the nightsongs challenge us to accept, as we write and perform, the predicament in which we live and, at the same time, to continue the search for accounts as truthful as possible of that which is like nothing on earth.

In the account that follows, I have adopted a writing strategy that, like the title of the book, highlights rather than obliterates the foreignness and shifts that mark ethnographic translation. The multilayeredness of isicathamiya performance invites this approach. And thus, instead of organizing my account around reified Western notions such as "music," "lyrics," "dance," "ideology," and so on, which are then encased and dealt with in their appropriate chapters, I constantly shift between sources and modes of analysis, introducing some, elaborating on and later discarding others.

The introduction, "A Unifying Force," was written by Joseph Shabalala, leader of the renowned isicathamiya group Ladysmith Black Mambazo. First delivered as a speech at the University of Cape Town, this text opens up a dialogue between the numerous authors whose voices went into the making of this book. The thread spun by Shabalala is then taken up in chapter 1 with some of my own reflections circling around some of the key theoretical issues in performance studies today. Through a critical appraisal of a number of influential ethnographies of the late 1980s and beginning 1990s, I attempt to position my account of isicathamiya within contemporary efforts to insert agency and performativity into anthropology. Following this, in chapter 2 I expand on the dialogue by offering three texts relating to an all-night competition, possibly isicathamiya's most salient performance context. Chapter 3, "The History of Isicathamiya," concludes part 1 of this book with a historical account of the nightsong tradition.

The chapters in part 2, "Spaces," focus on the construction of those imagined worlds beyond the here and now. Thus, in chapter 4, I explore the complex and heterogeneous life-worlds isicathamiya performers live in, while chapter in 5, I focus on the crucial spaces: home, family, and nation constructed in and through performance. In chapter 6, I then examine the dancing and clad body as the site and agent of aesthetic experience and as a signifier of an idealized community. In chapter 7 I look at the intertextuality of poetic genres in isicathamiya, arguing that the songs draw much of their rhetorical power and persuasive impact from the careful combination of poetic stylistic conventions within a performance frame. In chapter 8, I show how these spatial strategies are enacted and formalized within the context of competitions and are articulated in an aesthetics of power. The impact on isicathamiya of the mass media, the government, the industry, and other agents of the hegemonic order is the subject of chapter 9. Although the genre received strong media support during the 1960s and 1970s, I argue in chapter 10 that isicathamiya remains essentially a live genre which is anchored in small, closely knit communities whose survival depends on the ability of the performers to maintain their autonomy in self-supporting associations. If anything, these structures and patterns of social interaction, while frequently supportive of the hegemonic order, may contain the seeds of transformation.

In part 3, the narrative about the nightsongs comes full circle. In chapter 11, the word is returned to Joseph Shabalala, and an attempt is made to thread together the complex and sometimes conflicting strands of music history, autobiographical narrative, and anthropological analysis.

The research for this book was funded in part by the University of Natal in Durban, the University of the Witwatersrand in Johannesburg, and the Deutsche Forschungsgemeinschaft (DFG). Most of the writing was done while I was a Heisenberg Fellow of the DFG and, at the invitation of Georg Elwert and Ute Luig, a guest of the Department of Anthropology at the Freie Universität Berlin. To these institutions and colleagues I owe a special debt of gratitude.

I would also like to thank Rob Allingham, Christopher Ballantine, Gerard Béhague, the late John Blacking, Philip Bohlman, David Brent, Patrick Buthelezi, Charles Capwell, Jean Comaroff, Iain Edwards, Deborah James, Lindi Khumalo, Christine Lucia, Luyanda Mahlangeni, Cuthbert Mashego, Mpumelelo Mbatha, Henry Mdladla, Paulos Mfuphe, Khabi Mngoma, Paulos Msimanga, James E. B. Msomi, the late Bongani Mthethwa, Charles Ndlovu, Solomon Ndlovu, Bruno Nettl, Charles Ngema, Manqoba Nyembezi, Johannes W. Raum, Doug Seroff, Joseph Shabalala, Andrew Tracey, Thomas Turino, Charles van Onselen, Christopher A. Waterman, Edwin Wilmsen, Elijah Zondi.

Caesar Ndlovu for many years has been engaged in a parallel research project that has brought us together on numerous journeys through South Africa's townships and "homelands" and that generated a sustained dialogue from which I drew tremendous inspiration and sustenance. In addition, many of the materials quoted in this book are no less the product of his labors than they are of mine. For all this, he deserves my wholehearted gratitude.

Last but not least, I would like to express my gratitude to Jeremy and Judith Grest, Jürgen and Brigitte Bräuninger in Durban, and to Jennifer James in Johannesburg. During the final revision of the mansucript I was fortunate to enjoy their warm hospitality and generosity that are so crucial when a project of so many years comes to its completion.

PART I TEXTS

Cultures, Jacques Derrida tells us, always write themselves. They constitute themselves as texts, as a web of differential cross-references without confines, an open net irreducible to a meaning. This, of course, when taken to its last consequences, can hardly be the position of an anthropology of performance that concerns itself, as does in fact all social analysis, with culture as a set of practices that seeks to establish meaningful connections between different realms of human experience. Derrida's notions of writing and difference are, of course, one of many theoretical uses to which the term "text" has been put, Paul Ricoeur's and Clifford Geertz's hermeneutic version clearly being the single most influential in anthropology. Regardless of whether one shares or rejects one or the other textual paradigm, the profound epistemic shift underlying all of them continues to remind us of one of the oldest imperatives of anthropology and ethnography. Whether we conceive of reality as traces cross-indexing one another or as documents of human action endowed with a *noema,* both sets of assumptions force a notion of ethnographic representation on us that does as little violence as possible to the various *écritures* that so arrest us. The "other" may have retreated into the text; maybe it never existed. It is not for this book to decide such questions. But if anthropology is ever going to go beyond the never-ending intersubjective dialogue and self-styled nativism in which it now seems so helplessly caught up, some stories and some meanings will, however imperfectly and provisionally, have to be told and retold.

In this sense, the chapters that comprise this section of the present book stand for an ethnography of performance that takes the poststructural critique seriously yet does not dissolve into so many stories and viewpoints. The texts presented here are some of the (mostly written) materials from which my account is constructed. Yet others will be found scattered throughout the book, and one text that lies parallel to all these, the video, will even have to be "read" by other communicative means outside the literary mode. But ultimately, all serve to unfold before the reader's eye some of the constructs in which we, as ethnographers, are forced to traffic and that form the context, as it were, of the complex and conflicted relations we entertain with our interlocutors and audiences.

Figure 1. Joseph Shabalala in Cologne, Germany, 1991. Courtesy Veit Erlmann.

Introduction

Joseph Bekhizizwe Shabalala:

A Unifying Force

To some of you today it is going to be a complete culture shock, to some it's going to be a sociological study, to some it is going to be a revelation, but to all of you it's going to be home. It is indeed a great privilege and an honour to have this wonderful opportunity of sharing with you something I have always considered to be one of the biggest unifying forces in the world, music. Music transcends all divides.

If music is a unifying force as I have indicated, then it is of paramount importance that before we even start, we bow our heads and express our deepest gratitudes to the supreme unifying force, our father who art in heaven. Let us pray.

> Loving God you are wonderful
> You know that we need you everyday
> But today we need you more than yesterday.
>   Amen

The Chinese have a lovely saying, a woman is free to wear her dresses as short as she likes, but her dresses should be long enough to cover everything. I guess I am saying though my talk may be short, but it will hopefully cover everything. I came here to talk about my music. Isicathamiya, now I am talking about the Chinese, if you are not careful I'll end up singing in Chinese.

Anyway, I was very excited when I received your invitation to come and talk to you about the music that is so dear to me and my bank manager, the music called Isicathamiya. What is Isicathamiya? Where does it come from? How did it become such a significant phenomenon in our culture? These are some of the areas I hope to touch upon. I would like to also say something about one of my favourite subjects, me, me and my God. How he revealed himself to me and how his holy spirit inspired me too to compose songs that I believe have touched the heart of millions of the Ladysmith Black Mambazo fans not only in South Africa, but also, in Germany, Switzerland, Japan, U.S.A., United Kingdom, African continent, Asia, all over the world, including wait for it, USSR, our music is our idea of Perestroika.

3

Okay, let us come back from Russia, yes with love, music has always been part and parcel of African Culture. Isicathamiya is our tradition. Let me take you back, back to centuries ago. In 1795 the greatest king of the Zulu nation was born, King Shaka, from his early childhood to his manhood he was a super athlete, a great warrior, an incredible dancer and quality singer. He was also a visionary. He wanted the Zulu nation to become the strong force that it is today. To do that it was necessary to persuade the other tribes to woe [pledge] their allegiance to him and be part of the Zulus; as you might have suspected, this resulted to many wars being fought, many wars.

You are perhaps wondering, what is this man talking about, we want him to talk about music and he talks about Zulu wars. Ah . . . but you see, Shaka, being a great warrior, knew he had to keep the morale of his Impi high, and music did that for him. He composed a lot of songs many, many, many war songs. What we call in Zulu, *Amahubo empi*. When he died in 1828, he left us with an immense wealth of traditional music, he left us a heritage which today still influences all our lives. When an African is doing something physically strenuous, he breaks into a song. You have probably seen African men digging trenches, boy do they sing.

Allow me to jump a number of years, move to the following century in fact, to 1930. This is surely within the life time of some of you. I know all the ladies are saying, way before my time. Anyway, I want to introduce you to one of our many unsung heroes, Solomon Linda, God bless his soul. Solly was, like most of our great musicians from Ladysmith, Emnambithi. You are obviously aware that the Black Mambazo also originated from Emnambithi. We are the boys from Ladysmith, that is why we say "Kusho thina bafana baseMnambithi." Among the many songs that Solomon Linda composed was a song that, like a beer commercial would say, has stood the test of time. Sing with me,

> Mbube . . . ah . . . wimbube . . . ah . . . wimbube . . . ah . . .
> wimbube . . . ah
> mbube . . . ah . . . wimbube . . . ah . . . wimbube . . . ah . . .
> wimbube . . . ah

Okay, Okay, Okay, don't let me sing too much, I might be tempted to charge you. Anyway, you know there are so many people in this country and abroad who used to ask me about the music called "Wimbube" and I said to them, truly I don't know that type of music, until I realized later that they were talking about the song we have just sung, "Imbube." They thought the word *wimbube* was the name of the music. Now I can tell them, like I am telling you, "Imbube" is the title of a song which was composed by Solomon Linda. Look at it this way, Handel composed the famous Hallelujah chorus, we cannot then say all Western classical music Hallelujah chorus, can we?

Let me then answer these questions.

What is the Music I sing called?

Like Solly's song, my music is called Isicathamiya.

Why is it called Isicathamiya?

Before I answer that you must first understand that my people like to give names that are descriptive of what you do or that indicate what they want you to do. Let us take my name as an example, Bekhizizwe means one who looks after the welfare of nations. Please note, when I say nations, I do not mean any particular race, colour or creed. Obviously this is what my father wanted me to do in my adult role. I hope I am doing as you wanted me to do Dad. Let me give you another example, what is the sound that a motor bike makes. Does it not sound like this: thu . . . thu . . . thu . . . thu . . . thu . . . thu . . . so in Zulu we call it *isithuthuthu*, because of the sound it makes.

Okay lets go back to our question. Why is it called Isicathamiya? If one attempted to translate the word, *isicathamiya,* one would have to say, "Tiptoe guys." Yes that is the English translation of Isicathamiya, Tiptoe guys. So you see people who sang *cothoza* or Tiptoe music did not call themselves or name themselves, but they were named by their fans because of the action of the musicians. The word *cothoza* means act carefully, gently with your toes and with your heels off the ground, let me demonstrate again. So you see that it is the action realized then the word *cothoza* refers to: the action or the dance, not necessarily to the lyrics. You realize of course up to that point most of our music required a rather aggressive type of dance. Put the same action in the *cothoza* context and it looks like this. . . .

Okay, Okay, Okay, before I get carried away let me explain this. It was crucial for the survival of this music that the pioneers had to tiptoe. Tiptoe-ing achieved a very important thing: it shut the complaining neighbours up. They were complaining about the noise the musicians were making as they stamped hard on the ground during rehearsals. You must also realize that music moves you, so when our pioneers had been moved they could stamp so hard on the wooden floors that the floors would break and the cement floors would crack or doctors would mend their swollen feet and legs. So we taught ourselves to avoid these problems, that is when the gentle alternative was born, hence the late Alexius Buthelezi, one of the Radio Zulu announcers, used to say *Cothoza Mfana*. We thank you Alexius my brother for keeping our music heard, may God Bless your soul.

Now I want to talk briefly about myself, Bekhizizwe Joseph Shabalala, born in 1941 in Ladysmith. My father and some of his friends used to sing. They were the pioneers of this music. I can remember as a young boy, being at my father's side and listening to my father and his friends singing different songs. The music was the same. The melody expressed the sentiments of the people. I fell in love. I fell in love with the music. I knew then that this was the music I will grow up and sing, there was this drive in me that said, "What are you waiting for, start singing." I started. I joined and sang with several groups and when I wanted to sing my own compositions, my own repertoire, I decided it was time to form my own band. God was on my side. I organized a group of spirited young men, formed them into a group which I called Black Mambazo, in Zulu we said Ezimnyama. We worked hard, we worked very hard from obscurity to stardom. When we reached stardom we thought, well, maybe things are now going to be easier, but we have found that now we have to work harder. In all this, brothers and sisters, allow me to remind you that I believe, without the grace of God and the fellowship of the Holy Spirit, there would be no Ladysmith Black Mambazo today.

I love this music, I love it dearly. I realize that this music which we have helped to develop is part of our heritage, however it is not bound to Ladysmith, it is not bound to Kwa Zulu, it is not bound to South Africa, music is universal, it knows no boundaries. Having said all that, this music is our heritage and thus it must be protected, it must be nourished and it must be taught. It belongs to us, all of us. Eurocentric music is taught at universities. This is Africa. Why not African music? I have come to the conclusion that with the help of God we can build a school or university that will cater to all types of our cultural music. We are blessed in this country with such a wealth of diverse musical influences, we must not let it all go to waste.

Isicathamiya, isicathamiya. Just look at this wealth. Today there are more than ten types of music that are collectively called "isicathamiya." There is:

1. ISISHAMENI DANCE AMAHLUBI DANCE	This type of Zulu dancing is commonly found where it originated at Shameni district in the regions of Mhlumayo Mountain, east of Ladysmith.
2. IMASHI EMSHADWENI	These are songs sung at a wedding ceremony. They are normally led by a conductor, in Zulu we call him *Umbhidi*.
3. ISIGEKLE	Any form of a wedding dance which is accompanied by hand clapping and it is generally of a quick spirited nature and mostly sung by the golden oldies, old married women.
4. QHUQHUMBELA UMQHUMQHUMBELO	To dance in the rhythm of the handclaps or drums. This form of dance originated from the diviners or *Izangoma* as we know them in Zulu.
5. IKHETHO	These are songs sung mostly by the better halves of the golden oldies, old married men. At African weddings, you will normally find a musical competition. The bride will come with a group of singers who will compete with a group that will be brought by the bridegroom, this latter group will also sing *Ikhetho*.
6. UMGOBO WAMAMPEVU NGAPHESHEYA KO THUKELA	*Amampevu* dance whereby men pull off the stick of a shield and use it as a prop for their dance routine. An *Umgobo* is fitted at the point of the stick with a tuft of a twisted skin.
7. UMGOBO WAMAMPUMUZA EMAGCEKENI KWAMXHAKAZA	Amampumuza dance is performed with a shield fitted with *Umgobo* as an integral part of the dance routine.
8. ISICHUNU DANCE ESTCOURT WEENEN	It is dance performed by the Chunus.
9. AMAHUBO EMPI	War dance songs.
10. IZIGIYO	Perform a war dance, leap about brandishing a spear etc.

11. ISIBHACA	Dance performed by the Bhaca tribe at Umzimkhulu district.
12. UKUKIKIZELA EMSHADWENI	Utter shrill cries of pleasure, what we call joyous ululation.
13. UKULILIZELA KWEMPI	War ululation.

I have enumerated some of the traditional music, where they are found, their origin, their type and so forth. You realise, of course, that this is just a tip of the iceberg. There is still a mountain of a variety of styles out there, our heritage, that will either be lost forever or be preserved for eternity and for future generations to enjoy.

In spreading this music to the world the Ladysmith Black Mambazo has taken the world by storm. In the United States of America, our sound has been called, "Inexplicably physical and spiritual, a dramatic introduction to an indigenous African social tradition and culture."

The music of the Ladysmith Black Mambazo has its origin from Zulu songs and dances. Our music has evolved from its ancient form to its current style. In our culture every occasion has its own music. We have music done this way; someone calls, others respond, there is music sung during war times. Each age group has its own music and/or war cry. The mission of the Ladysmith Black Mambazo is to spread our culture and its traditions, to encourage musicians and composers that their music and compositions should remain as close as possible to their African roots. It is to spread the gospel of love, peace and harmony and to identify our Lord as the answer to most questions.

In conclusion then, ladies and gentlemen, I want to take this moment and express my deepest gratitude to our loving God for having made it possible for me and the Ladysmith Black Mambazo to move into the homes and the hearts of millions, spreading through our music the message of love, peace and hope. I want to thank him also for having made this meeting possible. I hope amongst you, enough people will say, yes Mshengu is right, yes we are sitting on gold in this part of the world, yes we can focus on our common ground, rather than our difference as we have been doing, yes we can come together and build, build stronger and lasting relationships. Yes our lives are one in the eyes of God.

I thank God for making me feel as I do that it is a shame, it is being ungrateful, it is being uncaring and unpatriotic to destroy God's gift to us by concentrating our efforts on foreign things. When we were touring the world with Paul Simon in our Graceland tour, the newspapers of the world had this to say about us, "A joyous voice of Africa and the darlings of the show." I think this was God's way of saying to us I have given you a beautiful thing, go out there and use it.

Ladies and Gentlemen, I thank you. May God bless you all. Love,
Bekhizizwe Joseph Shabalala.

I   Performance Theorized

"Kusinwa kudedelwana," a Zulu proverb says. "You dance and then let go." Meaningful human existence, in other words, requires more than one person, one viewpoint. It is essentially a matter of dialogue, of communication within a moral community. Likewise, in ethnography the view of the totality can only be a fragmentary, partial one. The production and interpretation of meaning—through systematic unpackings, figuring out what the devil they think they are up to, and so forth—becomes more and more like dancing, Zulu style: a shifting of vantage points, a patchwork of steps. The search for the system, the whole or whatever literary metaphor else has traditionally been invoked to mask the "discipline's impossible attempt to fuse objective and subjective practices," has been subverted by the juxtaposition of disparate and discordant realities (Clifford 1986, 109). Like the myriad steps that make up a dance, these realities compete with each other as centers of attention and can no longer be subordinated to authoritative, monologous representations. No bird's-eye perspective brings the field within the sight of any one individual.

But where, one might ask nonetheless, does one stand then? And what do the dancers see? What Joseph Shabalala's introduction suggests, at the very least, is the possibility of other vantage points, of a complete reordering of the context, style, intention, and object of the ethnographic discourse. Clearly, historical consciousness is no longer a property of the detached, supposedly scientific gaze alone; Zulus themselves have been engaged in reconstructing their own musical history, and they have done so decades before scholars in the West deemed it worthy of any attention. In much the same way, those whose entire professional ethos centered around the notion of being the subjects of a process rather presumptuously called fieldwork, now increasingly find themselves members of an audience, passive listeners, too, at worst, or, as Joseph Shabalala's address so persuasively and gently indicates, audiences invited to become partners in an emerging dialogue. Appraisal, questioning, and critique, just as they cease to be the exclusive privilege of one side only, are now being recognized as the essential constituents of a dialogical mode of discourse: the production of texts, videos, sound recordings, and so forth has become a relational process involving dissent, critique, and even rejection. As the dichotomies between subject and object dissolve, both lose their inner congruity. As our displayed professional self-confidence as ethnographers wanes, the fissures in the other's world, too, come to the surface.

None of this is new, of course—in anthropology, in any case, and perhaps in some allied human sciences, but it is considerably less new in ethnomusicology and popular music studies. The primacy of "the notes," for instance, as the central object of inquiry remains largely unquestioned even if the attractiveness of plain structuralist approaches has somewhat dwindled and most scholars now loosely contextualize the musical "facts" by establishing more or less unequivocal correlations between musical structures and social structures of some sort.[1] Similarly, although critiques of the reification of music as a product are now being voiced much more frequently, we lack as yet a substantial body of musical ethnographies that offer full-fledged, empirically rich portrayals of locally embedded and globally connected performance practices. Rather than offering here a critique of these and other established modes of ethnomusicological discourse, I shall attempt in this chapter to survey in part the theoretical terrain students of performance practice have traversed in recent years and how some of the most controversial and contested issues in anthropology today—the politics of interpretation, reality as enacted process, and so on—have been dealt with in ethnographies of performance. In order to ground my discussion in concrete examples of how authors have grappled with these issues within the discursive space of extended ethnographies, I have selected eight texts of the last decade or so that I believe occupy key positions in an emerging experimental ethnography of performance.[2]

Most of these monographs have appeared during the latter half of the 1980s, but they were prefigured in a sense by John M. Chernoff's *African Rhythm and African Sensibility: Aesthetics and Social Action in African Musical Idioms* (1979), and Steven Feld's *Sound and Sentiment: Birds, Weeping, Poetics and Song in Kaluli Expression* (1982). Both books, whose many merits have been extensively discussed elsewhere, are dazzlingly eclectic texts. At the same time diary, textbook, and life history of a West African drummer, Chernoff's book boldly remolded the Africanist discourse about music and performance. For its part, Feld's study charts in novel ways the production of meaning through the iconic representation of natural sounds in Kaluli performance. The issues that emerge from Chernoff's and Feld's texts as problematic for the study of performance have subsequently been refocused and developed by the authors to whose works I now wish to turn.

Ethnographic Authority

The first of the self-consciously experimental accounts I shall discuss is Vincent Dehoux's *Chants à penser Gbaya (Centrafrique)* (1986). The publication of Dehoux's text in 1986 went largely unnoticed (in the United States at least), but in many ways *Chants à penser Gbaya* marked a significant turning point in performance studies and ethnomusicology. The second text to which Dehoux's book may be compared is Anthony Seeger's *Why Suyá Sing: A Musical Anthropology of an Amazonian People* (1987). Seeger's study, although it is read much more widely than Dehoux's book, represents one of the most radical departures in recent years from the detached, objectivist tribe-and-tradition paradigm prevalent in monographs on performance, music, and dance. In addition, both texts, apart from their numerous other merits, stand out for the intense questioning of the role of the ethnographer in constructing authoritative accounts of performance practices. As the subtitle of Seeger's study suggests, the nature of the enterprise its author is engaged in and the genres in which the ethnographic discourse was conventionally cast, have in themselves been opened up to critical reflection. Seeger juxtaposes anthropology and ethnomusicology in novel ways by situating himself in the ambiguous space of a "musical anthropology," which examines "social life as a performance" (Seeger 1987, xiii). Dehoux's book, for its part, as the numerous evocative chapter headings ("Une lettre à un ami," "Something in Blue," "Echec," etc.) suggest, is really two books: one, a full-blown field diary full of personal reflections, the other, a meticulous analysis of the lamellaphone *sanzi* and its repertoire.

Seeger and Dehoux, then, do not reproduce the rigid distinction between scientific ethnographies and other more conventional strategies of constructing the Other such as diaries and travel accounts—a distinction that has long been recognized as a legacy of nineteenth-century objectivism, and one that is still largely maintained in anthropology and performance studies. Seeger's opening chapter, for instance, breaks up the idyll obligatorily opening most prefaces of the ethnographer's arrival and first contact by interlacing a low-key description of a Mouse Ceremony—deliberately set in the problematic, holistic present tense—with an almost casual, but nevertheless trenchant discussion of some of the discipline's most tangled issues. Seeger interpunctuates the rhythm of his argument by constantly shifting back and forth between extended diary entries and unadorned, matter-of-fact descriptions of ritual events. His is a prose that ultimately subverts monolithic readings and promotes incompleteness and multiplicity of interpretation. Similarly, the transcription and analysis of recordings of a single song made over a period of several decades and displaying a disconcerting variation of pitch, leads Seeger to a plea for methodological pluralism. But in the end, it is our confidence in scholarly discourse as a means of establishing historical continuity that is shattered: "There is little certainty in ethnomusicology" (103).

In Vincent Dehoux's book, the author is first and foremost concerned to show how and under which conditions the object under study slowly came to constitute itself (Dehoux 1986, 13). On some eighty pages of diary entries, a passive, pleasantly unobtrusive, and at times bored fieldworker emerges for whom everyday village life seems to hide no magic surprises ("reality is infinitely simpler than I feared: 'village Saturday night fever'")—any more than Europe does for his worldly-wise catechist neighbor Philippe: "France, capital Paris, Paris, Paris. Paris first. You, in which Paris are you? Paris sixième, that's good. Have you also traveled America? Gold digger, I am a gold digger, at the Mboumbé site, one kilometer from Zaoro-Mambèrè" (67). Dehoux's "object," then, is the product of a long historical entanglement between Africa and the West in which stereotypes, clichés, and texts, like the traveling individuals, have been in constant circulation.

Ultimately, of course, such shifts of the narrative register, and deconstructions of the conventional boundaries between discursive genres undermine ethnographic authority.[3] The truth in a sentence, in a performance event, or in a field recording is no longer one person's property. It is essentially a matter of conjunction and negotiation. The unruly, multiple meanings that emerge from this negotiation cannot be subjected to a unified portrait, a tableau vivant to be contemplated from a single vantage point.

Synecdoche

The repercussions on performance studies of these alternative modes of ethnographic representation—and of the concomitant weakening of ethnographic authority—are important. Thus, the answers to questions such as, Why do people make music, Why do they dance and tell stories, and What are these dances and stories about? are no longer to be found in the "facts." One of the anthropology's most fetishized procedures since Malinowski has been shattered: the assumption that the totality of a society is implicit in its constituent parts and that the truth of the whole can be educed by the careful observation and faithful description of as many of these components as the ethnographer might accomplish within the relatively short time span of his fieldwork. We can no longer treat emblematic performances, particularly condensed and compelling narratives and so on, as easy-to-use, symbolic representations of a totality. Unlike the perception of art, in anthropology an image of a system does not emerge from the observation of one of its components.

Although ethnomusicologists, dance scholars, and folklorists have always been engaged in attempts to consolidate the boundaries of genres, styles, and other such "facts" by inducing general organizing principles from a limited set of observed songs, melodies, and so on, they have been reluctant to consider musical structures, ritual, and performance as master narratives of society, to recognize metaphor as a central vehicle for the mediation of meaning. The reasons for this neglect are numerous, not the least important of them being the fact that context is an "abused term in the ethnomusicological lexicon" (Waterman 1990, 214). Context, in much writing devoted to performance, frequently plays little more than the spurious role of a "cultural background," a setting in which the drama of performance proper takes place. More often than not, the symbolic multivocality of performance effectively impedes serious cultural analysis. At the same time, contextualization of the sort described was one of the main narrative devices through which synecdochic representations of performance practices could be constructed. A melody, rhythmic pattern, structure, or a genre, because they may index anything from the agrarian cycle to worldview, can also mean nothing in particular.

Thus, some key ethnographies have boldly argued for relatively close-knit systems of symbolic referentiality in performance. Foremost among these texts is Charles Keil's *Tiv Song* (1979), a classic of African musicology. In his book, Keil deduces an entire worldview or what he calls "Tiv expressive grid" from the patterning of symbols—circles and angles—in such disparate fields as calabash ornamentation, body scarification, roof architecture, and song and dance. "Every song," he writes, "like every carved calabash and walking stick, is a unique configuration of angles incised upon circles. While it is the round elements that contain or sustain in these two kinds of objects, the angles being mere surface decoration, in song the angles (intervals) move, dominate, point to the sustaining elements (tonics)" (Keil 1979, 256).

In another part of the world, in Java, Judith and Alton Becker have found iconic equivalences between overlapping gong cycles in gamelan music and multiple systems of time reckoning as well as theater and puppet show plots (Becker and Becker 1981). Similarly, among the Aymara of highland Peru, Thomas Turino sees an iconic unity between musical form and activity on the one hand, and forms of behavior in other realms on the other. Aymara society stresses the collective over the individual, hence, musical performance tolerates little if any individual variation. Similarly, the layering of the parts in Aymara panpipe music corresponds to the binary opposition between two symmetrical halves from a center outward. In the Andes, then, musical performance "is not merely a statement about identity and worldview, rather it is the very essence of such statements" (Turino 1989, 29).

Paradoxically, the desire to transport the reader's (and author's) imagination from the part to the whole, to construct scientific accounts of concrete, closely observed microcosmic systems of sound, movement, and icon, conceived of as allegories of more abstract wholes—society, village structure, or global economic networks—also has another effect. It undercuts authoritative, monologic metanarratives. Thus, in the most critical ethnographies of performance, there is a noticeable attempt to juxtapose the making of wholes with a desire to unmake totalizing modes of representation. The picture that results from this hermeneutic circle, to use Wilhelm Dilthey's expression, from this oscillation between structure and context, context and structure, is complex and perhaps as opaque as Captain Marlow's famous analogy between the meaning of an event and "those misty halos that sometimes are made visible by the spectral illumination of moonshine." The meaning of a performance is seen as being embedded in the interstices between text and context, just as much as a performance becomes a context itself for human perception and action (Waterman 1990, 214). Performance is considered both as a web of meaning to be read from its surrounding context and as a form of communicative praxis in which meaning is always emergent, relational.

However, few ethnographies, if any, have fully adopted a radical anti-synecdochic rhetorical stance. In *Why Suyá Sing,* for instance, Seeger is careful not to jump to totalizing, ahistorical conclusions about correlations between music and the Suyá universe, a fact which may be due to the relative paucity of comparative and historical evidence about this small-scale community. At the same time, it is questionable whether such a position is indeed desirable, resembling as it does more the casting out of devils through Beelzebub. For if performances are described in nothing else but their thisness, a new kind of empiricist objectivism is bound to result which the critique of holistic representation in fact sought to eliminate in the first place. Thus if the study of performance as social practice is to be of any value, the "hopping back and forth between the whole conceived through the parts that actualize it and the parts conceived through the whole that motivates them" will remain central to the ethnographic project (Geertz 1983, 69).

The fine line that separates these two strategies and the constant juggling between them has rarely been thematized with greater sensitivity than in what could probably be regarded as the most sustained attack to date on authoritative, objectivist modes of ethnomusicological writing. Bernard Lortat-Jacob's book *Chroniques sardes* (1990b) is a slim volume of brief, carefully crafted vignettes that relate the author's experiences as field-worker, traveler, and musician in Sardinia. Populated by a variegated cast of highly original, headstrong characters—accordion players, hotel owners, and matrons—Lortat-Jacob's Sardinian villages throw into sharp relief a host of problems that many of our conventional ethnographies have failed to address adequately. How does one, for example, describe a culture and musical heritage as rich and varied as that of Sardinia and at the same time remain truthful to that most fundamental principle of Sardinian music and dance—a natural recourse to the explicit (68)? Lortat-Jacob's writing does not describe Sardinian music from a distant, disengaged standpoint. Nor are all the accordion players, instrument makers, and dancers depicted as analogies or mirror images of larger cultural and social matrixes. Each individual is left to stand on his or her own, with all their idiosyncrasies and in their nonreducible, ultimately impenetrable singularity.

There is, for example, Cocco, the chicken farmer, who interprets the heavenly constellation as a mirror of the earthly fauna, and who structures his chicken farm like an astronomer. And there is Pietro, soccer trainer and referee, schoolmaster, and postmaster in one, who—almost a Sardinian Florentino Ariza from Gabriel García Márquez's *El amor en los tiempos del cólera*—reads out the letters he carries to the villagers and writes the responses at the same time. But Pietro is also typical of a generation of Sardinians increasingly trapped between labor migration and tradition, local patriotism and modernist conformism. His music and that of his older friends—nocturnal guitar songs addressed to local bachelors—scarcely hide "an energy of despair" (107).

But Sardinia is also a land of *senso comune*. The recourse to the explicit is habitual in the native land of Gramsci. The villagers do not talk about the "little kitchen" that underlies their social networks, because it is evident, taken for granted, and ritualized. In turn, the potentiality and the recourse to the fantastic, Lortat-Jacob tells us, become the norm: the mythical discourse determines reality and, hence, it is the latter that has to conform to the imaginary (114). Thus, the way Cocco organizes his chicken farm is a conceptual scheme that is "created from nuances" (19), but its mythological grandeur by far exceeds the practical necessities of animal husbandry. In the same way, the four voices of the choir in Castelsardo, by producing the *quintina,* a fifth voice at the second harmonic, not only engender a commonsense, sensory metaphor of the village's communal accord but also the condition of that muscial reciprocity. The *quintina* does not become manifest unless the harmonic fusion of the vocal parts is perfect, until the choir is *cuncordu.* Here performance is simultaneously praxis and symbol, habitus and consciousness.

It is precisely through this kind of close-up description of almost self-contained microcosms and experiences that, however hazily, the whole world of the villagers, the impersonal behind the personal, and the social behind the individual comes into view. Not through allegorical generalization, but through a gaze that, like the villagers' perspective on the foreigner and ethnomusicologist, affirms real relationships (69), Lortat-Jacob manages to convey a sense of Sardinian life and music that nevertheless remains uncertain, incomplete, and personal. At the same time, through the cracks of the anecdotal discourse, and particularly the fissures produced by the encounter between radically different worldviews, almost imperceptibly a metanarrative, a second voice emerges. It is the voice of a heartbroken traveler, not an authority. It speaks of loss, pain, and of waning selves—among the men and women of Thiesi, Irgoli, and all the other villages, and, more important perhaps, within the ethnographer and narrator himself. Thus, the obsession with which Cocco pursues his celestial philosophy of the quotidian (or his earthbound peasant science of the firmament) contrasts starkly with the ethnomusicologist's indifference toward the inner mechanics of his sophisticated tape recorder. The taken-for-granted disposition of our high-tech world and ethnography's failure to demystify it, are the condition of the ethnographic project. Or, as Lortat-Jacob laconically concludes the anecdote on Cocco and his passage from Genova to Sardinia, "I entered the first bar to organize my trajectory with a glass of wine before me" (20).

Performance

What I have said about Lortat-Jacob's book perhaps also holds true of Johannes Fabian's book *Power and Performance: Ethnographic Explora-*

tions through Proverbial Wisdom and Theater in Shaba, Zaïre (1990), one
of the most important works on performance to have appeared in recent
times. In his book, Fabian advances a powerful critique of past performance
studies, by bringing the issues of the new, self-critical ethnography to bear
on the study of a popular play in Shaba-Swahili revolving around the proverb "Le pouvoir se mange entier." Having sparked off the creation of a
play by a casual inquiry about the meaning of the proverb, Fabian becomes
a close witness to the complex process of discussions, rehearsals, and script-
ing that eventually lead up to the first public performances of "Le pouvoir
se mange entier." But although Fabian devotes significant portions of his
book to meticulous transcriptions and verbatim translations of different
versions of the play from its initial conception to rehearsals and several public performances, he wrestles with the almost impossible task of presenting
a final version. The play is not so much the completion of a script, in the
original etymology of *parfournir,* "to complete, to furnish completely,"
but the "tip of an iceberg." Like culture, performance cannot be represented other than as a moment in a process: "culture" and "the play" as
such do not exist. And similarly, the resultant textual representations—
transcripts, videos, and so forth—are little more than fragmentary protocols, loosely strung together and accompanied by "remarks and apologies
on transcription and translation" (97).

Much of this may seem old hat. Victor Turner, in his later work, for instance, held that performances are more than mere enactments, framed by
certain rules. Plays, rituals, and festivals, he argued, may transform themselves and generate new symbols and meanings (V. Turner 1982, 79 ff.).
For a long time, Turner's insights remained theory. It was left to Johannes
Fabian to produce one of the first textual representations of a concrete,
highly localized performance in all its unfixed, processual unpredictability.

On a theoretical level, Fabian is interested in what he calls a performative ethnography: how to understand Shaba-Swahili cultural conceptualizations of power, not through the reading of a set of symbols, but through
enactment. Past theorics, Fabian argues, rested primarily on the notion
that ethnographic knowledge was produced through the transmission of
preexisting messages via signs, symbols, or codes, rather than through the
events in which messages are said to be transmitted (Fabian 1990, 11). In
contrast to such an informative ethnography, a performative ethnography
is one that is attentive to forms of knowledge that cannot be expressed in
discursive statements, but "only through action, enactment, or performance" (6). Here the ethnographer ceases to be a mere questioner and

becomes a "provider of occasions" instead. In this type of ethnography, performance appears as the ways in which people realize their culture and as the method by which an ethnographer produces knowledge (18). Thus, *Power and Performance* is as much an ethnography of the play "Le pouvoir se mange entier" as the play is an ethnography of the meaning of the proverb on which it is based.

Fabian combines his critique of the ethnographic discursive conventions with a powerful attack on what he calls the "sociologizing" of the concept of performance—Erving Goffman's "all the world's a stage" no less than Victor Turner's social drama analogies. Both sets of paradigms, Fabian writes, do not posit only a sociality of individual actors, guided by a common script of shared values, beliefs, and customs that predate concrete enactment (13). More significantly perhaps, drama analogies in the social sciences and views of performance as microcosmic mirror images of society assume an almost given, monosemic link between the two realms. Following Fabian, both axiomatic constructs have to be reexamined. Culture has to be disconnected from performance by making irreversible the proposition that performance is crucial to our knowledge of culture: "Not everything that is crucial to culture and to knowledge about culture is performance" (13).

It may be useful here, to briefly contrast Fabian's work with the views of James Fernandez, articulated most succinctly perhaps in his collection of essays entitled *Persuasions and Performances: The Play of Tropes in Culture* (1986). According to Fernandez, performance is an essential part of culture. It is to be understood as a set of transactions by which pronouns, the foci of identity, are moved about in quality space with the help of metaphorical operations. Most metaphors are rhetorical in that they try to persuade feelings to move in certain directions. Only rarely do such metaphors pass over into performance, that is, a condition where they become a "plan of ritual behavior," an "acting out of metaphoric predications upon inchoate pronouns which are in need of movement" (Fernandez 1986, 22, 23). Put forth in such a way, metaphors empower ritual practitioners or, as Fernandez aptly says, "More is involved in the games people play than the rules and boundaries by which they play them" (7).

This is not the place for an exhaustive critique of Fernandez's very penetrating argument. Performance, for Fernandez, clearly is an active category that seeks to explain human agency and the transformative power of symbols. In this, Fernandez's work is indispensable to any serious analysis of human experience. What remains unclear, is how persuasive metaphor becomes performance, how and why the acting out of an image becomes so powerful and compulsive for a collectivity. Although Fernandez, in a later reassessment of his major ethnography *Bwiti,* recognizes the "constancy of the body itself as the repository of the resonant images of past experience available for reassertion and re-enactment in the religious rituals" (1990, 108), he remains firmly within the tradition of symbology. The focus on metaphors as mental constructs, as Margaret Drewal has pointed out, while it does not completely ignore the bodily basis of metaphoric imagination, ultimately minimizes the very agency of performers Fernandez seeks to elucidate (Drewal 1991, 10).[4]

Power and Resistance

The returning to the whole, the tendency among many symbolic anthropologists to privilege, theoretically and empirically, behavior which affirms or enacts presumed societal values, as well as the desire to domesticate the unruly meanings of popular performance as deviance or drama, have entailed a marked lack of attention to power relations and to struggles of survival expressed in and enacted through performance (Fabian 1990, 16). The critique of this theoretical deficiency provides perhaps one of the strongest stimulants in recent performance scholarship for which Christopher Waterman's study, *Jùjú: A Society History and Ethnography of an African Popular Music* (1990), is exemplary. Although dealing with a radically different type of community than Seeger's Suyá and devoting markedly less attention to the problems of ethnographic authority and synecdochic representation, Waterman draws on Seeger's argument in important ways. At the same time, he is breaking new ground for the production of ethnographies by proposing to rethink the role of performance in the construction, expression, and legitimization of power relationships in the modern world. Waterman's alternative approach broadly supports the recognition that the power of performance "remains a vital source of nourishment for many of the world's peoples" (Blum 1991, 9). But Waterman's study also highlights some of the intricacies and mind traps involved in unraveling the dialectic of political power, empowering performance and resistance.

A performance tradition such as *jùjú,* Waterman maintains, has to be situated within the dialectic of social practice, identity, and power relations in a modernizing society. *Jùjú* emerged during the 1930s in the colonial city of Lagos from the confluence of a broad range of performance genres such as the Islamic *sakara* and the Christian *asiko* that served to position

Lagos's black strata in a complex network of links to the Nigerian Islamic hinterland, Europe, the Americas, and to the world market at large. Class relations in this nascent urban context were by nature shifting and ambiguous, and performers were highly dependent on the construction of patronage networks crosscutting social and cultural boundaries. By performing in elite parlors as well as in working-class palm wine bars, early *jùjú* musicians helped to bridge incipient class divisions within Lagos's growing black population and to some extent even contributed to the rise of anticolonial sentiment and Nigerian nationalism. But these processes were never simply a matter of a clear-cut political agenda. Embedded in large part in the fluid social milieu of Lagos's predominantly Yoruba-speaking informal sector and the Christian elite, itself precariously oscillating between colonial loyalty and looming proletarianization, early *jùjú* performance represented a highly ambivalent bricolage, at times subversive and yet frequently supportive of the hegemonic order. Thus after the Second World War, *jùjú*, while remaining firmly grounded in local patron-client networks, accompanied the rise to power and consolidation of the Yoruba comprador elite. But *jùjú*, as Waterman suggests, also masks its own apologetic role. Through ordering temporal experience and by framing social interaction in a performance context, *jùjú* provides powerful, commonsense images of an ideal society marked by traditional hierarchy, cohesion and equal opportunity: "good *jùjú is* good social order" (Waterman 1990, 220).

Most *jùjú* is praise-song and visually and aurally underlines a mode of transaction focused on the generous distribution of wealth in exchange for favorable portrayals of the social role of the rich and powerful. As early as 1949, and building on a tradition which started with Marcel Mauss's *Essai sur le don,* Georges Bataille, in his brilliant analysis of consumption and symbolic capital, as we would say today, has unraveled the ambiguity inherent in such transactions. Through displays of wasteful generosity by the wealthy, he argues, "the lies of the rich are changed into truth" (Bataille 1988, 74). Ostentatious squandering "places the value, the prestige and the truth of life in the negation of the servile use of possessions, but at the same time it takes a servile use of this negation. . . . Rank is entirely the effect of this crooked will" (73).

Despite the thick ideological layer of cultural cohesion and social justice, and embarrassingly obsequious song texts in modern *jùjú*, Waterman nevertheless believes in the ability of *jùjú* musicians to critique and resist the "crooked will": "Every expressive tradition discloses the gaps and contradictions that make transformation possible. . . . The contingent nature of *jùjú* performance patterns, the interpretive open-endedness of *jùjú* song texts, and the tenacity of values concerning the interdependence of leader and followers preserve, as they conceal, alternative 'readings.' . . . Talking drummers, the artisans closest to the wellsprings of Yoruba identity, are still feared for their ability to unmask the corrupt through surrogate speech and metaphor. Despite the progressive hardening of class boundaries, Yoruba musicians may retain the power to chasten and dethrone irresponsible leaders" (Waterman 1990, 228).

Body

The construction and celebration of social hierarchies, especially gender inequalities in a different part of the world—a small Greek town—is the focus of Jane Cowan's book *Dance and the Body Politic in Northern Greece* (1990). Rejecting the notion of culture as too consensus oriented and conflict unspecific, Cowan understands the construction of asymmetrical gender relations in and through dance events as a matter of dominance and subordination. But this hegemony, she argues, following Pierre Bourdieu and Anthony Giddens, is not simply the result of some kind of imposition of power from above. It is through "practical consciousness" and particularly the body as the chief locus of that habitus that hegemony is maintained. For Cowan, "meaning does not lie in the body" (Cowan 1990, 25); rather, the body is the carrier or recipient of the internalization of worldview, the agent of embodiment. Bodies are therefore not to be read as signs, but to be understood as processes of intersubjectivity. Their effectiveness derives not so much from the fact that they enable reflexivity, but because they are engrossing.

By examining three dance events—a wedding, a formal evening dance, and a private party—Cowan is able to isolate certain meanings about gendered bodies that are reiterated in various ways by each of these events. The wedding celebration, for instance, consists of bodily practices that recall the taken-for-granted bodily dispositions constituting the habitus, and "visibly invoke a particular gendered order of things" (91). At the same time, wedding events celebrate not only hegemonic representations of the proper relationships between a man and his fellows, but the coherence of the collectivity as such. The dancers are not only morally part of that collectivity, but quite literally "corporeally merged" with it (132). This poses a problem for Cowan, for collectivity and social cohesion seem to contradict the specific gender inequalities that these events construct and celebrate at the same time. But it is in the body, in the topography of the

body, Cowan says, that the two conflicting ideologies of iniquitous gender
relations and a communal utopia are "tangibly bound together" (133).
And it is this fusion of an embodied configuration of gender relations
with Greek everyday practice that make these social relations (and performances, I would add) so powerful and difficult to resist.

How the agency of the body can be reinserted in the worldly drama of
human history is also the subject of one of the most sustained efforts in
recent years at combining theoretical reflection and ethnographic description in a powerful cultural critique of Western industrial society and the
role of the arts and oppositional politics. Randy Martin's book, *Performance as Political Act: The Embodied Self* (1990), seeks to explore the significance of the body as a counterhegemonic political force against the manipulations of the mind that form the basis of advanced capitalism. For
Martin, the project of relocating the body entails, above all, an examination of the history of its repression, and of the division of mind and body
in particular. He identifies three different mind-body relationships that
broadly correspond to three major directions of capitalist development.
The first relates to early forms of capitalism where the social body is highly
visible and body and mind have yet to be disjoined. The second is found in
industrial capitalism where body is subordinated to mind as a source of
resistance to industrial legality. In the third phase of capitalist development, consumer capitalism, the body becomes veiled as an object of subordination behind a seemingly endless stream of signifiers (Martin 1990,
51 ff.).

But unlike Foucault, Martin does not view the body as only being
shaped by domination. It also organizes experience beyond social control
and becomes a site of resistance. The perfection and ubiquity of signs as
means of domination, Martin argues, can never be effective and pervasive
enough to make dominance complete. Thus, if there is more to social life
than the proliferation of signs, the analysis of social practice cannot be
based solely on the study of signs (16). And it is here that the study of
performance, Martin believes, provides a useful alternative to more established methods of investigating power relations. By taking advantage of the
fact that art serves as both laboratory and model in the study of culture, the
study of the performing arts, in particular, isolates the body's practice from
its submerged status in everyday life and thereby reveals the body's capacity
as an agent of change (11). The transformation of an empty space into a
kinetic architecture can reveal much about the felt but unknown reaches of
social experience.[5]

The mediation of bodily experience in dance and the social experience itself is the work in the work of art. Performance makes possible the interaction of consciousness—of the conceiver of the work and its consumer. Although itself not consciousness, the work of art mediates between forms of consciousness. And although the work of art is a form of mediation, that mediation is something other than an exchange which—like money—simply equilibrates. Performance, seen in this way, therefore not only creates the conditions for the meeting of consciousness, but, for the performers involved, it generates the conditions for the production of social experience itself (81–83).

On the basis of this notion of performance, it is perhaps not very surprising that Martin's ethnography of a New York dance company of which he himself was a member, departs in significant ways from our established paradigms of dance analysis. Thus, he refuses to base his narrative on conventional modes of representing the visual imagery of dance. His account is remarkable for the conspicuous absence of any form of dance notation, arguably one of the more conventional means of establishing the authority of the dance scholar in reading the body's symbols. Martin wants to leave his readers with a sense rather than an image of what the dance he describes was like (86).

The ethnography itself, of the rehearsal and performance of a dance, is a richly suggestive and highly personalized account, not of kinetic patterns but of the complex and shifting relationships between verbal communication and body movement, structure and intent, choreographer and dancer, meaning and technique, improvisation and repetition. Throughout, this narrative is informed by the problem of how to describe motion as an activity rather than a sign to be read. Verbal metaphor such as "soft" movement, for example, shifts the attention from what the body is doing to produce movement to the effects of that movement. "Soft" is an image that is evoked by a particular motion that is soft. Metaphors, then, move even farther away from the production of movement, for they deal with what the images mean to the dancers rather than the nature of the motion (104).

At the end of his narrative, finally, in a particularly charged moment of personal expression, Martin seeks to conflate the expression displayed through the dance on stage with the kinetic intent, the desire, of the performance in a verbal "journey through the work." After having related the work of seven intense weeks of rehearsals, Martin's ethnography reaches its climax with the description of the author's own experience of being "within dancing" during the final public performance. The almost breath-less flow of prose in a long, Molly Bloom–like monologue suggests that the unmediated communication of experience, the merging of the subject and the object in ethnography, are possible: "I am alone in here. We help each other inadvertently. We are pressed into a pyramid. There is no more singular action, there is no room. We are the available space. We draw our breath in. The audience deposits theirs with us. I am on top of the pyramid, my hand reaches up the center of the cone. The bob, almost brushing our skins, still revolves. The lights and music fade" (Martin 1990, 126).

Randy Martin's investigation into the attempts by Meyerhold, the Liv-ing Theater, and his own dance company to transcend the body-mind split is tied to a political project of the Left in the countries of advanced capital-ism. As such, as Martin admits, it is of necessity of reduced value in the kinds of society that most ethnomusicologists and anthropologists are con-cerned with: the impoverished and marginalized peasant-proletarian soci-eties of the Third World where the torture chamber has not yet dissolved into the shopping mall and in which the legions of order still brandish weapons instead of handing out gifts (3). Here the body is quite clearly the object of state control, a source of irrationality and of resistance to the ethics of the industrial order. Forcibly reshaped to fit the spatial and tem-poral dimensions of factories and mines, the body nevertheless is not as yet made to heal through the consumption of the commodified images of itself produced by late consumer capitalism. The resuscitation of the mutilated and interred body in industrial capitalism is still possible through the re-course to bodily practices that are tied to and form the basis of the earth as the source of socialized production. The rural home, regardless of how undermined it may be, at least still promises redemption, for the separation of the places of production, the factory, from the arena of reproduction, the home, has not yet developed. The producing body and the consuming body are still one and are not torn apart by the contradicting forces of need and fulfillment that perpetually propel the body on in industrial capitalism.

Gender

In this last section I want to offer a brief appraisal of a work whose theme is closely related to the issues of bodily practice, performance and consumer society already discussed. I shall introduce Robert Walser's *Run-ning with the Devil: Power, Gender, and Madness in Heavy Metal Music* (Walser 1993), one of the first attempts to fuse ethnography, cultural cri-tique, and popular music studies. The strengths of this monograph are many, not least of which is Walser's sensitivity to issues of musicological analysis. Thus, as Walser insists, the most pressing task for the study of popular music is to begin to "analyze the musical production of meaning within a discursive framework that is sensitive to many kinds of social experience even as it focuses on specifically musical practices" (41).

One of these realms of social experience, one that is of particular interest for my own argument in the present book, is the construction of gendered identities, particularly male identities. Not that ethnomusicologists in the past have neglected gender issues. Quite to the contrary, they have explored the gender base of musical performance to a possibly greater extent than popular music scholars. But frequently such ethnomusicological studies have exhibited, like much of the rest of the literature dealing with questions of performance and identity, a certain essentialist view of gender as a given biological condition that is simply reflected in performance roles and musical symbolism.[6] The advantage of a book such as Walser's, by comparison, is that here performance, like all other culture, is regarded as both enabling and being constrained by social practice. Heavy metal, Walser argues, offers occasions for doing "identity work," for "accomplishing gender." Overwhelmingly, the genre is concerned with the assertion of masculinity and the anxieties of men en-gendered by rapidly changing social worlds. And thus, without denouncing metal's politics of gender and without rescuing it wholesale, Walser engages in a serious dialogue with metal's constructions of gender and sexuality. These are based primarily on the "exscription" of women from the symbolic repertoire of heavy metal and on aggressively staged rituals of male bonding. But such celebrations of machismo are mediated in Walser's view by the androgyny present in some heavy metal, especially in glam metal. Here, Walser sees the exclusively male perspective opening itself up to several interpretations that blur hegemonic gender boundaries and call into question the "naturalness" of heterosexual male power.

Walser's analysis of metal's constructions of gender is broadened by a discussion of the alleged glorification in some metal songs of violence, death, and madness which have brought the genre under continual right-wing attacks. Refuting these as reactionary, Walser defends the celebration of evil, like the assertions of aggressive masculinity, as a "hodgepodge of referents" that deconstruct the exhausted and yet still hegemonic bourgeois ethics of the Enlightenment. The cryptic elements of mysticism, horror, alchemy, and images taken to be medieval, are not simply postmodern fantasies or blank parody. They are, rather, modern constructions of power offering resources that seem to exist outside hegemonic notions of economic and material power (154).

*

These, then, are some of the texts from which I have learned and with which *Nightsong* is caught up in a referential system like a "node within a network" (Foucault 1972, 23). But where do I stand? What is my part in the dance? In a sense, of course, *Nightsong* as a whole is an attempt to give a number of tentative answers to these questions. But rather than reiterating here the main themes of a theory of performance as practice, as it indeed appears to emerge from the ethnographies discussed, in the chapters that follow I shall add my own steps, turns, and leaps to the overall choreography. This, I hope, will not only contribute toward the establishment of a context for theoretical reflection, it should also reverse the received relationships between theory as the primary space for the representation of structure and empirical description as the sphere proper of the contingent and practical. Thus, although theory intervenes at various points in my account, my writing strategy resists the determinism inherent in notions of consciousness and human practice—to be observed and circumscribed by various ethnographic means—as outcomes of structure preconstructed in mostly ethnocentric theoretical models. Rather, in trying to explore the constitution of social practice, I wish to highlight the embeddedness of consciousness in everyday practice and the interdependence of transformative action and sociocultural form. Within this process, performance, with all its potential for ambiguous representation and expression, is one of the main arenas of mediation.

2 Isicathamiya Performance Represented

If is true that the field is already textualized, then the only referentiality the ethnographic discourse may legitimately establish is not a one-to-one correlation between a text and an object, a social reality, but that between numerous texts, produced from different social and subjective positions by authors with different interests and in a wide variety of modes and styles.

I offer three such texts in this chapter. The first text (pp. 29–38) was written by myself. It is an account of an isicathamiya competition that took place at the Umlazi Glebe housing complex near Durban on the night of 10–11 March 1984. Like all ethnographic texts, my account reflects a highly synthetic process of observation and interpretation and is more an extended comment than a complete, vignette-like description of a single event. The second and third texts (pp. 38–39) are protocols of a lengthy discussion that took place in June 1989 in Durban. I had invited the members of the Kings Boys, one of the finest isicathamiya choirs in the city, to view with me the videotape that accompanies this book. Caesar Ndlovu kindly joined us for this session and jotted down some of the spontaneous responses that came from the musicians.

Like the videotape with which these texts are, in a sense, made to compete, these texts, then, are not representations of something that happened in the past but accounts of what has been said in the past about something else. Thus, like the videotape, they only show what I saw, what Caesar Ndlovu and I heard, what he took down, and what I wrote in my diary. In this sense, both texts are fragments, partial renderings of an object that never comes into full view. As such, these texts, of course, only underscore the fact that ethnographic representation is not about the representation of some authentic "other," but, at best, a record of what performers say about what they think they are doing and of what ethnographers believe they saw and heard.

I.

The Umlazi Glebe "hostel," as it is euphemistically called, lies on the outskirts of Durban, near car and truck factories, the airport, oil refineries, and vast railway and container port facilities, the largest in Africa. There are other large and mostly older housing schemes for migrant workers in Durban and its surrounding townships such as Dalton Road in town, erected in 1922, the Jacobs and Wemmer hostels built in 1930, and several hostels in KwaMashu. But the Umlazi Glebe "hostel" is one of the largest of its kind in the greater Durban metropolitan area. When it was opened in 1968, it was designed to officially accommodate some twenty thousand men, but today the entire complex probably houses many more thousands of men who live here for the greater part of the year. To get there from the city, one has to take the highway and then branch off toward the black township of Umlazi. Most of the residents themselves, however, either walk or take one of the commuter trains that shift thousands of black workers each day from the "hostels," townships, and slums to their workplaces and back. At rush hour the station near Glebe is busy with workers rushing to do some last-minute shopping at the nearby fruit and meat stalls. A heavy smell of marijuana, called *dagga* in South Africa, and beer mixes with the stench of oil and exhaust of traffic.

When one enters the Glebe complex from the railway line and slowly drives uphill, past an abandoned check point and a beer hall, into the maze of uniform brick buildings, the drabness of "hostel" life becomes apparent. There is nothing hospitable here that would rightfully earn the place its official designation "hostel": no amenities that make life somewhat more bearable; no restaurants, libraries, public telephones, or cinemas. Far from being peripheral manifestations of industrialization, structures like Glebe are "labour batteries" (Wilson 1972) that have come to signify an entire system. Not quite as regimented as the mine compound, but not designed for normal family life either, the "hostel" has become the standard type of accommodation for most black migrant workers in South Africa; in other words, for a working population of some one million people.

10 March 1984, 10 P.M.

The *iholo*, or hall, as the Glebe residents call it, lies at the top of the hill, overlooking the airport, the oil refineries and the railway yards. From the outside it looks like a church. It is the only recreational facility provided by the administration. Boxing and judo clubs use this venue, but above all it is used by an association of isicathamiya choirs that organizes competitions every weekend of the year. The hall is dimly lit by neon lights that hurt the eye; plastic chairs that make a screeching noise when they are moved take up most of the space. The stage is a small elevated concrete platform. A group of men in black blazers and white pants are busy performing slow movements and singing at the top of their voices in parallel moving fourths and fifths. The group is called Kings Boys; they are the first choir to open the isicathamiya competition on this Saturday night of 10 March 1984 (video [1'10]; bracketed numbers identify location on video). For the next couple of hours, the Kings Boys, together with several other choirs, will run through their song and dance repertoire, interact with their fans, discuss details, and generally just warm up for the final contest. They are in practising time, *isikhathi sokuprakthisa,* in waiting time, *umlindelo.*

The Kings Boys are followed by the Jabula Home Defenders, a very successful choir led by Sikhosana [5'09]. The singers are dressed in black pants and blouses that are lined with white tassles that remind me of cowboy outfits. Underneath the blouses the men wear black shirts and glaring red ties. Mr. Sikhosana's attire consists of white pants and a black jacket over a white shirt and blue tie. The group moves in pairs, with Sikhosana at the head of the line. In slowly advancing toward the stage, the musicians execute a choreography called *ukureka,* raking. Derived from turn-of-the-century adaptations of ragtime movements, *ukureka* consists of two steps forward alternating with each other on each foot. When the group reaches the stage, they describe a circle and without interrupting the song leave the stage in the same slow marching procession.

The next choir is called Cup and Saucer. It consists of nine members, six basses, one tenor, one alto, and the lead singer, the soprano—all dressed in black pants, white sports jackets and licking clean black shoes. Tonight's *umdlalo* (entertainment) is for their "record," meaning that the proceeds of the night go to this choir. The following week they will go to another choir and in this manner some fifteen choirs belonging to the association take turns in raising funds for themselves. As Cup and Saucer move into the hall in two files and eventually reach the stage, they circle around in a single file. The song is about a rather familiar problem in the lives of young migrants, and the words have been used by several choirs from at least the 1950s [9'53]:

> *Akasangibhaleli,*
>> She does not write to me,
> *nom' incwad' encane.*
>> not even a small letter.
> *Uthul' ucabangani.*
>> I wonder what you are thinking.
> *Uzobuya nini?*
>> When are you coming back?

The movements that go with this song are similar to the slow marching steps of the previous choir, but all the steps fall on the offbeat. The arms, by contrast, are gently lifted and dropped on the beat. Sometimes the singers also sway the upper parts of their bodies, the arms held in a horizontal position, in the fashion of women at wedding dances. After this song, the musicians line up against the wall at the back of the stage while the leader gives instructions, arranges the collar of a bass here and adjusts the tie of another singer there. After a further song during which the choir marches around in a circle or shifts back and forth in a single line between the back of the stage and the front, the group leaves the stage.

Meanwhile, the hall is slowly filling up with spectators. The entrance fee is R 2 and goes directly to the host choir. Most of the spectators are the girlfriends of choir members, but some choirs also have a regular following of men. In recent years, however, the overall attendance at such events has been in steady decline and fewer patronize isicathamiya competitions for no other reason than to be entertained.

The Durban City Boys are a fairly small group of only six singers dressed in ordinary street clothes [11'51].

The song is a repetition of a short bass pattern, and the attention of the singers seems to be focused on a spirited choreography consisting of two basic types of foot movement: a marching movement with two steps forward and two backward, called *istep,* and a highly complex sequence of tiptoeing patterns on the spot.

Occasionally, these are interspersed with waist-high kicks of the legs. Generally, the flow of movements is gentle, characterized by seemingly effortless glides. Rapid, outward-moving leaps, for example, if they occur at all, appear as if they are withheld for split seconds. Like in some *ingoma* dance styles and the "near miss" of much vocal performance (Rycroft 1971), slight delays create an impression of pull-and-push, a "groove," a sense of a temporal order working against a strict metronome time. Unlike the marching in file or the standing line or semicircle, the floor patterns in this type of dancing also include a double row of singers who face each other as they move toward each other at a right angle with the stage.

The next choir are the Danger Stars, a group of four singers dressed in long, red overcoats with the words OK DS embroidered on the chest pocket and *Amanzimtoti* across the back. The dance pattern is similar here: two steps forward and two steps backward alternating with faster tiptoeing. A variation of the latter, however, is the dragging of a foot across the floor followed by a brief moment when the dancers keep the leg immobile in

the air at a right angle like a flamingo. Another interesting variation is a
kind of running on the spot performed on tiptoe that interlocks cross-
rhythmically with the song. This pattern consists of a cycle of twenty-four
pulses (= steps) (indicated here by X, x, or .) and starts after the leader has
given a cue. It is repeated twice before it reconnects with the back and
forward marching.

```
feet      l  r  r  l  r  l  r  l  r  l  r  l       r  l      r  l  r          l
          X  x  x  X  x  x  X  x  X  x  x  X  .  x  X  .  X  x  X  .  .  X  .  .

song      x  .  x  .  x  .  x  .  x  .  x  .  x  .  x  .  x  .  x  .  x  .  x  .
```

Then the Jabula Home Defenders, for a second time. This time they are
being led in by a woman dressed in an elegant pinstripe dress and a white
blouse, and although the group is singing "Somebody Is Calling My
Name," she is lustfully chewing gum [14′37]. The men move in an almost
crouching position, knees sharply bent in, torso leaning forward, the right
hand lifted shoulder high and with two raised fingers making a sign of religious faith.

"Somebody Is Calling My Name" is followed by another song before
the Kings Boys, too, appear for a second turn. The sequencing of these
repeated appearances of the groups is regulated by the "request fee," a sum
of money ranging from R 1 to as much as R 20, which choir members or
their supporters pay in order to appear on stage.

The next group is called Natal Universal [21′21]. Their uniform consists of white pants and blazers with a golden M embroidered into a crim-
son badge on their breast pocket. The musicians stand in a line, their shoulders touching. The torsos are almost immobile, while the entire line moves
back and forth very softly. The hands are clasped and pressed firmly against
the men's stomachs. After a while the dancers separate into two lines facing
each other, one line with its back to the audience, the other looking into
the audience. While the foot pattern continues, the two lines shuttle back
and forth.

They are accompanied by some four or five women. While the men
stand at the back of the stage, the women circle around in front of them,
shuffling slowly to the music. During the following song the men stand
still, but the women pace up and down in front of them, some applauding
noisily while others put long bead necklaces (*umgexo*) around the necks of
some of the musicians and point at their chests. "He is my boyfriend," they

are saying. "I sleep with him," another woman mimes, leaning her cheek against her clasped hands. Yet another one puts an arm around her man, while she raises her left hand to her mouth, her fingers moving up and down. Then, suddenly, a dismissive gesture toward the other women in the audience: "Don't you dare to talk to my man."

For the next hour or so, the Danger Stars, Kings Boys, Jabula Home Defenders, and Cup and Saucer alternate in occupying the stage.

11 March 1984, 2 A.M.

Two new choirs, Harding Boys and New Home Brothers. The first group, all dressed in dark trousers, immaculate white dinner jackets, and black bow ties, prepare for their appearance near the entrance [24'20]. The singers stand in a narrow circle, a position that choirs often take during rehearsals. Eventually the group proceeds toward the stage in the familiar formation of two rows and executing the usual *ukureka* double step pattern. The New Home Brothers follow the same pattern except that they advance in single file with simple marching steps [27'42]. On stage, however, this type of movement gets somewhat arrested as the men seem to be marching in place. During all this time their shoulders and slightly outstretched arms sway left and right in rhythm with the marching feet.

Much later—it must be around midnight—and after a further entrance of the Harding Boys, Sikhosana's Jabula Home Defenders put in another appearance, this time wearing completely different outfits: white suits, black shirts, red ties and pocket handkerchiefs, and stunning red gloves! The pattern onstage is much more formal than in preceding appearances, as the choir now stands in a straight line, the men bending forward at certain moments and then snapping back into an upright position. Their hands are folded as in prayer and during some sections of the song rhythmically point to the left and the right. The words of the song are as follows:

> *Ngifun' imali baba nomama.*
>> I want money, father and mother.
> *Baba, good-bye.*
>> Father, good-bye.
>> I want money,
>> you want money, everybody wants money.
> *Good-bye jelliman.*
>> Good-bye gentlemen.
> *Thula du.*
>> Be quiet.

As the group leaves the stage, they perform the familiar double-step pattern in pairs of singers, while their well-ironed jackets, neatly folded, dangle from their outstretched arms.

In the meantime, one of Durban's most formidable choirs, the SABC Easy Walkers, has taken up its position outside the hall. The team, as most choirs call themselves, is led by Alison Gumbi, one of Durban's most experienced choir leaders. Gumbi started the Easy Walkers in 1957 and now lives as a retired worker at the Jacobs "hostel." Although the Easy Walkers do not belong to the Glebe Association, they are frequent guests there.

11 March 1984, 4:30 A.M.

Most of the spectators have fallen soundly asleep on their chairs. Only the choirs present in the audience seem to take an interest in the further proceedings. The Kings Boys come back for a short while, only to be interrupted by the chairman in the middle of the song. The practice section, *prakthisa*, ends here. In front of the stage, a table and chair have been positioned, and after a short while a fair-skinned lady takes up this place [34'54]. She will not leave this spot until the late morning, for she is the judge; the competition, *ikompithi*, as such, starts. Competitions are not the only context for isicathamiya performance, but they are the one that brings the inherent dynamics, tensions, and aesthetic of isicathamiya into the sharpest relief. Other modes of performance of isicathamiya, apart from commercial recordings, include concerts and, above all, radio and TV shows.

Fifteen entrants have registered for the competition and paid a "joining fee" of R 10. The order of appearance has been determined by a draw [34'18] and thus Natal Universal enters the hall as number 1 [35'40]. After the group has reached the stage and put itself into position, the chairman addresses the judge, "Judge, this choir is choir number one. Start your time now. When there's more than ten minutes, just ring the bell to stop them." This is then repeated in isiZulu to the choir and Natal Universal presents its entry title. Their "showpiece" is a very staid song, the singers standing straight in one line with their gloved hands clasped firmly in the manner of classical concert soloists. The entire performance does not take more than ten minutes before choir number 2, the SABC Easy Walkers, comes into the hall.

Alison Gumbi has chosen for the entrance into the hall one of the big songs of the isicathamiya repertoire: Solomon Linda's "Mbube", composed during the mid-1930s and first recorded by Gallo in 1939 [37'43].

The effect of some twenty men singing the repetitive bass pattern of "Mbube" in deep resonating voices is enhanced by the magnificent uniforms: white pants and a black blazer with white lapels, black shirts and giant white bow ties. Gumbi wears an expensive-looking dark bown suit and a red shirt, while the whole procession is headed by a woman in a long black dress with golden tassles. The real eye-catcher, however, is a long red sash with the words "The SABC Easy Walkers" embroidered on it.

The next song onstage almost seems to be an invocation to the judge [41'22]. After the singers have made a deep bow, they sing in English,

> Come, my Lord, and help us!
> Beautiful and sing.
> We sing, so far, so far away.
> Yes, I'm traveling alone.
> *Thalila*.
> Amen.

The movements that accompany this and two further songs [41'22] are very restrained and carefully rehearsed. The group leaves the stage in the same marching style as during its entrance, and sings an English song that seems to be specifically directed at the judge:

> Oh my boss,
> please, baas, don't forget me.

Durban City Boys, the third choir in this competition [45'28], is followed by Nconyama Christ, a quartet of somewhat elderly gentlemen grandly dressed in tuxedos and white gloves. The presentation reminds me strongly of a barbershop quartet, but the group sings a series of religious songs in isiZulu as well as the African American spirituals "Judgment Day," "Where Is a Stone?" and "Mary, Show Me the Way." In much the same way as the term *isicathamiya* covers a broad range of styles and genres, isicathamiya competitions have always been open to choirs specializing in other vocal traditions outside of the nightsong mainstream.

Following Nconyama Christ, the Harding boys exhibit an even more impressive display of religious faith [47'03]. While the choristers slowly advance toward the stage, each singer crosses his forefingers and another musician reads aloud from a bible and occasionally points to the sky like a Zionist preacher. And in fact, one of the songs presented by this choir strongly resembles a Zionist funeral dirge, sung in an extremely high-pitched, strained vocal register:

Amagugu alelizwe ayosala emathuneni.
> The heroes of this world will be left at the graveside.

Ngiyolala ngingedwa ethuneni lami.
> I shall sleep alone in my grave.

Choir number 6, the New Home Brothers, now all clad in tuxedos, first dance around the judge, while the team leader performs a series of antics on the stage. He kneels down in front of the judge pretending to plead with her, then he crosses himself, and finally stretches his arms out as if in utter desperation. Exit in two rows, jackets in hand.

Next are the Danger Stars [48'15]. The group is sporting by far the flashiest outfit of the night: white sports hats, red and golden sashes with slogans such as "Look again," "Have a nice nite," and "Don't forget me"; colorful shirts, red gloves, and an assortment of accessories such as a mock-ruby-studded brooch and buttons form a dazzling bricolage of blazing colors and objects. To crown it all, the soprano wears an elaborate object on her head that looks like the aerial of an extraterrestrial. One of the songs strongly resembles the vocal styles of the Pondo, while another tune is "Gumbaya, My Lord." [49'18] There is hardly any movement here, the hands are folded in operatic fashion, occasionally the torso softly swings to the right, or the knees are bent in slightly. At certain brief moments of heightened emotional expression, the singers stretch and stand on their toes.

After this follow numbers 8 and 9; Cup and Saucer and the Harding Morning Stars. Apart from a new song entitled "Buya Evelina" (Come back, Evelina) and the revivalist hymn "Trust and Obey" [51'42], sung by Cup and Saucer, the other items presented have been introduced previously during *iprakthisa*. Eventually the Kings Boys reemerge with a selection of songs that emphasizes gospel-related material. They sing "Just a Closer Walk with Thee"[1] and "I Don't Care Where You Bury My Body," but also a folk song like "Thula Sithandwa Sami."[2] The Kings Boys are followed by Jabula Home Defenders *A* and the Hysters Brothers, and then—it has become bright sunlight outside—Sikhosana's Jabula Home Defenders. Their uniform has not changed except for the addition of an attractive little feature: a pen with a lit top that sticks in the chest pocket. Onstage, the group starts off with the hymn "Trust and Obey." But after a number of verses have been repeated, Sikhosana starts to "track" each verse, as South African black Christians would say, in the fashion of the choruses (*amakhorasi*). And then the song gradually shifts into the ground

pattern of isicathamiya with its cyclical bass pattern I IV I$^6_4$, V^7—a fascinating illustration in progress of the affinity of hymnody and isicathamiya.

"I Want Money" is the concluding song, but as the singers slowly file
past the judge and into the hall, they introduce an interesting variation into
the familiar slow marching pattern. The song is based on a cycle of sixteen
of these marching steps, but after each eighth step the singers perform a
quick double step on the spot and then turn their torsos slightly while their
feet remain motionless for another four steps. On step 13 they fall back
into the marching pattern.

Choir number 14 is Daily News, and the last choir of the competition
is GMC Good Boys with the familiar song "Somebody Is Calling My
Name." The adjudicator appears to have been taking extensive notes on
the proceedings, but unlike the method used in a number of associations
on the Rand, these are not entered into formal mark sheets. She writes the
numbers of the three *abaphumelele* (winners) on a blackboard [56'39].
The first prize of R 40 goes to Gumbi's SABC Easy Walkers, the second
prize of R 30 is given to Cup and Saucer, and the third prize, worth R 25,
is won by the Harding Morning Stars. While the distribution of prizes officially closes the competition, the choirs have some calculation to do. As
the chairman's book revealed on later inspection, this night was a fairly
successful one for the hosting Cup and Saucer.

2.

What were the girls doing here?
The key is too high.
Yes, we were singing right but the key was too high.
We were wearing nice.
What are the girls doing here, they are obscuring the vision; we should
exclude them in future video recording. Some of our dance steps, too, are
obscured. Had we known that the video recording was going to be a seri-
ous affair we would have excluded girls. Who is that girl? I don't know her!
The dance steps are okay except for the presence of the girls.
Our steps should be polished; some of us don't lift up their knees high
enough.
We should improve our steps when we disperse.

Our manner of stopping choreography by facing the wall must be discarded; you see it's not nice on video. We should face the audience.

The song wasn't fast; right speed; sometimes we do it fast this hampering execution of dance steps.

The front line isn't visible there.

Look at the feet.

This guy is an expert in steps.

The walking step in the first song was old style.

What is Mchunu doing?

Look at Khambule!

Look at how I execute my steps. Look, near!

That one is lazy.

That one is an expert.

These dance steps drain me out of strength.

In future the choice of songs to be videotaped should be ours; we have better songs than these.

Video viewing is good for rectifying our mistakes.

3.

After watching the video, the group carried on with the discussion and summed up the main points as follows:

1. Firstly, I think we should drop the key for voice balancing effect.

2. Secondly, when performing for video recording we should exclude the girls, or if we want them to appear on video, there should be some order of some kind.

3. Another thing as that for video recording our stance on stage must be uniform. When we disperse it should be clear that we are now dispersing.

4. When we dance the step of "writing our name by steps" it should be clear; otherwise it wasn't clear in this instance. We should also disperse in the right way.

5. Viewing is very good; we see our mistakes.

6. Another suggestion is that when we record in future we must be given the option of choosing songs ourselves. There are some songs which are just tailor-made for visual impact.

7. It should have mistakes because we hadn't practiced for video-recording.

8. The recording we did at Zululand is far better than this because we knew beforehand that we would be recorded and practiced hard for it.

3   The History of Isicathamiya, 1891–1991

> In any series of events that together form a story with a unique meaning, we can at best isolate the agent who set the whole process into motion; and although this agent frequently remains the subject, the hero of the story, we can never point unequivocally to the agent as the author of the outcome.
>
>   Hannah Arendt, *The Human Condition*

The writing of history is necessarily a competitive endeavor, a process that invites partiality and partisanship. The search for a first is not only a question of perspective, but also of power. The present chapter—as indeed the entire book—is one outcome of such competing projects. And like all allegories that, as Walter Benjamin says, seek to save the transient for eternity, this project raises a wide range of problems. As recent writings at the juncture of history and anthropology show (Beinart and Bundy 1986; Bradford 1987; Comaroff and Comaroff 1991; Murray 1992), scholars who attempt to chart the social and cultural transformation of southern Africa in the nineteenth and twentieth centuries are becoming increasingly attentive to the interplay of the agency and everyday experiences of ordinary people—a concern they inherited from social history—and the long-term processes of state formation, proletarianization, and political subjugation, traditionally the domain of political economists. At the same time, following earlier anthropological and historical work elsewhere, their studies have begun to raise—often more implicitly than explicitly—such important methodological issues as the relation of fact to allegory, the representation of historical process and agency, and the conceptualization and dialectics of structure and consciousness.

All this advances, without any doubt, our understanding of the making of modern South African society in important ways. Nevertheless, a number of critical issues remain to be addressed. For one thing, despite all the substantial empirical work done, it appears that South African historians in particular still by and large subject the representation of historical processes and of the experiences implicated in their making to a conceptual scheme, a narrative mode that, by virtue of its systemic, closed structure, negates the very subjective agency they seek to recover. Although this is not the place for an exhaustive critique of the "historiographic revolution" (Marks 1989a, 225) that emerged from the neo-Marxist school of historical thought, the point is worth making that much of this revolution, despite numerous assurances to the contrary, is marked by the persistence of older historiographic models, most notably by enduring teleological notions of history.

The most persistent narrative strand here seems to be one organized around the notion of class formation. The practices, worldviews, and social relations of the subordinate, even while they resist the hegemonic structure, are said to be constituted along inexorable lines of historical transformation. The working class only makes itself insofar as it becomes the subject of the revolutionary transformation of capitalist society. Or it does not make itself at all, and society remains a conglomerate of isolated and powerless individuals without any hope of determining their own destiny. This explains why, even in the most nuanced accounts, culture and consciousness ultimately remain little more than the form in which class articulates itself, temporarily, as it were, and against its true, objective dynamics. Take, for example, the persistence in modern South African society of race and ethnicity, for Marxist scholars traditionally one of the trickiest forms of everyday consciousness. Charles van Onselen, for instance, examining emergent class relations in the southwestern Transvaal, now admits to a "cultural osmosis" here, a social equality that reigned de facto, but not de jure between impoverished white landowners and only marginally better-off black peasants (van Onselen 1988). Similarly, William Beinart's studies on ethnicity in parts of the Transkei demonstrate that the social practice and forms of consciousness among Pondo migrants exhibit a certain "internal dynamic" that cannot be reduced to economic processes.[1] But for Shula Marks, on the other hand, ethnicity indicates more the incompleteness of proletarianization (Marks 1989a, 226), thereby suggesting some kind of finality and cohesiveness in social processes. In the end, this view projects the social dynamics of modern South Africa, uneven and contradictory as it may be, as a variation only upon the theme of the global expansion of capitalism and the objective course of history.

The study of performance in South Africa, needless to say, has remained relatively unperturbed by such epistemological and methodological concerns. With very few notable exceptions, the dances, songs, and rituals of black South Africans, by and large, are still being cast as the timeless realm of tribe and tradition tout court. Unchanging and communally based performance practices, we are told, reflect the collective state of mind of people without consciousness, of people without history. At best, in the most liberal accounts of African arts in South Africa, the music and dances of black South Africans are portrayed as mirror reflections of social order and less frequently as a mode of opposition to colonial conquest, racial domination, and poverty.

Against this and working from a critical reading of recent historical and anthropological literature, my account of the social history of isicathamiya is motivated by the attempt to think of the making of South African musical history as a process by which performers make themselves as social actors and subjects of the historical process. More specifically, I argue that the historical trajectory of isicathamiya cannot be cast in the preferred narrative logic of domination, development, and modernization, as the transformation, that is, of a once rural genre through the effects of labor migration and urbanization. Certain forms of migrant culture and migrant consciousness such as isicathamiya represent more than a historical phase, more than a passing moment in the inevitable transition of rural cultures toward the formation of urban working class musical cultures. It appears that the history and meaning of isicathamiya cannot be understood solely in terms of a rural-traditional performance style being used as a mechanism of urban adaptation. The participation of migrant workers in isicathamiya performance rather than in soccer, disco dancing, and other such solidly urban cultural activities as well as the choices different groups of migrant performers make about dress, dance, and vocal style in isicathamiya do not allow us to determine criteria of successful urban adaptation, to "tell the migrant worker who is urbanizing from the one who is not" (Coplan 1982, 114). As ethnomusicologists and anthropologists increasingly come to agree on the nonisomorphic relationship between performance and social structure, performers' and audiences' aesthetic choices can no longer serve as indicators of class position, nor can the stylistic development of genres based on such choices be accounted for in terms of urban adaptation alone (Waterman 1986, 25, 28).

What I argue, then, is that the making of historical subjects, although itself a structured process, creates its own structures. It is, in Anthony Giddens's felicitous phrase, not the outcome of a structure, but a process of structuration. But the representation of this process, as the following pages will show, poses numerous problems for the anthropologist and the student of performance. Not the least important of these is the question of history itself, of how to conceptualize process and structure, how to see, amid all the contingent and fragmentary, the totality. How do we conceive of the dialectic between the parts and the whole, and what exactly are we doing when we, as Clifford Geertz claims, seek to turn the parts and the whole into explications of one another (Geertz 1983, 69)? And if, as the Comaroffs argue, the relations between fragments and fields pose the greatest analytic challenge for historiography and ethnography, surely the representation of this process of structuration must amount to more than a question of tropology or the best-suited narrative mode. Likewise, more is required than the interrogation of the constructs through which disjointed stories are cast into master narratives (Comaroff and Comaroff 1992, 17). And, finally, it is not enough to make well-intentioned gestures in the direction of multistranded chronologies and to open up the historiographic operation to so many conflicting voices and viewpoints. In trying to bring the insights of an emerging historical anthropology to bear on performance and social practice in South Africa, we actually have to demonstrate—through ethnographic description based on a clear model of social analysis—the interplay of numerous social worlds, ideologies, and expressive forms setting each other into motion.

A number of key issues in this project—whether we call it a neomodern anthropology (Comaroff and Comaroff 1992, xi) or a realist historiography (Bozzoli and Delius 1990)—will have to be addressed with priority. To illuminate the endogenous historicity of all social worlds (Comaroff and Comaroff 1992, 24), for one, is a crucial prerequisite here. And, to be sure, so is the need to address the dialectic of indeterminate meaning and social determination in the colonial and postcolonial world. While I shall return to some of these issues later, notably in chapters 4 and 5, I would like to briefly concentrate here on the problem of periodization of the historical process.

To talk about periodization evokes the concept of mode of production, arguably one of those vestiges of totalizing modernist thought so utterly detested by some (postmodern) thinkers. And here I briefly have to return to the discussion at the beginning of this chapter. Seen in the light of the postmodern critique, the latter-day career in southern African studies of the concept of mode of production is indeed worth being restudied. The development of agrarian capitalism in South Africa, for example, is a case in point. Briefly, the position is this: while earlier studies argued that by the early twentieth century a fully commercialized agriculture had practically brought to an end a period vaguely described as semifeudalism, we now have in front of us a much more nuanced picture. The world of South Africa's farm laborers, labor tenants, and small peasants is no longer seen simply as the outcome of a unilineal transition from feudalism to capitalism. Without wanting to go into much detail here, it is clear what all this entails for the notion of a mode of production. The question here, patently, is not whether a distinction must be maintained between Marxist and non-Marxist social historians, as Charles van Onselen claims (Bradford 1990, 83). Nor does the dissolution of Marxist concepts, as Helen Bradford postulates (81), have to prove its usefulness. Rather, what emerges from the ongoing revision of the broader picture is the need to rethink our established models of social process generally, not just their place in a given intellectual tradition.

In this task, ethnography can be of major assistance. By being attuned, at least in theory, to the complexity and unpredictability of meaningful practices, by grounding individual action and consciousness in unified and yet multiply determined social processes, ethnographic inquiry constitutes a model methodology for the understanding of historically made social worlds. Ethnography, far from typifying history and from locking richly structured local worlds into the tight embrace of global models of historical development, contextualizes the fragmentary without losing sight of the fact that systems exist only in connection with and through the singular. We are not concerned, as historians might be, with the order of events, with finding "order in events by putting events in order" (Comaroff and Comaroff 1992, 26). Rather, we seek to understand how human beings use collective memory in the first place to conceive of the historicity of their world as an ordered and, hence, meaningful process.

Here, then, lies the challenge for us when we try to rethink the idea of periodization and modes of production, and what all these concepts ultimately fall back onto: history itself. A mode of production, then, on this view, cannot be a totality in the sense of an all-or-nothing. It is not a form in which, in an almost immutable constellation, actors, productive forces, and ideologies, happen to be contained, and which then passes over into another "stage." Rather, a mode of production constitutes a force field in which certain forms of power, practices, symbols, and meanings constantly converge and diverge. Internal differentiation is presupposed by this model, regardless of the type of society under consideration, be it modern capitalist societies or the so-called traditional social orders.

At the same time, however, to speak in this way about a society as a system necessarily entails some notion of a structure by which different phenomena can be meaningfully connected. In other words, to acknowledge the fact that social systems and forms of consciousness—including performances—evolve dialectically still demands that we separate the determining forces out from the merely varied and chaotic. All this may, of course, only seem to reflect a consensus reached long ago in some specialities of social inquiry. But for students of performance, the principal challenge will remain how to recast questions about the historical development of performance in relation to its context in terms other than those of some presumed base-superstructure relationship. Like the questions raised earlier about history, our investigations of the history of any given body of performance practices can only be interrogations about how such a corpus makes sense for those involved in its production and reception, and how exactly this sense is socially organized and controlled. In other words, a historical anthropology of performance must be able to show how, to paraphrase Susan McClary's words, disputes over musical propriety are themselves, ultimately, political disputes over whose rules of order shall prevail.

But how, then, does all this fit into the story of isicathamiya or, to be more precise, my account of it? How does one represent the history of a tradition as rich as isicathamiya, and one that does not, at that, appear to follow one single linear sequence? As it happens, a strong sense of periodization, of a temporal structure does impress itself on us merely from the performers' own taxonomies of isicathamiya substyles and their evolution in time. Broadly, three phases of isicathamiya history can be distinguished: an early formative period that begins in the 1890s and ends in the late 1920s to early 1930s; a period of differentiation and consolidation that lasts until the late 1960s and early 1970s; and, third, the present phase, a time of uncertainty, and at the same time a period of decline and a moment of renewal.

Before we turn to a detailed discussion of each of these phases, we have to consider the methodological implications of using such classifications. For these are more than simple "folk" taxonomies. They are, as Lévi-Strauss said in a related context, "good to think"—conceptual schemes proper that may indicate a moment of cultural consolidation (Keil 1985, 126) in which certain musical practices and the meanings attached to them become hegemonic. Nevertheless, such linguistic evidence must also be treated with some measure of caution. For Zulu linguistic practice allows for a degree of fluidity that makes the demarcation of performance styles on the basis of such a terminology alone problematic. Generally speaking, the class 4 singular prefix *isi*- refers to a particular manner of speech or of doing things. Thus, the word *isiZulu* in the most immediate sense refers to the Zulu language. But it can also mean "Zulu music," "Zulu custom," or "Zulu culture," and in this broader, and probably more correctly translated sense, the term, like the parallel Setswana or Sesotho, would signify all the conventions, symbolic forms, and practices; in short, everything that flowed from, and through life in a particular community (Comaroff and Comaroff 1991, 225). Similarly, isiMpondo does not necessarily denote a particular musical style only, but anything performed or done by a Mpondo.

Of course there is another aspect to this lexical practice. As Charles Keil has pointed out, varied and ambiguous lexical meanings suggest a great deal of collective and individual unconsciousness and, conversely, a greater power for "speaker's meanings" to define situations (Keil 1987, 275). In other words, the way in which people represent their history to themselves, be it linguistically or by other means, is always socially determined, culturally patterned, and, by virtue of its essentially dialogic, negotiated character, a constitutive element of the production of history itself. Semantic overlay, meshed situations, and discordant meanings are the very stuff history is made of.

"Coons," Ragtime and Wedding Songs—Early Isicathamiya

As might be expected, I begin my narrative of the historical development of the nightsongs not in some timeless tradition before time, situation in a virgin, rural space. On the contrary, the prehistory of isicathamiya starts in the second half of the nineteenth century or, as one correspondent to the Durban newspaper *Ilanga Lase Natal* (Natal Sun), a Zulu newspaper established in Durban in 1903, stated more precisely, it "dates back to 1890."[2] The 1890s were not only a period of rupture, in which all earlier African independent polities ceased to exist and South Africa grew into the largest colonial territory on the subcontinent, welded together into a single, all-encompassing economy. More significantly perhaps, the last decade of the nineteenth century also saw the complete reconfiguration of temporality altogether. For what was beginning to die in these crucial years was not just African independent power, but the idea and indeed the very possibility of different notions of social ordering coexisting in the same time frame and the same space. Time, henceforth, was to be structured and—in both meanings of the word—measured in the logic and categories of bourgeois ideology: progress and, in particular, technological advance.

It is at this juncture that isicathamiya was born of the meeting between two social worlds, two worldviews, in other words, two vastly different sets of images of personal identity, sociability, and aesthetic value. At the broadest level, a number of performance styles were wedded to each of these different domains. The world of wage labor, cities, and racial oppression during the late nineteenth century was perhaps most clearly represented in Christian hymnody and in the prevailing genres, characters, and themes of popular entertainment of the time: the minstrel stage. The other world— the realm of migration, rural poverty, and moral emasculation—found a somewhat more ambiguous expression in a string of dances rooted in great part in precolonial concepts and practices.

To begin, then, by disentangling, at least analytically, these strands, we first have to examine the repertoire, performance style, and musical instruments of the minstrel show. During the second half of the nineteenth century, American minstrel shows had become by far the most popular form of stage entertainment in South Africa's expanding urban centers (Cockrell 1987). Despite the crude caricatures of blacks in these shows, the genre was enthusiastically received by the growing black urban population of the late nineteenth century. More than any other minstrel troupe, one group of African American performers was to leave an extraordinarily deep and lasting impression on black audiences: Orpheus McAdoo and his Minstrel, Vaudeville, and Concert Company. Between 1890 and 1898, McAdoo, a graduate of the Hampton Institute in the United States, led this remarkable group of young men and women on two seminal tours of South Africa and introduced jubilee songs and the black minstrel repertoire to South Africa (Erlmann 1991, 21–53). In fact, his visits marked a turning point in black South African musical history and became so deeply ingrained in popular consciousness that Thembinkosi Pewa, a member of the legendary Durban Evening Birds declared, "Our oldest brothers, the first to sing isicathamiya, were the Jubilee Brothers. That was in 1891."

By the turn of the century, minstrelsy—complete with all its main accessories such as bone clappers and tambourine—had eventually reached even remote rural areas. Mission school graduates formed minstrel troupes modeled on McAdoo's company or on one of the numerous white blackface troupes that had established themselves in many South African centers and small towns. But the popularity of minstrelsy and music hall tunes was by no means restricted to the black urban intermediate class of teachers, artisans, and petty traders. Scenes such as the following, reported from a rural mission station in Natal were not at all uncommon: "One of the items was a march across the platform of all the urchins with a bone clapper, at the head of the line . . . and to the astonishment of all, one of the most heathenish boys stood up and sang 'Tiperary,' keeping time to his singing by the twirling of an invisible mustache."[3]

Similarly, in the mining compounds and barracks of South Africa's industrial heartland, migrant workers were able to watch and appreciate performances by the best vaudeville and "ragtime" troupes of the time, such as Reuben T. Caluza's Ohlange Choir, from as early as the First World War. Caluza was born in Edendale near Pietermaritzburg in 1895 and by the 1920s was regarded as one of South Africa's most successful and innovative black composers.[4] A protégé of ANC founding president John L. Dube, he wrote several dozen songs modeled on American and European syncopated music. From at least the turn of the century, black South African audiences had been accustomed to associate such music with ragtime and, accordingly, called it *ukureka*. In and around Johannesburg and in the Transvaal, Ohlange Choir member Selina Khuzwayo recalls, Caluza's show attracted "bigger crowds than anywhere else," while during concerts in the Natal countryside "the windows would be blocked up by people from all around." These audiences of farm laborers, miners, and compound residents were impressed by Caluza's skillful combination of dance, action, and topical lyrics in isiZulu. Above all, the slick entertainment reflected positive, black images of the ideal urbanite, the "coon." In the minds of South African migrant workers, the image of the sophisticated, self-conscious "coon" and its corresponding musical style, soon merged into *isikhunzi* (coons), the earliest prototype of isicathamiya.[5]

In Johannesburg during the mid-1930s, as Naughty Boys veteran Mbijana Shembe recalls, the *amacoons* used to parade the streets dressed in wide-sleeved shirts, playing military drums with their hands, and performing intricate kicks and steps with their feet. Despite certain overall similarities between "coon" parades and early isicathamiya, the interpretations of what really constitutes *isikhunzi* vary among veteran performers. Most singers, however, agree that it was a genre that was defined less in terms of what was sung than of the way in which and by whom it was performed. In the first instance, it was a distinctly urban, middle-class style, whose proponents were regarded by working class audiences and performers such as Thembinkosi Pewa "as a better group, as a different breed, a class of their own." Early isicathamiya protagonists such as Isaac Mandoda Sithole, onetime member of the legendary Evening Birds and Natal Champions, experienced difficulties in singing *isikhunzi,* because "they used to change voices. They sang like school choirs." Second, *isikhunzi* was a low-intensity and low-range idiom in four-part harmony. The isiZulu term *phansi* (beneath, below) designates both pitch and volume and in a more specific sense was used by the performers to refer to the Western way of balancing parts and the Western open voice quality.

This distinction between different voice registers, as we shall see in more detail later on, is fundamental to the way South African performers think about stylistic nuances. There are other parameters such as tempo, choreographic patterns, and overall rhythmic structure, but vocal register is by far one of the most important sonic aspects of isicathamiya performance discussed by its practitioners. And it is here that I must pause for a moment and invite the reader to reflect with me on a few theoretical issues relating to the problem of musical analysis.

All serious musical analysis must ultimately concern itself with music as meaningful practice. Musical analysis, it cannot be stated clearly enough, is not about structure per se, or even about semantic content. Rather, it seeks to uncover the processes by means of which certain people—socially situated and culturally determined actors—invest certain sounds with meanings. In other words, there may well be structures in music that may be transcribed and described. Yet they are structures only because certain people connect certain phenomena in certain ways that make sense to them. A song, a piece of music, thus become, to paraphrase Clifford Geertz, records of aural activity (Geertz 1983, 108). On the other hand, once they are invested with meaning, these structures do not simply reflect some kind of gray background called "sociocultural context" (Waterman 1990, 7). Rather, as aesthetic symbols, they are "primary documents; not illustrations of conceptions already in force, but conceptions themselves that seek—or for which people seek—a meaningful place in a repertoire of other documents, equally primary" (Geertz 1983, 99 ff.).

The analytical procedures with which intertextuality of this sort may best be tackled, of necessity have to be varied, and as Anthony Seeger suggests, must avoid rigidity. Transcriptions, so-called emic categories, although they are all fraught with their own epistemological problems, must come together to contribute to a methodological pluralism that aims not at the production of knowledge per se, but at "perspectives on a given problem" (Seeger 1987, 103)—vantage points from which to engage in some kind of interdiscursive practice and to produce stories that, at best, we hold to be true (Clifford 1986, 121).

As yet few critics and analysts of popular music have been able to engage analytically with concrete performances in a way that balances the many signifying levels such as the performers' physical motions, lyrics—traditionally granted disproportionate attention in popular music studies—and "music" and that, at the same time, grounds these components in culturally and historically specific contexts. A rare exception to this state of affairs is Robert Walser's account of heavy metal I discussed earlier in chapter 1 (Walser 1993). After having defined music as a form of discursive practice which is composed of concrete utterances that have meaning only in particular, socially grounded ways (29) and as the result of agreements over certain musical choices, Walser sets out to break up the discourse of heavy metal into "parameters" which he believes to be "primary bearers of meaning" (40) and as such crucial to the definition of the genre itself. He thus analyzes in turn the instrumental and vocal timbre, volume, harmonic, rhythmic, and melodic structures of heavy metal before he finally examines their deployment in van Halen's "Runnin' with the Devil." However, much of this discussion reads as though the only criteria for their analytical pertinence were derived, at best, from their functional role in the grammar of popular music generally. That is to say, Walser examines the musical discourse of heavy metal precisely from those abstractions which the concrete utterances are supposed to be prior to. It helps little, if these abstracted stylistic features of heavy metal music are then made over into bearers of concrete meanings by identifying their place in heavy metal performers' discourse. In the end, this procedure does more to illuminate the—unquestionably existing—"split between academic contemplation and popular understanding" (30) than performers' own interpretations of what they think they are doing.

In the case of isicathamiya, the difficulties of a methodological schematism such as the one hidden in Robert Walser's analysis—in fact, the danger of all analytic models—become even more apparent, not only because of the incompatibility of Western musicological precepts and migrant performance practice. Some terms, such as a number of isiZulu terms centering around notions of pitch and melodic shape, even demonstrate the fallacy of uncritically reduplicating whatever "emic" categories performers deploy in their own, often controversial attempts to make sense of their own music. A good example of this dilemma is the term *shuni,* tune. Many migrant guitarists, concertina players, and isicathamiya performers use this term not to talk about pitch relations but when they wish to designate a certain song, a particular piece of music. By contrast, most performers use a different term when they refer to the pitch contours of a vocal phrase. They talk about *indlela,* a path, and some performers even specify the "call" of a choir leader, the solo, as *isigqi sakhe endleleni,* footprints on a path, which the choir has to follow. The idea of something like melody, then, is not based here as in the term *shuni* on the Western reified notion that the essence and identify of a composition reside in its melody. Rather, the form a song takes is defined as quite literally the traces of collective interaction, of a group of people leaving their imprint on the normative conventions set by a community.

As a Western-derived term, *shuni* not only reflects the acceptance of the hegemonic order. As we shall see, it also bears within itself traces of isicathamiya performers' desire to appropriate from that order specific aesthetic criteria of power, for example, such melodic qualities as might be useful for the demarcation of alternative spaces of social action and identity. To be in the possession of that core fetish of Western music, the tune, becomes a crucial asset in the kind of competitive strategies of migrants of which isicathamiya performance forms part.

It thus goes without saying that a structural analysis of isicathamiya songs that, for instance, fails to illuminate the social relations that generate such "footprints" and that merely bases itself on one popular interpretation in opposition to an academic contemplative model, in the case of *shuni* would merely reproduce the very power processes and ideologies that isicathamiya performance seeks to combat by incorporating them. A better form of analysis, as Stephen Blum, in fact, convincingly argues, might thus ideally consist of more. It might reproduce the controversies among musicians and the stances they have adopted, "without resolving the disputes" (Blum 1992, 213). An analyst's choice of terms and models would then imply "an interpretation of the courses of action followed by a musician in a particular environment" (ibid.).

I now return to my story of early isicathamiya and how migrant workers use sound texture and vocal register as criteria for the construction and delineation of social position. A different set of symbols must now be considered, one that had emerged predominantly in the countryside from the encounter with the more urban performance practices already discussed. By the 1920s, the social formations in the Natal interior were being shaken to the roots by a turbulent process of social transformation. Massive evictions of African peasants from ancestral land had produced the farm labor required by the expanding white farms as well as a steady supply of migrant labor to the industrial centers around Johannesburg and Durban. It is from within the ranks of these dispossessed farm laborers that there emerged a cluster of performance traditions known as *ingoma*. The core elements of this body of light dances and songs form the second important source of early isicathamiya.

One of these *ingoma* dances was called *isishemeni* or, according to region, *umqonqo*. It is said to have originated from Shemeni in the Mhlumayo district, east of Ladysmith, although more specifically it was Jubele Dubazana, a migrant from the Natal midlands who worked in the mine timber industry in Johannesburg, who was largely responsible for working out some of its characteristic elements. In any case, in *isishemeni,* as Joseph Shabalala writes in a lengthy exposition on the sources of isicathamiya,

> The performers sit down and sing along with the "conductor" called *umshikishisi,* the one who is conducive to dancing. The group sing along until such time that the hands are clapped resulting in one of the performers standing up and doing dancing movements. Whoever feels the urge to dance or is called up by the men or women to do the choreographic movements or is even called by the 'conductor' to do the dancing. This goes on until the whole group dances as well.

More specifically, what Dubazana did was to combine the upright body posture of the *isishemeni/umqonqo* dance with raised hands and kicking, stamping leg movements. Few elements, if any, of early *isishemeni* dancing, such as an outstretched position of the arms, are preserved in present-day isicathamiya choreography.

Another important subgenre of *ingoma* that is closely related to *isishemeni* was *isiChunu.* To quote again from Joseph Shabalala's manuscript, this

> traditional dancing of the MaChunu tribe is called *phensuphensu.* It means the dangling of feet and may be compared to the chamaleon's hesitant move forward as if to probe the new environment. This stems from the fact that their feet first dangle once or twice in the air before the feet stamp the floor or ground. A dancer bends when performing this traditional dance and it is called *ukubhasha,* lowering of the body to a shorter height, and then slanting the body to the balancing foot. The performer then moves his body in a pretentious manner on the other foot and when he stamps his feet, it is as if he is rising up.

By far the most important set of songs and dances early isicathamiya performers adopted from the *ingoma* cluster, however, was one closely linked with the wedding ritual, both in its traditional and in the Christianized form. Of the enormous variety of wedding dances the ones called *isigekle, ikhetho,* and the marchlike *ukubika ibala* are the most relevant here. The *isigekle* dance, to begin with, is created and performed by women for marriage, and as Joseph Shabalala explains in the aforementioned text,

> This is a traditional dancing by women expressing their excitement at a woman who gets permission to get into the premises of a man in broad daylight (*gekle*). . . . The women dress traditionally. This means

the man is now the woman's partner and this is binding legally. All along, she has been entering the premises with stealth and at night, but now it is in broad daylight. Indeed, this one is the traditional wedding ring.

As for *ikhetho,* it is danced by the bridegroom's party, the *ikhetho.* The movements are "gingerly," as Shabalala puts it, "not haphazardly." The *ukubika ibala,* finally, often rather loosely called *izingoma zomtshado,* wedding songs, is much more common at Christian weddings. The choreography here differs from the other dances in that "the entry upon the premises while dancing in a group is called a march. There is a group that enters first, ahead of the wedding party and this is called *ukubika ibala,* the signal party of the arrival of the wedding party. The leader of the wedding party is called *umbhidi,* conductor. There are normally two conductors, i.e. one is involved with vocal conducting whilst the other navigates the march."

As early as the 1920s, dances such as the ones discussed by Shabalala began to absorb elements of the urban "ragtime" popularized by Caluza and his Ohlange Choir. Around 1925, near Pomeroy in the remote Msinga area and one of the most important regions of origin of the leading isicathamiya choirs of the 1930s and 1940s, Gilbert Coka, a thoroughly city-bred teacher, attended a female initiation ceremony and was pleased by the simultaneous performance of an "old Zulu dance of hand clapping" and a "Europeanized ragtime march" (Coka 1936, 286 ff.). By the early 1930s, in the area of Paulpietersburg, one of the remotest parts of Natal, these ragtimelike dances had first become known as *umgandyana* and later as *stishi* (stitches). *Stishi* dancers wore tap shoes that produced a clicking sound and executed shuffling double-steps reminiscent of Caluza's "ragtime."

In the context of present-day isicathamiya competitions, choirs have preserved a march-like form of dancing known as *ukureka* (ragging, ragtime) or *imashi* (march). Representing the Christianized version of *isigekle,* this type of dancing consists of slow steps that are danced as the choir enters the hall from the door, in files of two. The accompanying songs are called *amakhoti* (chords), and according to isicathamiya veteran Paulos Msimanga are "borrowed from wedding songs." As a result of the musical affinity between "chords" and wedding songs, Msimanga maintains, the corresponding dance movements "have got a similar effect of *reka,*" the "ragtime" steps of wedding songs.

And, finally, in another interesting semantic parallel that ties the entire nexus of weddings and isicathamiya back to minstrelsy, it should be noted that by the 1930s those wedding songs that were performed in a straight line became also known as *ameleki, boloha,* or *umbholoho*—terms the older generation of listeners still prefers to isicathamiya. According to Doke and Vilakazi, *ameleki* is a term that refers to the American Board of Missions—their practices, texts, and personnel—the predominant and earliest Christian mission in Natal. *Boloha* or *umbholoho* are etymologically related to Xhosa or Afrikaans for "polka" and are defined as a "dance with boots on (as on farms on festive occasions, Nigger minstrels, etc.)" and as a "rough concert or night carnival party" (Doke and Vilakazi 1972, 43).

But isicathamiya songs are equally indebted to the musical component of *ingoma* dancing. For performers such as Jubele did not content themselves with a new choreography; they also created a new song style in incorporating the more Western, hymn-based wedding songs *izingoma zomtshado* into traditional material (Clegg 1982, 11). Traditionally, wedding songs such as *isigekle* and *ikhetho* had been sung in polyphony, a fact which favored the transition to Western four-part structures. And it is thus that, with the increased missionization of the countryside, traditional wedding songs presumably became the first repertoire to be westernized. At least to isicathamiya veteran Paulos Msimanga it is therefore clear that "*ingoma* and wedding songs are closely related and have tremendously influenced isicathamiya."

As an example of the family resemblance of these genres I offer below the words and partial transcription of an *isigekle* tune from the area around Colenso (example 1). The song was performed by a group of women Joseph Shabalala had brought to the University of Natal in August 1993.

> *Izizwe zingibiza ngomuntu omnyama.*
>> The nations say I am a black person.
> *Angimnyama mina.*
>> (But) I am not black.
> *Akunani ngifuze ubaba.*
>> It does not matter, (because) I take after father.

As a quick examination of the score reveals, there are a number of elements in the song that can be identified as paradigmatic of "traditional" performance. Harmonically, the song undulates around a single tonality on E, with a slight shift toward something like a subdominant occuring in bar 4. As in much of Zulu music, parallel fourths and fifths predominate, although there are also occasional parallel thirds and octaves. The entire phrase (bars 1–4) was first sung by the lead singer and then repeated by the chorus—a clear responsorial pattern found in most African music. But

Example 1. *Isigekle*

there are also traces of Western influence, especially of Western hymnody. The melodic contour, for one, bears a strong resemblence to Wesleyan hymns. This link is reinforced by the rhythmic squareness of the first two bars and the homophonic parallelism of the vocal parts in the first two repetitions of the chorus.

As is to be expected, for the performers these affinities between wedding songs, *ingoma* dance songs, and early isicathamiya styles, speak less of an unruly juxtaposition of the symbols of the past and the signs of a new age than quite simply of a rather rectilinear historical scheme. Isicathamiya performers stress the conscious display of Western, "civilized" techniques implied in the use of four-part harmony. "In wedding songs there is no control," Durban Crocodiles veteran Job Kheswa points out. "A person sings whichever voice part he likes. But in isicathamiya you must be cautious and not produce a dischord." The notions of orderliness Kheswa evokes here hark back to the other major Western influence on early isicathamiya: Christianity and especially its role in the rural hinterland as a self-styled "civilizing mission."

   The Christian mission stations in South Africa, as is well known, not only sought to convert. Together with entirely new property relations, they introduced completely novel ideas of personhood, community, work, time, and space—in short, an entire worldview (Comaroff and Comaroff 1991). In this all-encompassing scheme of salvation, music occupied a privileged and, at the same time, a dangerously ambiguous place. On the one hand, it was supposed to be the language of the soul and thus be destined to express the true inner side of a person in search of God. On the other hand, music making everywhere has, of course, always been closely linked with bodily practice. In southern Africa it has been so in especially marked ways that render a distinction between music and dance meaningless, the term *ngoma,* over a wide, Bantu-speaking area, meaning both song and dance. It is especially on this fusion of sound and movement, of emotion and motion, that the missionaries cast their critical eye. And thus, in subduing matter to mind, in seeking to convert the "sinful" African forms of corporeality and sociability into their own conceptual designs of cleanliness, self-control and progress, they set in train a musical revolution that was to leave a lasting imprint on virtually every conceivable type of musical performance in South Africa.

   The concrete manifestations of this revolution—the near universality of the I–IV–V chord progression, the distortion of African language speech patterns in westernized song, and so on—have been discussed extensively in a host of writings and need not be repeated here. Suffice it here to point briefly to some of those sonic dimensions of isicathamiya that are particularly indebted to Christian hymnody. (Other aspects, such as song texts and body posture, will be examined later in this chapter as well as in chap. 7.) The most prominent feature here is the stolid, four-square phrasing in many, although by no means all, nightsongs. A further element that can be attributed to the impact of church hymns—and the education system in which they became the musical norm—is the elimination in some songs of such hallmarks of Zulu musical performance as the "near miss," the staggered entry between solo and chorus, and the preponderance of fourths as melodic intervals.

   By the late 1920s, the history of isicathamiya had completed its formative stage. What seems to emerge from my account of the "prehistory" of isicathamiya is a nuanced picture of urban-rural dynamics. The early history of the nightsongs can by no means simply be constructed as a case of transformation of a traditional rural performance style through rural-urban migration. Not only had the changed social relations in the countryside long produced cultural practices that contained strong admixtures of urban cultural practices, but the agents of these transformations were often the same within one generation. At the very least, both in the compounds and in the rural reserves the migrant laborer who admired Caluza's "ragtime" was in close contact with the farm laborer who preferred the virile dance steps of *isishemeni*.

Crocodiles and Evening Birds: The Formative Period of Isicathamiya

Both Johannesburg and Durban had witnessed periods of explosive urban growth immediately after the First World War that did much to sharpen the class contours of their black population. It is in this situation of intense social restructuring during the 1920s that the first full-fledged isicathamiya choirs were formed. But the reconstruction of the chronology of early isicathamiya choirs is complicated by both contradictory oral evidence and the fact that many choirs frequently did not record until ten or more years after their formation. However, irrespective of these uncertainties of research in South African black musical traditions, the choir that can be established with some degree of certainty as one of the oldest isicathamiya groups, was the Crocodiles. Founded in 1914 in Botha's Hill near Durban by Lutheran preacher and land-owning farmer Mzobe and members of his family, the Crocodiles initially confined their activities to rural wedding ceremonies in Umbumbulu and Inanda on the outskirts of Durban, performing *ingoma, izingoma zomtshado,* and folk songs (fig. 2). But when Isaac Mzobe assumed leadership of the group in 1920–21, the Crocodiles soon came to dominate male a cappella performances in Natal.

A further group that must be counted among the pioneer choirs, one whose history remains somewhat elusive, was called Amanzimtoti. Crocodiles veteran Enoch Mzobe maintains that Amanzimtoti was led by Caluza, after he had assumed the headship of the new school of music at Adams College in 1936. An alternative view is held by Ngweto Zondo of the Johannesburg-based Crocodile Singers which was founded in 1938 and is not to be confused with the Durban group of the same name (fig. 3). In Zondo's view, Amanzimtoti was a Johannesburg group, an assumption that is lent some credibility by the fact that in the early 1940s the Better label issued at least five recordings of a typical male choir called Amanzimtoti Male Voice Choir. Either way, Zondo is probably correct in suggesting that "singing really comes from these groups like Amanzimtoti. All these choirs that mushroomed were taking it up from these people, Amanzimtoti in Natal. . . . Amanzimtoti was singing *isikhunzi*." In the same period,

Figure 2. Enoch Mzobe as a young man. Courtesy Veit Erlmann.

Figure 3. Crocodile Singers, 1948. Courtesy Veit Erlmann.

another part of Natal, between Vryheid and Swaziland, became a second important center of isicathamiya music with choirs such as the Vryheid-based Boiling Waters under "Khabanyawo," Van Voice and a group called Germans being the most prominent.

The repertoire of these early groups consisted indiscriminately of anything from traditional and modernized *izingoma zomtshado* wedding songs to hymns, folk tunes, and material of the *isikhunzi* category. By the late 1920s and early 1930s, performance genres were anything but separate categories reserved for specific class uses. IsiZulu-speaking, urban mission-educated musicians performed Western music and ragtime in the style of Caluza known as *imusic* and *iRagtime*, at the same time maintaining a strong interest in *isiZulu*, a category that comprised traditional material arranged for choir. Conversely, some working-class performers such as Amanzimtoti occasionally sang *imusic* and *isikhunzi* tunes.

A fascinating example of the blurred and partially overlapping contours of elite performance repertoires and early isicathamiya is offered by "Jim Takata Kanjani," a folk tune that was extremely popular during the 1930s. It was a standing item in the repertoire of Petros Qwabe, a comedian and member of the elite vaudeville troupe Pitch Black Follies.[6] At the same time, the tune was recorded in 1932 by both the Bantu Glee Singers (HMV GU 137, reissued on Rounder 5025, side A, track 1) and Dhlomo's Double Quartette (Gallo GE 102). The Bantu Glee Singers were a solidly middle-class vaudeville troupe formed around 1931 by Nimrod Makhanya. The Transvaal-born Makhanya had been a member of Caluza's Double Quartette when it traveled to London in 1930 to record for HMV. Back in South Africa, Makhanya devoted his attention to a wide range of popular traditions, including sketches, folk songs, and *ingoma* dance songs. Dhlomo's Double Quartette, by contrast, was a far more short-lived enterprise initiated by dramatist-novelist Herbert Dhlomo. In any case, such recordings sold well throughout South Africa and both versions of "Jim Takata Kanjani" must have been widely popular among migrant workers. They were cited by Ngweto Zondo as one of the oldest *isikhunzi* tunes in the repertoire of the Crocodile Singers.[7]

> *Woza ngibone s'bari*
>> Come, let me see my brother-in-law.
> *uJim uthakatha kanjani?*
>> Jim, how do you bewitch people?
> *Wo, zasha mfana, ye hm . . .*
>> Wo, boy, here we go, hm . . .
> *Uyeza ngadilika*
>> He is coming, I descend.
> *Isewu la?*
>> Are you here?

Apart from records, live performances by tap dance troupes also provided object lessons for migrant performers. On some occasions, both repertoires shared the concert platform as, for example, in 1938, when the Darktown Strutters, the leading vaudeville group of the period, competed against the Crocodiles in Durban's Natal Workers' Club.

It was not until the consolidation and expansion of the country's manufacturing industry in the mid-1930s that working-class formation reached a stage where it produced the cultural forms, the dance clubs, trade unions, sports organizations, and musical performance practices that form the bedrock of present-day working-class culture in South Africa. It is against this background that the emergence of *imbube,* the first genuine isicathamiya style, and the career of its pioneer, Solomon Linda, have to be seen.

Solomon Popoli Linda was born in 1909 in the vicinity of Pomeroy, in the heart of Msinga, one of the most poverty-stricken rural areas of Natal.

But Msinga was also a wellspring of migrants' musical creativity and the home of such dances as *umzansi*. Solomon spent most of his youth at his grandmother's home in Makhasane, herding cattle and later also attending the nearby Gordon Memorial School. The school had been founded at the turn of the century and for decades remained the only institution of Western education open to black children for miles around. It is thus easy to imagine the profound influence the social style and worldview of this institution must have had on Solomon Linda's life. And in fact, when I visited the area and the school, what the older people remembered about Solomon Linda more than anything else was the fact that he attended "Golden" Memorial School in "Pomoloy."

After reaching standard 4 in school and having a series of short spells of employment in Johannesburg, Linda's "home people" Boy Sibiya and Gideon Mkhize agreed to employ him at their Mayi Mayi Furniture Shop in Small Street in 1931. Throughout this period, Linda sang in a choir called Evening Birds led by his uncles Solomon and Amon Madondo. But the group folded in 1933 and Linda found employment at the Carlton Hotel. Subsequently, he formed a new group that was to become one of the most successful and most innovatory isicathamiya groups of all times. The new Evening Birds consisted of Linda as soprano, Gilbert Madondo, alto, Boy Sibiya, tenor, and Gideon Mkhize, Samuel Mlangeni, and Owen Sikhakhane, basses—all Linda's "homeboys" from Pomeroy (fig. 4).

Initially, the Evening Birds performed at weddings for ten shillings, but eventually they became involved in the expanding network of choir competitions and concerts on the Reef that was concentrated in "hostels," location halls, and compounds. Hostels, in particular, were alive with creativity. In Johannesburg, Linda and his "homeboys" might have socialized with fellow workers at the Wemmer Barracks and in the Municipal Men's Hostel in Wolhuter Street. Both places were well known for their male choirs, while the latter was described by *Umteteli* journalist Walter Nhlapo as "an arsenal of song and songbirds" where "on any night, on the corridor, stairs, rooms, bathroom, kitchen you meet and hear good, bad and indifferent renderings."[8]

In 1939 Linda decided to take a job offer as a packer at Gallo's newly opened record-pressing plant in Roodepoort. His choir soon attracted the attention of Gallo's talent scout Griffith Motsieloa, and before long one of Linda's songs, "Mbube" (Lion) (Gallo GE 829, reissued on Rounder 5025, side A, track 5), topped the list of the country's best-selling recordings for the African listenership. Like most early isicathamiya tunes,

Figure 4. Solomon Linda and the Evening Birds, c. 1941. Courtesy Veit Erlmann.

"Mbube" was based on a wedding song which Linda and his friends had picked up from young girls in Msinga and whose words commemorated the killing of a lion cub by the young Solomon and his herd-boy friends (example 2).

> *Yekela yanini, yebo liyaduma amathamsanqa.*
> Leave it, indeed it thunders blessings.
> *Mbube ha, wembube.*
> Lion, *ha*, the lion.
> *Mbube, mama.*
> Lion, mother.

As the transcription of the beginning of "Mbube" shows, a marked contrast exists between the metrically free introduction and the main body of the song. Comparing the introduction to some of the earliest recordings available of *ingoma* dance songs, one discerns remarkable parallels in melodic structure. Thus, "Yayi Somela E Lomeni" (example 3), a slow-paced *ihubo*-type song recorded probably in 1932 by the celebrated Durban *ingoma* troupe of Mameyiguda Zungu (HMV GU 150), is based on a

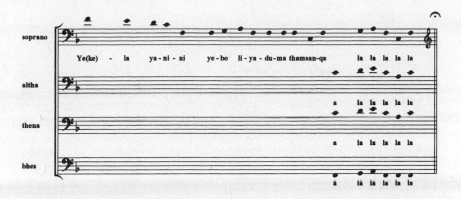

Example 2. (Continues on next page)

* Instrumental backing
starts here

Example 2. "Mbube," by Solomon Linda and the Evening Birds

Example 3. "Yayi Somela E Lomeni," by Mameyiguda Zungu

pentatonic scale, with a solo introduction in a free, declamatory style and a drawn-out choral section starting on a descending fourth so typical of ancient Zulu performance. Introductory sections such as the ones analyzed still remain the hallmark of all isicathamiya substyles today, and in an extended and harmonized form, in some cases have even come to occupy as much as a third of a performance.

To return to our analysis of Solomon Linda's "Mbube," the main body of the song clearly displays only a few features which can be said to be rooted in traditional performance practice. Thus, Linda's falsetto echoes a female vocal texture. However, the overlapping of solo and chorus, so crucial in traditional performance, is reduced to a minimum, and apart from a few instances of near-miss, Linda's solos always coincide with the beginning of the refrain on the tonic F. Similarly, the harmonic progression moves strictly with the beat, with one change of chord per bar: I (bar 1),

IV (bar 2), I$^6_4$ (bar 3), V^7 (bar 4). Linda's solo in turn moves in relation to this harmonic framework, thereby contradicting the traditional image of Zulu polyphony as the converging horns of a bull. This basic triadic structure linked *mbube* to other westernized genres popular among the upper strata of South Africa's urban black society, because it formed one of the lowest common denominators of all early urban African music regardless of class origin and specific ideological functions. Neither the words of "Mbube" nor its musical texture and partial anchorage in a wedding song were particularly original. Nevertheless, the song became canonic for an entire generation of performers, while certain of its musical characteristics such as the booming I-IV-V bass patterns became a mainstay of all subsequent stylistic developments.

In the view of Evening Birds member Gilbert Madondo, however, it was a number of other innovations that really revolutionized migrant workers' choral performance. First, the Evening Birds were the first migrant workers' choir to depart from the *isikhunzi* principle of one singer per voice part and to augment the bass section by several singers. While this alteration in the eyes of many of its practitioners "modernized" early isicathamiya performance, in substance the strengthening of the bass section meant a return to traditional choral practices of ceremonial performance genres. Here, such as in *amahubo* regimental songs, it was the bass parts that grounded the performance harmonically and temporally in a frame of collective expression.

At the same time, the relationship of these voice parts among each other was redefined. Henceforth, all parts were modeled on those of a mixed choir. That is to say, the terms used to designate the parts sung by female voices—soprano and alto—were used to refer to the lead solo part and the top choral part. In other words, the distribution of vocal parts was as follows. The lead part sung by the leader of the group was called soprano or *fas pathi*, first part, whereas the part sung by the two or three choir members singing falsetto was called *altha*. Tenor and bass, parallel with Western usage, were called *thena* or *bhes*. Alternatively, the tenors were called *izibhalantoni*, baritones, while the basses were called *doshaba*, those who sing the *do*.

Although as a result of Linda's "invention," early isicathamiya groups rarely numbered more than six to eight singers, when larger groups became fashionable in the 1950s, the principal of proportional preponderance of bass voices remained untouched. As Elkin Sithole asserts, "If the choir has eight members, the distribution of voices would be: first part (leader), one voice; second part (alto), one voice; third part (tenor), one voice; and fourth part (bass), five voices. If there are ten or more members, the next to be reinforced would be the third part, or tenor, for example: first part, one voice; second part, one voice; third part, two voices; and fourth part, six or more voices" (Sithole 1979, 277 ff.).

In 1938, in addition to his musical innovations, Linda became the first isicathamiya performer to introduce group uniforms and striped suits signaling urban sophistication at a time when Durban choirs still preferred the more old-fashioned baggy trousers called "Oxford Bags" immortalized in Caluza's song "UBunghca" (HMV GU 1). Both striped suits and "Oxford Bags," however, represented attempts on the part of migrants to work on their own mutilated physicality by appropriating (essentially Western) practices and images of the body that promised the possibility of a bounded identity and that spoke of the desire to fuse the bodies social and natural, to merge the outer shell with the inner "I." Stylish elegance, then, the consumption of the commodified signs of wholesome bodies, even in its most modest form as in isicathamiya uniforms, is inscribed with the contradictions of bourgeois society and power relations. Even today, neatly pressed suits and sports jackets, as we have seen in chapter 2, remain one of the main attractions of a successful isicathamiya performance, and at least since the 1960s many weekend competitions have been combining both choral music and "swanking" shows.

A sense of all this is perhaps conveyed by the words of Dan Twala, then chief organizer of the Bantu Men's Social Centre, one of the most important venues of black entertainment in Johannesburg during the 1930s and 1940s. In 1938, in a letter to his fiancée, he writes about a typical isicathamiya concert. "To-night I am locked in my office. Listening again to some queer and weird African-Englishised Music. The Koloni Choir is singing 'Hiki, No Mama! uyandibiza u Ma Radebe!' and if you want to see uniforms and tail-coats, you could find no better showroom than the Bantu Sports Club to-night. The Hall is half empty but these poor people are having the time of their lives, in their own fashion, and I tell you they are satisfied with 'very little' "(Couzens 1933, 6).

To interpret Linda's innovations, however, as indications of a clear shift toward an adaptation to urban values and life style is to misunderstand the space in which migrants such as the Evening Birds developed and pursued strategies of survival that made use of the best of both worlds, the urban and the rural. Striped suits and Western chord structures are certainly expressions of migrants' subjective desire to become "modern." At the same time, this antirural stance does not contradict a more critical perspective on urban ways as it is expressed, for instance, in the words of "Hamba Phepha Lami" (GE 874), a song by Linda that describes the bitter experiences of a Durban migrant.

> *Sahamba sahamba safika eThekwini.*
>> We went to Durban and we were robbed of our money.
> *Basitshintshela ngemali eluhlaza.*
>> They took our money and gave us ordinary paper in exchange.

Throughout the 1930s and 1940s, and until their demise in 1948, Linda's group maintained a leading position among South Africa's isicathamiya choirs. But this position was fiercely contested by other prominent choirs in Johannesburg and Durban, most notably the Crocodiles under Isaac Mzobe, the Dundee Wandering Singers, and the Durban Evening Birds. The history of these groups and the biographies of their most prominent members are linked in intriguing and at times mysterious ways that are difficult to illuminate more than half a century later and with little more evidence beyond the testimony of a handful of now rather aged contemporaries.

The fact that there should be such close connections between the three leading choirs of the 1930s seems hardly surprising, for most of its singers hailed from the same area in the Natal midlands. Linda, as we have seen, was born near Pomeroy. His in-laws, the Madondos, for their part, lived in the area of Mhlumayo. The Mkhizes, in turn, came from the area of Dundee. All these places lie in close proximity to each other, in a perimeter of less than thirty miles, in what could be rightfully called the heartland of isicathamiya.

As for the Dundee Wandering Singers, this choir had been founded in Johannesburg during the late 1920s to early 1930s by a Dundee-born man named Alson Novemu Mkhize "Bomvu," the "red" Mkhize. According to his son Sidney Mkhize, himself a seasoned performer and founding member of the celebrated Inqaba Yabesotho, the copper-skinned Alson Mkhize then left Johannesburg and took some of the members with him to Durban. Here the group reconstituted itself as Durban Evening Birds. The choir consisted of the Mkhize brothers, Alson, Edwin, Alpheus, and Josiah, and as a soprano, Alfred Siqokoma Nxumalo (fig. 5). All the singers lived together at the Msizini "hostel" on Somtseu Road, next to the Loram Secondary School. The choir dominated Durban's isicathamiya scene until well into the 1940s and produced numerous offshoots such as the Winter Roses, the Beam Brothers, and many others, but during this period and

Figure 5. Durban Evening Birds, 1941. Courtesy University of Cape Town Libraries.

under different names, they only recorded some seven discs for HMV and Columbia.[9]

The rivalry between the Durban Evening Birds and Solomon Linda's group was fueled and exploited by the record industry. As Solomon Linda's widow recalls, on record, Mkhize's voice was difficult to distinguish from Linda's, a fact which led to frequent disputes among isicathamiya groups about the identity of the Johannesburg and the Durban Evening Birds. This and the fact that both choirs were called Evening Birds might have induced some producers to swiftly rename Mkhize's group Singing Birds for a series of records on the Columbia label (YE 42, 43, 51).

Somewhat less popular than the two Evening Birds groups and the Crocodiles were the CTC (Cape to Cairo) Choir, Johannes Duma's Morning Starts from Estcourt, the Orlando Naughty Boys and Maktshwa's Alexandrians.[10] The last group also affiliated with the Industrial and Commercial Workers Union (ICU) in Johannesburg and recorded extensively during the late 1930s and early 1940s (1163, 1166, Gallo GE 143, 145, 185). The linkages between isicathamiya performance and political and union militancy illustrate an important aspect of early working-class consciousness. Contrary to the assumption that isicathamiya is one of the prime musical examples of a co-opted working-class consciousness, protest against oppression and exploitation has always been one of its main components. Until the late 1940s, politically motivated *mbube* songs were even aired from the Durban studios of what later became the South African Broadcasting Corporation (SABC). "Poll Tax" (1750) by the Dundee Wandering Singers is one such song, and so is "I Colour Bar" by the African Pride Singers.

> *Bayenzeleni iColour Bar?*
> Why are they practicing the colour bar?

An even harsher indictment of the regime of class and racial oppression than "I Colour Bar" is Solomon Linda's "Yetulisigqoko" (Take off your hat) (Gallo GE 887), equally a regular item on early SABC broadcasts. The song evokes the inquisitive atmosphere and debasing treatment of blacks at a Pass Office, before it bursts out into a cry for the lost autonomy.

> *Yethul' isigqoko sakho.*
> Take off your hat.
> *Igama lakho lasekhaya ungubani?*
> What is your home name?
> *Uyihlo ubani?*
> Who is your father?
> *Inkosi yakho ubani?*
> Who is your chief?
> *Uthelaphi wena?*
> Where do you pay your tax?
> *Uphuza maphi amanzi?*
> What river do you drink from?
> *Sikhalela izwe lakithi.*
> We mourn for our country.

Beyond such outspoken lyrics, choirs such as Maktshwa's ICU group and Linda's Evening Birds illustrate the fusion of two quite diverse sets of ideologies in emergent migrant culture. In the early 1930s, when Maktshwa's choir was presumably formed, the ICU had been reduced from a mass organization with a predominantly rural following of farm laborers to a middle-class organization based on nationalist rhetoric (fig. 6). Choirs like the Alexandrians and the Evening Birds bridged the gap between these two class-based forms of ideological discourse in performing the rural songs of the migrants as well as nationalist hymns propagating ICU and ANC slogans. One of the offspring of this peculiar aesthetic marriage is "Mayibuye IAfrika" (Come back Africa) by the Evening Birds (Gallo GB 3040). The

ISAZISO.

IIIIIIIIIIIIIIIIIIIIIIIIIIIIIIIIIIIIIIIIIIIIIIIIIIIIIIIII

Ngolwesitatu JUNE 15th 1932.   Sobane

Concert Enkulu

Yabantwana bas' eManzimtoti Institution,

I.C.U. HALL HEADQUARTERS,

117 Prince Edward Street,

Kusihlwa ngo 7.30 p.m.

Ukungena iziNtombi neziNsizwa 6d.

Futi ke sobana ma Taxi Car akututa abantu ebusuku abayise emakaya abo. Siyani mema namanye amaCollege abekona.

IIIIIIIIIIIIIIIIIIIIIIIIIIIIIII

NAZI IZICOMPANY EZIYOHLABELELA.

1. Midnight Follies, Amanzimtoti
2. Moonlight Six of I.C.U., Durban.
3. Evening Birds. Durban.
4. Tulasizwe Choir, Durban.
5. Zulu Male Voice Party, Durban.
6. The Famous Broadway Entertainers.

7. The Famous B.E. Company of P. M. Burg.

IIIIIIIIIIIIIIIIIIIIIIIIIII

A Grand Musical Show and Dance

which will be held at

I.C.U. HEADQUARTERS HALL,

117 Prince Edward Street, Durban on

WEDNESDAY, JUNE 15th 1932.

Ladies and Gents are cordially invited to come and witness the above "Show of Shows" which will be given by the African Youngsters.

"THE MORE WE ARE TO-GETHER THE HAPPY WE WILL BE."

Admission : 6d. all around.   Commencing 8 p.m. sharp.

H. MSOMI.
Stage Manager.

Figure 6. Program of an ICU concert, 1932. Courtesy University of Cape Town Libraries.

tune is traditional, but it was arranged by Walter Nhlapo, a Gallo talent-scout and journalist on the Chamber of Mines-funded black weekly *Umteteli wa Bantu*. Likewise, in the late 1930s Maktshwa's choir teamed up with the popular dance band Merry Blackbirds for a series of Gallo records (1163, 1166, GE 143, 145, 185).

Such musical enterprises across class barriers were designed to broaden the constituencies of a somewhat isolated middle-class leadership (Coplan 1985, 134). At the same time, they represent a musically ill-informed attempt by the expanding record industry to deepen its hold on a highly fragmented market. Lindi Msane, for example, ex-star of the elite vaudeville troupe Pitch Black Follies, recalls not without some contempt that concerts by the Follies were sponsored by Gallo and therefore had to feature renderings of Linda's "Mbube" in order to boost the company's sales figures of that record. But for all the marketing strategies and commercial categorizations of listeners' tastes, audiences elaborated their own criteria for what was popular. Sometime in the late 1940s, the highly polished vocal quartet Manhattan Brothers had to discover that an audience accustomed to *mbube* was perfectly familiar with American swing. Manhattan Brothers member Dambuza Mdledle recalled that during a competition against the Dundee Wandering Singers and Natal Evening Birds at Johannesburg's Bantu Sports, the Manhattan Brothers felt "that we had to teach the gospel of jazz to an audience that was still new to it. For it seemed that everybody looked down on us and did not like our music. . . . Our pianist took his seat and played the introduction to 'Walking my baby back home.' To our surprise, the audience picked up the tune and joined in the singing."[11]

The main format in which early isicathamiya was being performed was that of competitions. Musical contests had, of course, long been an established forum for school and mission choirs and in part overlapped with the conventional Western concert format. Until at least World War I, the concert (*ikhonsati*) had been the sole form of musical entertainment available to urban black South Africans, and in many instances it was also the most important and popular form of African social gathering in town. Although a novel feature of musical performance in a society in which a strict separation of performers and (paying) audience was, if not entirely unknown, fairly exceptional, returning migrant workers adopted the idea of the *khonsati* and staged concerts during Christmastime and at weddings. Apart from migrants' wage remittances and clothes and other consumer goods purchased in town, these concerts with their attendant ritual niceties provided migrants with the opportunity to demonstrate to their kin their achievements in town and, more important perhaps for the younger ones among them, the prospects and rewards of independent strategies of economic accumulation.

Linked to middle-class notions of concerts as the ideal format for musical performance is the idea that competitions are organized around set pieces which all choirs have to perform. This explains why some of the popular tunes of the time were recorded by most isicathamiya choirs and all classes of performers in general. Apart from the famous "Jim Takata Kanjani," another song, "Igama La Le Ntombi" (This lady is now famous), was a favorite with isicathamiya audiences and admirers of vaudeville alike. Consequently, the song was recorded by the Evening Birds (Gallo GE 145) and the Darktown Strutters (Columbia YE 15).

Related to the *khonsati,* even though it incorporated more distinctly African forms of social organization, was the *stokvel,* a combined fundraising and musical event that was practiced in every conceivable type of black working-class organization from soccer clubs to women's unions. In a peculiar mélange of performance and voluntary association, black mission choirs from early in the century—under the distrustful eyes of their white mentors—had begun to transform the structure of concerts into, as Durban missionary F. Bridgman called it, "a form of combined auctioneering and gambling." [12] The following is an early account of such "auctioneering" in Durban in 1917:

> Messrs. William Gumede and Z. L. S. Made from Ladysmith argued about which choir should sing. Gumede said that the Ohlange Choir should sing, whereas the other wanted the boot dance (*isicathulo*) by Skuni Jojilanga. The whole concert stopped because of the two gentlemen who eventually engaged themselves in a kind of 'bidding.' The money started from 1s and Mr. Gumede failed to go beyond £1.0.6. Mr. Made's 'bidding' went up to £1.4 and the other one surrendered. Mr Made's home team mates took him to the stage on their shoulders, followed by a great applause from the audience. Then Skuni Jojilanga went up the stage with his choir and sang nicely. When T. D. finished announcing the money paid by the two, he had already lost his voice. [13]

On a small scale, fund-raising such as the one described has also been a component of isicathamiya performance from the start. As such it was a practice that caught many a contemporary observer's eye. Ralph J. Bunche, for instance, an African American touring South Africa in 1937 and 1938, was one such observer. During a chance visit to the compound of the

WNLA (Witwatersrand Native Labor Association), an organization re-
cruiting labor for the gold mines, Bunche was able to watch two choirs
sing "Zulu songs, weird and with shuffling steps." Moreover, as his travel
notes tell us, money

> was being paid to "buy" dances and to "buy" singers not to sing. In
> the hall there was a chairman (sitting before a table laden with oranges
> and large bottles of "Society Pop"—not Kaffir beer) to announce
> items and to receive cash for the request of a choir to sing or stop sing-
> ing. That is, if one wishes a choir to sing one should go up to the
> chairman and "buy" that choir to sing. Small sums of even a penny are
> accepted. If, however, one is tired or not interested in the singing of a
> group, one can go up and "buy" the choir "off" with a slightly higher
> sum than the person who has bought them. There are cases where bid-
> ding in this fashion has been very keen and, of course, the highest bid-
> der wins. (Edgar 1992, 191)

Throughout the late 1930s and 1940s, black working-class organizations
such as the ICU held weekly concerts in Durban's Msizini hall that were
organized along similar lines and that involved vaudeville troupes and isicathamiya choirs. "Groups from Johannesburg, Ladysmith, Dundee etc.,"
T. Pewa recalled,

> would meet there and sang and huge gains—moneywise—were made.
> Well, we also sang for Champion. This was a special request. Then
> spectators paid to enter the hall and watch us. This was just for enter-
> tainment over weekends. He did not pay any money. We did not expect
> money, in any case, because we were actually enjoying ourselves. We
> used to have everything on the house, that is the singers. Champion
> would buy food, cakes, etc. There was food for the singers which they
> had for a song, and the rest of the food was sold to the spectators. It
> worked the same way as the *stokvel*.

Another example of how such early events were structured is a skit in isi-
Zulu by Lindi Makhanya and Company, entitled "Ikonsati eBantusport"
(The Concert at Bantu Sports) (Gallo GE 879), that is worth quoting at
length. Recorded in the early 1930s, the skit describes the frustrations of a
young sewerage worker from Durban's Point, aptly called "Reserve," who
left Durban, "because places like Tusi's and Mini's have all been closed,"
and who subsequently gets attracted to isicathamiya competitions in
Johannesburg.

A: Did you get the news that there is a music extravaganza at Bantu Sports today? Linda's group [Solomon Linda's Evening Birds], Mchunu's group [Orlando Flying Birds], and the ICU group [Maktshwa's Choir] will be there. . . .

B   (*Reserve*): You know very well that I don't want to move around here in Johannesburg and you also know that people tend to stab each other in gatherings like music competitions.

A: Hey, go away! You always beat about the bush when people are inviting us. Let's go man!

The sketch then describes how the young migrant "with the five shillings which I earned after hard labor at the Point [Durban's harbor] by carrying human excrement" gets involved in the bidding process that rapidly heats up to a general tumult:

C: [in English] Order please, order please, be quiet. With this ten cents piece, I am saying you do not know anything about music.

B: *Sis,* this is no music at all, is this the way how you sing in Johannesburg? With my penny I am saying that they must sit down, they do not know music. I do not want to see them here, they must sit down.

C: [in English] Order please, order please! You do not know music. Someone has paid a penny instructing you to sit down. Let us now give that Durban lady and her boyfriend "Reserve" a chance to sing so that we can listen to their music.

B: They are fighting. Stop it! I told you that I do not want to attend such gatherings. Just look now, we will be arrested during the very first days of our arrival here in Johannesburg.

The representation of popular practice by members of the black intelligentsia in forms of expressive culture such as "Ikonsati eBantusport" serves as a useful methodological device in deciphering the more subtle, inner workings of popular culture and power politics. For not only does the skit reveal more about underlying class interests than overtly political discourse, it also provides everyday images of power, authority, and order—fittingly couched in the language of the dominant culture ("order please, order please")—that were designed to become accepted as the normal way of life by urbanizing migrants such as "Reserve." Fighting during or after such competitions was indeed common, rivalries over women being one of the most frequent causes. But the meaning of such disputes was interpreted in quite different ways by the migrants themselves and their middle-class would-be mentors. The control of women, their reproductive and productive capacities, has been one of the strongest components of male identity in precolonial society and under the strained conditions of the apartheid economy continues to shape present-day gender relations. As a result, men place a premium on the skills required to win the favors of women. A *soka,* an unattached male who is popular with girls, is a hero among his peers, and *ubugagu,* expertise in performance, is one of his principal attributes. And thus, the disorder that Msane and Co. bemusedly perceived at the Bantu Sports was only one of the ways in which migrants structured their lives in town under conditions that were not of their own choosing.

The name that probably summarizes best this intense atmosphere of heroic contest is *isikambula,* or *ukambul.* It is by this term that Johannesburg audiences first became acquainted with what later became known as *isikhwela Jo.* Here we briefly have to consider the etymology and meaning of *isikambula.* As Sidney Mkhize suggested, the term is the Zulu-ized form of "gambling," and in fact, in trying to elucidate its meaning, he compared the game of chance to migrant performers' habit of shuttling between different performance venues in one night in order to win as many prizes as possible. This, he said, was similar to taking chances and, as I shall explain more fully in chapter 4, in a deeper sense represents an attempt at rooting the experience of migration in a time and a place.

For middle-class observers of the early isicathamiya scene, as we have repeatedly seen, all this was a book with seven seals. They could not understand that migrant performers had their own aesthetic criteria that stemmed from the intensely competitive and power-riddled context of the urban labor market, slums, and degraded rural lifestyle and had nothing to do with the more sedate forms of sociability fostered in the missions. The middle-class incomprehensibility is captured quite crisply in the comments about other concerts held at Bantu Sports before the Second World War, such as the following account by Walter Nhlapo of a competition in February 1941 involving the Home Defenders, Tulasizwe, Universal, Happy Boys and Orlando Flying Birds. In *Bantu World,* in the column "Spotlight on Social Events," Nhlapo wrote the following under the heading "Primitive Art": "The musical rendering was good though there was less singing but more shouting. To our entire disgust, the sketches by the Orlando Flying Birds are those of late Mtetwa and his Lucky Stars of Durban with scarcely a change. Their interpolated sketches were mostly of witchcraft and love instilled by medical potion. Mtetwa brought this and everybody is doing it. He is dead and nothing new in primitive vaudeville has cropped up." [14]

"Shouting" was of course a rather inadequate term for the kind of vigorous singing and sometimes tense voice quality that isiZulu-speaking musicians had traditionally been accustomed to in *amahubo* regimental anthems and other genres of group performance. As a result, many migrant performers remained unmoved by the efforts of music educators and critics to "improve" the robust sounds of the countryside. Similarly, the buying of choirs continues in present-day *prakthisa*. Even though it has never been fashionable in isicathamiya to buy a choir off the stage, it is still possible to buy it onto the stage by means of the request fee.

When early isicathamiya choirs began to compete against each other they also merged the aesthetic of the concert stage and the symptoms of the increasing commodification of social relations with the more rural format of *ingoma* dance competitions that had evolved in response to intensified struggles over land and job opportunities. In this, isicathamiya competitions resemble the *beni* dances of the East African coast described by Terence Ranger. Although this dance form was first and foremost "deeply rooted in the pre-colonial dance and competitive modes" (Ranger 1975, 7) expressing Swahili urban dualism and moiety solidarity (19), later as all sorts of divisions and antagonisms among the migrant and highly heterogeneous population of the coastal towns began to emerge, *beni* also mirrored these essentially modern, colonial conditions (165).

Equally essential to the idea of competitive performance was the notion that a man had to build himself, to acquire a name through the accumulation of prestige and wealth. The identity of a man was shaped in comparison, if not in contestation, with that of other men. To know oneself meant to know one's adversaries. The means to achieve this power were manifold. In performance, as we have seen, the level of volume was one indicator of a group's stamina. Another means was to distance oneself from the influence of women who were thought to have a weakening effect on men. Thus, on the eve of a competition the members of a choir used to spend the night together so as to avoid contact with women. Another widespread method was to apply a liquid charm called *isiphungo* to one's eyebrows. This was to ward off the negative influence of competitors and, more important, *isifufunyane*, a much feared possession by evil spirits.

Isicathamiya during the 1940s and 1950s

If Linda's Evening Birds were generally regarded as the most advanced isicathamiya group in terms of musical structure, Isaac Mzobe's Crocodiles have to be credited with the introduction of fast synchronized tap dancing called *istep*. Whereas the Evening Birds preferred slow "step by step movements, first backwards, then forwards," the Crocodiles, according to Gilbert Madondo, usually won the favor of Johannesburg audiences by the display of fast, fidgeting footwork. Previous styles had been characterized by stiff, immobile body postures, but dancing by early *mbube* groups featured intricate footwork contrasting with a straight, uninvolved torso. Samson Ntombela recalls that in early *mbube* dancing, dancers "were told to fidget with their feet, but the body had to be straight and uninvolved. And people would turn slowly."

The models for this kind of choreography, if the available evidence does not deceive, were films featuring Fred Astaire and Ginger Rogers that from the mid-1930s had become a powerful influence on the emerging popular dance forms of the African elite and the lower strata of the black population. Examples of extravagant ballroom dancing as well as tap dancing were copied by black audiences from these films, although virtuoso step dancing, in the early years, seems to have been the speciality of the Crocodiles only.

The contrast between the virile, fighting movements of *ingoma* and the subtle, almost silent footwork of early isicathamiya groups such as the Crocodiles, signifies the transition from the pastoral symbolism of "bullness" in *ingoma* to slick city behavior, and has been aptly described by South African ethnomusicologist Elkin Sithole. The steps in isicathamiya "have to be gentle, as if stepping on eggs or tiptoeing on forbidden ground . . . in *cothoza mfana* an upright posture is desired. Legs are stretched or kicked out as gently as possible. Even if the halls are uncemented, there is little or no dust at the end of the dance" (Sithole 1979, 279).

Yet if elaborate movement was admired by urban audiences as a skillful adaptation of the models suggested by local tap dance troupes and American movie stars, other predominantly Natal-based isicathamiya groups drew on older models of the ideal African inspired by rural missions. It is these models and their origin in the Natal midlands that gave rise to *isikhwela Jo*, the second major substyle of isicathamiya to have emerged in the 1930s and 1940s. In practice, there was hardly any difference between *isikhwela Jo* and *isikambula*, even if some veteran performers insisted that *isikhwela Jo* used much higher vocal registers. Another term, finally, that was broadly synonymous with *isikhwela Jo* and *isikambula* was *jazibantshi*. The term is derived from the Afrikaans word *jaasbaaitjie* for a knee-length waistcoat. Uniforms of this type became popular during the late 1940s or thereabouts but were soon replaced by sports jackets.

Be this as it may, etymologically *isikhwela Jo* is related to the verb *khwela,* according to Daniel Mabutho, a "strong word." The term is best translated as "attack, Jo!" and refers to the cues given by the lead singer to the choir before they burst out into the high-pitched yells that are the hallmark of this style. And, in fact, much of the aesthetic appeal of *isikhwela Jo* is grounded in the ability to beat competing choirs in terms of volume rather than poetic imagination or structural ingenuity. Something of this aesthetics and its realization in competition is captured nicely in a newspaper article written in 1956 by an anonymous author on the *jazbaaitjies.* The article appeared 13 October 1956 in *Ilanga Lase Natal.*

> The history of the *jazbaaitjie* singers dates back to 1890. It becomes clearer after 1925 and usable after 1939. The legendary Champions were led by Mabhulukwana Mbatha of Baumannville. There are hundreds of them in Durban alone. There are the Crocodiles of Enoch Mzobe, the Home Tigers of Samson Ntombela, the brothers of Victor Khanyile, the Five Roses of Aaron Ntombela, the New Stars of Amos Khanyile, the Tafitta Bros. Ltd. of Albert Ncala, to name but a few.
>
> The *jazbaaitjie* musicians have their own mannerisms. Educationally they are generally literate only in their own language. They dress well and are simple in style. They believe in the principle "as loud as your voice can take it" when singing. Each member of a group almost tries to sing louder than his comrades. The audience are in most cases men. The few women you see now and then, are admirers of certain individual singers.
>
> The *jazbaaitjies,* as they are commonly known, love to compete among one another and the popular trophy in Natal is a nice live goat for the winners, £5 for the second prize and £2.10 for the third. Their adjudicators are usually picked at random in the street so that they may not know or have any special interest in any individual group or competitor. If they are Africans, they stand a good chance of being beaten up should their verdict be queried.
>
> Attempts to bribe adjudicators are often made by some competitors. The competitors pay as much as £2 or more in order to enter a contest and there is a lot of money being made by organizers of such contests. The money comes from the musicians themselves and the spectators are entertained almost free of charge.
>
> The *jazbaaitjie* concerts are an attraction for the semi-literate. The

music has grown so popular among Whites that it has been mistaken for pure Zulu traditional music. The "step" of the *jazbaaitjies* remains unequaled in its uniqueness, while their beautiful compositions remained original and simple.

If we are to believe the Warden-born (Orange Free State) Mbijana Shembe, who joined the Johannesburg-based Naughty Boys in 1937, *isikhwela Jo* was introduced to Johannesburg by Mkhize's Durban Evening Birds. Other veteran performers such as Thembinkosi Pewa maintain that *isikhwela Jo* was pioneered by the Natal group Shooting Stars. Originally from northern Natal, Pewa recalled, "these singers were used to church singing. They came down to Durban and brought in the influence of the higher tones that they were introducing into male only singing." Although only recorded in the mid-1940s, the high-pitched, yelling choral sound pioneered by the Shooting Stars in songs such as "Yek' Emarabini" (HMV JP 23, reissued on Rounder 5025, track 8) had already become known in Durban in the late 1930s. A few years later, during the war, audiences compared the choral yells with exploding bombs and renamed the style *'mbombing* (bombing).[15]

Choral fortissimo yells and falsetto, as I have said, were of course not entirely unknown in traditional vocal music, especially in regimental war songs. In *isikhwela Jo,* however, the high-pitched sounds more likely represented a far less masculine attempt at substituting the female parts of Western hymnody with male falsetto singing. As Thembinkosi Pewa explained, "We first heard of [Western] music at school and were encouraged by teachers to sing church hymns. . . . By singing in church we got to know that there is soprano, alto, tenor and bass, and not singing in unison as the *ingoma* dancers do. . . . After we left school, we continued to sing. We just wanted to show that the males could do it alone without females."

That migrant workers accustomed to male only performance genres should have drawn on middle-class aesthetic metaphors of urban status is hardly surprising. As I pointed out earlier, the social style practiced at mission stations such as Gordon Mission in Pomeroy—the choirs, soccer clubs, bible classes, and so on—were the most readily available symbols of successful urban adaptation and upward social mobility. But the identification with middle-class urban behavior was not restricted to four-part harmony. It even reinvigorated older forms of stage behavior predating Caluza's "ragtime" and action songs. *Isikhwela Jo* performers banished all dancing from competition because church choirs, according to Natal Champions veteran Isaac Sithole, "don't move when they sing. Girls stand in front and boys at the back. So we also stood like that, 6 or 8 boys."

Mbube and *isikhwela Jo* remained the dominant styles throughout the 1940s and 1950s, but for reasons that can only be discussed in the context of postwar socioeconomic developments in South Africa, isicathamiya performance generated little stylistic innovation until the early 1970s.

"Tip-Toe, Guys!"—the 1970s

The years of the 1970s were, in many ways, a crucial decade in South African history. It was a period in which, as Alf Stadler writes, "the cumulative effect of apartheid practice marked every aspect of society, and constituted the central element of South Africa's recurrent political crisis" (Stadler 1987, 11). It was the era that saw the apotheosis of grand apartheid—forced mass removals, the constitution of the "homelands"—but also the first rumblings of a storm—the armed struggle, growing black labor union militancy, and the decolonization of Angola and Mozambique—that was shattering the entire system to its very foundations. At the same time, the 1970s marked a watershed in the political economy of the country. Thus, compared to the immediate postwar period, African employment had more than doubled, and the number of blacks living more or less permanently in urban areas had risen from 2,329,000 in 1951 to 5 million in 1970 (Stadler 1987, 59). Important shifts also took place in the situation of "migrant labor" itself, especially in the mining industry, the core of South Africa's migrant labor army. Following a number of government measures restricting the influx of foreign labor and particularly after a significant, if by no means lavish, increase in mine wages in the 1970s, traditional migrant cultures and "migrant values" (Moodie 1991, 41–44), straddling as they did two modes of production, gradually gave way to more proletarianized cultural practices. Whereas prior to the 1970s no man could survive on the pitifully low mine wages without a rural subsistence base or a racket on the side—in other words without being part of a migrant culture—after the mid-1970s this migrant culture began to disappear and with it the bridge between country life and the mines. As a result, present-day miners are likely to be "professional miners whose families continue to reside in the countryside" and who perceive themselves as "wage-workers rather than farmers working to fund rural homesteads" (1991, 41). In short, they have become, for all practical purposes, rural commuters. The same, of course, holds true of the manufacturing industry in which most isicathamiya performers work, even though wages there have always been higher.

All of this, as I have said, is not to suggest a direct link between political economy and performance, between social structure and artistic practice. New forms of social organization do not necessarily engender new songs; changing social structures, as I have said throughout, are not reflected in some reified compositional structure. Nevertheless, as the social position and cultural practices of large sectors of South Africa's migrant labor force change, so do their ideologies (Mayer 1980), leisure-time activities (Møller 1991), and performances qua forms of practice themselves. As the social identity of migrant workers began to be reformulated in the 1970s, and as the distinctions between mine workers and other migrants began to dwindle, performance, too, as one of the means of this definition of self-hood, began to be restructured. From the 1970s the cultural practices of migrants for the most part reflected the increasing homogenization of the labor force, but also a despairing conservatism. And it is thus, I argue, that post-1960s isicathamiya was marked by the dual tension between performers' attempts to preserve a retrospective, somewhat encapsulated, almost antiproletarian stance and the desire to reposition themselves by forging new symbolic alliances with the life experiences and expressive repertoires of other strata of the black laboring population.

The dwindling resonance and practical effectiveness of migrant culture led to two kinds of responses from isicathamiya performers. The first consisted in the widespread cooperation with the apartheid media which, starting in the early 1960s, had been greatly expanded and delivered the ideological rationale of the state's "homeland" policy (see also chap. 9). Given all its emphasis on "home" and rural values, isicathamiya became one of the most effective means of this media strategy that was eagerly accepted by most choirs in their pursuit of power and a positive self-image. In fact, without the SABC's strong interest, as Joseph Shabalala asserts, the night-songs would have "really nearly died." The second response, as chapter 10 will show more fully, consisted in the foundation of a number of choral associations structured along the lines of revolving credit associations and *stokvels*. This move enabled choirs to raise their own prize money and made them potentially independent of outside donors or concert agents and even larger audiences. Most isicathamiya competitions today offer the specter of tightly knit, insulated circuits of choirs performing for each other.

The remodeling of isicathamiya, the dialectic of restoration and reform in the third and most recent phase of isicathamiya history, is reflected in two related stylistic developments. The first of these is the growth of a genre called *cothoza mfana*. The term translates as "tread carefully, boy" and is said to have been coined by SABC broadcaster Alexius Buthelezi. It enjoyed only a relatively short period of popularity before it was superseded by the term *isicathamiya*. Derived from the verb *-cathama*, to stalk, to stand on tiptoe, isicathamiya could be roughly translated as "stalking style." Although more or less identical in sonic structure, *cothoza mfana* and isicathamiya differ with respect to the kinesic component in that isicathamiya choreography is generally considered to be of a more brisk and fast-moving nature.

The transition to the "stalking style" is epitomized, more than by any other single development in recent nightsong history, by the music of Ladysmith Black Mambazo. The creative work and life of Joseph Shabalala, the leader of this greatest isicathamiya choir of all time, is the subject of the final chapter, and I must limit myself here to a discussion of the most important innovations in his compositions. Established in the late 1960s in Durban, this group quickly rose to national fame as the result of Shabalala's attempts at "modernizing" isicathamiya in four major areas: choreography, song texts, sound texture, and professional practice and organization of the group. To understand these adjustments, we first have to consider some of the changes that had occured in the music of migrant workers after the 1950s, more particularly in guitar-based *maskanda* music.

Rooted in various styles of traditional bow music, guitar music by the 1950s was at its peak. Largely promoted by the Troubadour label, *maskanda* and related musics by the mid-1950s to early 1960s came to dominate the record market, Troubadour at times selling two million records a year and for a time controlling as much as 85 percent of the entire market (Allingham 1989). A musician by the name of John Bhengu was one of Troubadour's most successful artists. In 1971—Bhengu had by now acquired the epithet *Phuzushukela* (drink sugar) this Nkandla born guitarist became the first *maskanda* to switch to the electric guitar that had by then become universally accepted as the main instrument of popular band music in South Africa.

The music that resulted from this and other innovations became known as *mbaqanga* because, like the maize porridge it is named after, it became the subsistence basis for scores of township and studio musicians. A typical *mbaqanga* number by, for instance, the Soul Brothers or Amaswazi

Emvelo would feature a band of electric guitar, bass and drums, and sometimes keyboards and a horn section. Over a basic harmonic scaffold of four
bars, a solo singer would alternate with short instrumental riffs, or with a
backing chorus in the call-and-response pattern. This formula had a powerful impact on some of the isicathamiya performers of the 1960s. Thus,
Joseph Shabalala was an ardent guitar player before he switched to isicathamiya, and Scorpions leader Gershon Mcanyana played a self-made tin guitar and socialized with musicians in *mbaqanga* circles. He also admired the
Beam Brothers, and before he eventually assumed leadership of the Scorpions, he encountered Roxy Jila, then leader of the Scorpions and later a
manager of the female *mbaqanga* group Qeue Sisters.

Moreover, *mbaqanga* and *isikhwela Jo* were musically related and could
be easily adapted to one another. The genre in which this fusion seems to
have been experimented with first is called *umgqashiyo*. The term may be
related to *gqashagqasha*, a word describing, according to Doke and Vilakazi's *Zulu-English Dictionary*, a "person of brisk, spirited gait." And indeed, as we shall see further below, the *umgqashiyo* choreography is characterized by light and quirky movements. Although the term itself may
have been coined by radio broadcaster K. E. Masinga, it was the female
vocal group Mahotella Queens who pioneered *umgqashiyo*. Other celebrated male groups such as the Soul Brothers and Abafana Baseqhudeni
later followed suit. The songs by these groups that are most closely related
to isicathamiya, feature a *mbube*-style vocal arrangement backed by a guitar
band in which the bass guitar provides the harmonic framework interspersed with short glides and in which a solo guitar plays short formulas
reminiscent of the *ukupika* style of *maskanda* guitar music.

As for the thematic subjects of *umgqashiyo*, many songs share with isicathamiya a concern for the values and practices of an idealized past. The
following two songs by the Abafana Baseqhudeni show this quite clearly.
The first song, "Bumnandi Lobutshwala" (Igagasi IAL 3001, A6) comments on the changed role of alcohol in the degrading environment of
"hostels," starvation wages, and loneliness.

> Chorus: *Bumnandi lobutshwala.*
>   Nice, this beer.
>   *Utshwala bumnand' eKoloni madoda.*
>   The beer in the Cape is nice, men.
>   *Sibuzwile utshwala bumnandi.*
>   We have tasted the beer; it's nice.

Leader: *Yizwa!*
        Taste!
Chorus: *UKhumalo, uKhumalo ulibele utshwala.*
        Khumalo, Khumalo, you are wasting your time in beer.
        Umuzi uyachitheka.
        Your home is disintegrating.
        Tshwala udlalelani ngomtanomuntu?
        Beer, why are you troubling this man?
        Uma wenzanjena ubulala abantu.
        If you do like this, you are killing people.
Leader: *Iza!*
        Come!

Beer, an essential marker of male identity and a nourishment of male bodies and as such an indispensable ingredient of meaningful social intercourse, is seen here as a killer of people and a destroyer of the homestead,
the *umuzi*. As such, beer becomes a potent symbol evoking the dramatic
effects of labor migration on core social relations. A similar theme, equally
suggestive of the disturbing impact of labor migration on domestic life
and gender relations, is addressed in "Ayisekho Intombi," (Igagasi IAL
3001, B4) a song that voices the typical male complaint about "immoral"
women.

Chorus: *Ayisekh' intomb' ethandwa yimi kulomhlaba.*
         There's no longer any lady that deserves my love in this world.
Bass: *Awu!awu, ethandwa yimi.*
         Awu! awu, that I love.
    O, ngiyesaba.
         Oh, I am afraid of them.
Chorus: *Izintombi zalonyaka zilal' emaphathini*
         These days ladies sleep at the parties
    zivuk' emashibhini.
         and wake up in the shebeens.
Leader: *Kungcono ngiziphekele.*
         It's better if I cook for myself.
    Kungcono ngiziwashele.
         I would rather wash my own clothes.
    Ayisekh' intomb' ethandwa yimi kulomhlaba.
         There's no longer any lady that deserves my love in this world.

The destruction of the homestead, then, and its symbolic reconstruction
in performance forms a rich poetics of labor migration cross-cutting nu-

merous genres of migrant performance. In the case of *umgqqashiyo* and isicathamiya, these intertextual linkages are made even more evocative by one further aspect of *umgqashiyo*. For the most prominent innovation introduced by the Mahotella Queens was a new dance style that, like so many components and styles of the nightsongs, was based on girls' wedding dances. Journalist Alf Gwebu has written a detailed description of *umgqashiyo* choreography that is worth quoting in full.

> Basically, jive Mqashiya is almost the same as jive Motella, only faster. As in jive Motella, jive Mqashiya starts with the stamping of the feet in the "Zulu war dance" way, but instead of lifting the feet up in jive Mqashiya you lift both your heels and then move them rhythmically outward. After counting four you clap your hands and then repeat. Then you bend your right knee slightly forward and twitch your hands to the left four times. The position of the hands should be in the same position as it would be if you were stopping the light of a torch from reaching your face. The count for the twitching is also four.
>
> Then you put your hands on your stomach, fingers stretched, and stamp your feet rhythmically forward and backward in turn as you would do in an African wedding dance. At this stage you throw your arms wildly in the air, the "pepezela" style.
>
> For the final step you turn left, clench your fists as though holding a hoe or golf stick and then, standing partly on your toes, wobble your knees rhythmically like a Coon in action.
>
> This is jive Mqashiya. Its variations consist of the hysterical shaking of the breast, the rocking of the buttocks and the spiralling tangling of the arms above your head. If you get this right you'll be in fashion and very welcome at any mbaqanga party.[16]

From Gwebu's account and the accompanying remarkable photographs showing the Mahotella Queens in action (fig. 7), it is easy to see that *umgqashiyo* is the product of a long articulation of rural-traditional performance elements with some of the oldest models of urban black performance—the wobbling knees of a "coon." More fundamentally, however, Gwebu's report demonstrates the close links between *umgqashiyo* and some of the dance steps still performed by Ladysmith Black Mambazo. (fig. 8). The incorporation of these *umgqashiyo* dance routines into their performances was the first major reform of isicathamiya performance in the 1970s. In fact, the blending of *umgqashiyo* and *istep* in the performances of Black Mambazo did much to reinvigorate some of the older *cothoza* choreography and helped to form the essence of present-day isicathamiya choreography. The stealthily moving bodies of isicathamiya, the "soft

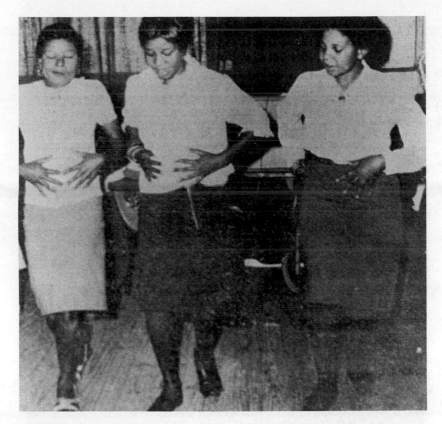

Figure 7. The Mahotella Queens dancing *umgqashiyo*, 1965. Courtesy Republican Press.

touch," as Thembinkosi Pewa called it, signals not only urban sophistication but also a shift in the relationship between embodied emotions and feelings of corporeality. The "gentle alternative" (as Joseph Shabalala explains in the introduction) was born when performers learned to control their emotions that had traditionally compelled them to stamp their feet vigorously. Although isicathamiya choreography is not devoid of emotional depth and requires no more control than *ingoma,* it seems that a link has been severed here between movement and ground, a link, that is, in which emotional intensity was coterminous with earth, dust, and a downward thrust. It is as if traditionally emotion was mediated by a grounded body, whereas in the isicathamiya stepping, kicking, and *umgqashiyo*-type of dancing, emotional expressiveness and the sensory experience of being a body passes through notions of lightness and detachment from the earth.

Figure 8. Ladysmith Black Mambazo. Courtesy Frans Schellekens.

Song texts are the second important area in which Joseph Shabalala set new standards in isicathamiya composition. Although the majority of his songs, like those of other choirs, express extravagant self-praise, Joseph Shabalala was the first isicathamiya composer to base his compositions on extended narrative sequences. The juxtaposition of disparate textual segments that characterizes the song texts of other choirs and that, as I shall demonstrate in chapter 7, in itself represents an important statement on the dislocation of migrant life, plays only a minor role in Shabalala's songs. The following example conveys some of the narrative logic in Shabalala's songs. It is drawn from "Hamba Dompasi," a track on the album *Journey of Dreams* that was composed on the occasion of the abolishment of the passbooks, one of the most odious and detested measures of the apartheid regime.

Leader: *Woza.*
    Come!
Chorus: *Woza s'hambe siye lena kwelakithi eSouth Africa.*
    Come, let us go to our country South Africa.
    Yizwe lokuthula.
    The land of peace.
    Yizwe lamaKristu.
    The land of Christians.
Leader: *Woza.*
    Come!
Chorus: *Woza sidl' igolide ne dayimani.*
    Come, let us enjoy the gold and the diamonds.
Leader: *Thina* . . .
    We . . .
Chorus: *Sihloba ngegolide nedayimani.*
    We dress with gold and diamonds.
Leader: *Lena kwaZulu siphila ngokuthi*
    Down in Zululand we usually say
Chorus: *ubothand' umakhelwane wakho.*
    you should love your neighbor.
Leader: *Kodwa ungilahla kanjani?*
    But how can you reject me?
Chorus: *We makhelwane wami, ungilahla kanjani na?*
    Oh, my neighbor, why are you rejecting me?
Leader: *La dum'izulu.*
    The thunder roars.

Chorus: *Wathi wafel' usulu mawuthanda izulu.*

         If you die because of being impolite, it was your choice.

Leader: *La dum'izulu*

         The thunder roars

Chorus: *nalizulu.*

         and it is raining.

Leader: *Kwaqhaqhazel' abantu, kwashayisanwa ngamakhanda.*

         And the people are shivering and confused.

Chorus: *Duma laduma izulu.*

         Thunder, thunder and rain.

Leader: *Ladum' izulu.*

         Thunder roars.

Chorus: *Wathi wafel' usulu mawuthanda izulu.*

         If you die because of being impolite, it was your choice.

. . . .

Leader: *Lapha . . .*

         Here . . .

Chorus: *lapha kwelakithi eSouth Africa*

         here in our country South Africa

         sidl' igolide ne dayimani.

         we enjoy the gold and the diamonds.

         Kuneng' okunye, singeze sakubala okuhle laphaya.

         There is a lot more, we can't count all the beautiful things there.

Leader: *Sibathanda bonke . . .*

         We love all . . .

Chorus: *sibathanda bonke abantu,*

         we love all the people,

         kodwa munye umuntu esimxoshile.

         but there is one person we have chased away.

Leader: *Hamba, hamba dompas.*

         Go, go away pass book!

Chorus: *Hamba dompas.*

         Go away pass book!

Leader: *Ubuyele kwelakini.*

         Go back to your home!

Chorus: *Ubuyele kwelakini. Wo, buyela kwelakini.*

         Go back to your home! Oh, just go back to your home!

Leader: *Hamba dompas thina asisakufuni kulelizwe.*

         Go away, pass book, we no longer want you in this country.

         Ubuyele lapha waqhamuka khona.

         Go back to where you came from.

> *Bazokulandel' abakuthandayo.*
>> Those who love you will follow you.
> *Hamba wena.*
>> Go away, you!
> *Songoba thina, songoba simunye songoba sihlangene.*
>> We will win, we will win being one, we will win united.

Chorus: *Songoba simunye.*
>> We will win being one.

Leader: *Hamba wena. Ukube uyazi ukuthi amadoda kudala ebengizonda . . .*
>> Go away, you! If only you knew that men have hated you ever since
> *bedlula bengishisa. Ngo 1960 bangenz' isilo sengubo.*
>> they made fun of me. In 1960, people burnt me.

Chorus: *Ngo 1960 bangenz' isilo sengubo.*
>> In 1960, they burnt me.
> *Hamba dompas.*
>> Go away, pass book.

Leader: *Songoba simunye, songoba sihlangene.*
>> Together we will win, united we shall win.

Leader: *Hayi.*
Chorus: He.
Leader: *Kumnandi . . .*
>> It is beautiful . . .
Chorus: *Kumnandi kwelakith' eMnambithi.*
>> It is beautiful, our place Mnambithi.

One of the most significant effects of a linear textual progression such as in the foregoing example lies in the fact that the performer becomes a voice that speaks from a position of authority. Instead of almost disappearing behind the jarring contrasts between stark images drawn from widely discrepant realities, this composer foregrounds his subjective position as a storyteller who impresses on his listeners a singular vision of the world. A song, Joseph Shabalala once told me, "is like a book. It tells people about the past and the future."

Joseph Shabalala's experimentation with a new sound texture was another factor that revolutionized isicathamiya, even though in essence the changes probably represent Shabalala's most conservative reform. Although *cothoza mfana* contained some low-key, close harmony material, Joseph Shabalala's group sang all his compositions in a soft, velvetlike tone. The top parts, alto and tenor, while still being sung falsetto, were tuned

down and reduced in volume and made to blend more with the rest of the
bass parts that, over the years and with new members joining the group,
began to sound less wiry. This technique, whose significance can only be
compared to Solomon Linda's augmentation of the bass parts in the 1930s,
was even applied to songs that, strictly speaking, belong to the *'mbombing*
category. Thus, to name but one example, in the track "Iya Bhompa" on
the album *Ushaka* (Motella BL 129) the cues given by Shabalala and the
sudden outbreaks of the responding choir are vintage *'mbombing,* pack-
aged in the fluffy sound of isicathamiya.

It is arguable whether the new sound can be attributed to Joseph Shabalala's creative genius alone. Some of the low-key, gently flowing choral
harmonies had been tried successfully by the King Star Brothers, a slightly
senior group from the Transvaal town of Standerton, that enjoyed tremendous popularity in the late 1960s to early 1970s. Moreover, as some of the
best informed connoisseurs of isicathamiya such as SABC announcer Patrick Buthelezi argue, the Natal midlands and particularly the area around
Weenen, Harrismith, and Standerton had traditionally known more down
tempo and middle-register forms of vocal performance, and even in the
majority of Solomon Linda's recordings the overall sound is less compact
than in *'mbombing* songs from other areas. In any event, today's performers and audiences have come to discern and appreciate an entirely unique
aesthetic in Joseph Shabalala's music that differs fundamentally from the
ethos of fiercely contested manliness and vociferous regional pride expressed in previous substyles. The most telling expression, perhaps, of this
new aesthetic are terms such as *isithululu, pholile,* and *ubumnandi* used to
designate the music of Black Mambazo. The ideophone *isithululu* is derived from the verb *-thula,* to be quiet, peaceful, and connotes the rolling
roundness of Shabalala's songs. In fact, during particularly satisfying moments of collective involvement, isicathamiya performers at times abandon
themselves to the gentle flow of their choral harmonies and sing short
phrases on words like *thululu,* or, as in some of the older genres, *wi wi wi.*
The term *pholile* means "calm," "polite," and roughly conveys the same
sound qualities as *isithululu. Ubumnandi,* for its part, means sweetness, a
key aesthetic category in many African societies (Stone 1982).

Even though the vocal skills of Shabalala's group by far exceed the
usual, we should equally keep in mind that the soft textures—for which
Ladysmith Black Mambazo is now world famous—like the emergence of
cothoza mfana earlier are in part also the result of far-reaching advances
in recording technology and fundamental changes in studio and market-

ing practice. As a comparison between the early LPs of the 1970s and the most recent recordings of the late 1980s—such as the 1973 recording of "Nomathemba" from the album *Amabutho* and the same song from the Grammy-winning album *Shaka Zulu* of 1987—reveals, the perfect blending of voices in the later recordings is enhanced by a more pronounced echo and a softer sound space. I attribute these developments equally to a greater willingness on the part of producers to creatively work on a product rather than, as was commonly done in earlier times, to invest as little money and effort as possible in what was generally regarded as an artless culture.

Joseph Shabalala's fourth reform—one in which so far no other choir has followed his example—concerns the organization of his professional praxis. In the early 1970s, after the phenomenal success of the first LP *Amabutho,* Shabalala decided to become a full-time composer and performer. Above all, this decision had major repercussions on the composition of the choir. In the beginning, in addition to Walter Malinga, the majority of the members came from the Shabalala family—Headman, Enoch, and Joseph Shabalala—and Joseph's in-laws Milton, Albert, and Joseph Mazibuko. In later years only Albert Mazibuko and Joseph's brother Headman—tragically murdered on December 10, 1991—remained from this nucleus. Most of the members that came in after the mid-1970s— Thamsanqa Mdletshe, Russell Mthembu, Jabulani Dubazane, and Ainos Phungula—were recruited because of their professional qualities, although Ben and Jockey Shabalala as well as Abednigo Mazibuko are also related to Joseph. But the professionalization of Black Mambazo in large part is also responsible for an unparalleled degree of perfection in their performances, even though other isicathamiya choirs spend a considerable amount of their spare time rehearsing. At the same time, this move enabled the group to build up a large following which in turn helped the sales of their albums.

Days of Miracle and Wonder—Isicathamiya Today

From the mid-1970s Ladysmith Black Mambazo has been steadily consolidating its position as the leading isicathamiya group of the postwar era and, beyond this, as one of the biggest-selling recording artists in South Africa. Joseph Shabalala's strategy to reach audiences outside the narrowing microcosm of isiZulu-speaking traditionalist migrant laborers was further enhanced by the release of a number of LPs of a purely religious nature, and of several tracks sung in English or Sotho.

By far the most climactic point in Joseph Shabalala's career, however, and probably one of the most spectacular moments in the history of isicathamiya was the involvement of Ladysmith Black Mambazo in Paul Simon's Grammy Award–winning album of 1986: *Graceland*. At the height of the international antiapartheid campaign during the intensely experimental takeoff phase of "worldbeat," and for the first time since Miriam Makeba's rise to stardom in the mid-1960s, Simon had managed to bring South Africa's black musical traditions back into the limelight. The role of Ladysmith Black Mambazo in the making of the album consists, in a nutshell, of the coauthoring by Paul Simon and Joseph Shabalala of "Homeless" and of the introduction in "Diamonds on the Soles of Her Shoes" (see also chap. 11). On both tracks, Joseph Shabalala and Ladysmith Black Mambazo perform as lead singers and also in the background vocals. The success of *Graceland* and a subsequent world tour was capped off with Shabalala's own Grammy in 1987 for the album *Shaka Zulu,* basically a compilation of rerecorded classic Mambazo songs such as "Nomathemba," "Golgotha," and "Hello My Baby." *Shaka Zulu* and subsequent albums such as *Journey of Dreams* and *Two Worlds, One Heart* also featured a growing number of titles sung in English, and from 1991 the group also began experimenting with instrumentally backed songs such as "Township Jive" on *Two Worlds, One Heart.* While this musical marriage between isicathamiya and *mbaqanga,* as we have seen, is not entirely new, this joint venture of Black Mambazo and lead guitarist Ray Phiri of Stimela does represent an attempt to once again align the experiences and hopes of the most oppressed and underpaid members of South Africa's black labor army with the spirit of defiance and exuberance of an entire people in one of the darkest and most difficult moments of its history. Or, as the lyrics of "Scatter the Fire" say,

> Scatter, scatter the fire, spread the music all over the world.
> Music is Love! And Love is Power!

While all these startling developments without question signified for Joseph Shabalala and his men the dawning of veritable "days of miracle and wonder" (to quote Paul Simon's apt formula for the age of the global village), the effects of *Graceland* on the future of isicathamiya at this stage remain uncertain. Although Shabalala's "journey of dreams" has become a powerful source of inspiration for numerous lesser-known choirs, one that inspired the Mthunzini Brothers (RPM 7064, A1), the Thulisa Brothers, and many others to compose songs in praise of Black Mambazo, isicathamiya performance remains firmly grounded in the social organization, ideologies, and aesthetics formulated in the early 1970s. No other choir has succeeded in securing even a fraction of the local record market. Albums by groups other than Black Mambazo rarely if ever sell more than one thousand copies, a fact which is to be ascribed less, as Reamusic chief executive Clive Risco speculated, to allegedly mysterious black buying habits than to highly discriminating tastes among the black record-buying public. Ultimately, it is to be feared, such a speculative approach is also exemplary of some white promoters' ignorance of black musical preferences and, in the last instance, redounds on Reamusic and other labels that have been loath to provide proper promotion and royalties for their artists.

At present, Joseph Shabalala himself, together with a number of prominent isicathamiya aficionados in the media and in education, work to anchor the now century-old tradition of the nightsongs in the culture of a new South Africa, facing the task of finding a place in a vastly changed global order. The challenge embodied in this task appears to lie in the bringing together and mutual enrichment of the meanings of locally embedded and yet globally connected worlds. Performance may then become a potent means of breaking up the received conceptualizations of colonialism and neocolonialism that turn those at the margins into the subjects of our texts and scenarios. If history, on the periphery of the modern world-system perhaps more than elsewhere, is the rooting of personal experience in the inert structures of a world ordered according to exogenous designs, it is also the power to reverse the received subject-object relationship of colonialism in which the "civilizing mission" was paralleled by an academic practice, a historiography that colonized "others" (de Certeau 1988, 72). But the representation of such history poses a challenge to anthropology, history, and particularly the study of performance as one of the potentially most unfixed, open domains of cultural practice; a challenge that, as Hannah Arendt reminds us, consists in the need, as we write "our" and rewrite "their" stories, to recognize the indeterminacy of human action and, hence, to reject monolithic modes of representation and reductionist determinations of agency and meaning. In the same way, writing history as historical anthropologists requires from us an analytical approach to the role of consciousness that sees in the contingency of social knowledge, individual, and collective experience the creative source from which may emanate, if not "authors of outcome," then historical subjects.

PART II SPACES

In the preceding chapters I have offered a number of texts—a speech by Joseph Shabalala, the transcript of a discussion with performers, a mixture of oral narratives, and several others—all of which, even in their specific form as modes of verbal discourse, reflect the notion inherent in almost all present-day anthropology that culture—the socially maintained and historically constituted practices, beliefs, and symbols—is a system of texts to be read and endowed with multiple meanings. The results of this textual turn in anthropological theory—in which, to be sure, my own account has its own modest share—are well known, and so are the main lines of contention in the debates this paradigmatic shift has generated. None of this needs to be reiterated here.

One critique, however, increasingly being voiced in recent times, is worth recalling. The preoccupation with the text, the "epistemocentrism," and indeed the sheer obsession—observable in much of current anthropology and in the social sciences generally—with social processes as theater and semantics, appear to be the result in part of the profound changes in the role of knowledge and the social position of intellectuals in modernity. It is thus that a number of theorists working from a critical reevaluation of science, scholarship, and the role of intellectuals in a broadly antihegemonic politics, insist on a difference between theory and practice. The world, apart from whatever it may be to intellectuals who cast their theoretical eye (*theorein*) on it, is a totality of concrete problems that call for practical answers (Bourdieu and Wacquant 1992), even if these problems and the answers now overwhelmingly seem to be located in the realm of culture.

The development of an alternative notion of space as a central category of a politics of resistance has proved to be particularly crucial in this project. The work of Edward Soja (1989), Fredric Jameson (1991), and especially the later work of Henri Lefebvre (1991), in my view, can be read as an attempt to recover space and spatiality—the "dead, the fixed, the undialectical" of former philosophical thought (Foucault 1980, 70)—as a concept countering the triumph of the sign, that profoundly mystifying logic of late capitalism which makes (real) relations of domination and subordination disappear under a giant metatext. Global capitalism, Lefebvre argues, has hidden from critical scrutiny an all-embracing spatiality which is built on uneven development and which is central to the maintenance of the power relations that mark this social order. To uncover these spatial orders and to make ideas leave their mark on space, in other words to produce space, is therefore the first step in demystifying this world as socially produced and thus transformable.

More than a medium, a frame, or worse, a fashionable formula for the reshaping of social theory, space then for Lefebvre is above all a "materialization of social being" (1991, 102). This notion of space may perhaps be illustrated by a distinction of which Michel de Certeau has reminded us. Space, de Certeau says, must be distinguished from place, a term which denotes a location in which two things cannot be at the same time. Place is ruled by the law of the "proper." Space, by contrast, is "actuated by the ensemble of movements deployed within it" and has none of the stability of the "proper"; it is a "practiced place" (de Certeau 1984, 117).

Lefebvre and the other authors mentioned limit their discussion of space to the industrialized societies of the West. They might have found interesting evidence, however, in the growing body of literature addressing itself to the spatial organization of societies on the margin of the First World (e.g., Moore 1986). Although increasingly swept up by the spatial regime of global capitalism, these societies often exhibit a practice in which the disjunctures between the sign and its referent and the concomitant loss of spatial anchoring of human practice typical of modernity are still, by and large, absent. Here the body still maintains a relationship with space that is more immediate and not yet veiled by the pervasiveness of the commodity sign. Although social practice everywhere is constituted in the dialectic of action and meaning, and societies everywhere and at all times have been culturally saturated, the signifying practices of societies differ and so does, within these, the role of space in ordering and representing human practice.

Taking these considerations into account, I shall argue in the chapters of this section that in isicathamiya performance the vanishing symbols and crumbling orders of the past are returned to and remade in a complex set of spaces. But instead of asking what these mean as signs, I see these spaces foremost as embodiments of an imagined order, located in a heroic past beyond the here and now and constructed through multisensory communicative means such as sound texture, dress, and dance.

Space, then, as I understand it, is not another "cultural text among many" (Moore 1986, 189). Quite to the contrary, as a socially guided process, isicathamiya performance seeks to "establish authoritative traditions, discrete temporal and spatial parameters in which it is made singularly clear to cultural subjects and their others what is (and who are) to belong within these parameters, and what (and who) not" (Scott 1992, 375 ff.). Like all local discourses, the production of space in performance is animated by the desire to fetter the random play of signifiers and the very disappearance of the signified imposed by the relentlessly disembedding logic of an extrinsic system.

4   The Unhomely: Performers and Migrants

Sihamba nje sizulazula senziwa yindaba zokuhlupheka.
We are wandering about and experience hardship and suffering.

Greytown Evening Birds

Ikhaya lami alikho lapha.
My home is not here.

Scorpions, "Ikhaya Lami"

"It is the hostels that produced this idiom," said Paulos Msimanga, a prominent and experienced isicathamiya promoter. Commenting on the pervasive osmosis of isicathamiya and the life and experience of migrant laborers, he continued, "The living of males alone created loneliness and nostalgia. This therefore led to singing which gives relief to the tedium of work, nostalgia and loneliness." The juxtaposition of isicathamiya and the world of migrant labor that Msimanga evokes here, points to one of the most crucial aspects of the nightsong tradition. But Msimanga's observation also mirrors another important theoretical premise of much current work on performance. Theater, dance, and music are not simply embedded in some context vaguely described as "sociocultural background," a set of external conditions that exist prior to and independent of the performance. Performance practices such as music making are socially and historically located, meaningful configurations of symbols and practices and, hence, any adequate analysis of such practices "must be informed by an equally detailed understanding of the historically situated human subjects" that perceive, learn, interpret, evaluate, produce, and respond to these symbols and practices (Waterman, 1990, 6).

Yet the exact nature of the linkages between performance as practice and its social context remains one of the key critical and unsolved issues in the contemporary anthropology of performance. Thus some recent musical ethnographies convincingly demonstrate that performance is every bit as embedded in social interaction as it becomes a context for social action. Similarly, performance practices are increasingly understood as interactions with and constructions of social processes beyond pristine communities with primordial roots. In the most experimental ethnographic accounts, the focus has shifted markedly from the demarcation of parent cultural traits in syncretic musical systems (Bohlman 1988, 120; Wachsmann 1961,

148) to the description of socially and culturally heterogeneous communities and their musical practices. The pervasiveness of syncretism in the modern world has largely rendered obsolete closely observed and isolated cultural worlds as the normative descriptive space of ethnographies. How and through which social agents cultural identity and musical practices came to be constructed as self-constituting and essential among the Yoruba of Nigeria or the Aymara of Peru, for instance, may be of greater relevance to ethnomusicologists today than the putatively intrinsic features of these practices (Turino 1993; Waterman 1991b). Taking these interventions into account, in this chapter I seek to formulate a critique of the prevailing ethnomusicological paradigm of tribe and tradition. Rather than defining stylistic configurations and practices from the cultural core, I argue that the multiplicity of migratory strategies and the heterogeneity of life experiences of isicathamiya proponents undermine the notion of a singular social position as a monocausal determinant of performance practice. Performance, I suggest, does not emanate from a social base, it is itself a field of changing and conflicting social relations.

This position, it is true, echoes a growing theoretical concern in the social sciences and the humanities with the text, that is to say, with social practice as nothing but a web of free-floating signifiers. On this view, meaning does not reside in the music, as one of musicology's most entrenched fictions would have it, but is essentially produced in the ever-shifting interaction between actors, interpreters, and performers. How and why certain social actors, by producing and perceiving certain patterns of sound and movement, make sense of their world, is more a question of discursivity and intertextuality than of knowing some presumed, a priori truth or meaning. In taking into account, as I indeed proposed in the introductory remarks to this section of the book, these and other tenets of postmodern theory, I nevertheless wish to sharpen our awareness of those aspects of South African reality that have remained hidden under the thick conceptual layers of structuralist and neo-Marxist thought. Power relations in South Africa, to be sure, the numerous cleavages of race and class cutting through its social fabric, apart from being tied to and activated by material processes, clearly rest on a relatively coherent semantic terrain that allows people to construct themselves and their image of others. At the same time, as we have seen in chapter 3, the attempts of historians and social scientists to provide realistic accounts of the ongoing transformation of South African society have tended to underestimate the signficance of culture and consciousness in this process. Individual experience, the emergence of multiple, fractured identities and the indeterminacies of meaning and social action have all been dealt with rather inadequately.

Perhaps it is this instability of meaning amid the persistent divisions and semantic polarities of class and ethnicity in the postcolonial world that has led some scholars to reexamine the relationship between, inter alia, place and culture. Thus, Akhil Gupta and James Ferguson in a recent critique of anthropology's all-too-monadic notion of culture explore ways of dealing "with cultural difference while abandoning received ideas of (localized) culture" (Gupta and Ferguson 1992, 7). The authors propose to rethink difference through connection, as the product, that is, of a "shared historical process that differentiates the world as it connects it." Similarly, Homi Bhabha, discussing recent South African literature, speaks of the "unhomely" as a paradigmatic experience whose resonance can be heard in a wide range of historical conditions and social settings (Bhabha 1992). To be unhomely, he writes, does not simply mean to be homeless. Unhomeliness is a condition in which the border between home and world becomes confused, in which the private and the public become part of each other. The home no longer remains the domain of domestic life, nor does the world simply become its counterpart. The unhomely, Bhabha concludes, "is the shock of recognition of the world-in-the-home, the home-in-the-world" (141).

The unhomely, then, could, in a wider sense, be taken as that condition in which the making of an individual experience may well happen in one place while its actual coordinates lie in a reality far beyond the limited space and often beyond the conceptual capacity of any one individual. The result of this strange dialectic of the private and the public, the near and the far, the local and the global is, to use Fredric Jameson's phrase, a "new play of absence and presence" (Jameson 1991, 411). Isicathamiya performance, I would argue, like all forms of performance located at this particular juncture of the world-in-the-home and the home-in-the-world, not only captures this moment, it is also inconceivable without this figurative play. To understand this, we now have to turn to the varied and multiply determined social worlds that govern isicathamiya performers' immediate experience. In particular, we have to reexamine labor migration, one of the most powerful—and problematic—constructs used to account for the complex experiences of a significant portion of the country's black population.

Men of No World? The Economic Strategies and Cultural Practices of South African Migrants

Labor migration, as even the most cursory inquiry into South African history and political economy will tell, is without any doubt the cornerstone of South Africa's entire social, political, and economic landscape. It is the linchpin of an entire system that within a few decades transformed the country into one of the most powerful economies in sub-Saharan Africa. "Never in modern times," the sociologist Bernard Magubane wrote in 1979 on the growth of capitalism in South Africa, "has a country made such an extensive use of migrant labor as has South Africa, where more than 70 percent of the labor force is made up of migrants. . . . The root and basis of the migrant labor system and the reservations reaches deeply into the history of how African labor power has been exploited in South Africa" (Magubane 1979, 93). This fact, as other authors have argued, even contributed to a certain homogenization of African labor (Stadler 1987, 89), a process that was supplemented by several decades of apartheid legality which defined millions of black South Africans of quite diverse social and cultural backgrounds rather uniformly as migrants or interim urban sojourners. In fact, this system, with its "hostels," compounds, prisons, trains and pass laws, was so comprehensive and powerful that earlier analyses portrayed labor migration and the attendant reserve system as a structure set entirely in place by capital, overseen by the South African state, and designed to serve the interests of a handful of mine magnates. Thus, Harold Wolpe and Martin Legassick, two of the foremost proponents of this theory, argued that access to a subsistence base in the so-called reserves reduced the cost of labor by providing (in whatever rudimentary form) for welfare costs and the reproduction of the black labor force (Legassick 1974; Wolpe 1972).

Recent scholarship, in the aftermath of the so-called revisionist school of South African historiography, has, of course, done much to give us a more nuanced overall picture of South African capitalist transformation than the sweeping and detached analytical mode of earlier political economy suggests. Beginning in the 1980s, an enormously prolific school of researchers have produced accounts of highly differentiated processes of the formation of a migrant labor force. One of the insights that emerged from this literature is a "growing picture of structural relations within African societies acting every bit as powerfully on the actions and consciousness of migrants as any 'pull' of market forces, growth of 'new wants' . . .

or the 'determining role of the South African state' on the other" (Marks and Rathbone 1982, 19). Thus, labor migration and migrant consciousness, especially when examined in the light of migrants' own conceptualizations, are not simply manifestations of the all-encompassing capitalist system.

And they are far from constituting a homogeneous realm, either, be it geographically or historically. For the conditions under which vast stretches of the Southern African continent were gradually being transformed into seemingly inexhaustible labor reservoirs differed from region to region and during particular historical periods. By no means had the South African countryside been welded, during the early decades of the twentieth century, into a sphere with uniform social, economic, and moral relations and rules. In Natal, for instance, the area with which we are mostly concerned here, the 1920s and 1930s were perhaps one of the most dramatic phases in the long process of dispossession of the African peasantry. But even here, in a geographically small area and during a relatively short historical period, striking differences in the socioeconomic position and prosperity of the African population can be observed. Although sharecroppers, squatters, and labor tenants throughout Natal have all been reduced over time to little more than hired farm hands, some fared better than others. Reserve dwellers, for instance, were generally regarded as more prosperous than labor tenants on white farms (Bradford 1987, 61). In some magisterial districts of northern Natal such as Newcastle, Dundee, and Utrecht—all strongholds of early isicathamiya—the vitality of subsistence farming remained fairly unbroken even into the mid-1930s and made migration and wage labor relatively unattractive life projects for many African farmers (Harris 1985).

In more recent times, of course, the depressed situation of South Africa's black rural population has become all-pervasive, and any niches and alternative escape routes from the lot of labor migration that may have existed in earlier times have now very nearly all disappeared. As one study of a rural slum in TabaNchu shows, the households locked away into the bleak settlements, camps, and shantytowns of South Africa's so-called homelands are no longer tied to a rural lifestyle and are therefore better understood as segments of dislocated urban communities (Murray 1988). Similarly, in Natal, a functioning rural subsistence base has become but a very remote possibility for the vast majority of isiZulu-speaking migrants. Thus, a survey of the rural links among Durban's black residents revealed that for 77 percent of them it is impossible to live by farming alone. The land most of them own in reality represents little more than a retirement plot (Schlemmer and Møller 1985; 161, 165). Nevertheless, more than 60 percent of migrant workers in Durban have access to some form of arable land and continue to entertain hopes about supporting themselves and their families through farming or a combination of farming and wage labor (159). All in all, the majority of today's black migrant population appears to fall into a category that can best be described as "men of no world."

Clearly, then, being a migrant from a northern Natal farm during the 1930s meant something quite different from entering the urban labor market from the reserves. The situation of the migrant workforce in the 1930s in turn differed markedly from the lot of most migrant workers in the 1970s and 1980s. And even then, the experience of a KwaZulu "homeland" resident who commutes between his shack and the factories at Isithebe may have little in common with that of Mr. Job Kheswa, a member of the Durban Crocodiles and a truck driver, who has been living in Umlazi on the outskirts of Durban for the past twenty years. Thus whether we think of these "men of no world" as migrant laborers, peasant-proletarians, or members of displaced urban communities is only of secondary importance here. The point is that, more than anything else, it is the heterogeneity and fluidity of experience at the interstices of the world of wage labor and the world of subsistence production that characterize the situation of South Africa's laboring masses, and not any particular fixed class position as such. These shifts and displacements occurred historically between different generations of migrants, but often they also characterize the life trajectory of a single individual.[1]

Labor migration in modern South Africa, then, is more than a facet of the country's political economy, more than the movement between "two different modes of production, capitalist wage employment on the one hand, and some form of pre- or partially capitalist subsistence or peasant production on the other" (Stichter 1985, 1), as one influential text on migrant labor puts it in rather schematic terms. The making of this social universe is not a matter of structural constraint alone and, in any case, it is much more difficult to account for in qualitative terms than the cut-and-dried statistics of the labor market. Involved in these structural processes were living human beings who were both their object and their creative subjects and whose experience and response differed widely as a result of varying cultural and personal backgrounds. Thus, the lives that millions of black South Africans are forced to live in the insecure interstices between wage employment and other forms of production, in the language of anthropology could perhaps be better described as an all-pervasive state of off-centeredness, of fractured identities, and of perpetual displacement. It is a whole social microcosm in itself, a complete way of life with its own sets of rules, symbols, and meanings.

But this world is one we know very little about. There are a great number of surveys (e.g., Møller 1985; Møller and Welch 1985), to be sure, as well as a substantial literature on such issues as the breakdown of rural social life, the role of migrant labor in the maintenance of rural domestic production, strategies of resistance, and so on. But this rich output is not quite matched by equally vigorous attempts to penetrate the manifold forms of consciousness and symbolic expression among black migrant workers. The reasons for this relative academic indifference may not be entirely dissimilar to those Charles van Onselen discovered with regard to the dearth of studies on domestic service (van Onselen 1982, 1–2), after all one of the major forms of migrant labor. Although migrant workers stand in the front line of production, van Onselen argues, everything that is not directly related to their role as providers of cheap labor and producers of profits was of little value as object of investigation and examination. In addition, a great many of the activities of migrants, both at and away from the workplace, were directly opposed to the law of these institutions and therefore not readily accessible to outside inquiry.

In the light of these obstacles, scholars have been slow in realizing that to concentrate only on how migrants responded at the workplace, was "to capture only a very partial view of their diverse consciousness" (Beinart 1987, 305). Consequently, alcohol consumption, criminality, prostitution, stick fighting, and numerous other cultural practices of this universe of transition and displacement have only recently attracted scholarly attention. Thus two studies, Jeff Guy and Motlatsi Thabane's article on Basotho miners and shaft sinking (Guy and Thabane 1988) and John and Jean Comaroff's paper on Tshidi Barolong concepts of work and labor (Comaroff and Comaroff 1987) have persuasively demonstrated how closely technological processes, the experience at the workplace, and migrants' consciousness are connected. Philip Bonner, for his part, has looked at alcohol brewing and prostitution among migrant Sotho women in the 1930s (Bonner 1990), while Patrick McAllister has written on beer drinking rituals for returning Xhosa migrants (McAllister 1981).[2] The criminal gangs of migrant domestic servants have been the focus of a series of studies by William Beinart (1987); Paul la Hausse (1990); Charles van Onselen (1982); and Jeff Guy and Motlatsi Thabane (1987).[3] Finally, in a field even further removed from the usual haunts of academic curiosity, Dunbar Moodie has explored migrants' homosexual relationships (Moodie 1988).

These and other studies not mentioned here not only paint a rather somber picture of migrant life in South Africa's townships, "hostels," and reserves—of disrupted relationships, violence, and great emotional distress. More important perhaps, they argue that such cultural practices are expressions and reinforcements of migrants' hidden forms of resistance to capitalist legality and proletarianization. What is lacking in these accounts, however, is the description and contextualization of closely observed microcosms of social interaction and of the meanings and interpretations that the social actors concerned invest into these local worlds. Several important exceptions must not be overlooked, however. Thus, Rian Malan, in a haunting account of a journey to Msinga, of a pilgrimage that, as he writes, left him begging for the "eyes to go blind" (Malan 1990, 277), has described the hunger, destitution, and murderous politics of one of South Africa's worst reservoirs of migrant labor. Another writer, David Robbins, giving testimony to the Second Carnegie Inquiry into Poverty and Development in Southern Africa in 1984, found harrowing evidence in the same area of malnutrition, thuggery, ecological devastation, and abject poverty (Robbins 1984). Finally, Mamphela Ramphele's exceptional *A Bed Called Home,* a study of life in the migrant labor hostels of Cape Town, provides a compelling account of what the author calls the "survival culture" among migrant hostel dwellers (Ramphele 1993, 133). Ramphele is concerned to show how hostels, as the "logical outcome of the process of conquest" (15), impose severe constraints of physical, political, and psychological space on the residents. The picture she draws of this environment is a grim one, and can only be expressed in a stark numerical imagery: the bed occupancy in these hostels is 1.8 persons per bed, the persons-toilet ration is 31 : 1, and so on. Furthermore, the residents are organized in what she calls "bedholds." These are units of social relationships that superficially resemble households, but in reality are marked by various linkages of patronage, with ill-defined norms of reciprocity between a male bedholder and various dependents such as wives, children, and girlfriends (20 ff.). But far from casting a detached gaze on the world of Cape Town hostel dwellers, Ramphele also describes the practices migrants have devised in coping with this degrading environment.

In the area of performance, the music and dances of migrant workers likewise have long remained in the shadow of academic curiosity. Here David Rycroft's analysis of violin music (1977), while not explicitly addressing issues of labor migration and performance and although it echoes the premises of an earlier period of anthropological thought, must count as a pioneering exception. The same goes for a number of more recent studies, most notably Jonathan Clegg's four evocative essays on *ingoma* dancing and concertina music (1981a, 1981b, 1982, 1984), and Harold Thomas's as yet unpublished thesis on thirty-three Durban *ingoma* dance teams (1988). What limits these and three other brief studies of isicatham-iya by the dramatist Peter Larlham (1981); musicologists Elkin Sithole (1979); and David Rycroft (1957) is the focus on the structural continuity of rural-traditional performance in town rather than on the historical pro-cesses of transformation.

Studies of migrant performance that go beyond this approach are a se-ries of interrelated articles by David Coplan on *lifela,* one of the core per-formative literary genres of Lesotho migrants (1986, 1987a, 1987b, 1988, 1991). Coplan's studies are exemplary in that they do not content them-selves with the analysis of structure. Rather, their author shows the perfor-mance of *lifela* as being grounded in social practice, both set in motion by broader social processes and powering the perception and consciousness of social actors. What we lack, at this point in time, are detailed ethnographies of how these processes are located and enacted in specific sets of circum-stances and how the cultural practices of migrants travel through different geographical and social spaces. There are relatively few studies that, like Thomas Turino's (1993) study of migrant performance in the altiplano of Peru and its capital Lima, are based on multilocale fieldwork in both the rural and urban settings of migrant life.

On the whole, the remarkably broad range of heterogeneous cultural practices emerging from all these accounts constitutes perhaps what one might call a poetic of labor migration, an expressive map of the no-man's-land between the here and there. For what all these practices have in com-mon is their insistence on migrants' creativity in shaping the world for themselves. By articulating the language and idealized images of the rural homestead with the aspirations and suffering of town life, migrant workers struggle to re-center their fractured life worlds around powerful (and em-powering) symbols.

This is not to say, however, that all these activities and symbols, as at least one author has indeed suggested, form a "migrant culture" sui ge-neris (Moodie 1991, 50–53). In fact, on the evidence available it is open to debate whether anything as discrete and unified as suggested by such a term exists at all. Take, for instance, migrants' own taxonomies of social grouping: an extensive vocabulary captures the experience of people whose world is not circumscribed by well-defined boundaries and whose movements are described in words that convey a sense of disorientation, a lack of direction and collective identity, an acute awareness of distance, even death. Tswana miners, for example, are often called *makonteraka,* contract laborers, and among the Tshidi Barolong, wage labor in town, *mmereko,* is distinguished sharply from the work at home, *tiro. Mmereko* is alienated labor, while *tiro* is "doing" proper, work that has meaning (Comaroff and Comaroff 1987).

Similarly, in isiZulu, phrases commonly used among migrants are "to roam around" (*zula zula*), "to live like birds." The women who stay behind say that the men working in the mines and the industries are *wezintaba,* "beyond the mountains." They are travelers (*abahambi*), they are going up and down (*behla benyuka*). In a another widely used, if somewhat dated, terminology, reserve residents in Natal, including many migrants, refer to themselves as members of one of three distinct categories of people: the *amakholwa,* the believers, or *abantu basesikoleni,* the school people, whose cultural practices are informed by Christian values; the *amabhinca,* the traditionalists, who "adhere tenaciously to the Zulu traditional patterns of life;" and finally the *amagxagxa,* the driftwood of society, the people who are neither Christian nor pagan (Vilakazi 1965, 94).

Today, migrants are, of course, likely to be found in any of these categories. As H. Thomas's recent study on *ingoma* dance teams in Durban suggests (Thomas 1988, 44), the discrete occupational backgrounds of migrants and their leisure time activities and dance styles only in part coincide with participants' own taxonomies of social grouping. Thus although the vast majority of *ingoma* adherents saw themselves as *amabhinca,* there was a certain overlap between dancers' subjective categorization and the kind of practices they engaged in and that, as traditionalists, they were not supposed to be interested in. The difficulty with such taxonomies clearly lies in the fact that they are socially constructed and as such subject to a great number of constraints, both material and ideological. But be this as it may, what all these terms seem to indicate is of the very essence of the migratory experience: the blurring and dissolution of boundaries, the interim state, the liminal position. Labor migrants, whether *makonteraka* or *amagxagxa,* are the modern wanderers of a world in which the dichotomies of the past—here and there, dwelling and travel, center and periphery—increasingly become enmeshed with each other.

In order to fully understand the subtle interplay of migrants' economic

strategies and symbolic practices in a field like isicathamiya, it is necessary
to first examine some of the material coordinates of the migrants' worlds.
Evidently, not all that is crucial about a society—or even a small fraction of
the activities taking place within it—is constituted at the symbolic level
alone. We therefore now have to ask a few questions such as, Where do the
singers come from, where do they work and live, and what are their relationships with other singers in a choir?

The uneven development of capitalism in South Africa, and the complex and heterogeneous realities subsumed under the term "labor migration," are related to and reflected in a great deal of regional variation of
labor markets, flows, and patterns of labor migration. Thus, for a number
of reasons such as racial segregation and enforced ethnic particularism, it is
possible in South Africa to broadly discern certain ethnically and regionally
exclusive segments of the labor market. A great number of Pondo migrants, for example, for the better part of the early twentieth century have
gravitated toward the Natal sugar cane fields, while mining and the highly
specialized shaft sinking have been monopolized by Sotho migrants. Similarly, the early washermen's guilds of the Witwatersrand and certain forms
of domestic labor in the early phases of industrialization have been reserved
for isiZulu-speaking migrants. In Durban, finally, even finer ethnic and regional ties seem to have played a role in structuring the labor market from
as early as the turn of the century. There is evidence to suggest that certain
groupings of the urban workforce such as ricksha pullers, policemen, and
sanitary workers have become identified with individuals from Mahlabatini, Mapumulo, and Bhacaland, respectively (la Hausse 1990, 86). Clearly,
the point where the journey began in the countryside to a certain extent
also determined the sector of wage labor in which it ended.

It is not possible here to enter into a detailed discussion of the reasons
for the ethnic segmentation of the urban labor market, but from the examples quoted it should come as no surprise that the cultural practices of
this regionally divided workforce were deeply imprinted with a sense of
local identity.[4] The rural home, the workplace in town, and migrants' cultural practices in the urban context were often contingent on each other.
And thus, given all this regional diversity, it is not very surprising to find
that in a tradition such as isicathamiya, so deeply concerned with the rural
home, issues of locality and regional identity in general are so significant.
As we shall see further in the course of this and subsequent chapters, the
various aspects of isicathamiya are impossible to understand without taking
into consideration the profound processes through which South Africa's

modern geopolitical matrix was being shaped. The spatial linkages constructed by migrant performers in particular, and the factors that affected
them in doing so, is what interests us here; in other words, the networks
that have been and are being created between performers from neighbor-
ing rural locales and foremost, of course, their regions of origin. As we shall
see, the reasons why some isicathamiya styles are being sung in one region
and not in another, why isicathamiya performers originated from one part
of the country rather than another during a certain historical period, are
not to be seen as final causes. But these connections are not arbitrary, either. They were also conditioned in part by the broader processes of labor
migration just as much as they helped to shape the formation of the migrant workforce in certain ways.

The overwhelming majority of isicathamiya performers, then, are isi-
Zulu-speaking men from Natal. This fact has led many observers, including
numerous isicathamiya practitioners, to a view of the nightsong tradition
as a significant symbol of Zulu ethnic identity, an assertion that we shall
examine in more detail in chapter 5. In any case, like "Nguni" and other
terms denoting some kind of presumed collective identity in the southeast-
ern corner of the African continent, the notion of a Zulu community is an
extremely delicate construct (Wright 1986). It may be prudent, therefore,
to deconstruct the assumption that isicathamiya can be defined in ethnically and regionally homogeneous terms by first pointing to a few variations and exceptions. Thus, a small number of isicathamiya choirs have
emerged in recent years in areas beyond the isiZulu-speaking core of Natal.
A handful of Xhosa choirs, for instance, are now operating in the Transkei,
and at least one group, the Ndebele choir Amanzi Okuphila, has been in
existence in Zimbabwe for almost a decade.[5] In Swaziland, isicathamiya
enjoyed a certain measure of popularity during the 1950s, and the influence of certain Bhaca genres is evident in some tunes currently being performed. Lastly, a few mostly Natal-based choirs such as the Tugela Ferry
Home Singers, Lucky Stars, Madidi Messengers, Venanda Lovely Boys,
Mavukela Chiefs and Inqaba Yabesotho have recorded a number of tracks
or even entire albums in Sotho and so have Ladysmith Black Mambazo.[6]
None of these groups is, of course, Sotho speaking originally, thus the appearance of a Sotho variety of isicathamiya is more a phenomenon of marketing strategies that needs to be discussed more fully in another context.[7]

These examples of choirs singing in Sotho or Xhosa are, of course, little
more than the famous exception that confirms the rule. Nevertheless, the
notion of isicathamiya as a Zulu genre pure and simple is questionable for

yet another reason. Zulu-speaking musicians have always differentiated between a variety of regional styles, whether they played concertina, guitar, or sang work songs. *IsiNdwedwe,* for instance, was a concertina style from Mdwedwe district, while *isiChunu* originated from the Chunu clan in Msinga, and so on. Similarly, as was shown in chapter 3, the world of isicathamiya is divided up by numerous finely drawn regional lines that are rooted in, as they symbolically maintain, the regional and ethnic segmentation of the migrant labor market.

Three major regions of origin can be broadly distinguished: (*a*) the Natal midlands and the southern parts of the Orange Free State, (*b*) the Durban metropolitan area and the Natal South Coast, and (*c*) Zululand. Similarly, two broad periods can be distinguished in which the various geographical centers of isicathamiya and the spatial patterns of migration among its practitioners developed. In the early decades, two regions clearly stand out as wellsprings of musical creativity and migrant musicians' homes: the area around Durban and the Natal midlands. The causes of this regional preponderance are complex and, as we have seen, are to be sought in economic structures as well as in other cultural factors. The city of Durban, for instance, had been founded in 1824 and with its rapidly growing European population and expanding port facilities, soon came to constitute one of the most important regional urban labor markets on the southeast African coast. Naturally, it was the adjacent reserves that were among the earliest suppliers of migrant labor to the city's docks, railway yards, or white households. The Nyuswa reserve or, what is today better known as Botha's Hill, was one such labor reservoir on the outskirts of Durban. The first labor migrants from this area began streaming into the seaport city as early as the 1850s (Mbatha 1960, 102–17). It is thus small wonder that Durban's premier isicathamiya group, Mzobe's Crocodiles, hailed from the Nyuswa reserve.

As for the Natal midlands, their prominent role in early isicathamiya history is explained by the fact that large tracts of this part of the isiZulu-speaking territory had been marked as reserves from very early on. These impoverished, drought-stricken areas had soon deteriorated into huge labor reservoirs whose residents were among the first and numerically most important sectors of Natal's black population to experience migration. As was discussed in chapter 3, some of the earliest isicathamiya choirs— Solomon Linda's Evening Birds, Alson Mkhize's Dundee Wandering Singers, the Morning Stars—came from Msinga or the adjacent white farmland in the vicinity of towns such as Dundee, Estcourt, and Newcastle.

Apart from these economic reasons, the migrants from the midlands and the Durban region were also the first to absorb the kind of values and cultural practices that were being spread in mission stations and urban locations and that were to have such a crucial effect on the evolution of early isicathamiya. In other words, migrant performers from the reserves in Inanda, Msinga, or Amanzimtoti were the first to discover the appeal of the minstrel shows and choral singing cherished by the black elite in Durban and on the surrounding mission stations.

With the outbreak of the Second World War, however, more and more migrants were pouring into the cities from all over Natal. It is around this time that other regions, too, began to produce choirs, sometimes, as we have seen, with their own specific styles. Eventually, by the 1950s, a dense network of choirs had developed in Durban and Johannesburg with links to virtually every corner of Natal, and since then no particular area seems to have asserted some kind of stylistic supremacy.

The geographical origin of isicathamiya performers is as diverse and varied as their social background. To be sure, the vast majority of isicathamiya practitioners have always been and continue to be firmly wedded to the countryside. But as the life stories of numerous performers suggest, there has never been uniformity in their rural social milieu, and considerable variation exists in the degree of attachment to a subsistence or peasant economy among these musicians. Here, two biographies from the formative period of isicathamiya history, 1920s–1930s, may serve as an example. As I have said, social relations in Natal consisted of a great variety of forms: labor tenancy and sharecropping existed side by side with black land ownership and farm wage labor. It is from this mix of social and productive relations that the first generation of isicathamiya practitioners emerged. Thus Solomon Linda's family appears to have been one of the many small impoverished peasant households—the household is the important social unit to consider in matters regarding labor migrancy—in the crowded and hopelessly unproductive Msinga area. Conditions must have been so desperate indeed that virtually all young males, including the young Solomon, had been driven into migrant labor.

Enoch Mzobe's family, by contrast, does not seem to have relied exclusively on the wage remittances of the younger generation. The Mzobes lived in the Nyuswa reserve, close to the river Umgeni. Enoch's father was a priest in the Lutheran Church in Clermont, a position from which he derived a small but regular income. In addition, Enoch's father owned extended property that was being looked after by his mother. The produce from these lands was kept for the family's own consumption. "I was surprised by food shortage in the cities," said Mzobe. "Here we would have a surplus of food especially pumpkins which would be given to cattle. You know the first time for me to see a white man was when I was fourteen years old. We were self-sufficient and there was no need of going to town." Although probably none of this meant extraordinary wealth for the Mzobes, with some of the money Enoch's older brothers were making in Johannesburg they were able to send the fourteen-year-old Enoch to Amanzimtoti mission school where he even went as far as standard 5.

If the rural background of performers, varied as it is, accounts for a significant portion of the social universe in which isicathamiya is situated, the urban segment of this universe must also be examined. In particular, it is the two most crucial aspects of migrant life in town—work and housing—that interest us here. A cursory glance, for instance, at the sectors of the urban economy to which isicathamiya performers have been drawn over the past seven decades, reveals a striking phenomenon. Despite the dramatic shifts in industrial development in South Africa and the profound changes in migratory patterns, isicathamiya performers have consistently been gravitating toward employment in the manufacturing industry. An early performer such as Enoch Mzobe, as we have seen, worked as a laborer in a tie factory. Others, like Solomon Linda, were unskilled workers in the Carlton Hotel and at the Gallo record-pressing plant, while most of the members of the Johannesburg-based Crocodile Singers were employed in the timber industry. This pattern has not changed significantly to the present day. A choir such as the Durban-based Cup and Saucer, to quote only one representative example, in 1985 recruited the majority of its then twenty-nine members from the Toyota assembly line and the packaging manufacturer Nampack. Some members worked for the South African Railways and others were employed as laborers in smaller companies producing carpets, kitchen utensils, and other consumer goods.

Somewhat singular, by contrast, are performers such as Zephania Mzolo of the Mzolo Mbube Group who has become a self-employed diviner (*isangoma*). Some members of the King Star Brothers, in turn, have been experimenting with taxi businesses of their own, while Solomon Ndlovu, the erstwhile chairman of the Glebe association, although no longer an active performer himself, in the mid-eigthies tried his hand at a number of enterprises such as a barber shop and a grocery store. But for Ndlovu and most musicians, the switch from wage labor to small-scale entrepreneurial activities has rarely been accompanied by lasting success, a dilemma they share with South Africa's proletariat as a whole.

What is remarkable about the job distribution among isicathamiya performers is the fact that two broad sectors of the South African labor market that have always been occupied by migrant workers, mining, and domestic service, have never produced significant numbers of isicathamiya singers. As a result of this, the repertory of isicathamiya song texts, choreographic patterns, and dress seldom bear a direct relationship to the experience of migrant workers in these major sectors of the country's economy. However, in the Transvaal a few singers have known spells of employment in the mines before they took up other jobs and, it must be emphasized, before they became engaged in isicathamiya performance. And there are also a few groups such as the Mtwalume Young Aces, who deplore in their songs the fate of the miners and beseech the Lord to have mercy on "the poor brothers who suffer in the gold mines" (*lezongane ezihlezi kabuhlungu emgodini*). Ladysmith Black Mambazo, in an ambitious attempt to reach the record-buying migrant miners, in 1981 even recorded an entire album entitled *Phansi Emgodini* (In the mines) (Mavuthela/Ezomdabu BL 321). The cover photograph shows the choir in typical miners' gear underneath a shaft head, but only in the first track "Nansi Imali" (Here is the money) do the lyrics seek to capture some of the jubilant feeling families express over the return of their men from the mines. In recent years, the group has also occasionally performed to international audiences in overalls, crash helmets, and carbon lamps, no doubt because of South Africa's image as the world's leading gold producer. Irrespective of these isolated examples, it would be misleading, however, to characterize isicathamiya as a miners' performance genre.

The world of kitchens and suburban gardens, traditionally one of the major sectors of the urban labor market occupied by isiZulu-speaking migrants, plays even less of a role in isicathamiya. Nonetheless, some musicians did enter the labor market from the bottom end as severely underpaid domestic servants. Thembinkosi Pewa, Alison Gumbi, and Enoch Mzobe, for instance, at first worked as kitchen "boys" in and around Durban. But this was a road that many young newcomers, disparagingly labeled *okishini* (kitchen people) by more settled township residents, had to take before they were able to gain access to more lucrative jobs in the industries.

The heterogeneous patterns by which South African migrants have been drawn into the wage economy historically and structurally had major repercussions on the structure and content of these genres as well as on their linkages with other genres created by black South African migrants. Examples of such genres are the *lifela* oral poetry of Basotho miners and the *ingoma* dances of isiZulu-speaking domestic servants. Both these types of competitive migrant performance differ not only with regard to structure and expressive extent but also in relation to the types of labor and rural cultural background from which their respective adherents are drawn. Right from the earliest period, *ingoma* dancers, for example, recruited themselves from within the ranks of domestic servants and, as far as Durban was concerned, from the mass of stevedores and dockworkers laboring in the city's port. *Lifela,* by contrast, is a partly narrative, partly lyrical genre of sung poetry composed in performance by Basotho miners. Together with other genres such as the dance and xylophone instrumental suites of Chopi migrants, *lifela* and *ingoma* emerge from and thrive in two quite distinct contexts of migrant labor with their own sets of work procedures, patterns of residence, and leisure-time activities. While these links between migratory patterns and forms of expressive culture will continue to occupy us throughout the rest of this book, it may suffice here to highlight those aspects of the intertextuality of migrant performance genres in South Africa that are related to the political economy of migrant labor.

Broadly speaking, as a result of the specialization and ethnic fragmentation of the migrant workforce and in conjunction with the resilience of more rural-traditional forms of expressive culture among these migrants, the emergence of literary, musical, and other performance genres such as *lifela* and *ingoma* among sectors of South Africa's black migrants cannot be divorced from the experience of workers in each of these encapsulated sections of the migrant population. Thus it has been noted frequently that the pursuit of these leisure-time activities served to differentiate migrants ethnically as well as to mark status differences between migrants of common ethnic background. Furthermore, such divisions often played into the hands of the industry, and *ingoma* performances were transformed into effective mechanisms of social control (Erlmann 1989).

More important, however, than the scarcity of miners and domestic servants among active isicathamiya practitioners is the fact that a change of workplace and an upward move toward better-paid positions was typically accompanied by changing patterns of performance activity. Thomas Mtshali of the Kings Boys, for instance, on entering the labor market in

Durban, first became active as an *ingoma* dancer. Subsequently, as an employee of the King Edward Hospital, he joined a soccer team and eventually founded his own isicathamiya choir. Likewise, Alison Gumbi, before joining a number of isicathamiya groups, participated in *isicathulo* (gumboot) performances. From this evidence it could be argued that a marked hierarchy of cultural practices, leisure-time activities, and performance genres corresponds to the highly stratified and competitive market of unskilled labor of black migrant workers. Within this system, gambling and *ingoma* dancing clearly seem to have occupied the lower ranks, associated as they were with the least urbanized segments of the migrant workforce. Soccer and isicathamiya, by contrast, were regarded as somewhat more prestigious leisure-time pursuits. Boxing, ballroom dancing, or classical music, however, signaled the fact that a person had crossed the fine line that separated the mass of laboring poor from the thin layer of preachers, teachers, and clerks that constituted South Africa's black middle class.

This fact should, of course, come as no surprise in a society where there existed few means to express status differentiation other than by the subtle appropriation of symbols provided by an order that regarded all blacks as little more than underdogs. Furthermore, from at least the 1920s, such distinctions were actively reinforced by companies and municipal welfare schemes in an attempt to deepen the real fissures within the black workforce and to prevent the growth of a black intraclass solidarity. Or, as indeed one agent of such social control, Durban's Native Welfare Officer Sidney Shepstone, suggested in 1935, assessing the town's welfare policy, "[*Ingoma*] Dancing Troupes . . . supply the vigorous recreation that the Tribal Native requires, just as Football does for the de-tribalised Native." [8]

Some choirs, nonetheless, saw little meaning in such rigidly staked-out domains of lawful leisure-time activity. They created their own scheme of things. Crocodiles leader Enoch Mzobe, for instance, was not only a passionate performer but also an ardent soccer fan who recorded elaborate praise-poems of South Africa's leading teams of the 1950s (GB 3015). Similarly, the Easy Walkers, a team that had emerged from the soccer club New Tigers in the mid 1950s, saw no inherent contradiction between singing and kicking the ball and, as Alison Gumbi pointed out, combined the two activities in the following manner: "At night we sang, during the day we played football."

Where do isicathamiya adherents live and what influence do residential patterns have on the performance style? Questions such as these are not without relevance in a country that enjoys the dubious repute of having invented the closed compound and having instituted other highly regimented forms of urban housing. For it is clear that the cultural practices of migrants also evolved in direct response to such restrictive conditions, hence have to be seen in close relationship to South Africa's many forms of artificial, involuntary communities: the "total institutions" of mine compound, prison, "hostel," and the township.

Among all of these institutions of regimented living, as performers unanimously agreed, the hostel is the archetypal space of isicathamiya. "Most of the followers of isicathamiya were from the hostels," King Star Brothers public relations officer Sipho Xulu stated. Concrete figures for some of the choirs affiliated with the association at Glebe, for instance, demonstrate that most present-day isicathamiya practitioners live in hostels. Thus, of the twenty-one members of the Kings Boys, ten live in the Glebelands "hostel", while the rest stay at a "hostel" in KwaMashu, the S. J. Smith hostel (Wemmer) and various other hostel-like dwelling places in Umlazi. The Glebelands "hostel" is also "home" to the majority of singers in the Cup and Saucer choir. Of the twenty-nine singers no less than fifteen live in this complex, while the rest live scattered over the S. J. Smith "hostel" and Umlazi township.

Although what has been found here with regard to these two choirs probably applies to the overwhelming majority of isicathamiya practitioners, two important points must be made here. The first is a caveat against the tendency to overconstruct a link between patterns of urban dwelling and cultural practices in South Africa. Even though the state apparatus, mine management, and private enterprise have always put a premium on segregated and highly authoritarian housing structures, and patterns of housing have rarely been the result of deliberate choices on the part of black South Africans, the link between the class position and form of urban residence of an individual is rarely a clear-cut one. Evidence currently available from a wide range of townships, shantytowns, and small country towns suggests that homogeneous communities in which cultural traditions and ideologies blend into each other, are, in fact, the exception rather than the rule (Bozzoli 1987, 29; Smith 1992). Contrary to the mythology of apartheid with its tales of happy township communities, profound cleavages exist within many urban state-initiated communities. "Hostels" in particular have acquired a sad reputation for being the breeding ground of strife and division. In other words, the involuntary allocation of living space is is in no way a reliable index of the class position, let alone of the cultural practices of those who occupy it.

Conversely, like any black migrant in South Africa, isicathamiya singers have, of course, always sought to obtain other, more comfortable kinds of accommodation than a crowded and filthy room in a "hostel." Thus Solomon Linda was a Sophiatown resident during the latter part of his life, and Thembinkosi Pewa was a lodger in the slum of Mkhumbane. The important observation to be made here concerns the danger of reading some kind of contradiction into the fact that more permanently established town dwellers belong to isicathamiya choirs. Thus, a house in town, the use of certain clothing, and of such items as radios and motor vehicles by migrants who consider themselves *amabhinca* cannot be explained, as H. Thomas in his study of *ingoma* dancers has argued, in categories of ruralness or urbanness. These goods are neither "culturally ambiguous" nor are they ineffective in assessing migrants' responses to town (Thomas 1988, 142). Rather, migrant workers do not appear to have adopted uniform approaches to forms and symbols of urban living but instead have made a situational use of such practices and strategies.

The second point concerns the role and potential of "hostels" to function as sites of communication, of creative experiment and innovation. As has frequently been noted, the institutions of labor coercion such as the compound and the "hostel" served to divide and police the black workforce. Considerable evidence has been gathered to prove the existence of strong animosities between compound and "hostel" dwellers on the one side and township residents on the other side. The formation of country-oriented associations such as the *indlavini* among Xhosa-speaking migrants has often been seen as a result of the encapsulated living of migrants in heavily policed mine compounds that have little connection with the outside world of townships (Mayer 1980). Consequently, it is argued, compound dwellers have shown little interest in adopting the practices and symbols of the urban working class.

While this may be true to a certain degree for the more isolated mining compounds, recent evidence also suggests a more differentiated picture at least for "hostels." In most cases, these not only lie near urban agglomerations, in some instances they have even been erected right in their midst. In Durban, for instance, during the formative period of isicathamiya, a network had developed close to the very heart of the white city that spread concentrically from Cartwright's Flats, the most strategically situated and the busiest site of working-class leisure-time activities during the 1920s and early 1930s. It consisted of some of the most important areas of migrant housing such as Msizini Barracks (Somtseu) and the Greyville South African Railways Barracks in Depot Road, the Central Togt Barracks, as well as the Goal Barracks. As the network of "hostels" expanded even further after the Second World War, the life worlds of Durban's migrant population amalgamated even more. Thus, a Pondo migrant, M., whose life story has been told by William Beinart, recalls that in the late 1940s the S. J. Smith "hostel" had little of the tight male organization which he had encountered earlier in the mines. "Women were not allowed to go in," he remembered. But they did. Access to town was also easier. "We were just together—Zulus, Shangaans" (Beinart 1987, 297). In addition to these "hostels," within each walking distance lay a maze of beer halls, shebeens, and dance halls in the surrounding smaller streets and lanes. Among these were the Victoria Street beer hall, C. D. Tusi's dance hall in Fountain Lane, John Nduli's African Social Club at 117 Prince Edward Street, and the African Workmen's Club chaired by James Ngcobo at number 71, which counted some eight hundred domestic servants as its members. In Etna Lane, at one time the International Amusement Club served as a meeting place for homosexual domestic servants and compound residents. At the northern end of the recreation grounds, finally, was Alpheus Seme's dance hall in Umgeni Road, a very popular den that even featured a resident pianist. More sedate venues were the ICU Yase Natal hall at 45 Prince Edward Street and the Bantu Social Centre in Victoria Street (Erlmann 1991). As is to be expected, a dense network such as this could spur intensive interaction not only within the black community but also between the black labor force and the white city. Thus although it is possible to speak of a certain hostel culture and although isicathamiya may be one of its components, this culture was never hermetically screened off from the other urban cultures surrounding it.

As all this clearly suggests, the world-in-the-home and the home-in-the-world constitute a total reality for migrants and isicathamiya performers, not an exceptional situation. Whether they resist the uncertainties of this unstable condition, or turn it to their own advantage, the performers of the nightsongs always do so on practical terms. But practice, as I have repeatedly pointed out, both as everyday social conduct and as performance, is never just the unthinking reproduction of the given. Consciousness intervenes at every step. And so I conclude this chapter by exploring a set of key tropes of the 'unhomely' that isicathamiya performers constantly revert to in order to structure, reflect on, and ultimately render their practice meaningful.

The Crowd, the Machine, and the Whore

To the multiple spaces occupied and activated by migrant performers in the city correspond certain images of the city. Or, to be more precise, the urban milieu is characterized by a certain, historically specific dialectic and even disjuncture of symbolic and material practice. For early migrants, in fact, the urban experience itself was defined by the irreconcilable difference between a former subjective experience tied to a place and a world that has become veiled behind a web of signs, inaccessible to direct personal experience. The city itself is the image. In concluding this chapter we will now have to examine the ways in which the practical experience of the unhomely is mediated and configured symbolically in three fundamental tropes: the crowd, the machine, and the prostitute. Together, these three tropes stand for the profound distinctions labor migrants perceived between the social worlds—the country and the city—which they inhabited simultaneously and whose symbolic significance, ironically, seemed to grow in inverse proportion to their disappearance in structural terms. In discussing these tropes here, I shall draw particularly on the work of Walter Benjamin on Baudelaire and the Paris of the mid-nineteenth century, especially the essays "Paris—the Capital of the Nineteenth Century" and "Some Motifs in Baudelaire" that are key to the aesthetics of urban society and modernity (Benjamin 1973).

To start with the first trope, the crowd, the first observation here that will strike even the most uninitiated listener to the nightsongs, is that there is in them, as in Baudelaire's *Tableaux parisiens,* what Benjamin calls "the secret presence of a crowd" (1973, 122ff.). As in Baudelaire's poetry, in isicathamiya songs the crowd is rarely named. (Later, in chap. 6, we shall see how the corporeal experience of being in and moving with a crowd is enacted in isicathamiya choreography.) And yet, it is through the crowd that migrant workers see the city as though through an "agitated veil." The following song by the CTC (Cape to Cairo) Choir (Bantu Batho BB521), recorded in 1951, illustrates this well:

Leader: *Sengine* . . .
       I have . . .

Chorus: . . . *kula lam' eThekwini.*
        my coolie in Durban.
        Langithengel' ubhanana.
        He bought me a banana.
Bass: *Wen' uMama lo.*
        You, mother.
Chorus: *Hamba mfowethu, hamba siye Thekwini.*
        Go, brother, let's go to Durban.
        Abavumi nokubuya.
        They don't want me to, for fear of my not coming back.
        Sebekipitis' is'ponono
        People are living with a concubine.
        Behla benyuka ngo Berea Rodi.
        Going up and down Berea Road.
        Ngoba ilanga leshonile.
        Because the sun has set.
        Sebekhumbul' eSamseni.
        They are thinking of Samseni.

In the first part, the song sets up an intriguing opposition between the benevolent Indian trader—despite its racist connotation the white term "coolie" is also used by Africans—and the concubine, the urban sweetheart, *isiponono*. Much more to the point, however, that I want to make here are the ways in which the song describes the dangers of the city. For, in the second half, the song seems located in an almost archetypal set of chronotopes, as Mikhail Bakhtin would have said (Bakhtin 1981, 7). First, the familiar image of the night is evoked as the quintessential setting of evil and mystery. But then, the CTC singers complete this image of urban peril with a description of some of Durban's most transient spaces of migrant life. Berea Road is one of the main thoroughfares leading out of Durban into the western suburbs and slums. It was—and to some extent still is—a favorite gathering place for black people working in the adjoining shops and white homes, and up until 1960 led straight past Mkhumbane, or Cato Manor, as one of South Africa's most notorious urban slums was known to Durban's white inhabitants. Samseni, the place mentioned in the last line of the song, was a section of Mkhumbane that was particularly known for its numerous drinking dens and dance halls.

The urban space that is figuratively mapped in the CTC song and others like it, ordered as it may appear at a first glance, is in fact the epitome of disorder: a space hinging on the experience of shock. The words of one further song may illustrate this. The example is from "Eloff Street," a song by the Dundee Wandering Singers (GE 902) that was released in 1941 and is about Johannesburg's elegant main shopping street.

> *Safika eGoli.*
>> We arrived in Johannesburg.
>
> *Safika eGoli kwandonga ziyashunqa*
>> We arrived in Johannesburg, in the heat-chamber,
>
> *kwantaba zikhala amanzi.*
>> where the mountains are pouring out water.
>
> *Ngangihamba noMqothukanwele esahamba.*
>> I was accompanied by "Bald-headed," when he was still alive.
>
> *Awukhalime wethu awele man damn it!*
>> Give direction, brother, cross, man, damn it!
>
> *Safika eGoli sabona intombi nensizwa zehla ngo Eloff Street.*
>> We arrived in Johannesburg and saw young ladies and men walking down Eloff Street.
>
> *Sanibona siyanibingelela.*
>> Greetings, we are greeting you.

Not only does the song articulate the same fascination with the strolling crowds as the CTC song, it also registers the rough and truncated mode of communication—ambiguously couched in English, the language of the colonial city—corresponding to the shock experienced in the urban traffic: "man, damn it."

Beyond this, it is worthwhile to compare the two songs quoted above with what appears to be one of the earliest models for such depictions of urban life in song: Reuben T. Caluza's "ragtime" songs. Based on British syncopated music and vaudeville, Caluza's songs, as we have seen in chapter 3, exerted a certain influence on early isicathamiya performers. One of these "ragtime" songs is "Ematawini or Excuse Me Please" (In town or excuse me please), composed shortly after World War I. The title "Excuse Me Please" is a pun about the *ooscuse-me*. This is what Xhosa and isiZulu-speaking migrants, until well after World War II, called the slick, well-adapted early town dwellers, in whose deferential demeanor and polite manner of speaking they saw only a thinly disguised submission to foreign domination (Wilson and Mafeje 1963, 15). In the main body of the song, Caluza makes a mockery of the language, eating habits, and dress code of the *ooscuse-me:*

Sadlula lapho kesafik'eThekwini.
>   We went to Durban.

Nisaka ngwa'zintombi kanye nezinsizwa
>   Our attention was caught by young ladies and gentlemen

zasehlaze nyuka emgwaqweni.
>   walking up and down the streets.

Zihamba ziqenya zingen' impahla.
>   They are proud of their clothes.

Abanye bey'olwandle abanye kwaMadala.
>   Some of them were going to the beach, some to Madala.

Zabethi Excuse me please gidedele.
>   They say: Excuse me please, can I pass?

Me want some cup-a-tea, because me hungly.

Insizwa zifake izigqoko,
>   The young men were wearing hats,

nentombi zihambis' okwamada ngez'cathulo.
>   and the young ladies were walking like ducks.

Abany'ubonenj'ukutina bo besikholo.
>   Some of them were quite visibly students.

The song then ends with the following "morals":

Kunjal' wematawini.
>   It is like that in town.

Kukhon' inhlobo izinhlobo zabantu.
>   There are all kinds of people.

Ababin' abahle
>   Ugly ones

abaziqenya yo kanye nabathobile.
>   and beautiful ones, proud and simple people.

Although, like "Eloff Street," seemingly painting a realistic picture of the hustle and bustle of urban life, the subtext of Caluza's song, not without a certain sarcasm and frisson that is difficult to translate from the original isiZulu, portrays the urban landscape as a more or less chaotic assemblage of people without a shared moral foundation (Erlmann 1991, 127–35), a space people of every conceivable variety inhabit side by side. But the real horror at this scenery is only expressed in the last line of "Ematawini":

Kukhon' abaghafi nabulungile.
>   There are vagrants and upright ones.

A similar expression of shock is found in Peter Abrahams's novel *Mine Boy,* written in 1946, at about the same time that the song "Eloff Street" was recorded. The text describes the experiences of the young Xuma, a new-comer "from the north." On his arrival in Malay Camp, then one of Jo-hannesburg's many notorious slums, Xuma is overcome with confusion. "He shifted the little bundle from his right hand to his left, hitched up his pants, and continued up the narrow street. A dark narrow street full of shadows, he thought. But then this whole Malay Camp is full of shadows. I wonder where I am, he thought. He had lost all sense of direction. Still, one street was a good as another" (Abrahams 1946, 13) Later, Xuma's new acquaintance Joseph introduces the newcomer from the north to another aspect of urban life: "'It is always like this on Saturdays. People have money in their pockets and it makes them move in the streets and they spend the money. Saturday is so here,' Joseph said. It was so in all the streets. One street was as crowded as another. Groups of men and women milled up and down. It was Saturday" (13).

Obviously, there are numerous differences among these different poetic subjects speaking through Reuben Caluza, the South African poet and composer of the turn of the century who casts his eye on Durban, the novelist Peter Abraham visiting the slums of Johannesburg, and Charles Baudelaire, the poet of Paris of the nineteenth century. For Durban, Jo-hannesburg, and Paris, in their socio-spatial matrix as well as in their class structure, are clearly characteristic of quite diverse historical moments and manifestations of global capitalism. But there are parallels here, too, most notably in the gaze on the city by those not totally lost in and to the city. For the horror that is expressed in Caluza's song—or in Xuma's confusion, for that matter—is the same as the fear of the Parisian urbanite of the middle of the nineteenth century to whom, as Walter Benjamin says, the "masses appear as the asylum that shields an asocial person from his perse-cutors" (Benjamin 1973, 40).

At the same time, the experience of difference—the "going up and down" on Berea Road, Eloff Street, and the streets of Malay Camp and the multitudinous and yet socially differentiated crowd—is here not the same as the ambulant mode of Baudelaire's urban *flaneur.* The *flaneur,* accord-ing to Benjamin, relishes the shock caused by the new urban technology that intersects with older habits of bodily perception. He "develops forms of reaction that are in keeping with the pace of a big city. he catches things in flight" (Benjamin 1973, 41). For Baudelaire's *flaneur,* unlike Caluza's observer of Durban town life, the crowd is "not only the newest asylum of outlaws; it is also the latest narcotic for those abandoned. The flâneur is someone abandoned in the crowd" (Benjamin 1973, 55).

"Going up and down" to "cross" is thus less an indication of urban adroitness, of the individual blending in with the amorphous crowd, than a symptom of acute disorientation and loss of sense of spatial and moral direction. The migrant does not seek to endow the crowd with a soul, as does the *flaneur*. Unmoored from any recognizable moral and social use of the natural environment, the migrant experiences the urban built-up space and the soulless masses as diametrically opposed to his or her centeredness within the circular enclosure of the *umuzi* and to the anchorage in a network of pathways and spatial divisions linking semiautonomous yet interdependent homesteads and districts. Movement in physical space for inhabitants of the old precolonial world thus always entailed a building of, and engagement with, webs of reciprocal exchange. Moving about town, by contrast, is a metaphor for dislocation.

The role of the crowd as the most archetypal symbolic figure of the perceived opposition between town and country finds a correlate in another image: the machine. As is well known, in his work on Baudelaire and Paris, Walter Benjamin linked the experience of the city and the shock in the crowd with the experience of the worker at the machine. The pedestrians in the street, he writes, "act as if they had adapted themselves to the machines and could express themselves only automatically" (Benjamin 1973, 133 ff.). But like the crowd, the machine and industrial technology for the most part hardly ever are present in isicathamiya songs, with two exceptions. One is in the form of the train that carries migrant workers to the city, the other consists in the enactment, indeed in the mode of performance itself prevalent during the 1940s and 1950s, called *isikambula*: gambling.

The train, on the periphery of the modern world system, is the machine in its ur-form, the machine before the machine. Its presence rings through the arts in the whole of southern Africa, from Zimbabwe to Namibia, from Mozambique to Zambia, from *maskanda* music and Hugh Masekela to Zambian *kalindula*. For millions of black South Africans *stimela*, the steam train, has been the key vehicle and, at the same time, the archsymbol of physical bondage and spiritual alienation. For many the train is the most fundamental image produced by the encounter with Western technology and worldview. In isicathamiya songs, however, the image of the train is frequently an ambiguous one. On the one hand, the train is often por-

trayed as a predator that abducts the girlfriend, but sometimes it is also
invoked to convey messages to the relatives at home, as in "Isitimela Samampondo" by the Crocodiles (SABC LT 10, 158, B1):

> Leader: *Isitimela saseMampondweni sihamba njalo sibange enyakatho.*
> > Here is a train bound for Pondoland, also heading for the North.
> *Nas' is'timela s'qudl' uMtata.*
> > Here is a train going past Umtata.
> Chorus: *Isitimela saseMampondweni sihamba njalo sibange nyakatho.*
> > Here is a train bound for Pondoland, also heading for the North.
> *Nas' is'timela s'qudl' uMtata.*
> > Here is a train going past Umtata.
> Leader: *Si . . .*
> > It . . .
> Chorus: *Sisuk'e Thekwini, kwashis'a phantsi.*
> > It is from Durban, you can see sparks from the rails.
> *Hamba njalo ukhonze kubazali.*
> > Go, train, and send greetings to our parents.
> *Nas' is'timela sawa maBhunu.*
> > Here is the train of the Boers.
> *Sisho sithi "khu-khu-khu."*
> > It is going "khu-khu-khu."

What we have here differs markedly from the depictions found in other
genres of migrant performance, such as in Basotho *lifela* where the train is
often quite simply—albeit very eloquently—personalized and demonized
as a madman. The Crocodiles song, by contrast, sets in motion a rather
basic metaphoric operation. In the main body of the song, it appears, the
singers mainly content themselves with offering a seemingly neutral map of
the space traversed by the train before they then turn the train into an ally,
asking it to symbolically bridge the very space that separates the young
migrants from their kin. This strangely ambivalent situation of the train as
the machine that creates space in the first place and, at the same time, as
the means to transcend those spatial divisions, is then metaphorically filled
with an onomatopoetic "khu-khu-khu." But this almost unadorned and
yet sensuous representation of the train, in its very rhythmic structure
probably comes closer than a rich poetic imagery to the essence of the experience of the worker at the machine. The "khu-khu-khu" produced by
the train represents the drill of factory work, the unceasing motion, as
Marx puts it, of an automaton (Benjamin 1973, 132 ff.).

The second form of the invisible presence of the machine, as I have suggested, is inscribed into the very organization of performance itself. And it is here again that Benjamin's work on Baudelaire reminds us of an important parallel. In the section in "Some Motifs in Baudelaire" that follows his reflections on the machine, Benjamin explores one further extension of factory and machine work: gambling (1973, 134–38). Briefly, Benjamin's argument is that gambling shares with wage labor in the factory a sense of futility, emptiness. The gambler no less than the factory worker is unable to complete something. Starting all over again is the regulative idea of the game and of work for wages. Both are devoid of substance, they are a matter only of a reflex action. Enslaved to a relentless mechanism, a drudgery that makes them start all over again, and to a time that reaches only as far as the next card or the next operation at the machine, the gambler and the wage laborer "cannot make much use of experience" (1973, 136).

In chapter 3 we have seen that a style of isicathamiya had emerged in Johannesburg during the 1940s called *isikambula*. The meaning of this term, however, was seen to be ambiguous. While some isicathamiya veterans thought *isikambula* referred to the practice of buying choirs on and off the stage, others believed the term reflected the way in which choirs "took chances" by shuttling between different venues. Either way, it is clear that in both interpretations, performance itself is likened to a game of chance. What resonates through both interpretive options of the term is a deep sense of frustration, not so much about life being, as in an analogy, like a game of chance, but about the impossibility of desire as such. Like Baudelaire's gambler, isicathamiya performers are out to win prizes and prestige. But like him, all they gain is a time that is not their own. The intention to win, for the performer of the nightsongs no less than for the gambler, does not equal a wish. It does not, like experience, reach out in time, as Benjamin says. Wanting to win in a competition is not to fill and divide time; it means to submit to "time in hell" (Benjamin 1973, 136).

This linkage between machine, wage labor, and industrial time is not only highly indicative of the way in which the very social relations of capitalism are inscribed into isicathamiya. In a sense, this linkage also contradicts what I have said earlier about nighttime as a protective zone, thus highlighting yet again the ambiguity of performance. The freedom which the night promises from the merciless clock time of the factory nevertheless is not a total one. The chronological net that imperceptibly and yet powerfully holds captive the performers' consciousness is perhaps the form most effective and difficult to resist, in which the hegemonic order asserts and reproduces itself.

What we have seen so far in the first two tropes of the crowd and the machine is the quintessentially ambiguous nature of the migrant perspective on and experience in the interstices of the urban and the rural world. We now have to turn to the third trope, the whore, as perhaps the new social order's most ambiguous symbol of all. In southern African arts and expressive culture—from Modikwe Dikobe's novel *The Marabi Dance* to Basotho *lifela*—the world of the "marabi girls," as these women are frequently called, or *matekatse*, as they are referred to in Lesotho, is one of the inexhaustable sources of poetic imagination. But this imagination, it will be noted, was one that largely originated from and confirmed a male perspective. Prostitution, to be sure, has been one of the most contested issues in southern African societies undergoing capitalist transformation. For one, African men rather indiscriminately (and pejoratively) applied the term prostitute, "marabi girl" or *matekatse* to any unattached woman who had relinquished her traditional obligations toward her kin and husband (Marks 1989b). In addition, prostitution became a "problem" of white urban politics (Bonner 1990; van Onselen 1982). As such, the term and the category of women subsumed under it, are the product of two interdependent forms—the one black, the other white—of male domination.

In the performing arts, too, this particular category of women was a perennial theme of commentary by men (Ballantine 1993, 81–84). "Intombi Zasi Parktown" (The girls of Parktown), for example, was a very popular tune during the 1930s about the women of Johannesburg's posh suburb Parktown. Although not exactly loose women, these women— often the domestic servants of white households—were one of the prime and most vulnerable objects of black (and sometimes white) male desire, not quite tied any longer to the fiber of South Africa's countryside and not accepted as permanent urban residents, either. A tune such as "Intombi Zasi Parktown" was just one of many songs voicing the ambiguities of male desire and anxiety. Like many others, it was popularized by the vaudeville troupes of the 1920s and 1930s such as the Darktown Strutters and Pitch Black Follies, and later also found its way into the isicathamiya repertoire.[9] Typical of these early isicathamiya songs on the marabi girls, for instance, is "Ngasuke 'Kaya" (I left home) by the Natal Champions (Decca DC 44), a song recorded in 1941:

Ngasuk' ekhaya ngiqond' omsebenzi.
    I left home to look for work.
Nga bon' intombi engomarabi.
    I saw a marabi girl.

What is remarkable about this song is how the familiar stark logic of the "here" and "there" is translated into a dichotomy between "home" and "marabi girl." At one level, this opposition between the home—the quintessential representation of a morally ordered social universe—and the whore reflects, of course, the traumatic displacements that had occurred in precolonial relations of productions and their gender base in particular. For as Cherryl Walker has pointed out, the role of African societies in shaping the migrant labor system was integrally dependent on the gender relations that operated in the precolonial chiefdoms (Walker 1990, 168). The ability of precolonial societies to export male labor rested on a mode of production in which women were the primary producers. This, she argues, explains the violent opposition of chiefs and men in general to female migration. And, consequently, the image of the irresponsible town woman stems from this conflict (179).

At another level, however, there is also a deeper experience, a profoundly unsettling sense of ambiguity that is being registered in these verses. For it is striking to observe how the opposition between the domestic (with its concomitant role of women) and the public represented by the prostitute is put in place by work. Clearly understood in this context as wage labor, work is seen here as both the symbol and the process whereby male labor power and the female body itself become commodities. It is wage labor that brings the migrant to the city, but it is also wage labor that creates the social environment in which the prostitute and her customer come into contact with each other. Labor, then, fuels ambiguous social relations. It does not, unlike work in precolonial society, yield positive value, and it does not fashion an identity. Or, as the Comaroffs say in their discussion of Tswana and missionary concepts of work, unlike work, the notion of labor does not evoke "an image of social life as a continuous, creative flow of events through which persons worked to construct themselves in relation to others" (Comaroff and Comaroff 1991, 141).

To understand migrant performers' perceptions of the ambiguity of a kind of social fabric that enhances production without producing people, we again have to return briefly, in closing, to another time and another

place. In Walter Benjamin's "Paris—the Capital of the Nineteenth Century," there is a passage in which Benjamin discusses some of the root images produced by the ambiguity of social relationships in Paris during this
era. It is one of the main features of the modern, Benjamin writes there,
that it "always conjures up prehistory" in ambiguous images. But this ambiguity of images is only the "figurative appearance of the dialectic, the law
of the dialectic at a standstill." Commodities and the arcades of Paris are
such ambiguous images. And, Benjamin concludes, so is the whore, "who
is seller and commodity in one" (Benjamin 1973, 171).

Clearly, then, the unhomely enters into isicathamiya performers' daily
practice at every moment. At the same time, as we have seen, it resonates
strongly through a stark imagery, both verbal and embodied, that speaks
of disorientation, uncertainty, and ambiguity. But far from submitting to
the shock of the world-in-the home and the-home-in the-world, the performers of the nightsong also tell of a past and a future in which a truthful
existence and an ordered social universe are anchored in, and thus mutually
enabled by, the homely, a firmly framed world of local rootedness, tradition, and of sexual and collective identity. To harness, then, the instability
of social action and meaning in capitalist society, to bring to a standstill the
restless "disembedding mechanisms" (Giddens 1991) of industrial society
and its constant relocation and redefinition of people, things, and meanings is the alternative isicathamiya performers pose against the unhomely.
In the following chapter we shall see how the antithesis, the homely, is
enacted in performance and how, in the process, it is in turn itself marked
by other ambiguities.

5 *Ekhaya:* The Past, the Home,

and the Nation Revived

Mas' buyele kwezomdabu.
    Let us return to our roots.
                Empangeni Home Tigers, "Niyezwa Yini?"

In the previous chapter I dwelt extensively on the pragmatics and semantics of labor migration, examining in detail how this profoundly unsettled and unhomely world shaped a poetics of displacement and shifting identities. The nightsongs, rooted in the experience of a deranged social universe as they are, were shown to be one of the most engrossing expressions of this poetics. But, as the line above, quoted from a song by the Empangeni Home Tigers, also suggests, a strong desire for wholeness resonates through isicathamiya performance.[1] In fact, the genre seems to be driven by a quest for the source (*omdabu*), some prior state of grace. Isicathamiya performance is tantamount to a mode of homing, its practitioners are—both figuratively and in real terms—homebound. In short, to sing isicathamiya is to be at home, *ekhaya.* This unmaking of the unhomely and the remaking of the home through a complex edifice of symbols and bodily practices in performance is the subject of this chapter. Thus, on the pages that follow I shall attend to three major arenas of homing, three particularly contested semantic terrains on which South African migrants and isicathamiya proponents in particular enact the symbolic return to the source: the past, the home, and the nation.

These terms describe the most fundamental destinations of a journey that is to take the performers of the nightsongs to a realm of wholeness, a world of tradition, custom, domestic cohesion, and political allegiance. But this journey, to be sure, is first and foremost one of the imaginative kind in which the pure and simple invention of practices taken for historical fact and a more realistic reconstruction of the past, constantly influence each other (Ranger 1993). As such, these moves that seek to recapture a past partake of the goal of all symbolic practice: the returning to the whole. In a seminal article, "The Argument of Images and the Experience of Returning to the Whole," James Fernandez has written that to construct an imaginatively integrated context, a stage for satisfying performance, is the ultimate and recurrent strategy of the human experience. In performing the contiguous experiences of one domain, he goes on to state, a sense of resonance or relation by analogy arises with some part or related parts of the contiguous structures of another domain. Performance, then, Fernandez seems to suggest, is at base an exercise at restoration, a redemptive activity in a profoundly afflicted and unsettled world (Fernandez 1986, 184).

But the reassertion of alternative spaces of social practice also hinges, quite ironically, on another important process: the creation of temporal frames. It is to these that we briefly have to turn before we examine the main themes of this chapter.

Time

Performance, as Richard Bauman pointed out long ago, frames ritualized, "playful" communication between the participants in a ritual, show or other type of event by creating spheres of interaction bounded and coordinated by time and physical space (Bauman 1984). Subsequent elaborations of Bauman's theory have tended to fetishize these frames as marked-off "events," as a reified "social product" (Stone 1982, 25). But performance fames are more than a mere realm of metacommunication. Rather, performers such as the isicathamiya singers and dancers construct spaces, protective spheres of "virtual power," as Suzanne Langer might say (Langer 1953, 175), that renounce the law of the given and now by asserting their own spatiotemporal order. This modified notion of performance frames as spaces finds it most striking expression perhaps in the fact that isicathamiya performances take place at night. Although scholars of African performance have encountered problems in linking musical time structures to patterns of social or ecological time, it is evident that the experience of shared time in probably all performance events involving music is shaped by flows of sound and motion, just as proper musical relations in turn usually require some form of synchrony (Merriam 1982; Stone 1985; Waterman, 1990, 215–16). African performance, in particular, constructs "another world of virtual time" by virtue of overlapping, repetitive cycles that have no common pitch or metrical reference points (Blacking 1973, 27; also Drewal 1991, 33–38).

In isicathamiya, the construction of virtual time frames as both the context and product of performance, is reflected in the broad distinction performers make between day and night as appropriate time for performance, a distinction, as we have seen in the preface, which is articulated in the highly ambiguous term *ingoma ebusuku*. But the linkage between song/

dance and night in *ingoma ebusuku* suggests a further-temporal distinction. For whereas daytime belongs to the realm of work (*sebenza*) and the exigencies of physical survival, nighttime is time for play (*umdlalo*). The distinction between work and play is, of course, recognized in a number of African societies as significant for the ordering of human activity, and as such it frequently serves to distinguish musical performance from other activities (Adams 1974). But by using the term *umdlalo* for their all-night competitions and by conflating the idea of play with nighttime, isicathamiya practitioners take account of and challenge the hegemonic temporal order. Nightsong performances, then, build relatively unpatrolled and unmonitored locations, alternative spaces which untangle the participants from the "chronological net," as Keletso Atkins calls the complex fabric of industrial time and leisure time, in which migrants are caught (Atkins 1993, 87).

Mobilizing the Past—Historical Consciousness and Narrative

The reconstruction, then, of an integrated universe, of a totality of practice and worldview entails narrative, historiography, in fact, a restructuring of time. As recent work on the production of historical consciousness in modernizing African societies amply demonstrates, the reinterpretation of tradition, of selected master metaphors, is the fundamental strategy the displaced, marginalized, and powerless of Africa's neocolonial societies mobilize in the service of the creation of a positive self-identity.[2] History, as the growing body of texts documenting the resilience of African traditions equally shows, is not simply deadwood, tradition preserved in allegedly immutable and timeless customs and narratives. History is above all a matter of consciousness, of agency. It is for this reason that attempts to distinguish between different forms of the appropriation of the past, such as Eric Hobsbawm's much quoted, but often incompletely cited distinction between tradition and custom (Hobsbawm 1983), must ultimately remain unconvincing (also Ranger 1993). For custom as organic, embedded, and taken-for-granted practice, is as much constituted by discursive practice as is the "invented" tradition of the industrial era. Likewise, in contrast to what many of our scholarly accounts of African repositories of historical consciousness are wont to suggest, the cultural forms and practices themselves—the performances, texts, and artifacts—are more than literal representations of the past. As Leroy Vail and Landeg White, in a critique of the Oxford Library of African Literature (which comprises collections of southern African poetry) observe, many of our scholarly treatments of African oral traditions reify oral poetic genres and other narratives by reducing them to a set of complex historical allusions. The authors take Isaac Schapera, M. Damane, and P. B. Sanders to task for being concerned, in their exegesis and annotation of southern African heroic poetry, primarily with "decoding the alternative history of the text." But history, Vail and White go on to state, is history as metaphor, and not simply history as code. "It is history as drama, evaluation, and judgment: history with the metaphysics included. The metaphors, elaborated into patterns of interpretation, are not simply vehicles for the events themselves. They are the means of comprehending those events in terms of permanent or changing systems of values, a means of being equal to events and hence of transcending them" (Vail and White 1991, 73).

This notion of tradition as essentially dialogic practice must inform all our attempts to understand black South African cultural practices, including isicathamiya performances. Perhaps the best illustration of this idea of tradition as socially constructed was provided to me in conversation with Alpheus Kuzwayo, then leader of the Durban High Stars, a choir whose performances and songs on aspects of Zulu history always impressed me. One of these songs, "Siyolila Sonke" (We shall all lament) is about the Mendi, a ship that was carrying black South African soldiers to the European war theater when it sank off the Isle of Wight in February 1917, taking 615 men with it. The words are as follows:

Leader: *Siyolila sonke mhla kuvela izindaba.*
             We shall all lament on hearing the news
Choir: *Siyolila sonke mhla kuvela izindaba ezivela*
             We shall all lament on hearing the news from
Leader: *phesheya* . . .
             abroad . . .
Choir: *phesheya, kolwandle zokuhlupheka kwalamadoda,*
             abroad, about the hardships of those men,
     mhla kushona inqanawe enguMenzi.
             when the Mendi perished.
Choir: *Hhayi ulwandle lwabagwinya,*
             The sea swallowed them,
Leader: *bonke* . . .
             all of them . . .
Choir: *bonke bephilile,*
             all of them alive,
     mhla kushona inqanawe enguMenzi.
             when the Mendi perished.

After these verses, the song in performance leads seamlessly into a different section, a stanza with different melodic material:

Leader: *Sikhala* . . .
　　　　　We are yearning . . .
Choir: *Sikhala ngezwe elathathwa yizizwana.*
　　　　　We are yearning for our land, which was snatched from us by
　　　　　foreigners.
　　　Zinayo indawo yokulala elizweni lokhokho bethu.
　　　　　These foreigners are now residing in the land of our ancestors.
Leader: *Woza!*
　　　　　Come!
Choir: *Woz' woz'!*
　　　　　Come, come!
Leader: *Woza!*
　　　　　Come!
Choir: *Woz' woz'!*
　　　　　Come, come!
Leader: *mSuthu* . . .
　　　　　Sotho . . .
Choir: *mSuthu nomXhosa hlanganane!*
　　　　　Sotho and Xhosa, unite!
Leader: *Nani* . . .
　　　　　And you . . .
Choir: *Nani maZulu hlanganane!*
　　　　　And you Zulus, unite!
Leader: *Elizwe* . . .
　　　　　In the land . . .
Choir: *elizweni lokhokho bethu.*
　　　　　In the land of our ancestors.

The Mendi disaster had inspired many earlier composers, including Albert M. Jonas whose composition "Ama-Gora E-Mendi" was taught widely in schools beginning in the 1930s. Jonas's song as well as a "Mendi Memoral Anthem" whose words almost completely match the transcription above, may well have been the models for the Durban High Stars song.[3] But when I discussed this song with Alpheus Kuzwayo, he denied any connection between his song and the Mendi incident. "It does not say the Mendi [uMendi], it says the creator [umenzi]." Instead he suggested that the song was about Shaka's famous prophecy. "When he died, he prophesied that the new rulers of the country would emerge from the sea, and that on the arrival of these people we would all cry and suffer." When

I asked whether the second stanza, beginning with "Sikhala," was part of the same song, he responded that the second section of the song had a different theme. "It registers a different mood, for the first theme is a prophecy. The second theme then captures the arrival of the Europeans, who would come to change the mood of the country."

"Did the people arrive in the ship?" I asked.

"Yes," he answered, "meaning that the sea swallowed the whites from Europe and disgorged them here in the country."

"So the second section of the song describes the situation as it is, of whites ruling the country?"

"Yes, up to now," he replied.

Interpretations such as this one about particularly traumatic moments in South Africa's black annals, situated at the watershed between the dying precolonial past and the inescapable dawning of modern capitalism, are symptomatic of the kind of refashioned heritage with imagined reference to the past (Comaroff and Comaroff 1987, 195) invoked by isicathamiya performers. The departure of African soldiers to the European war theater, although widely regarded as an act of loyalty toward the empire that would hopefully lead to some form of political compensation for blacks, was also bitterly resented (Willan 1978). In this sense, Alpheus Kuzwayo's fusion of images of death, oppression, Christianity, and the glorious Zulu past forms a historical icon of great rhetorical force that alters the way the past is read and brought to bear on the present. As a form of historical consciousness, this arrangement of tropes does not offer us easily recognizable distinctions between history and its representation. But it does merge history and the stories told about it into a mode of present-ing the past.

A similar example is the following passage from "Sengiyabalisa" (Now I am brooding), a song frequently performed in Durban competitions by the Mtwalume Young Aces:

> *Madoda sekunzima lapha emhlabeni.*
>> Men, things are bad here on earth.
> *Kubaba wami nakumama wami zangishiya izihlobo zami.*
>> Oh, father and mother have passed away, my relatives.
> *Nikuzwile ukukhala kwalababantu baseGoli abahlezi kalukhuni emgodini.*
>> You have heard the cries of the people who live dangerously in the gold mines of Johannesburg.
> *Sithi baba nkosi thethelela lezongane ezihlezi kabuhlungu emgodini.*
>> Oh Lord, we say have mercy on the poor brothers who suffer in the gold mines.

. . . .

Sebethi uQueen uwelile udabule amanzi, siwutholile umbiko ovela kuye.
They say the Queen has crossed the seas, we have heard the news.
Lalelani, lalelani maZulu.
Lend her your ears, Zulus.

The invocation by the Mtwalume Young Aces of Queen Victoria—a very common trope in Zulu folklore—as the imperial savior whose imminent arrival sets all wrongs right, is of course not to be taken as historical ignorance. Nor is Kuzwayo's interpretation of the modern predicament through the past—and the implied investment of traditional knowledge with the power to provide authoritative explanations of the modern world—a misrepresentation of the historical record. The traditionalism voiced by Kuzwayo is not simply a relic of dead generations weighing, as Marx suggested, like a nightmare on the brain of the living. Rather, his account has to be seen as the highly articulate expression of a historical consciousness through which "human actors deploy historically salient cultural categories to construct their self-awareness" (Comaroff and Comaroff 1987, 205).

Tradition, then, or, the source (*umdabo*), as the Empangeni Home Tigers sing, is a remarkably flexible instrument, one that tells us a great deal more about those who use it than about its "content." We shall now have to consider a specific set of "traditions," or rather, a specific site of tradition making in isicathamiya performance: the "home," by far isicathamiya's most important trope.

Homestead, Household and Family—Spaces of the "Home"

As a space that is predominantly anchored in an imagined past, the "home" represents an inverted utopia of a sort, a counterimage of the "unhomely." Consequently, the "home" as a symbol does not so much stand for the possession of a home. Rather it denotes a condition in which the blurred boundaries of the world-in-the-home and the home-in-the-world are redrawn so as to keep distinct from each other the world and the home and to protect the latter from the destructive impact of the former. A clear indication of this, as in fact a cursory glance at the song repertoire reveals, are numerous song titles such as "Ikhaya Lam" by the GMC Choir (HMV JP 826); "Ngilangazelela Lelo Khaya" by the Ladysmith Naughty Boys (Rainbow ZCN 1025); "Likude Ikhaya Lam" by the Durban City Choir (SABC LT 7941); and "Kwe Lakithi" by the Dundee Wandering Singers (2019, Unissued). More pointedly, however, the importance of the home as the spiritual and moral hub of migrants' lives is observable in the plaintive, mournful tone of many songs.

> *Bhekani baba wami nawe mama wami, sekunzima lapho ngikhona.*
>> Look, my father and mother, it is now difficult where I am.
> *Ngiyalivuma icala lami, yebo ngonile.*
>> I confess, I did wrong. Yes, I did wrong.
> *Ngihlulekile; sehlulekile thina.*
>> I have failed; we have failed.
> *Kungcono masiphinde kwelakithi eMphumulo.*
>> We'd better return to Mphumulo, our home.
> *Ubandlululo kulomhlaba.*
>> In this world there is apartheid.
> *Kungcono masiphinde kwelakithi eMphumulo.*
>> We'd better return to Mphumulo, our home.

Although the term *kithi* here refers to a particular locality or, more precisely, a district—a definition of "home" that we shall encounter again later on—a song such as the one quoted does not permit us to determine what exactly the notion of home entails. It is here that I must pause for a moment and offer a few explanations of this ambiguous term. In the first instance, "home," as the words of the song quoted and others show, can be a variety of spaces. Apart from *kithi* (home), *abazali* (parents), or *izihlobo* (relatives), the term *khaya* is used most often in these lyrics. But *khaya* is anything but an unequivocal term, either, for it denotes a whole range of spatial and social forms. Following Doke and Vilakazi (1972), *khaya* denotes the home, a dwelling, an inhabited place, a place to which one belongs, or even the members of a family. *Khaya*, by all accounts, then, seems to be the root symbol for a "practiced place," a domain of social practice engendered and integrated by rules of moral conduct and material production as well as by images of shape and process.

Second, I must alert the reader to two mistakes frequently made in southern African studies. Although terms such as "relatives" or "parents" may be acceptable as rough translations of the corresponding isiZulu terms, we must be careful not to read narrow Western ideas of family and home into a rich set of social practices that have nothing to do with Western reified notions of social relations. In an article, "Migrant Labour and Changing Family Structure in the Rural Periphery of Southern Africa," Colin Murray (1980) has cogently criticized the fallacies of essentialism inherent in kinship analyses based on the imposition of Western categories

such as that of the nuclear family or the extended family. Traditional kinship relations, he argues, are constantly dissolved and conserved as essential
components of the political economy of the labor reserve. The nuclear
family is therefore not an antipode of the extended family, a form of kinship
system logically standing at the end of a modernization process, but rather
it is to be identified as one among numerous types of household compositions and as one typical phase of the developmental cycle. Therefore, Murray concludes, the notion of family structure must "encapsulate diverse
temporal processes by which individuals constitute their kinship universe"
(Murray 1980, 151 ff.).

Another caveat to be made in regard to the semantic polyvalency of
the term "home" concerns the articulation of town and countryside, what
Dunbar Moodie has called the migrants' "purposive organization of life-
worlds" (Moodie 1991, 44). While the antonomy of town and countryside, as I have noted in the previous chapter, is without doubt one of isicathamiya's most powerful tropes, the poetic oppositions between "here"
and "far," "past" and "future" are not to be taken as absolute master
tropes. In southern Africa, images of the countryside and the city are "necessarily conditioned both by the politicosymbolic demands of the urban
present and, at the same time, by the political and economic character of
the social relations linking the country and the city" (Ferguson 1992, 90).
And thus, while such dichotomies clearly reflect the fabric of a society in
which powerful and seemingly insurmountable lines separate the center
from the periphery, the various levels of performance—singers' uniforms,
dancing, choir names—provide a multilayered picture of migrants' experience of their multiple worlds. The "home" is far from being enshrined in
the countryside alone.

The best sense of the ambiguous space called "home," of the *intermun-
dia* between town and countryside, may be gained perhaps from the performers' own interpretations of their social position. Enoch Mzobe, for
instance, felt that he had "lived too much in town. I am like someone who
grew up in town. I experienced farm life and also experienced town life.
Town life is nice but it's not a place where one can nurture one's children.
There are many beautiful things of course. Most of the guys we went to
Jo'burg with never went back to their families. Then I saw that this place
doesn't want weak people. There were two boys here in the farm with
beautiful voices who wanted me to take them to Johannesburg to sing. But
I was afraid of taking them lest they don't come back and my name would
be blemished."

Something of the highly ambiguous semantic field surrounding migrants' notion of home, of the advantages and disadvantages of either space, or of the push and pull of the urban and rural contexts is perhaps even more compellingly expressed in the following two song texts. Alison Gumbi's song "Vela Mfowethu" (Reveal yourself, brother), for instance, is quite unambiguously sung from the perspective of those who have stayed at home. The countryside here is quite patently the quintessential embodiment of the idea of home. The song unequivocally reminds the far-away brother of his duties toward his rural relatives:

Choir: *Sawubona baba!*

> Greetings, father!

Sawubona mama!

> Greetings, mother!

Sawubona bhuti!

> Greetings, brother!

Sawubona sisi!

> Greetings, sister!

Size lapha nje ngendaba enkulu

> We have come here for an important matter

yokufana umfowethu.

> of search for our brother.

Washiy' umakoti

> He left his wife behind

nabantwana bayahlupheka ekhaya.

> and the children are suffering at home.

Leader: *Selokhu, . . .*

> Since he departed, . . .

Choir: *ahamba ethi uyosebenza.*

> saying he was searching for work.

Manye sekuphelile unyaka welishumi. Singazi ukuthi washonaphi.

> It is about ten years now. And we do not know his whereabouts.

Sifuna ukuya nawe mfowethu siyobon' abantwana.

> We want to go home with you, brother, to see the children.

Choir: *O vela vela vela mfowethu. Woza musa ukucasha ngabanye.*

> Oh, appear, appear, appear, brother. Come, do not hide behind others.

Woza sifun' ukuya nawe, o mfowethu siyobon' abantwana.

> Come, we want to go with you, oh, brother, to see the children.

Leader: *Kunje! Kunje, nje mfowethu!*

> It's bad, bad, brother!

> *Washiya ikhaya kanye nabantwana.*
>> You left your home and children.
>
> *Yasuk' insizwa.*
>> The gentleman went away.
>
> *Yayosebenza eGoli.*
>> He went to work in Johannesburg.
>
> *Yafik' eGoli kukuhle kunjena,*
>> He found good things in Johannesburg,
>
> *yabalahla bantwana ekhaya.*
>> but he deserted his children at home.
>
> *Obuyel' ekhaya mtaka baba!*
>> Go back home, brother!
>
> *Izingane zilala zingadlile mfowethu.*
>> The children go to sleep without food, brother.
>
> *Uhlala nent' ebomvu.*
>> Yet you are staying with a red thing [beautiful lady].

By contrast, a song such as "Savumelana" (We agree) (Gallo GE 1049), by Solomon Linda's Evening Birds, recorded in 1940, suggests a somewhat unsympathetic attitude toward the "small-moustached in-laws" in the countryside:

> Leader: *Hhayi amadevana asemzini esibiza ngabafokazana.*
>> No those small-moustached in-laws call us little men.
>
> Leader and choir: *Sizowashaya lamadevana asemzini uma esibiza ngabafo-kazana.*
>> We will beat them if they call us little men.
>
> Leader: *Savumelana.*
>> We agree.
>
> Choir: *Savumelana.*
>> We agree.

What we see here, then, are the poetic expressions of the marked contours of South Africa's sociogeographic spaces and, at the same time, the paradoxical and polysemic representation of home, town, and countryside in the nightsongs. But regardless of these contrasting representations of the homely, it is the paramountcy of a bounded community—centered on, but not exclusively defined by, the homestead and the family—as the reference points of all meaningful social life that isicathamiya performers seek to revitalize in performance.

At the most fundamental level, this meaning of the home as a bounded community is intimately linked with *umuzi,* the homestead. The center of a spatially rooted and culturally and morally integrated social universe, the embodiment of all that is good and important in life, the *umuzi* constituted the economic and social basis of preindustrial society. "Ideally inviolate" (Vilakazi 1965, 24), the web of social ties, relations of production, spatial arrangement of dwellings inside the *umuzi,* and their symbolic representation in virtually every aspect of cultural practice formed an indivisible whole, a multistranded and yet unified alliance of actors and interests. In short, the *umuzi* was, in the words of Eileen Krige, a space "in which a complete life can be led" (1950, 39).[4]

The loss of this sphere of the "homely," the disconnection from the *umuzi* as the moral, spiritual, and cultural center of gravity of social life, is perceived by migrants as the most troubling symptom of a derelict social order. And it is the source of intense discomfort. As a recent survey conducted among migrant workers throughout the country revealed, more than two-thirds of the respondents expressed grave concern about the enforced separation from their families (Schlemmer and Møller 1985, 138–40). Others worried about not sending enough money home, about insufficient food at home, or about the ill health of their wife and children. In fact, better than any statistics, a song by the New Home Brothers brings the matter to the point:

> *Kwathi ngenye imini mina ngilele ebusuku, ngaphupha usizi olukhulu.*
> One night, when I was asleep, I dreamt of a great calamity.
> *Kwathi kusenjalo kwafika nombiko ovela kuzo izihlobo zami.*
> At that very moment, I received a message from my relatives.
> *Zangitshela ukuthi sengisele ngingedwa, bangishiyile abazali bami.*
> They were informing me that I was left all by myself and that my
> parents had passed away.
> *Uma ngicabanga ngayo leyomini ebuhlungu sekuvele kufike izinyembezi.*
> The mere thought of that grieves me and makes my cry.
> *Zaphalala izinyembezi mangikhumbula mhla ngisele ngingedwa emhlabeni.*
> Tears run when I remember that I am left all by myself in this world.
> *Umama wami nobaba wami sebengishiyile.*
> My father and my mother have passed away.
> *Sengisele ngingedwa namuhla.*
> I am alone now.[5]

In the following, I shall examine four highly polyvalent semantic grounds on which isicathamiya performers reconstruct the "homely." The first of these arenas of homemaking, as it were, is the social organization of choirs in networks centered on "home people." As the second of these spatial semantics and "localizing strategies" (Fardon 1990), I shall discuss the extraordinarily rich topo-poetry that is expressed in the names of isicathamiya choirs. The third terrain is the more personal realm constructed in and by intergender relationships, while the fourth and last type of strategy emerges from the interaction between different generations. At this point in our analysis, the discussion of these sites of the "homely" will concentrate on song texts and other textual forms of representation. Other levels, such as bodily movement and choir uniforms, will be examined more closely in chapter 6.

Home People, Workmates, and Neighbors: The Social Organization of Isicathamiya Choirs

"They were also from Standerton, so they were my home boys." This is how King Star Brothers bass singer Phillip Mabizela, sitting in the posh, brand new Protea North home of Herman Pelo in Soweto and reminiscing about his musical career explained why he joined this choir after having sung for other choirs for a number of years. The isiZulu term *basekhaya* he was using literally means "those from home." It is related to other terms such as *abakhaya* and *omkhaya* (home people), all of which reflect the idea that neighbors or people from a certain rural area tend to regroup in town in relatively tightly knit and closed networks of social relationships. In the anthropological literature such networks of home people have customarily—and somewhat obliquely—been called "home boy" networks. In fact, networks that are based on common regional ties have been among the earliest and most enduring organizational patterns devised by migrant workers throughout Africa in an attempt to minimize the effects of proletarianization and to provide some measure of stability in an uncertain environment (Epstein 1958; Little 1957; Harries-Jones 1969).

In the South African context, the role of regional solidarity as an important basis of South African migrant workers' cultural activities has been noted by some authors (Mayer 1980; Beinart 1987), although much less concrete evidence has been gathered here. Beer drinking, for instance, has been one of the privileged areas in which anthropologists have been able to observe the operation of such home-people networks (McAllister 1981, McNamara 1980). In a field closer to isicathamiya and performance, H. Thomas, in his study of Durban *ingoma* dance teams, found "a strong tendency towards involvement with 'home people'" (Thomas 1988, 122). Half of the dance troupes he investigated were, in fact, composed exclusively of home people (1988, 115). Similarly, J. Clegg has argued that the opposition and competition among the former districts and chieftaincies of the autonomous Zulu kingdom over access to farm land and employment on white farms are still at the root of *ingoma* dancing, and as such eventually "became part of the home boy structure" (Clegg 1982, 10).

In isicathamiya the home-people theme is only one, albeit very strong, motive in a complex design of social relationships among the choirs and musicians. Three types of organizational structures are used in isicathamiya choirs. A small number of choirs are exclusively based on bonds of kinship while in other, mostly younger choirs a more fluid internal composition is evident which seems to be grounded in shared workplace or patterns of joint urban residence such as accommodation in the same "hostel." Some choirs, such as the Durban groups Nongoma Morning Stars and White Water seem to have adopted the latter principle. Thus all but one of the fourteen members of the Nongoma Morning Stars reside in Umlazi township south of Durban, and all the singers of White Water not only live in Umlazi, but many also come from the same section of the township.

In most choirs, however, membership seems to be determined by a combination of kinship ties together with other factors such as common regional origin. A number of Durban choirs are good examples for the latter category. The overwhelming majority of singers in Gumbi's Easy Walkers, for instance, hail from the surrounding area of Port Shepstone on the south coast, and although this kind of regional homogeneity has become somewhat exceptional, the Danger Stars, for example, all come from Amanzimtoti. Even more typical of the third category are the Jabula Home Defenders in Durban. The group was formed in 1978 by Bhekeni Sikhosana and attracted numerous singers from Ezingolweni. But in 1984 the choir split in two and singers who joined either half after this date came from such diverse places as Maphumulo, Melmoth, Bizana in the Transkei, Nongoma, and elsewhere (table 1). Interestingly, it was Hamilton Sukhozi's split-off group Jabula Home Defenders *B* that maintained a much higher degree of regional cohesion. Of its eleven members, nine came from Ezingolweni, while two new members who had been recruited in 1984 came from Umbumbulu and Ulundi, respectively. Although the conflict that led to the secession of Sukhozi's group from the main body under Sikhosana is said to have been related to mismanagement of the group's financial affairs, it is possible that the formation of the breakaway group also involved, among other reasons, regional loyalties of the Ezingolweni home people.

Table I Choir Members by Home Area

Home Area	Jabula Home Defenders A (Sikhosana)	Jabula Home Defenders B (Sukhozi)
Ezingolweni	6	9
Nongoma	3	0
Port Shepstone	1	0
Mahlabatini	1	0
Bizana	1	0
Maphumulo	1	0
Estcourt	1	0
Melmoth	1	0
Umbumbulu	0	1
Ulundi	0	1
Total	15	11

It is tempting to construct a line along which these forms of choral organization developed historically from an earlier, more rural and predominantly kin-based category to the third, modern group of choirs structured according to principles of urban residence. Speaking of Xhosa Red migrants, for instance, Philip Mayer has suggested that they have organized themselves in two basic kinds of networks. The first is an encapsulating network comprising only people from one's own rural location, while the second includes migrants of diverse regional origin (Mayer and Mayer 1961, 290). While most isicathamiya choirs would certainly fall under the first category, this by no means implies that it constitutes a more rural, historically dated form of cultural practice among urbanizing migrants.

Nevertheless, in the formative period of isicathamiya during the 1930s, kinship seemed indeed to be the only bond that kept a number of choirs together. The Crocodiles, for instance, initially recruited themselves from within one single family, the Mzobes. As time went by, this nucleus extended to include the in-laws of the Mzobes, the Molefe family.

Similarly, when Solomon Linda first came to Johannesburg in the early 1930s, he joined his uncle's group. In his own new choir, the Evening Birds, however, Gilbert Madondo remained the only member from Linda's extended family. All the other members were home people from Mhlumayo. The Johannesburg-based Crocodile Singers, finally, like their Durban namesakes, belong to only two families, the Zondos and the Khumalos. At the same time, the singers were all migrants from the immediate rural surroundings of Paulpietersburg.

Although these early examples demonstrate the presence of networks of kinship in isicathamiya choirs, common regional origin was by far the most important criterion of membership. More recent examples of younger choirs illustrate the continued relevance of such mixed patterns of membership based on kinship and the system of home people. Two singers of the King Star Brothers, for example, originate from Bethlehem, one from Newcastle, and one from Greylingstad. But the majority of five members come from Standerton and, in fact, these singers belong to the Hletshwayo family. It is the preponderance of these ties of kinship that led to the name of the group, the "Brothers" being the Hletshwayo brothers and "King" signifying their numerical superiority.

The complex layering of patterns of internal organization in isicathamiya choirs finds a parallel in the words the performers used to refer to their entire group. Apart from *kwaya,* choir, many performers talk about *thim,* a team, or a *khlaphu,* a club—both designations, of course, that stem from the world of industrial labor and urban leisure. At the same time, these terms are used interchangeably by traditionalists and more thoroughly urbanized performers alike.

In sum, home-people networks, patterns of workplace, and urban residence are not only poor indices of the historical formation of modern, urban, working-class principles of association among isicathamiya performers, they often depend on each other and complement each other as resources in migrants' strategies of survival. Black urbanization in South Africa has often been accompanied by coercive mechanisms, and few migrants ever exercised much control over where they wanted to work and live and with whom.

The necessity to foster some sense of community and to create structures for the organization of mutual support are clearly among the most pervasive functions of home-people networks. Although such networks are not the only social basis of isicathamiya choirs, a good deal of their internal cohesion stems from the successful functioning of such networks. The solidarity among the members of a choir is a valuable asset in the daily struggle for survival and comprises all aspects of life from job hunting and financial matters to sick care. Thus some choirs will offer financial assistance to a member needing to attend a funeral in the countryside; in others, support is given to those members who lost their job. Expenses for uniforms and transport are shared as are the money prizes won in competitions.

Internal solidarity and mutual support are also recurrent themes in numerous isicathamiya songs. Thus, "Hey Wemfana" by the Scorpions

(SABC LT 10 247), even in its present recorded, heavily censored, form is about singers with "deviant behavior," as leader Gershon Mcanyana put it.

> Leader: *Hey wemfana.*
>> Hey, you, boy!
> Chorus: *Hey wemfana, wena wemfana.*
>> Hey, you, boy, you boy.
> Bass: *Hamba juba lami.*
>> Go, my dove.
> Chorus: *Hamba juba lami.*
>> Go, my dove.
>> *Bayokunqanda phambili.*
>> They will stop you yonder.

"Initially," Mcanyana commented upon the genesis of the song, "I meant to say, 'Go my love, they will need you at your place.' Then I would say, 'A person who doesn't listen to advice usually runs into difficulties.' But the SABC said, if you say, 'A person who doesn't listen to advice usually runs into difficulties,' it doesn't sound right, because it's like you are threatening that person, as if you wish that he should run into difficulties. Therefore they suggested that I should say what I want to say, but omit the part that sounds like a threat." And then he added, "Some members have deviant behaviors. Whether all members of the group cooperate, one won't give us problems by being a wet blanket of the group. Music needs united people. So if you can't tolerate rules of decorum in the group, then 'go, but you'll run into difficulties.'"

But for all the benefits of togetherness and home-people ties, for at least one experienced isicathamiya adherent the home-people principle also held clear disadvantages. As Crocodiles veteran Enoch Mzobe pointed out, a more kinship-oriented and geographically diverse internal composition gave the Crocodiles a certain musical lead over the majority of home-people-based choirs. "Having members from different regions," Mzobe observed, "gained us fame, because we used to travel a lot. Again this brought us invitations to many places, because all our members would make it a point that we go and perform in their home town. The idea of having group members from the same region is fine, but the disadvantage is that it is easy for a group to fade out. For instance, there was a very good choir in the region which was comprised of guys from this same region. This choir did not last long, because it used to sing in this neighborhood and in this way they did not get exposed to other places and meet different groups, hear other styles of music. As a result this group died a natural death, because they didn't move around, they stuck to this place because all of them were from this place."

But mutual support and fraternity are also embedded in more rigid and hierarchical structures of authority and seniority. The focal point of these structures is the leader, or as most groups would say in the Zulu-ized version of the English term, *ilida*. The leader assigns duties and performance roles, he controls the group's finances, and leads rehearsals. Most often he is also the composer of the group's entire song repertoire and in many cases he is responsible for the choreography as well. In performance the leader is highly conspicuous; he heads the lines of choristers when they move into the hall and he leads them out of it. On stage he often stands in front of the choir, giving cues. In short, nothing that affects a choir directly or indirectly happens without the knowledge of the leader; in fact, the *lida* reigns supreme.

A number of additional terms besides *ilida* symbolize even more vividly the extraordinary powers wielded by the leader. Thus some choirs refer to their leaders as *ukhondakta* (conductor), while three somewhat older and rarer titles appear to be *umbhidi, umpishi,* and *onandisayo,* the improviser or, as Crocodile Singers veteran Ngweto Zondo explained, "the person who starts the song." The most current term, however, is *ikhontrola* (controller). It signifies both the performance-related functions of the leader and his more general directive powers. As with other aspects of the social organization of choirs, an even more telling, if somewhat unusual, signal of the leader's superior position are the names of some choirs. Thus the Mzolo Mbube Group is named after its leader and founder Zephania Mzolo, whereas a name such as Mshengu White Mambazo derives from the praise name of Joseph Shabalala and his family, whose sons form the core of this group. The names of some older choirs, however, such as Phillip Msimango's Zulu Choir, were probably invented by the recording industry.

Experience and age are the two most crucial qualities that make a choir leader. Seniority was, of course, one of the fundamental principles of precolonial social ordering, but one whose continued relevance can be observed in many spheres of modern social life. Its significance in isicathamiya choirs cannot be better illustrated than by the role it played in the career of Joseph Shabalala and the formation of Ladysmith Black Mambazo. As a young man and before migrating to Durban, Shabalala had joined a choir of age-mates whose singing to him appeared to be "incongruous." The problem for the young Joseph, however, was how "to teach older people." "It was difficult," and he concluded that "I couldn't change their singing. Then I left them just like that." Fortunately, for Shabalala this disappointing experience resulted in the insight that "when you sit down and arrange music critically, it sounds good. But I also saw that you need people who are going to listen to you. Then I thought that people who could listen to me would be people who are younger than I am. Then I decided that when I go home I would take my younger brothers and teach them what I feel inside me and see how it goes. Then at Christmas time in 1960 I gathered my brothers. They listened to me and I gave them what I want and feel, which is what invokes me every time I sing. . . . They didn't ask me where I had got it from since I said I was going to teach them. They just took what I said and accepted it from a person who at home has been a hero in charge of weddings, conducting, playing a guitar."

As for the rank-and-file members no special titles seem to be assigned to them other than the ordinary age-related designations *umfana* (young man) or *indoda* (man). Nevertheless, in most choirs a strict distribution and hierarchical ordering of performance roles is considered a prerequisite for the proper functioning of the choir and as such is mirrored in special terms. As I have discussed in chapter 3, the most current division of roles is that into *bes* (bass), *thena* (tenor), *altha* (alto) and soprano or *fas pathi* (first part). The spatial positioning of the musicians singing these parts is fixed according to a principle that seems to have been in force from the earliest days of isicathamiya performance. The leader—and soprano—is at the head of the file of singers as they move into the venue, followed by *altha* and *thena*. The basses, the main body of the choir, form the end of the line, and again here the youngest and most inexperienced basses come at the very end. Some of the larger choirs also have a junior team in which these newcomers serve an apprenticeship of some time, before they are allowed to take part in competitions. A choir such as the Durban-based Kings Boys, for instance, in 1986 had a total of twenty-three singers of whom five were "unqualified," as leader Thomas Mtshali put it.

A much more elaborate distribution of roles and titles is that within the King Star Brothers. This choir not only has an executive committee but also a manager and a public relations officer. The former is named Herman Pelo and although he is not an active performer himself, he has been serving in that function for over ten years. The public relations officer is Sipho Xulu, a dynamic young salesman who recently opened an office in downtown Johannesburg from which he intends to promote cosmetics. Xulu's position, in particular, is a result of the decision, after a long and steady decline of this once-popular choir, to attune its image more to the changed role of isicathamiya in today's entertainment industry and to muster the professionalism to challenge Ladysmith Black Mambazo.

The distribution of performance roles, anchored in precolonial concepts as they partly are, reveal broader concepts of social ordering. Although similar patterns of leadership and seniority are being observed in a great many forms of modern African associations, clubs, churches, and societies and thus are not characteristic of migrant laborers alone, the arrangement of vocal parts in isicathamiya choirs, leadership roles, the apprenticeship of young musicians, and the spatial grouping of performers on stage deserve closer examination. For the sources of these patterns and their transformation in isicathamiya have a great deal to tell us about the kind of human order migrant performers imagine amid the chaos and disorientation of urban life. Their significance in isicathamiya performance is perhaps best assessed by a comparison with the terms for related positions and roles in *ingoma* dance troupes. As J. Clegg has observed, *ingoma* dance teams are compared to oxen plough spans (*isipani*) or war regiments (*impi*). And further, within this imagery of farm life and war, the most current denomination for an *ingoma* team leader in the Durban area is *igoso* (war-leader), while in some teams the dance leaders are also known as *ifolosi* (lead oxen) (Clegg 1982, 13). Interestingly, in other parts of Natal, *igoso* was also used for a leader of a group of herd-boys (Thomas 1988, 172). In a similar mix of pastoral and military symbolism, intermediate positions are called *iphini* (inferior officer), and *isikhulu* (elder), while the rank-and-file dancers are given titles such as *isosha* (soldier) or *inkabi* (ox). Quite clearly, these titles recall the precolonial Zulu kingdom and its foundation of cattle and military organization. But others like *iphoyisa* (policeman) and *isosha* also reflect the institutions of colonial power and modern capitalist society.

The contrast between these terms and those used in isicathamiya choirs could, of course, be interpreted as an indication of the greater integration of isicathamiya performers into the modern urban environment. But as the name of at least one choir suggests, pastoral symbolism is not a domain of *ingoma* dancers alone. When Joseph Shabalala formed his choir Ladysmith Black Mambazo, he not only deliberately built a reference to his home area Ladysmith into the name, but by adding "black" he also chose a farm and pastoral image. "The name Black Mambazo," he said, "is a name that I had been using at home, because where I come from, it is a place of music, and musicians are called oxen. I'm sure you know that oxen on a white man's farm are called span, sixteen of them. Now singers in our district are called oxen. Now coming to the word Black, it is like this: a span of black oxen, among other spans which are black, red, white and coloured, being three types of spans the black span was very strong. This is why I decided to call my span Black."

Ladysmith Black Mambazo is not the only choir whose naming practice is based on pastoral symbolism; a number—albeit a very small one—of choirs such as the Black Bulls and Shabalala's own junior team Mshengu White Mambazo have adopted the same principle. But bulls, oxen, and their attributes do not symbolize the world of farms alone; in Zulu folklore bulls are one of the most common symbols of strength and masculinity. Therefore, as will be seen in chapter 8, bulls and much more frequently, wild animals are vivid expressions of the concern with power relations and the assertion of power in competitive performance.

Thus it would seem that the titles and roles of isicathamiya choirs are not merely urban adaptations of rural models of social organization; rather, both the social organization and the structure of these choirs are clearly the result of the heterogeneous realities of black migrants. It also became evident that the construction of the various networks of home people, workmates, and neighbors within the choirs is based on highly malleable notions of "home" that enable migrants to constantly reposition themselves within their multiple and interconnected life worlds.

Localizing Strategies—Choir Names and Codas

One of the most visible levels, perhaps, at which the rift between this world of cities and segregation and the "home" is being bridged and figuratively transcended, are the names of isicathamiya choirs. As the partial list of choir names indicates, these names represent a rich inventory of the topographic divisions that play such an important role in the South African migrants' world. More than half of the choir names listed contain the name of a place—a town, a region, a country. In other words, they organize the spatial experience of the migrant performers by repositioning them in spaces that are less ambiguous than the amorphous "here" of the factories and cities. They articulate a "geo-poetry" of the homely that opens up the spaces of migrant life to rich and unexpected meanings. Possibly one of the most elementary forms of metaphoric predication, names here are turned into compact maps of spatial experience, complex topographic tropes, employed in the conception and transformation of South Africa's political,

economic, and cultural landscape. Through choir names, migrant performers redraw the cartography of a profoundly upset moral universe.

Abafana Baseqhudeni [Boys of the
Rooster]
Abafana Bentokozo [Happy Boys]
Abahambi Bezwe [Travelers]
Abaphuzi Begazi [Blood Suckers]
Abathandazi Zulu Choir
ABC
Abyssinian Eight
African Male Choir
African Male Voice Choir
African Music
African Zulu Male Voice Choir
Alexandrians
Allenhome
All Stars
Amabhungu Amnyama [Black
Entertainers]
Amanzi Okuphila
Amanzimtoti Male Voice Choir
Amashinga Amnyama [Naughty Black
Boys]
Amavuthela [Blowers]
Amazulu Amnyama [Black Zulus]
American Stars B
Ample Fire
A Natal Try Singers
Apollo 11
Arnot Home Singers
Assembly of God

Babazani Boys [Shouting Boys]
Batshe Brothers
Bayeni Black Mahlabatini
BB Tigers
Benoni Tycoon
Bergville Express
Bergville Mavuthela
Bergville Ngwadi Ndukuzibomvu
Black Bull
Black Bush Bucks
Black Stars
Black Tigers
Blood and Snow
Blue Hams Choir
Boiling Waters Choir
Bomber C
Brave Lion Singers

Brave Lions Mbube Choir
Bright Stars
Buhle Bemvunge
Buhle Benala
Buhle Betheku [Beauty of Durban]
Buhle Bethelezi

Cape to Cairo Choir
CCX Brothers
City Walkers
Clairmont Happy Boys
Clermont Home Defenders
Combela Small Boys
Come to See
Crocodiles
Crowdville Olympics
CTC Choir
CTC Mbube Choir
CTC Zulu Choir
CTL Mbube Choir Volksrust
Cup and Saucer

Daily News
Danger Express
Danger Stars
Dangerous
Dannhauser Flying Stars
Decca Wandering Minstrels
Dhlamini Home Defenders
Dundee Wandering Singers
Durban C to C
Durban City Boys
Durban City Brothers
Durban City Choir
Durban Crocodiles
Durban Evening Birds
Durban Heavy Stars
Durban High Stars
Durban Home Tigers
Durban Humming Bees
Durban King Express
Durban Letter Stars
Durban Opera Stars
Durban Royal Stars
Durban Stars

Easy Walkers
Emdeni Ituthuko

Empangeni Flying Stars
Empangeni Home Tigers
Empangeni Messenger
Empangeni Messengers: Durban

Fear No Harm Choir
Flying Birds
Fountain Brothers
Free Walkers
Funny Voice
Funny Voice Mbube Choir

GMC Choir
GMC Good Boys
GMC Mbube Choir
Green Mamba
Greytown Evening Birds

Hamlet's Male Voice Choir
Happy Boys Mbube Choir
Happy Brothers
Happy Walkers
Harding Boys
Harding Lucky Stars
Harding Morning Stars
Harrismith Boys
Harrismith Twin Brothers
Hlabisa Happy Stars
Hluhluwe Black Tigers
Home Defenders Male Voice Choir
Home Rovers
Home Singers
Home Tigers
Humming Bees
Hysters Brothers

Ilanga Elihle
Imfumi Male Voice Choir
Imi Zwilili Choir
Inala Ladysmith
I'ngqongqo Ama—Allenhome
Inhlaba Boys
Inhlangano
Inkandla Cothoza Stars
Inkatha kaZulu
Inqaba Yabesotho [Sotho Castle]
International Singers
Intokozo Yamaswazi [Happiness of the Swazis]
Inyanda Yesizwe [Child of the Nation]
Izingilozi Ezimnyama [Black Angels]

Izingwenya Zasenkuthu [Nquthu Crocodiles]

Jabula Home Defenders
Junior Natal Champions

KC Choir
Khanyisani Mbube Choir
Kings Boys
Kings of Mountain
King Star Brothers
K-Team
Kwaitos-D
Kwa Thema High Jumpers

Ladysmith Allenhome
Ladysmith Black Butterflies
Ladysmith Black Mambazo
Ladysmith Fountain Brothers
Ladysmith Gumba Gumba
Ladysmith Heralds
Ladysmith Home Comrades
Ladysmith Lemon
Ladysmith Lion Cubs
Ladysmith Lion Danger
Ladysmith Naughty Boys
Ladysmith Ntuthuko Brothers
Ladysmith Red Lions
Ladysmith Well Try
Leslie Shooting Stars
Lion Side
Loving Boys
LP Try Again
Lucky Boys
Lucky Stars
Lucky Stars Champion
Lucky Strike A

Mahlabatini Bekimbazo Brothers
Manekwane Red Stars
Mashona Brothers
Mavukela Chiefs
MCC
MCC Choir
Melody Masters
Mfolozi Emnyama [Black Umfolozi]
Morning Lights
Morning Shine Choir
Morning Stars
Morning Tigers
Moroka Swallows
Mountain Side Tugela Ferry

Moving Stars
Mpiyake Mabizela
Mpumalanga Happy Boys
Mshengu White Mambazo
MTA
Mthunzini Brothers
Mtsueni Nezi Nkonkoni
Mtubatuba Brothers
Mtwalume Young Aces
Mvunge Boys
Mzolo Mbube Group

Natal AB
Natal Champions
Natal Express
Natal Junior Champions
Natal Medium
Natal Universal
Natal Wandering Singers
Naughty Boys Choir
NBA Champions
NBA Happy Brothers
Newcastle Five Roses
Newcastle Star Roses
Newcastle Wanderers
New Germany
New Home Brothers
New Law
New Lucky Boys
New Members—IMemba Ezintsha
New Morning Stars
New Mountain King Boys
NF Brothers
NHL Home Defenders
Nkandla Aces
Nkandla Brothers
NKA Special
NND New Morning Stars
Nongoma Happy Stars
Nongoma Morning Stars
Nongoma 100% Brothers
NQ Home Division
Nsimbi Kayigobi [Iron Does Not Bend]
NTU King Brothers
Ntuthuko Messengers

Ocean Blues: Estcourt
Orlando Flying Birds
Orlando Naughty Boys
Over Silence

Phazamisa
Phillip Msimango's Zulu Choir
Piet Retief Jealous Down
PMB Young Fiders
Pretoria Rolling Stars

Ringer Stars
Rockcliff Tigers
Royals

Scorpions
Sesela Smiling Boys
Shining Stars Male Voice Choir
Shooting Stars
Silver Stars
Soshanguve Black Tycoons
Springs Bomber Boys
Stirtonville Sweet Melodians
Super Stars
Swaziland New Lucky Boys
Swaziland Singing Seven
Swazi Male Voice Choir

Thembisa Lemon High Stars
Thulisa Brothers
Thulisa Choir
TJ Highlanders
Transvaal Champions
Tugela Ferry Home Singers

Ubuhle Bemvunge
Ukhukhu Zulu Stars
Umlazi Male Voice Choir
Umoya Omsha [New Spirit]
Umthetho Omsha [New Law]
Umtwalume Flying Swallows
Umzi Omsha [New House]
Unhlanhla Nezimbali [Prosperity of Imbali]
Union Express Company
UTC

Venanda Lovely Boys
Vienna Stars
Volksrust Try Singers
Vultures

Watersmeet Morning Stars
Welkom Morning Stars
White Water
Winter Roses

Xolo Home Boys

Young Brothers	Zulu Tiny Boys—Qhudeni Zulu
Young Star Brothers	Zulu Vultures
	Zulu Wandering Singers
Zulu Assegai	Zulu Zebras
Zulu Champions	

But these toponymic strategies and the meanings they generate are far from homogeneous. Nor are they necessarily, as Michel de Certeau asserts, "liberated spaces that can be occupied" (de Certeau 1984, 105). Writing about *les arts du faire,* the tactics of the quotidian in the city, de Certeau argues that in spaces "brutally lit by an alien reason, proper names carve out pockets of hidden and familiar meanings" (104). Detached from the places they were supposed to define, even the most common place names, like worn coins that have lost the value engraved on them, retain their ability to signify. By virtue of a rich indetermination that opens up unforeseen itineraries and invents new spaces, names constitute a discourse of local authority that makes places habitable.

The spaces that de Certeau has in mind, are, of course, those defined by the ubiquitous city. As such they are fully known, mapped spaces that do not tolerate alternative modes of linguistic appropriation, outside of the official designations. Although the city presents itself as a dense arrangement of tightly clustered places, it is, in fact, itself an "immense social experience of lacking a place," a mere "network of residences temporarily appropriated by pedestrian traffic." It is, ultimately, only a name: the City (103). It becomes clear here that it is because of the all-embracing presence of the city, its role as the master sign of modernity per se, that de Certeau can conceive of place names as "supererogatory semantic overlays" (106) and, hence, of places as "fragmentary and inward-turning histories, pasts that others are not allowed to read, . . . symbolizations encysted in the pain or pleasure of the body" (108).

The gaze of isicathamiya performers on the city—and on the countryside from the city—is a different one, at least as it is translated into such choir names as Durban City Boys, Durban High Stars, Pretoria Rolling Stars, Clermont Home Defenders, Soshanguve Black Tycoons, or Umlazi Male Voice Choir. (Later on, in chap. 6, we shall see how some song texts and certain choreographic elements articulate a topopoetry similar to the signifying practices analyzed by de Certeau.) These examples speak of a gaze that still emanates from an outside, a place anterior to the city. The narratives—stories, songs, names—which it prompts are not constructed from the verbal debris left by the heterogeneous urban syntax. The city, to the isicathamiya performer coming from the outside, is still an Other, the

essence of which can be captured in a name. The act of naming the city—
especially by its English name rather than by an isiZulu synonym such as
Thekwini or Pitoli—makes sense of the alien space by appropriating, in a
synecdochic operation, the entire toponymic system of making sense.

A reverse expression of this logic of the proper are those choir names
that contain a memory of another place elsewhere, names that resonate
with other spatial practices and that organize an escape from the gaze of
the city. Here again, some of these names do not designate final destinations as much as they localize temporary stopovers en route to a dreamed-
of identity. Names such as Nongoma Morning Stars or Dundee Wandering
Singers fall into this category. They indicate the home area of the majority
of the choir members. Some names even include the term "home," as is
the case of the celebrated Empangeni Home Tigers. But, as I indicated,
the meaning of "home" in each particular case is a matter of a great deal
of variation and of a complex fusion of images. Beyond this, a more careful
comparison between a great many of these names with the singers' places
of origin reveals that in numerous names these home regions are not the
rural areas as such, but the regional urban centres. The members of the
Harding Boys or Newcastle Five Roses, for example, do not actually come
from these towns in Natal, but from the immediate rural surroundings.
"Home," then, is frequently understood by isicathamiya practitioners as
the district into which they were born. Names such as Nkandla Cothoza
Stars for a group from Nkandla district and Mahlabatini Bekimbazo Brothers for a choir from Mahlabatini district reflect this perhaps more clearly.
Furthermore, in the majority of cases these districts do not conform to the
precolonial districts (*isigodi*), which still play such a significant role in the
names of *ingoma* dance teams. In most cases they refer to the modern magisterial districts drawn up in the colonial period and, hence, most choir
names—unlike the song texts in which isiZulu toponyms tend to be pre-
fered—use the official designations of districts or towns. There are Ladysmith Red Lions, Ladysmith Heralds, and Ladysmith Fountain Brothers,
but no Mnambithi Tigers or Mnambithi Stars.

By contrast, an even wider grid of regional identification is manifest in
names such as Transvaal Champions, Natal Champions, or Natal Universal.
With the exception of the Swaziland Singing Seven, a Swazi male choir of
the late 1930s whose recordings belong to the *isikhunzi* tradition (1247–
1249, Gallo GE 153), few other choirs have chosen the names of larger
administrative units such as those of South Africa's four provinces or even
those of sovereign states.

The most striking naming practice, however, seems to have been inspired by more visible manifestations of regional pride and modernity than administrative boundaries: automobile license plates. The NBA Champions, for instance, echoing a practice not uncommon throughout Africa, quite unmistakably indicate the fact that they are migrants from Babanango in Natal by using the number plate abbreviation NBA for that place, and to isicathamiya amateurs versed in automobiles the CCX Brothers are easily recognizable as original residents of Matatiele district in the Cape Province on the borders of Natal. The TJ Highlanders, finally, clearly indicate their identification with the Transvaal province and the city of Johannesburg.

For the sake of correctness, it should be said here that the workplace, too, although hardly the embodiment of home, is an important point of identification that is reflected in choir names. In most cases, the teams quite simply adopted the name of their employers such as the Durban group Dunlop of the 1940s. An even more politically outspoken choir such as the K-Team with its strong trade unionist stance, has chosen to identify with their employers Kellogg's, for the *K* stands for the name of that company. Other choirs convey a more complex message such as the GMC Good Boys of the Durban General Motors assembly line, while the team of the municipal cold storage houses in Durban during the 1950s rather poetically named themselves Blood and Snow.

It would be misleading to abstract some kind of unilinear development of urban consciousness from such naming principles. Identification with the home area, as I have stressed, does not equal rural consciousness, just as names such as BB Tigers (Baumann Bread Tigers) or Durban High Stars do not automatically suggest a higher degree of urbanization and proletarian consciousness among the members of these choirs. Thus, although an early group such as Alson Mkhize's Evening Birds were mainly composed of Dundee-born musicians, the choir was primarily known as Durban Evening Birds. Another case in point are the many choirs that have emerged from, in, and around Ladysmith. The area around this midlands town has been one of the cradles of isicathamiya, but this fact was of little significance to early groups from the Ladysmith area such as Linda's Evening Birds. We know of only a handful of choirs from the area whose names before World War II, contained the name of a town or place from the area. However, when Ladysmith Black Mambazo became a national success, dozens of choirs such as Ladysmith Fountain Brothers, Inala Ladysmith, Ladysmith Naughty Boys, Ladysmith Heralds, Ladysmith Lion Cubs, and many others sprang up in the area who not only sought to pattern themselves after Shabalala's group musically. By choosing to attach the name of Ladysmith to their name, the choirs hoped to benefit from the prestige their home area had gained in the isicathamiya world.

How diverse the patterns of identification with the rural home-area, town, and the factory can be among different choirs is further illustrated by the cadenza-like formulas that serve as a kind of name tag for the choir and are attached—with identical words and music—to every song in a choir's repertoire. Early examples of such cadenzas or codas are found in some of Solomon Linda's songs, such as "Zingango Kwela" of 1940 (1630, Unissued):

> *EmaQongqo kwelakithi.*
>   The Maqongqo mountains are our home.

The practice, although rare prior to the 1960s, recalls the *izihlobo* section of *maskanda* guitar or concertina music in which the performers praise themselves and indicate the "river from which they drink," that is to say, their home area. Today, most codas contain some statement of religious belief such as "Khanyisa nkanyezi yezulu" (Light up, heavenly star) in songs by the Welkom Morning Stars, for instance. But many also include a direct reference to the singers' home area. The most famous of these tags is, of course, that of Ladysmith Black Mambazo.

> *Kumnandi kwelakithi eMnambithi.*
>   Ladysmith is a sweet place.

Two things can be learned from the contrasting types of symbolic representation of the "home." First, the growth of the capitalist wage economy and the closing of escape routes into alternative methods of reproduction have spawned rather than weakened networks of regional solidarity and the home-people system. Isicathamiya performers have increasingly resorted to symbolic practices that heighten rather than diminish their implication in this system, articulating local worlds and the exogenous structures encompassing them. In a more fundamental sense, perhaps, the different degrees of relevance assigned to images of home and countryside in such symbolic layers as choir names and song codas also suggest the complex manner in which migrants reflect and act on the ambiguities of their lives. To sing about one's place, as James Fernandez has observed, does not mean to assume all the musical colloquialisms of that place. Unlike the duels between Asturian poets examined by Fernandez, metaphor

in isicathamiya competitions is not transformed automatically into meto-
nym (Fernandez 1988, 31).

Women with Trousers

The symbolic reconstruction of the "home," despite all its ambiguity, also involves a certain notion of a gendered order of the social universe.
For the redress from the alienation and intractability of urban life not only
entails a rezoning of geographical space but also a search for the deepest
moral and social foundations of human existence within the parameters set
by the domestic unit, the homestead. It was two sets of relationships in
particular that were crucial in keeping the *umuzi* intact: subordination of
women and control over the younger generation. An element of the reproduction of the polity, these inequities were ritualized in an elaborate set of
practices such as the forms of respectful address (*ukuhlonipha*) wives employed toward their husbands. In a sense, isicathamiya performances can
be seen as another form of ritualizing such inequities.

We have already seen in chapter 3 how the genre in part emerged from
a repertoire of wedding songs, thus celebrating in its very musical essence
the virtues of marriage and progeny. But as has frequently been the case
when the sociomoral integrity of African societies was undermined by the
intrusion of the forces of colonial domination and the world market, the
victims of these processes perceive the breakdown of their universe as being
caused from within the very moral core of their societies. Often lacking any
means to directly confront these anonymous forces, those marginalized by
the encroaching world system first and foremost conceive of the threat to
the cohesion of their moral system as stemming from an inner virus, some
kind of internal disorder. And, to be sure, it is the most vulnerable and
dependent members of society, women and the young, that are considered
to be the immediate sources of such disorder and those most easily affected
by it. Thus, a song like "Shanelani Amabala Wezingane" (Sweep the yard,
children) by the New Home Brothers, as performed in the competition
described in chapter 1, puts the blame for the destruction of the old moral
cosmos rather squarely on the woman's shoulders:

> *Shanelani amabala wezingane.*
>> Sweep the yard, children.
> *Nanguya nje umakoti uzongena nemikhuba emibi.*
>> Here comes the bride with bad manners.
> *Wamuhle umakoti, wamuhle usafika.*
>> You are beautiful, bride, upon your arrival.

Uyothi angajwayela akhahlele indoda.
>Once she has familiarized herself with the place, she will kick her
>husband.

Lomakoti akahloniphi, ufaka amabhulukwe.
>The bride lacks respect, she puts on trousers.

Ayi isimodeli sibi madoda.
>Oh, the modern times are bad, gentlemen.

Thina nabafowethu sasithandana wafika wasixabanisa.
>We got on well with our brothers until she came and we started
>quarreling.

Another, if earlier, example of migrant men's concern over the endangered moral code is "Intombi Nezintsizwa" (Boys and girls) by the Evening Birds, recorded in 1937 (GE 144). The song does not so much articulate a critique of urban immoral behavior as such as it reflects the concern with which older migrants perceived the threat to the moral foundations of the homestead economy as the backbone of migrants' reproduction through the growing independence of young men and women:

Choir: *Izintombi nezintsizwa zihamba amashende.*
>Men and women are getting used to having extramarital affairs.

Nans' indaba yamashende.
>Here is the story of concubines.

Nant' usizi luvela emashendeni.
>These concubines bring shame to the families.

Peculiarly, the Evening Birds are accompanied on this recording by a jazz band, often decried by middle-class Africans as the musical archsymbol of urban immorality. Be this as it may, songs such as "Intombi Nezintsizwa" clearly demonstrate the bias that exists in isicathamiya toward a male-centered conception of the ideal homestead. This ancillary role of women is also represented in the role women play during isicathamiya performance, both on- and offstage. During *prakthisa,* as we have seen in chapter 2, the women sometimes join their favorite choir when they move into the venue by simply extending the tail end of the *ukureka* dancing line of singers. Much less frequently, though, do these women join the men on stage, and in some of the smaller venues with a small stage they remain entirely in the liminal space between stage and audience while the men occupy the stage. On the other hand, women heroize their male counterparts through a complex gestural language, described in chapter 2, and gift tokens bestowed on their favorite singers. On other occasions, I observed some women miming household chores and some of the actions, such as sweeping the ground, that are routinely being performed in wedding cere-monies. During *kompithi* the women, like the audience in general, with-draw into almost complete passiveness. With one exception. In recent years, a number of choirs such as Alison Gumbi's Easy Walkers have begun to incorporate one or two women into the group. In performance, these women always occupy a prominent position. They lead the men into the hall or stand in front of the choir onstage. This new approach, as Gumbi said, was designed to enhance, to "embellish" the appearance of the choir and to influence the judges. The move has been hotly contested by other choirs and, as a result, some choir associations adopted a policy in which choirs wishing to incorporate women must compete in a separate category. In sum, then, women constantly move into and out of the performance frame. They comment on the men's performance, they occasionally take an accompanying part in it, but they never control the performance from within.

But why did isicathamiya remain an exclusively male performance genre and did any parallel female genres emerge among women laborers? Al-though the topic would deserve a much more detailed investigation than is possible here, the available evidence suggests that the music closest to a female isicathamiya is the music of the internationally known female *mba-qanga* group Mahotella Queens. Belonging to the *umgqashiyo* genre of which both male and female varieties have emerged, the music of the Ma-hotella Queens articulates specifically female perspectives on labor migra-tion within the stylistic confines of a predominantly male genre. Thus, on older recordings, such as the album *Izibani Zomgqashiyo* (The flashing lights of Gqashiyo) (Shanachie 43036), the group is heard providing little more than background vocals. Fronted by the male *mbaqanga* group Aba-fana Baseqhudeni whose leader singer Robert Mbazo Mkhize sings the equivalent of the soprano solo part of isicathamiya, the female vocalists sing the remaining parts. The bass guitar of the accompanying Makhona Zonke Band provides the usual I-IV-V harmonic groundwork. The distribution of performance roles, then, clearly suggests the subordinate position of women in the symbolic discourse established by isicathamiya performers about the imagined rural "family." Women are relegated to a position on the margins of migrant performers' imagined world, because this margin-ality of women is part of isicathamiya's very symbolic strategy.

This situation contrasts sharply with the role of women poets among Basotho migrants. Driven into a stubborn independence by despotic chiefs and absent (and often irresponsible) husbands, Basotho women have long been fighting their own struggles within South Africa's informal sector, most notably in the liquor trade. And thus, modeling their performances on the *lifela tsa litsamaea-naha* (songs of the inveterate travelers) of their menfolk, Basotho women have created shebeen songs that "proclaim a resolute, individualistic, and adventurous spirit, . . . deliberately contrary to the stationary domestic commitment expected of adult women in Lesotho" (Coplan 1991, 173).

This is not to say, of course, that women did not develop their own strategies of countering male hegemony and that these have not found expression in long-established performance genres. As Rosemary Joseph's study of Zulu women's bow songs shows, the amorous feelings of rural women, as might be expected of the genre, are mainly depicted as a pining for the distant lover, frequently a migrant who sojourns behind the mountains. But because "the texts of the bow songs reveal many of the poetic qualities previously only associated, among traditional categories of performance, with Zulu praise poetry" (Joseph 1987, 105), these women's songs are an essential component of female self-definition. As modified praise poetry, they represent attempts at asserting normative female roles in the face of an alien system and its disrespect for kinship, marital security, and custom. In this, women's bow songs can be seen indeed as a parallel genre to isicathamiya songs.

Patriarchs and Youthful Proletarians

The central place of parental, and thus ultimately male, authority in the moral code and its importance for the unity of the *umuzi* is, of course, rooted in the organization of productive relations and the sexual division of labor within the homestead. And so is the clear demarcation of age groups, the second major aspect of the homely reconstructed in isicathamiya performance. Interestingly, the forcible transformation of South Africa's independent black peasantry into a rural proletariat, the degradation of the domestic domain to the periphery of the urban centers, cemented rather than weakened the moral claims to obedience made by seniors over their youthful dependents. From at least the turn of the century, as Helen Bradford has shown, the brunt of labor on the white farms generally fell on the shoulders of black youths (Bradford 1987, 38–39). To escape the drudgery and backbreaking tasks on the farms, youths therefore often resorted to all kinds of acts of resistance—overt and hidden—against the white landlord and their own parents. Not the least important of these options was to join the ranks of the urban laborers.

Even then, most families depended bitterly on the wage remittances of these migrants, a fact which is reflected in some isicathamiya songs such as "Yise Kamfana" (Father of the boy) by the Scorpions (SABC LT 15 646, A5) that exhorts young migrants to be loyal to their families.

Chorus: *Hamba kahle nje usithumelel' imali.*
    Go well and send us money.
    Ubokhumbula abantwana bayalamba.
    Remember, the children are starving.
Leader: *Se . . . sesiyabonga.*
    We . . . thank you.
Chorus: *Sesiyabonga imali siyitholile.*
    We thank you, we received the money.
    Usisizile wasithumela imali.
    You helped us by sending money.
Bass: *Uthumel' imali.*
    You sent money.
Chorus: *Usithumelel' imali.*
    You sent us money.

Interestingly, in isicathamiya—at least at the level of song lyrics—these acts of defiance have not found the same boastful expression of youthful pride and manly self-assertion as in Sesotho-speaking migrants' *lifela* (Coplan 1988, 346 ff.). One of the few exceptions is the song "Nansi Imali" by Ladysmith Black Mambazo (Mavuthela/Ezomdabu BL 321).

Nants' imali, elandwa zinsizwa phants' emgodini.
    Here is the money, earned by the men underground.
Saze sayibon' imali elandwa zinsizwa le kude la ungek' ufike khona wena
    ngob' unovalo phants' emgodini.
    We have finally seen the money which the men earn far from here
        where you would not reach, because you would be afraid
        underground.
Zinsizwa zukithi siyun' hulalisela nyamandla nangesibindi ngokuz' inikela
    kwenu.
    We congratulate you, men, for the strength and bravery and for
        sacrificing your lives.
Sisho ngoba nina nizinsizwa zoqobo nisebenzel' isizwe,
    We say this, because you are real men who work for the nation
Ngokusilandel' umcebo nezinto zonk' ezikhona phants' emgodini.
    by fetching all the riches and the wealth from underground.

Izinto zonk' ezikhona zenziwa ngayo lemali eniy' landa phants' emgodini.
      Everything exists because of the money which you fetch from
          underground.
Halala. Sinethulel' isigqoko baholi bomgodi ngokunqob' ingozi.
      We salute you, masters of the mine, because you have overcome the
          danger.

"Nansi Imali" is exceptional in that it is part of an album aimed primarily at Basotho miners. As a rule, however, a remorseful tone of submission and regret breathes through many songs. The following song by the King Star Brothers, for instance, from their album *Yashimizi* (LYBOL EO 313, side B, track 4), is an example of the way in which the youthful challenges to parental authority are conceived:

Leader: *Uxabana nobaba nje ubukade uleleph' izolo mfana.*
          You are quarreling with father, where did you sleep yesterday,
          young boy?
        Wen' uxabana nobaba nje.
          You are quarreling with father.
Chorus: *Uxabana nobaba nje.*
          You are quarreling with father.
        Ubukad' uleleph' izolo mfana?
          Where did you sleep yesterday, boy?
Leader: *Bakubonile bathi mfana eChawelo.*
          They say you and said: Boy from Chawelo,
Chorus: *Uhamba nabangani ababi abahamba bekhuthuza.*
          You are going with bad friends who are pickpockets.
Leader: *Kodwa awulalele ngani?*
          But why don't you listen?
Chorus: *Wemfana yini, yini ungalaleli ndoda.*
          Boy, why? Why don't you listen, old as you are,
        imiyalo yabazali bako.
          to your parents' moral codes?
Leader: *Thuli-la la.*
          Thuli-la la.
Chorus: *He! Khuluma Nkosi kimi.*
          He! Speak to me, Lord.

The next example, "Ngikhumbula Usizi" (I remember the sorrow) (SABC LT 8765, B3) by the Crocodiles, is typical of the kind of nostalgia for the abandoned homestead recalcitrant but unsuccessful young migrants, caught between the wonders and repressiveness of town life, might feel:

Chorus: *Ngikhumbul' usizi olwabonwa ngiye umzali wami.*

>   I remember the sorrow that gripped my mother,

. . . .

Engalali ebusuku.

>   She could not sleep at night.

Ngikhula njalo kodwa wabekezela.

>   I was still growing up, but she persevered.

Namhla sengikhulile sengimshiyele yedwa elel' ekhaya.

>   Today I have grown up and left mother alone at home.

Yek' uhambo lwami lungivezele usimanga.

>   Oh, my journey has shown me wonderful things.

Songiko ngaboshiswa kwenkomo mika.

>   I was once bound like a cow.

Ukulahl' umzali wami.

>   Because I left my mother.

Sengizibuyela kuyena uwazali wami

>   I am going back to my mother

ngiquqa ngaphambi kwathi.

>   and kneel in front of her.

Leader: (spoken) *Mzali wami, ngiyazisola phambi kwakho.*

>   Mother, I am ashamed of what I have done.

Ngonile, bengiyintsizwa enkulu endobheni.

>   I have sinned. I was a famous gentleman around town.

Ngiyintsizwa enkulu ethembekile.

>   I have been a famous and respectable gentleman.

Namhlanje sengizibone ukuthi angilutho.

>   Today I have realized that I am nothing.

Ngiboshiwe eGoli kodwa anginalutho.

>   I have been arrested in Johannesburg, but I am alright.

Ngicela uxolo kuwe mama wami.

>   I beg for forgiveness from you, mother.

Ngithi xola ntombi kababa.

>   I say, forgive me, fathers, lady.

Xola mama.

>   Forgive me, mother.

Zulu Ethnicity and Black Racial Pride

The ultimate guarantee of the homestead with its hierarchies and divisions of social roles, the space that is the supreme embodiment of this imagined world of orderliness and cohesion, the roof under which the homely resides, is the Zulu nation. The notion of national identity, how-

ever, that is inseparable from a history, language, and culture shared by all
Zulus is a historically recent phenomenon. Zulu ethnic consciousness in
Natal, as the work of Shula Marks (1986b, 1989b), Nicholas Cope (1990),
and Carolyn Hamilton and John Wright (1993) amply demonstrates, has
been the product of intense ideological labor by the black intelligentsia and
the white ideologues of South Africa. Designed to diffuse the formation of
radical class-based political organization in the increasingly sharpening social conflicts of the 1920s and 1930s, a new type of discourse cobbled from
a wide range of reconstructed and invented symbols and practices representing a heroic Zulu past came to dominate black politics in Natal.

But this conservative politics of "patriotism, patriarchy and purity," as
Marks is careful to point out, was not built on domination or authority
alone. The relationships between the Zulu monarchy and the people and
between the state and the monarch are best described in Weber's term
Herrschaft, a term that retains notions of reciprocity, of the acceptance of
the rulers by the ruled (Marks 1986b, 131). Historical evidence from the
interwar period suggests that the identification with this "imagined community" cut across all sectors of the black population. Class consciousness,
if it existed at all in the fragmented framework of Natal's society, frequently
overlapped with other loyalties and allegiances of race and ethnicity.

Elsewhere I have shown how the politics of race and ethnicity determined and in turn was shaped by performance practices across the entire
spectrum of social relations in the South African countryside and the urban centers (Erlmann 1991). Performance genres as diverse as *makwaya,*
iRagtime, and *ingoma* were not only located in different settings of social
interaction, but because the experiences and life-worlds of the performers
of each of these genres frequently intertwined, they also served to symbolize the imagined bonds of a society long transformed by capitalist relations
of production.

Space and the paucity of evidence on the subject, does not allow for a
detailed discussion of the emergence of ethnic consciousness among migrant workers. Instead, I wish to examine the production of ethnicity in
isicathamiya against the background of the evolving traditionalist discourse
of the 1920s and 1930s. The period between the two world wars, as we
have seen, saw not only a vastly changed socioeconomic landscape of rural
poverty and mass exodus into the growing urban centers but also the
origins of the nightsong tradition as such. In fact, as I have stressed time
and again, both processes were connected in numerous ways. Interestingly,
in some of the earliest recorded examples of isicathamiya, this nexus be-

tween rapid social change and the personal experience of dislocation is pro-
jected back in time and space, as it were, to a fictitious period when the
nation was at one with itself. "Anoku Gonda" (You must know how to
pray), a song recorded by Solomon Linda and the Evening Birds in 1940
(1637, reissued on Rounder Records CD5025, track 7), is one such example. Built on an enormously popular tune—later to resurface as "Madoda Inzondo" in a HMV recording by the Bantu Glee Singers (GU
127)—the song juxtaposes, in an interesting metaphoric operation, the
experience of migration and the uncertain future of the nation.

> *Asazi Zulu lapho siyofela khona.*
> > We do not know, Zulus, where we will end up.
> *Lapho sibizwayo thina siyoya khona.*
> > We will go to any place where we are called.
> *Anoku qonda ukukhuleka thina sazi ndodana.*
> > You must know how to pray. We know the son.
> *We Ndabezitha sisho kuwo amakhos' ohlanga.*
> > We are saying this to the kings of the nation.
> *Sithi bayethe.*
> > We say hail to our kings.

On the surface, the line, "We will go to any place where we are called,"
refers, of course, to the fact that the Evening Birds were invited to perform
in many parts of the country. But in the same line the singers also lament
their uprootedness and homelessness as migrant workers. Read against the
previous line, "We do not know, Zulus, where we will end up," the predicament of migration, that is, the growing penetration of the countryside
by the capitalist mode of production, is seen as the result—and not the
cause—of the decline of the kingdom. For, in fact, the phrase evokes Shaka's famous prophecy that after his death Zulus will be dispersed like birds
and the country ruled by foreigners.

These were common sentiments in the interwar period, ones that were
expressed in a wide range of performance genres. The following passage is
from "E Zintsukwini Zo Tshaka" (In the days of King Shaka), a *makwaya*
tune recorded in 1938 by elite music critic Mark Radebe and his African
Male Voice Choir (Columbia YE 12):

> *Wathi lapho mhla efayo*
> > When he died,
> *wathi thina maZulu siyosala singahlangene,*
> > he said that we Zulu shall never be united,

siyofana nezinyoni.
    and that we shall be scattered like birds.
Kodwa ke nempela siyabona
    We have already seen this
ngokusuka ezintabeni amakhosikazi ashiya amakhaya.
    in leaving the mountains, wives left their homes.

But such nostalgia for the heroic past did not remain confined to the period before World War II. The following examples show that ethnic sentiment and traditionalist viewpoints have been alive and well in isicathamiya performance ever since Linda's "Anoku Gonda." The following song, "Ngeke Salungelwa Lutho," (Nothing will come right) was recorded for the SABC by the Welkom Morning Stars in 1974 (SABC LT 14 417, A2):

Leader: *Ungeke mfana wam' ungeke . . .*
    You won't come, my son, you won't . . .
Chorus: *Ngeke salungelwa ilutho thina.*
    Nothing will come right for us.
Leader: *Ngoba thina . . .*
    Because we . . .
Chorus: *Ingoba asiwagcin' amasiko akwaZulu.*
    Because we do not keep our Zulu customs.
Leader: *Kodwa namhlanje . . .*
    But today . . .
Chorus: *Aph' amabheshu?*
    Where are men's loin-skins?
Leader: *Amabheshu.*
    Loinskins.
Chorus: *Siph' isidwaba.*
    Women's leather-skirts.
Leader: *Webaba.*
    Yes, father.
Chorus: *Aphi wonk' amasiko akaZulu?*
    Where are all our Zulu customs?
    Uyadela owaziyo.
    I wish someone knew.
Leader: *Namhlanje, lalela ndoda.*
    Today, listen man!
Chorus: *Ubuphithiphithi, no buyaluyalu.*
    Confusion and disarray.
    Ukuhlafuna kwentshebe kwaMashu
    Even a bearded man in KwaMashu

> *yakhala ngaphantsi.*
>> went under.[6]

Leader: *Thala-la*
Chorus: *Thala-la.*
Leader: *Kumnyama.*
>> It is dark.
Chorus: *Khanyisa nkanyezi yezulu.*
>> Light up, heavenly star.

Our next example, "Zinsizwa Zomdabu" (Indigenous gentlemen) by the Empangeni Home Tigers (SABC MKB 818, A), was recorded a few years later, in the early 1970s. It reflects a similar retrogressive mood.

Leader: *Ezombadu, izintombi zomdabu.*
>> Indigenous, indigenous ladies.
> *Nenzani nilahl' isiZulu?*
>> Why throw Zulu culture away?
Bass: *Zinsizwa zomdabu.*
>> Indigenous gentlemen.
Leader: *Aphi?*
>> Where are they?
> *Kinina?*
>> To you?
Chorus: *Aph' amabheshu?*
>> Where are the loin-skins?
Bass: *Zintombi zomdabu.*
>> Indigenous ladies.
Leader: *Kambe,*
>> By the way,
> *sengiyabuza*
>> I am asking:
Chorus: *Baph' onomndeni?*
>> Where is the family?
Leader: *Kinina-ke bobaba*
>> And you, old men:
Chorus: *Uph' ungiyan' ekhanda?*
>> Where is the head-ring?
Leader: *Asambheni manje.*
>> Let's go back now.
> *Sukumani sambe.*
>> Let's stand up and go.
Chorus: *Asambheni sonke, siyocela isiZulu kwaNongoma.*
>> Let's go and ask for our Zulu culture at Nongoma.

Sibe kwe engolobaneni
> It is stored in the barn
yamaguq'a kwaZulu.
> of Zulu wisdom.
Leader: *Ufik' ucaphune khona nje.*
> Just dip your hand in the barn.
Chorus: *Ufik' ucaphune ngezandla zombuli.*
> Just dip both your hands.
Ngek' usiqede mude lomlando wethu maZulu.
> You won't finish it, we have a long history, we Zulus.
Leader: *Hayi!*
Chorus: *He!*
Leader: *Sasala sodwa.*
> We are left behind.

The next example by the Empangeni Home Tigers commemorates the battle of Blood River (Ncome) of 1838 in which Dingane's forces were defeated by the Voortrekkers. After a lengthy description of the battle, full of evocative images, the song culminates in the call for continued Zulu resistance against foreign domination.

Leader: *Nhlanezwe yahlangana, yesuka*
> In the north, a fierce war erupted
eNcome, eNcome bo.
> at Ncome, at Ncome.
Chorus: *eNcome, eNcome yahlangana yesuka.*
> At Ncome a fierce war erupted.
Leader: *eNcome enhlanezwe, madoda.*
> At Ncome in the north, gentlemen.
Chorus: *eNcome, eNcome yahlengena.*
> At Ncome, at Ncome the war started.
Leader: *Yesuka, sayibamb' ezindala bo!*
> The war began; we fought fiercely.
Chorus: *Lwaye bamb' undloko kwathul' umoya.*
> It was a frightening battle.
Leader: *Zayibamba ezindala izintsizwa mfana.*
> The men fought fiercely, my son.
Chorus: *Lwayubamb' ukhanda mpevu.*
> Even the old men were fighting.
Kwasuk'uthuli lwaqonda KwaMoshoeshoe.
> You could see dust heading toward Moshoeshoe's country.

Leader: *Kwabalek' umama, mfana.*
        Women ran away, son.
Chorus: *Kwabalek' umama nezingane no dubi.*
        They fled, mother, children and the entire household.
        Bayophephela emiphemeni yezintaba namawa.
        They fled seeking sanctuary in the mountains and cliffs.
Leader: *Kwakukhal' uve ndoda.*
        You could only hear the sound of swords and spears.
        Kwakukhal' uwe
        You could hear war cries,
        luth' nyadela wen' osulapho,
        saying to the dead "I wish I was you."
        Hayi mbamb' enyalo maZulu usuthu.
        No, fight on Zulus, great nation.

Finally, the last example was recorded in 1984 by the King Star Brothers on their album *Yashimizi*. The song is entitled "Esanlwane" (L4 BOL EO 313, B1) and celebrates the battle of Isandlwana of 1879 in which the defeat of the Zulu forces brought about the final downfall of the Zulu kingdom:[7]

Leader: *Asambheni bafana siye khona le eSandlwana.*
        Let us go, boys, let us go to Sandlwana.
        Asambheni bo.
        Let us go.
Chorus: *Asambheni wemadoda, siye khona le Sandlwana, lapho kwafela khona amaqhawe.*
        Let us go, men, let us go to Sandlwana, where our heroes died.

The journey to Isandlwana, although essentially a symbolic move back to a "home" and a past that will remain for ever out of reach, in most isicatha-miya songs and Zulu lore stands for the construction of an order that, while drawing for its images on the sanitized and heroic vision of the past, is nevertheless tooled on the logic and institutions of the dominant society. Ethnic consciousness, while pretending to be the product of a seamless continuity with the past, is thus in fact an integral component of modernization, reacting against the estranging effects of modernity and at the same time modeling itself on it. A song like "Phansi Imikhonto" (Down the spears) by the Empangeni Home Tigers (SABC MKB 818, B) illustrates this clearly:

Leader: *Phans' imikhonto, phans' izagila.*
    Down the spears, down the assegais.
    Phans' imikhonto Zulu.
    Down the spears, Zulus.
Chorus: *Phans'imikhonto.*
    Down the spears.
Leader: *Bekani izagila.*
    Put down the assegais!
Chorus: *Phans' izagila.*
    Down the assegais.
Leader: *Bekan' imikhonto.*
    Put down the spears!
    Yilomhlaba, osabuswa ngegazi
    The era of reigning with blood is over,
    lokho kwakwenzek' emandulo.
    that used to happen in ancient times.
Leader: *Akekho noyedwa namhlanje.*
    There is no one today.
Chorus: *Akekho noyedwa namhlanje*
    There is no one today
    ongafuya amelw' umnotho ngomkhonto.
    who can be a farmer and merchant while being threatened by
    spears.
    MaZulu, hayi, maZulu qhababo
    No Zulus, no Zulus.
    Ake siqhubekele phambili.
    Let us progress.
Leader: *Nakhu kukhanya ke.*
    There is a light.
Chorus: *Nakh' ukukhanya kithi kufikile.*
    It is the dawning of the age.
    Nans' imfundo maZulu ifikile.
    Here is education, Zulus.
Leader: *Manje-na* . . .
    Now . . .
Chorus: *Ohubani izingane ziye es'koleni.*
    Lead children to school.
    Ziyothola ulwazi olungena kuphela.
    Let them receive endless knowledge.
Leader: *Hayi!*
Chorus: *No!*

Leader: *Sasala sodwa*.
　　　 We are left behind.

It is a message such as this one, together with isicathamiya's general emphasis of the rural, the traditional, and the nation, that have earned isicathamiya practitioners the reputation of being followers of Chief Gatsha Buthelezi's Inkatha. True, some performers such as Ladysmith Black Mambazo have, on occasion, expressed their confidence in Buthelezi's politics of reconciliation and generally in an organization that, in the words of Gerhard Maré and Georgina Hamilton, offered "elements of an historical pride through membership of an organization that had its roots in that history, a leader that was as firmly part of it, and that expressed itself in the rhetoric of 'cultural liberation'" (Maré and Hamilton 1987, 76).[8] As a blanket statement about isicathamiya performers' political affiliation, however, such allegations are misleading.

Few symbolic carriers of isicathamiya performance other than song lyrics exhibit the politics of Zulu ethnicity so vividly. Some of the choir names listed earlier in this chapter such as Amazulu Amnyama, Inkatha kaZulu, Inyanda Yesizwe, and Zulu Champions might be mentioned here, but also some stage uniforms. Although this is a topic that will be discussed at greater length in chapter 7, I would like to briefly describe a uniform here that is frequently worn by Ladysmith Black Mambazo. It consists, apart from trousers, of a golden or silver silk shirt with a shield and crossed spears printed on it—a symbol that is used in a number of black political organizations and that more generally, especially in its commodified form as a tourist souvenir, evokes images of past tribal grandeur.

The bricolage in song lyrics, choir names, and uniforms of images and symbols representing an imagined Zulu collectivity rooted in an ancient past is not the only form in which the desire for a secure place and positive self-image is conflated with the notion of national unity. As I have pointed out in chapter 3, concurrent with the more parochial forms of Zulu ethnic pride, a pantribal nationalist rhetoric has informed isicathamiya performance from the start. Yet it is in the ferment of the antiapartheid struggles of the 1980s and 1990s and the ensuing rebirth of politically conscious arts that isicathamiya reemerged as a vital component of a politics of popular resistance. One of the most visible signs of this, at least on the international stage, has been Paul Simon's appropriation of isicathamiya on the *Graceland* album and the incorporation of isicathamiya songs and dance routines in the grand finale of Mbongeni Ngema's phenomenally successful musical *Sarafina!* In both productions, the nightsongs have come to signify the indestructable resilience of the black South Africa.

On a more local level, isicathamiya has also regained an important place in the new radical unions. Thus, from the mid-1980s on, numerous theater groups, gumboot dance teams, and creative writers have emerged who put their work in the service of black working-class politics. On occasion, isicathamiya choirs such as the Clover Team have participated in FOSATU (Federation of South African Trade Unions)-sponsored rallies, and a choir known as K-Team has dedicated itself entirely to the union cause. Composed of migrants from Kwaceza in Natal working at Kellogg's, the K-Team was founded in 1984 by Agrippa Xaba, the composer and choreographer of the group.[9] As an example of their work I reproduce below the lyrics of "USomandla" (Almighty) (Shifty 24L4, A2):

Leader: *Somandla uyashesh' ukuzwa, uyephuz' ukuphendula.*
        Almighty, you hear immediately, but you take time to answer.
        Somandla.
        Almighty.
Chorus: *Uyashesh' ukuzwa, uyaphuz' ukuphendula.*
        You hear immediately, but you take time to answer.
Leader: *Asazi . . .*
        We don't know . . .
Chorus: *Asazi noma uyosizwela lolusizi esinalo.*
        We don't know whether you will pity us in our misery.
Leader: *Yini . . .*
        Why . . .
Chorus: *Siyahlupheka kulomhlaba.*
        We are poor in this world.
        Siyakhala kulomhlaba.
        We are crying in this world.
        Lomhlaba wakithi
        In our land
        owathathwa izizwe.
        that was taken by other nations.
Leader: *K'dala ke . . . thina . . . hayi . . . yiyo lena.*
        For a long time . . . we . . . no . . . this is the one.
Chorus: *K'dala sidliw' izinja singaphethe nduku.*
        For a long time we have been beaten by dogs, and we did not
        have sticks (to hit them).

Nathi sesingay' induku kuCOSATU.
          We can also be a stick for COSATU.
Botha, o'deda endleleni.
          Botha, get out of the way.
Thanana.
Leader: *Awu, suka la uhleli ukhona Mnumzane.*
          Ah, get out of the chair, Mister!
Suk' endleleni Botha.
          Get out of the way, Botha.
Kuhlal' uMandela Mnumzane!
          Mandela wants the chair, Mister.
(spoken) *Angena amaAfrika madoda.*
          The Africans have moved in, men.
Angena kwashung' uthuli.
          They move in, you can see it by the dust.
Kade sisho sithi soze sifike la esiya khona.
          We have long been saying that we would reach our aim.
Obanayo nongaboni uyabona manje.
          Even the blind can see now.
Sekuseduze lasiya khona madoda.
          The aim is high, men.
Qiniselani, sizwe siNtsundu.
          Persevere, black nation!
Leader: *MaComrades.*
          Comrades.
Chorus: *MaComrades, phambili ngomzabalazo.*
          Comrades, forward with the revolution.

On the basis of songs such as this one, it might be argued that because of the radicalization of black politics in the second half of the 1980s and the enormously increased international attention to black South African arts isicathamiya is now beginning to be remolded as a black performance tradition rather than a expressive form of Zulu migrants only. As we shall see in chapter 10, the foundation of SATMA (South African Traditional Music Association), designed to promote and organize the development of isicathamiya nationally, in part represents a response to the radicalized cultural politics of the late 1980s as it reflects the growing role of South African music on the international pop markets. In much the same vein, Joseph Shabalala, always a keen observer of shifting public moods and alliances, provided a telling illustration of the changed role of isicathamiya in the age of "worldbeat" when he explained the etymology of Ladysmith Black Mambazo to American video viewers on Spike Lee's music documentary *Do It a Capella*. Whereas in previous years Shabalala had derived the word "black" from the color of the oxen spans his choir is meant to symbolize, he now interpreted the name as referring to his and his singers' skin color.

To recapitulate, in my analysis I have shown how the remaking of a meaningful social order involved complex symbolic constructions that re-situate key arenas of human practice, displaced by an alien and oppressive system, in a set of spaces at once "traditional" and modern, homogeneous and paradoxical. In the following chapter we shall see how these purposive strategies of reconstruction extend into even deeper reaches of isicathamiya performers' experience occupied by the consuming passions of the dancing and dressed body.

6   The Home Embodied:

Dance and Dress in Isicathamiya

There our house was; and I lived in it as I lived in my body.
                    Nadine Gordimer, *The Lying Days*

The suppression of the body—and to a much lesser extent the domestication of the mind—has been at the heart of the colonization of
southern African societies. The subjugation of black male and female bodies, rather than the battle for African minds, was the decisive factor in the
production of an industrial labor force on a scale unprecedented on African
soil (Comaroff and Comaroff 1991). The process was a long one, ironically
entailing a "bitter contest of conscience and consciousness" (Comaroff
and Comaroff 1992, 235), and resting on the separation of body and mind,
on the double process of a reification and desymbolization of the black
body. For in the preindustrial societies of southern Africa, the body was
primarily an agent of the transformation of the earth. And it
was a signifier whose visibility and agency in social practice had been
clearly marked through a rich symbolic vocabulary. Among the precolonial
Tshidi-Barolong of Botswana, for instance, as Jean Comaroff has shown,
the female body served as the primary symbolic model for the physical
structure of the house, the quintessential domestic unit (Comaroff 1985,
132 ff.). The female reproductive organs were the primary symbolic referent for the conjugal hut, just as the intimate matrimonial union was referred to as "entering the house" (56). The male domain, by contrast, was
symbolized by the mouth. Through artful speech and carefully controlled
social communication, men ensured the social reproduction of the polity.
Similarly, among rural Zulu, the center of a homestead, the hut (*umsamo*),
is divided into three parts that are metaphorically associated with the realm
of procreation: the interior of the hut is like a woman's womb (*inimba*)
and to cross the threshold of a hut is considered to be the equivalent of
sexual intercourse (Berglund 1976, 102, 168).

Given these taken-for-granted, embodied conceptions of the social universe, it is not surprising to find that the missionaries—the benign pioneers
of colonial subjugation—first concentrated on the body in order to undermine the autonomy of this universe and to undo the unity of the bodies
natural and social. To be sure, the model for this attack on the black body
was to be found in a long history of scientific and moral discourse about

the nature of man—a discourse closely tied to Europe's encounter with the larger world around it. With the dawning of the Enlightenment in eighteenth-century Europe and the expansion of global commercial networks, a general biology of mankind had developed that assigned the lowest position in the "great chain of being" to the African. In the rhetoric of evolution, race, and color, white bodies were thought to incarnate rationality, whereas dark skins were associated with fogged minds. Blind to the profound significance of African polities, scientific racism reduced Africans to a natural essence, to mere bodies shackled to their primordial nature, disrobed of any symbolic meaning fostered by socially ordered human intercourse. Black bodies, like women in general, were thought to be held in bondage by the sensory stimuli of the environment and the dark and unreasoned forces of their own needs and functions.[1]

It is in this reduced state as a moldable natural essence whose possibility for symbolic representation is undercut, that black bodies in South Africa were becoming available as free wage labor—free from the nexus that tied the body to the sociomoral universe of domestic production with its ancestors and symbols, but also free to seek fulfillment in a world beyond nature. As the work of John and Jean Comaroff on concepts of work and labor among the Tshidi has shown, the colonized subjects increasingly came to experience wage labor as a gradual weakening of the idea of work as the primary measure of personal value. Industrial labor required the physical operation and interaction of bodies increasingly cut loose from any referentiality in nature.

Coinciding with this, in the world of industrial production, the domestic sphere ceased to a place where the body might reside for itself. The house has become no more than a site of consumption, severed from the direct appropriation of the earth and at the same time physically segregated from the sphere of production: the mines and the factories. In South Africa's industrial capitalism, the gun and the *sjambok* (whip) of colonial conquest increasingly yield to the train, the Putco bus and the minitaxi ("Zola Budd") as the chief instruments of the oppression of the body. And it is this contradiction between production and consumption that mutilates the body. The distance of the body from the workplace only generates more need and the necessity to return to work in order to satisfy it. Thus, unable to find a home, the body roams in an never-ending pursuit of satiation. The unleashed body, abandoned to its own devices, eventually comes to be perceived as an afflicted, homeless thing whose pathology in turn indicates the disturbed social order.

The symptoms of disease and the interpretation of its causes indicate the great significance medical practitioners and the afflicted patients alike attach to the disruptive effects which the disintegration of the preindustrial patrilineage and its attendant ancestor cult had on the body. Thus, among the Nyuswa-Zulu on the outskirts of Durban a type of malevolent spirit possession called *indiki* appeared shortly before World War I that is generally associated with industrialization. *Indiki* is said to have been introduced by migrants from the north who died in the mines of South Africa without having been integrated into the spirit world through the appropriate funerary rites. Their spirits wander about, taking possession of the local people and causing illness. As the signs of physical disorder, the *indiki* spirits simultaneously signify an ailing social order, and Nyuswa-Zulu typically attempt to resocialize the afflicted body by replacing the alien spirits with male ancestor spirits (Ngubane 1977, 142–44).

The affliction of the body is, of course, not always expressed through the signs of physical disturbance. In a more general sense, the complete reordering of space and time engineered by the modern social relations in South Africa has entailed a marked shift in some basic bodily practices and the cultural meanings attached to them. Among the Tshidi, as Jean Comaroff notes for example, the political oppression by the state is metaphorically linked to the compression of bodily space (Comaroff 1985, 201). Another astute observer of South African performance and ritual provides an insightful and empathic interpretation of black women's sluggish weariness. Describing a meeting of the Mothers' Union at Soshanguve township, Helen Kivnick cannot help but notice the stark contrast between the jubilant exuberance of these women united in prayer and singing and the kind of shuffling, trudging body postures these same women would adopt in the streets of the white cities and in the white suburban households. Here, in the protected and unpatrolled space of the black church, bodies that were too cumbersome for activity other than serving tea, were suddenly transformed into a community bristling with energy and vitality. Weary deference, Kivnick concludes, is what black women have been socialized to show toward whites. It is safe. It camouflages rage and frustration at being forced to shoulder responsibility for the fabric of a family life worn thin by generations of legislative assault (Kivnick 1990, 40–43).

Given, then, the long and troubled history of the suppressed and diseased body in southern Africa, it is hardly surprising that, as Jean Comaroff's study on Zionist ritual illustrates, the efforts to reclaim the agency of the body in human history, in the broadest sense, involve practices focusing on healing as a mode of repairing the tormented body, and through it, the oppressive social order itself. Ritual, Comaroff goes on to state, works on the body so as to refashion the continuity between social, natural, and personal being. The Zionist cult seeks to reformulate the constitution of the everyday world by dealing with contradictions inadequately addressed in dominant ideology (Comaroff 1985, 8 ff.).

In a similar sense, I argue in this chapter, through dance and dress isicathamiya performers seek to reform the offending system by rehabilitating the body. Isicathamiya choreography and dancers' uniforms reinsert the body's potential for symbolic representation. The bodies of isicathamiya dancers cease to be the mere individual parcels without social or historical referent to which they have been reduced in the factories and become potent metaphors evoking the lost continuity between the bodies social and natural. The majority of these embodied images, as we shall see, corporeally merge the dancers with a collectivity bound by regional identity and common values about a certain gendered order of the world and thus become metaphors for the ideal community itself.

But the dancing and clothed body not only resists its submission; it also attempts to encompass and to recapitulate the history of that submission. The therapy which the dancer administers to his own body is not only meant to compensate for the debilitating modern social environment. The images of slick and smoothly gliding bodies, as we shall see, equally suggest that relief for the tormented body is to come from the consumption of the commodified images of the body molded in and by the city. In the topography of the dancing and fashioned body, the abdication of the body as a signifier and the utopia of the body as the socialized means of appropriation of the earth are tangibly bound together.

Given this ambiguous reappearance of the body, I am reluctant to see the dances of isicathamiya as a quintessential representation of the body politic. This suggests a view of dance that differs from other dance scholarship in several respects. For instance, I am not concerned with the question whether dance constitutes a "primary modeling system" (Blacking 1985, 65) through which ideas and feelings can be expressed before they are articulated in speech. Likewise, I am less interested in approaches that view dance primarily as a means of constructing social cohesion and unified cultural systems of meaning—be it through cathartic release of tension, the competitive display of boundaries, or the like.[2] Taking these and similar strands in dance research into account, I see the dance as a special form of human communication that has implications beyond its immediate social uses and functions. Dance is essentially a medium and context of social action and thus an agent of the bodily construction of worldview in all its fluidity and heterogeneity.[3]

Here I follow the critique some scholars of dance and ritual have directed against Pierre Bourdieu's views of embodiment as a passive incorporation of dominant social relations. Together with these scholars, I argue that dancing is both embedded in ordinary social relations and at the same time a special mode of social interaction itself. In other words, it is text and context at the same time. But because its site is the body, dancing is a form of social practice that is only partially subject to reflection. Through the body's preeminent potential for ambiguous perception and semic polyvalence, dance can both celebrate the taken-for-granted constitution of the world and it can reflexively act on it. Dancing seems to be a special mode of bodily behavior which enables dancers to be more reflexively conscious than usual of their bodies. In dancing, the performer is not only aware that he has a body but also that he is a body. Thus, dancing can reproduce the givenness of the dominant order, but it can also provide the models for its transformation. To dance is to produce not only signs but also social experience itself.[4]

The production of this experience, I suggest, is contingent on notions of space and bodies moving in space and time. Any study of dance must therefore pay attention to the entire spectrum of ordinary bodily movement habitually deployed in any given type of socially constructed space. Because dance styles, patterns of movements, proxemic structures, and regimes of spatiality constitute each other, we must first consider two facets of the performing body normally neglected in scholarly discourse about African music and dance: the dance floor and its environment and the sensory articulation of performance and social experience.

Performance Venues

The allocation of space, the architecture of the built environment, and frequently even the naming of places and how to move between them—all these things have rarely been of black people's choosing in South Africa. In addition, the scarcity of space for black occupation in a land of vast, open expanse has imposed a bland and uniform type of urban landscape on the vast majority of black South Africans. Drably regular street plans and monotonously shaped houses in the townships of South

Africa are the symbols of a world in which consumption for the sake of the reproduction of labor power is contained in places—physical locales designed to keep a laboring populace in place.

Of course, black South Africans have never simply accepted this state of affairs. Quite to the contrary, as a growing number of studies suggest, a central theme in the history of black urban communities was "to create and defend illegal space" (Bonner et al. 1989, 2). Nevertheless, even those physical structures and spaces—the community halls, lofts, and cultural centers—that have been set up as repair stations of laboring bodies, offer one advantage: they protect and seclude. This is an important point to make in a society where such protection is in itself the less than taken-for-granted result of intense struggles over property, shelter, and privacy. And it is a point worth recalling in a society in which some practices deliberately defy the hegemonic spatiotemporal order such as in Zionist open-air prayer meetings, and in the "people's parks" that emerged in some South African townships during the 1980s (Sack 1989). In other words, how to turn a place into a space—a site of practice—how to remodel a given architecture into a lived space, is at the heart of isicathamiya performers' tactics. By appropriating the objectified symbols of the dominant order—its roads, townships, buildings, and so forth—migrant workers sign their existence as authors on these structures (de Certeau 1984, 31). The halls, sheds, and lofts cease to be mere built spaces and begin to signify the operations whose object they have been. The consumption of the built environment is at the same time a use of a system and an operation performed on it. A profoundly ambiguous process in which the users subvert and escape the world of technocratic rationality without leaving it, this consumption is characterized by its fragmentation and invisibility. It shows itself not in its own products but in an art of using those imposed on it (31).

Access to these venues is the first act of appropriation. It requires advanced skills in the art of urban mobility. Some venues, for instance, are inconveniently located on the fringes of downtown Johannesburg and Durban and cannot easily be reached except by those spectators living in nearby "hostels," servants' quarters, and so on. Conversely, some venues that are part of larger complexes of migrant housing are often too remote to get to from the townships or the city. For the performers, in any case, the journey to and from these venues depends on the availability of taxis, and until the late 1980s at least, the ability to maneuver through the maze of curfews and pass-laws that were in force at the time. Thus, Solomon Ndlovu, the chairman of the Glebelands association in Durban until the mid-1980s, had to use a *laissez-passer* issued by the Durban authorities for his nocturnal travels to procure adjudicators.

At the macrolevel, the setting inside the halls reflects Western notions of spatial order. In contrast to the importance and symbolic potency of the circle and its derivatives in precolonial communicative praxis, linear and square arrangements predominate in isicathamiya performance venues. These can be grouped in four distinct areas: the stage, the audience, the space between stage and audience, and the section occupied by the chairman and his assistants. In some venues, a fifth area is sometimes set aside where refreshments are served. As a result of architectural constraints, there can, of course, be little variation in the layout of these four or five areas in a venue. The chairman and his assistants almost invariably position themselves along one of the side walls, diagonally across from the stage, while the refreshment section takes up the rear portion of the hall. As no backstage area is provided in most venues, access to the stage is only possible through the hall, either through a passage dividing the audience area up in half or between the audience and the wall. It is clear that this rigid plan reinforces as it reflects predominantly Western concepts of performance space. The strict separation of stage and audience, during *kompithi* at least, physically marks a mode of performer-audience interaction that invites contemplation and reduces participation.

As for the liminal space between the stage and the audience, it also serves a more ambiguous function. In *kompithi* it is taken up by the adjudicator and thus removes the audience from direct contact with the performers. But the adjudicator is fixed in this liminal space. He or she may not leave the assigned place unless accompanied by the chairman or one of his assistants. During the *prakthisa* phase, by contrast, this space becomes an extension of the stage. Most stages are small and as a rule cannot accommodate groups larger than thirty or more members. Thus when the female spectators join in the dance routines, the proceedings frequently spill over into the area in front of the stage. The area occupied by the chairman, finally, is strategically placed so as to enable the chairman to monitor the entire venue without obstructing anyone's vision and freedom of movement.

The movements between these areas are relatively codified and depend on the actors. But in either case, it is again the critical area between stage and audience that is constantly being staked out as the space on which the entire performance hinges. During *kompithi* it becomes an invisible boundary that disconnects the audience from the flow of communication between the judge and the choirs. Similarly, to cross that line during *kom-pithi* is to drastically switch between an offstage mode of bodily behavior (dance) and an onstage pose (stand still). To cross it as a spectator during *prakthisa* signals a shift between performance frame and out-of-performance frame. The (female) followers change from a position of observer to that of participant. Likewise, the chairman, who instructs the adjudicator from this in-between area, mediates between the two halves of the hall. By using a megaphone he also signals the fact that his instructions are public and contain no hidden information belonging to only one side.

Le Grain de la voix

The construction of space, as proxemics and acoustics tell us, is, of course, not a matter of bodily movement alone. Just as much as communication through speech and music is shaped by the spatial positioning of those who participate in it, sound patterns in turn influence our perception of space. Thus, to make music and to sing is to produce configurations of sound that literally define a space, mark its boundaries: high sound levels often make a given room to appear smaller, and low levels may widen a space. Given the fact that music making and dancing are often coterminous throughout Africa, African musicologists have generally been highly perceptive to the interdependence of the two domains of performance in the production of cultural knowledge. They have, however, been considerably less attentive to the physicality and tactile qualities of performance, the corporeal exigencies and pleasures of singing, playing, and dancing and to performers' own conceptualizations of these bodily sensations.[5] But if the meaning of performance in Africa has been not "to reflect a reality which stands behind it but to ritualize a reality that is *within* it" (Chernoff 1979, 36), and if, hence, performance is to be understood as a form of social experience, we will need to redirect our attention from the textual qualities of sound and movement to the sensory experience as an integral component of their meaning. An anthropology of performance, in the full meaning of the term, is inconceivable without an anthropology of the senses (Stoller 1989).

We have seen that performers often categorize isicathamiya styles according to the vocal register and level of volume used. *'Mbombing, isithululu,* or *sithuthuthu* are all terms which are, if not plain and simple onomatopoetic, emblematic of the quality of the overall sound produced within the genre. Other styles, such as *Isikhwela Jo, cothoza mfana* and *isicathamiya* are differentiated by the bodily movement required for the performance. In a sense, then, performance style is essentially conceived of as a manipulation of physical matter—body parts, space, air, and so forth—which is then linked to the social world via metaphor. Correspondingly, to know a style amounts to the ability to physically engage in its production. Reading the relationship between performance and the "embodied self" (Martin 1990) in this way, the "truth" of isicathamiya songs would primarily reside not in their expressive content but in the unique, grainy texture of the voices that generate them. Isicathamiya songs are *geno-songs*, to use Roland Barthes's expression, in which meanings emerge from the materiality of language itself and reside in the very act of the activation of a voice, in the fact of having and feeling a voice.

What terms like *isikhwela Jo* and *'mbombing* do not convey, of course, is the bodily experience itself of singing *isikhwela Jo* and of dancing "like a cat." From some performers' own comments and my own experience, however, a few things can be inferred about what it feels like to engage in isicathamiya dance and song. I suggest that the basic sensation produced through vigorous singing and dancing is a form of purification, of catharsis. After a considerable buildup of energy and immersion especially during *prakthisa*, and often not finding an end, performers emerge from a competition drained and sometimes even euphoric. The filling of the vacuous given and now with vigorous step dancing that "drains you out of strength" and strenuous falsetto singing that "burns one's voice" simultaneously saps performers' energies and cleanses them. Being a member in an isicathamiya choir, as Easy Walkers leader Alison Gumbi once remarked, "makes one respectable and also gives one self-respect, like being always clean and tidy. This is why I chose to sing isicathamiya music." The cleanliness that Gumbi alludes to, refers equally, of course, to a state of being that is free from the pollution of a threatening, evil social environment. Like the *amahubo* on which they are in part based, the nightsongs are the music of the "socially and spiritually clean person" (Xulu 1992, 350).

Dance

At the beginning of my account of the transformations of the body under colonial dominance and industrialization, I argued that the formation of a centered individual involves the recourse to the body as a signifier and practical agent of a spiritually animated social and natural world. I would now like to pursue this thought by examining the dancing bodies of isicathamiya performers as a principal means of this self-constitution and of the symbolic redefinition of notions of human relations in space and time.

We have seen in chapter 3 that isicathamiya dancing grew out of a complex and heterogeneous body of indigenous and Western dances which I do not wish to review again here. Rather, I shall concentrate on a central set of ritual practices that has particular relevance for the symbolic reconstruction of a centered social universe: weddings. Together with these practices, I shall examine a number of tropes that are connected with interdependent foci of social life: the homestead and warfare. In doing so, it is not possible to describe the extraordinary density and complexity of movement characteristic of isicathamiya dancing. Dance and speech are two modes of discursive praxis that, while not being completely independent of each other, cannot directly be translated into each other. Dance analysis, like the analysis of the sonic aspects of performance, is concerned not with structure per se, nor in fact only with the meaningful connections performers and their audiences make between different texts and genres. As I have stated in chapter 3, ethnomusicological analysis should ideally aim at an interpretation of the activity that is required to produce meaningful patterns of sound and physical motion. Thus, what follows in the next couple of paragraphs should be read as an examination of the social and performance activities (and of the reasons of people engaging in them), that have to take place in order to invest isicathamiya dancing with specific, albeit contested and ambiguous meanings.

It is hardly surprising, of course, that wedding ceremonials should assume such a central place in the metaphoric structure of isicathamiya performance. As I pointed out in the previous chapter and at the beginning of this one, homing, the return to the home, *ekhaya,* centered fundamentally on the house as the nucleus of an ordered web of sociomoral relations uniting production and consumption, the private and the public. Thus, in precolonial society, marriage was a multilayered, partly ambiguous alliance between domestic groups rather than a contract between freely acting individuals. Any wedding, with its delicate preparations and complex rituals of exchange, illustrates this vividly. But it is the dance, generally considered by Zulus as the highest form of worship and spiritual communication with the ancestors, that constitutes the most sacred ritual activity in a wedding. A wedding is considered incomplete, indeed spiritually empty and profane, unless the bride has danced. Hence, the most common question asked in determining the stage of the ceremonial proceedings is, *Umakoti usesinile?* Has the bride danced? As Bongani Mthethwa has written, it underlines the fact that "no man, witchdoctor, diviner, chief or priest can solemnize a wedding. It is the dance *ukusina* that sacralizes the marriage" (Mthethwa 1986, 4).

Probably the most telling symbols isicathamiya dancers appropriated from the realm of weddings (as Joseph Shabalala indeed suggested in his enumeration of isicathamiya styles in the introduction and as I repeated in chapter 3) are select key elements of dances such as *ikhetho, ukureka,* and *isigekle.* To begin with *ikhetho,* as its name suggests, is the dance associated with the *ikhetho,* the bridegroom's party at a wedding. It is danced in a single line, in a mock confrontation with the *umthimba,* the bride's party, equally positioned in a straight line. As for the *isigekle,* it is generally considered to be one of the most profound expressions of lineage identity. It is a slow dance performed in a straight line in which the main thrust of movements consists in the pointing of a spear toward the ground and in the stately raising of the feet and subsequent fast stamping down in relatively slow-paced intervals. As a core dance genre of heightened spiritual and ritual significance, *isigekle* is also at the root of the sacred choreography of Isaiah Shembe's Nazareth Baptist Church.

In addition to these dance forms from the past, *ukureka* (ragtime) constitutes an essential, if relatively more recent component of isicathamiya choreography indexing the sociomoral web of the house. *Ukureka* is danced in a single or double file, the dancers executing simple walking steps in time to the song. Although there are numerous variations to this pattern, such as stopping the forward-walking thrust at a certain recurring moment in the vocal cycle, the file is the principal formation. Among the reasons performers give for the prevalence of this formation in these dances is the spatial order imposed by the traditional homestead. Thus, when the bride's party, the *umthimba,* bring the bride to the bridegroom's homestead, they cannot pass the narrow gate all at once. They have to form an *uklele,* a straight line, that allows them to enter one by one while singing *ukureka* and *ameleki* songs in the case of Christians and *isigekle* songs in the case of traditionalists. It is thus that, through their association with "chords" and wedding songs generally, *ukureka, ikhetho,* and *isigekle* play a key role in the real and symbolic travels between and into the houses that are in the process of affiliating through the marriage: they are lineage reciprocity embodied.

It is obvious that of the features that *ikhetho, isigekle,* and *ukureka* have in common and of the ones that are adapted to isicathamiya performance, the formation of the dancers in straight lines carries the greatest symbolic

weight. Because of the march-like character of all these dances and probably as a result of the fact that the linear arrangement was acceptable to the
Christian missionaries as dignified and orderly, *ikhetho* and *ukureka* are frequently called *imashi,* "march."

But the march-like formation of these dances also connotes another
crucial aspect of precolonial social practice: warfare. The most telling symbolic cross-reference performers make in this respect is to the formation of
regiments in single lines (*ukuklela kwamabutho*) or to the breaking-up of
a unit into strands led by a "war-leader" (*ukudabuka amafolosi*). This image of a marching regiment going to war, as Jama Lucky Stars leader Wel-
lington Dlamini told Caesar Ndlovu, is in the minds of performers pro-
ceeding to the stage. "When we go to the stage," Dlamini said, "we go
there *ngomdlandla wamabutho,* with the enthusiasm of the regiments."

One final prominent feature of isicathamiya choreography remains to
be mentioned: the use of circular floor patterns. Before a choir moves onto
the stage, the members form a ring, and with the leader in their midst, start
the opening song in hushed voices. This circular pattern is also common
during rehearsals and is associated by most performers with *isibaya,* the
cattle enclosure in a traditional homestead. The cattle enclosure is the most
sacred, the most symbolically charged place in a homestead. It is a practiced
place, a place of power and, hence, a male domain. It is here that men
convene before they go to war to invoke the ancestor spirits and to gather
spiritual strength. By positioning themselves in the shape of an *igoda,* a
coiled rope, until the song is *vuthiwe,* cooked, and then meandering (*gu-
duza*) toward the stage, isicathamiya performers behave like men gathering
in the cattle enclosure.

A circular floor pattern is also common onstage when the performers
describe a circle by agitatedly moving around with slightly shuffling feet.
Called *isifekezeli,* this type of choreography is associated with homeward
motion and closely resembles the kind of bodily behavior prevalent in Zionist ritual. In the most general sense, this type of kinetic "architectonics"
reshapes the rectangular architectural frameworks of the alien order by
evoking the "feeling tones" of the precolonial concentrated circularity
(Fernandez 1984, 38).

Not all choirs appropriate all these dances and floor patterns in like
manner, nor do all performances incorporate all these choreographies into
one pattern. Ladysmith Black Mambazo, as we have seen in chapter 3 for
instance, have chosen to highlight *gqashiya*-type movements in their performances and hardly use any *ukureka*. Other choirs, by contrast, construct

their choreography mainly from *ukureka* and a number of tapping techniques. The main point here is the fact that isicathamiya dancers, in freely selecting from a number of bodily patterned and therefore gendered roles, construct, as men, spheres of corporeal interaction that metaphorically speak to the contrary location of the house in the white city and its alienating set of social relations. By singing and dancing in the style of women, the dancers are not simply crossing gender lines. Rather, like solo singers who sometimes try to render the idea of a song by singing the call and response at the same time, isicathamiya dancers complete the context required for ordered, meaningful social interaction.

But the choreography of isicathamiya is no less polymorphous than the images evoked in the lyrics of the nightsongs or the patterns of social organization underlying isicathamiya choirs. In industrial capitalism, as I have said, the body ceases to be the integrated and centered agent of the construction of worldview. It becomes the site for a never-ending conflict between production and consumption, need and fulfillment. Increasingly, the body experiences the feeling of being "homed" only in consuming industrially manufactured goods and images of itself. As the unity of the producing and consuming household dissolves, the TV commercial for that cereal and that special garment is framed in scenes of domestic happiness.

In its most basic form, the corporeal regime of the city and the world of commodity relations is concentrated in the step, *istep,* the earliest form of isicathamiya choreography. Similar to *ukureka,* it consists of a simple walking, almost lilting gait, executed in such a manner that two steps forward are followed by two steps backward and so on. This is done with a lot of vigor but without the rigidity of a fast-pacing person. A variation of this basic step is a rapidly sliding, forward movement of one foot which is then kept suspended in the air, slightly crossed in front of the other leg. From here, many choirs launch into the intricate tapping which, historically, is derived from African American tap dancing. Subtle turns of the feet, slanting positions of the shoes, and tiptoeing are the hallmark of these elaborations of *istep.* As in most African dance, these kinetically crucial body parts are highlighted by gleaming shoes and flashy socks which the dancers display by carefully lifting their trousers a few inches, pulling them up at the top. To further intensify the impression of effortlessly *catham-*ing bodies the dancers execute waist-high kicks—trousers still slightly pulled up—while they slide the other foot to the side. The raised leg is then gently brought down on the floor.

The meaning of all these micropatterns can only be understood when seen in relation to the reconfiguration of space and movement engineered by the industrial city. In his brilliant reflection, "Walking in the City," Michel de Certeau (1984, 91–110) has argued, perhaps somewhat optimistically, that the city not only produces its own "urbanizing" language of power. The city, he wrote, is "left prey to contradictory movements that counterbalance and combine themselves outside the reach of panoptic power" (95). Walking, de Certeau argues, contains within itself the possibility of a "proliferating illegitimacy" (96), of a rhetoric that, like the drifting manipulations of figurative speech, diverts and subverts the proper and normative meanings constructed by the grammarians.

In the south African city, that most disciplinary and disciplined space of spaces, the normativity and rigidity of the spatial order imposes severe restrictions on its black inhabitants' everyday choices—not to mention the brutal "mass removals" of the 1960s and 1970s—of organized space. A black person encountering a white pedestrian on a sidewalk has to step aside and use the street. Curfew regulations that were in effect in many South African cities prevented black people from walking certain sections of the city at night. To socialize with their fellow domestic workers next door, the maids of the white suburbs can only use the sidewalks. Clearly, a black person has virtually none of the means at his disposal to actualize and create spaces. He or she lives in no space at all, and does not, in practice, constitute a "near" and a "far," a "here" and a "there." Thus, the black "user" of the white city is derobed of what de Certeau calls the phatic function of walking, of the ability to ensure communication by creating sequences of phatic *topoi* (99).

Inevitably, this lack of choice, this absence of a place—the primordial black experience of the white man's city—sheds an ambiguous light on a type of dancing such as the step. Although dancing might be fruitfully conceptualized as a bodily rhetoric, whose turns and figures operate on culturally codified systems of bodily communication, it does not always manipulate hegemonic spatial organizations in the same way that the turns of phrase of a speaker create metamorphoses of grammar and order. *Istep,* I argue, in its basic form celebrates the body finding its proper place in the normative space of the engineers of the apartheid city. The walking of *istep,* as the most condensed rhetorical figure in isicathamiya dancing, does not constitute a displaced, wandering semantic. The to and fro of the step does not, like the evocations of the rural home in *ukureka* and *ikhetho,* counterpose its own spatial enunciation against the rigid grid of the segregated city. *Istep* is the omnipresent sign itself of the city. It has no direction and it does not articulate places in relation to an "I." It is walking in the neuter and thus ratifies the absence of a place and the continuous search for a proper locus that propels the mobile individual in capitalism. As de Certeau aptly writes,

> The moving about that the city multiplies and concentrates makes the city itself an immense social experience of lacking a place—an experience that is, to be sure, broken up into countless tiny deportations (displacements and walks), compensated for by the relationships and intersections of these exoduses that intertwine and create an urban fabric, and placed under the sign of what ought to be, ultimately, the place but is only a name, the City. The identity furnished by this place is all the more symbolic (named) because, in spite of the inequality of its citizens' positions and profits, there is only . . . a shuffling among pretenses of the proper, a universe of rented spaces haunted by a nowhere or by dreamed-of places. (103)

Something of the haunting vacuum of the city is also mirrored in at least two choir names. Thus a name like Easy Walkers, although ultimately stemming from African American culture, in the South African context could be read as a metaphor for the ease with which these performers imagine themselves moving about the urban space and that compensates for the lack of place (fig. 9). Another example, if a slightly more ambiguous one, is Green Mambas. This is what black people in Johannesburg call the segregated busses that transport them to and from the workplace. Feared and poisonous as mambas, these busses, like trains, are both the symbols of urban mobility and the icons of alienation.

But the walking step, as I have indicated, also often leads into spirited tapping, as though the dancers were executing a movement from the naked sign into style, from the abstract symbolic into figure. This transition, marked by intensified emotional immersion and almost whispered repetitions of the key bass line, is a digression from the ordered up-and-down of the walking step. As such, the tap in isicathamiya performance recalls a statement by African American tap veteran Chuck Green. "Maps," Green said, "are full of limitations. But when I tap, I can get lost in dancing. I don't have no maps on my taps" (Hanna 1983, 52). The "unmapped" situation of tapping, the feeling of being lost in dance, is contrasted here with the limitations imposed on space by the sign which obliterates the traces of those who produced the knowledge on which the map rests. Tapping would thus appear to be challenging the rule of the sign and of the space that engenders it. The identity that is constructed from this rhetorical

Figure 9. Easy Walkers, c. 1970. Courtesy Veit Erlmann.

freedom finds its expression in the phrase "writing the name by steps" which isicathamiya dancers use to refer to their choir's particular form of choreography.

Adding another layer of meaning to the tapping and the stealthiness of *cothoza mfana*, we must recall Joseph Shabalala's assertion (see introduction) that the "gentle alternative" was born from the performers increasingly controlling their emotions, from the domestication of a supposedly "traditional" spontaneity and lack of formality. While Shabalala's narrative may, in fact, reproduce the familiar tale dear to numerous performers of isicathamiya history as one of progress and improvement, to other isicathamiya practitioners the stalking, held-in character of *istep,* instead of keeping it under control, highlights the expressivity of the music. "*Sinyonyobela ingoma ukuze ingabaleki.* We move stealthily so that the song does not run away," performers say. "It is like proposing love to the ladies. You have to approach them cautiously, lest the women will run away." Controlling, feigning, and holding in, these performers seem to imply, keep the dance movements and the sound balanced and in touch with each other. To achieve this balance, a man must be balanced himself, and as in social interaction in general, patience and delay are the mark of a skilled performer. Like a performer who does not allow his song to run away, a mature person will strive to keep a cool distance from his own actions, thereby never allowing them to take on a dynamic of their own.

To conclude our investigation of isicathamiya choreography we finally have to consider the rich gestural language that is combined, juxtaposed, or contrasted with the more bounded, stylistically codified dance genres discussed above. Most of this complex inventory is activated during the *kompithi* section when full-blown dancing as such is prohibited. The formal, concertlike atmosphere of this part of the performance and the almost immobile stance adopted by everybody around—the semicircle of singers fixed in standstill pose, the strict temporal limitations imposed by the adjudicator ("Five minutes"), the dozing spectators—is, of course, indicative of the stage entertainment practiced in the mission stations. More specifically, the dramatic impact of hands imitating flowing water or of nodding heads signaling approval derives from a performance genre known as "action song." First created in the missions to replace "heathen" dancing and to accommodate the irrepressible drive among African performers to transform sound into movement and movement into sound, action songs could be understood as spatial stories. This is to suggest that, rather than organizing spaces into a linear progression, the gestural elements built into many songs in *kompithi* align narrative structures with spatial syntaxes.

A useful example of such spatial narration is the song "Vela Mfowethu" by the Easy Walkers discussed earlier in chapter 5. In the following synopsis from the middle section of the song, I try to give an idea of the way in which song text and gestures are synchronized. At the beginning of the section, the lead singer and another singer move out from the rest of the choir—aligned in a semicircle with hands clasped—and position themselves in front of the choir at the left and right end of the line. In the entire section, they perform all movements in synchrony, framing the relatively immobile choir with action.

Text	Gestures
Selokhu ahamba	Walking a few steps forward
Since he departed	
ethi uyosebenza.	Digging
saying he was searching for work.	
Manye	Throw both hands forward as if in despair
Now	
sekuphelile	Right hand stretched out to right side
unyaka welishumi.	Both arms stretched out in front of body
ten years.	

Singazi ukuthi washonaphi.
    And we do not know his
    whereabouts.
Sifuna ukuya nawe
    We want to go home with you   Pulling arms toward chest
mfowethu   Both arms stretched out to the sides
    brother,
siyobon'   Waving hands as if calling someone
    to see
abantwana.   Moving hands from left to right nearer to
    the children.   the ground

At this point the second soloist steps back into the chorus and the woman with the sash takes his place. She also executes her gestures in time with the leader Alison Gumbi.

Vela vela vela mfowethu.   Swaying body from left to right
    Appear, appear, appear, brother.
Woza   Bending knees (together with the choir)
    Come
musa ukucasha ngabanye.   Both arms pointing to the right (with
    do not hide behind other people.   choir)
Woza   Both arms stretch out wide to the sides as
    Come   in welcoming gesture
sifun' ukuya nawe   Moving hands quickly from left to right, as
    we want to go with you,   if arguing,
o mfowethu   at the same time switching between palms
    oh, brother,   pointing upward and downward
siyobon' abantwana.
    to see the children.

The effect that is achieved through this syntactic alignment of verbal and bodily narration, on one level, is a tremendous multiplication of semantic layers. At the same time, the gesticulating blurs the signifying and expressive levels of performance. While a number of the gestures described above are highly emblematic and thus clearly belong to the ideographic and physiographic categories, most appear to relate more to the mode of the action they enact, to the structure of the narration, the emotional state of the author, or all of these at the same time. Thus they initiate primarily not a relationship between a sign and a not-sign, a semiotics proper, but a practical relationship in which the message and the production of the message coincide. It appears therefore that a bodily practice, such as the gestures of the action-song type, shows not to signify, as Julia Kristeva writes, "but to *englobe* in one and the same space (without the dichotomies of idea-word, signified-signifier), let us say in one and the same semiotic text, 'subject' and 'object' and practice" (Kristeva 1978, 269). The gesticulating

body, standing in this way before (though not anterior to) the act of sig-
nification, within the context of isicathamiya performance becomes one
that defies, as it reflects, the binary logic of body and mind.

Dress

The symbolic inscription of the body through clothing is another
major facet of isicathamiya performance. But like the dancing body, the
dressed body, both in- and outside the dance, is as yet poorly understood.
Thus the conventional wisdom, articulated by a prominent dance scholar,
that clothing is an "extension-shaper of the dancer-self" in which the cos-
tume becomes part of his person (Keali'inohomoku 1979, 80), seems to
be based on a rather static view of clothing as though the relationship between body and clothes and the meanings inherent in it are a given, situated outside the social forces that determine it. Against this, an enormously
prolific branch of social inquiry has come to regard fashion as a process of
consumption. But rather than being the mere realm of fetishism with its
undertones of a "self-indulgence, greed, vanity, and irrationality" (Mc-
Cracken 1988, xiii), consumption is seen as a sphere of social practice in
which identity is achieved through the individual accumulation of otherness. More than the simple satisfaction of a need, the consumption of the
coded commodities of capitalism amounts to a desire to be like another.
The "social skin" signals the "internalized others," the social meanings
and values of the collectivity (T. Turner 1980), and the restless drive to
advance in society through the endless consumption of goods and images.

In South Africa, the colonial encounter proved to be a particularly rich
field in which new commodities and new regimes of local consumption
would "conjure new desires, exertions, even forms of society" (Comaroff
1993, 1). Thus, in two richly textured ethnographic studies of women's
dress and the political uses of traditional regalia within Inkatha, Sandra
Klopper has shown how these transformations and the meanings ascribed
to them have become part and parcel of ongoing redefinitions of power
relations (Klopper 1989, 27). Beadwork, a crucial component of traditional female apparel, for instance, underwent significant transformations.
Whereas formerly different beadwork styles served to identify specific geographical areas, Inkatha appropriated these as a communication of some
generic "Zuluness" (12). Similarly, since the late nineteenth century, both
state officials and male traditionalists came to regard dress as an increasingly
important symbol in their efforts to retain control over women: the former
in the desire to preserve the role of female rural subsistence production in

subsidizing the reproduction costs of migrant workers in town (Marks 1989b), the latter with the aim of maintaining a rural base in times of urban economic crisis. The ensuing folklorization of female dress, then, was not so much the sign of an alleged inbred female conservatism as of the very modern processes of marginalization and feminization of the countryside (Comaroff 1993).

Examining the transformation of the clad body from the lower end of the power spectrum, Jean Comaroff has studied the dress code of Tshidi Zionists. The garb prescribed by mainstream Methodist churches, she argues, was based on the code of the West, "setting off sacred from mundane, men from women, production from consumption, and productive from nonproductive activity" (Comaroff 1985, 220). By contrast, Zionism developed a code that reformulates these established categories. Long, flowing robes and gleaming white skirts protest against the pragmatic implications of proletarianization, the one-dimensional functionality of somber and threadbare clothes, by crowding Zionists' outward appearance with signs rebuilding a rich and meaningful synthesis of bodies personal and social (221).

This search for a synthesis of the semiotic and the pragmatic, the body and the mind, as I have persistently argued in my discussion of isicathamiya's many expressive layers, also informs performers' sartorial practice. The fashionable body fashions itself, in hologram-like manner, after the juxtaposed and incompatible realms of social experience—the subordinated rural world and the unattainable spheres of white exclusive power—produced by the neocolonial system. This reworking of the precolonial unity between the acting and the signifying body and, hence, the working on the neocolonial rift between the two bodies can be observed at a diachronic level, in the historical development of isicathamiya dress and in the sequential ordering of present-day performances. But it can also be seen at the synchronic level, in the combination of different sartorial styles in one performance and even within one choir. The boundaries between these two regimes of self-fashioning are fluid and in themselves constitute a form of enacted social relations.

In the early days of isicathamiya, as I have noted in chapter 3, suits and sports combinations—both attributes of the nonproductive and affluent classes—were the only form of attire. Although it is not possible to determine the exact historical moment when this relatively strict code began to break up, it appears that concurrently with the rise of the low-key sounds of *isithululu* in the 1970s, variation in dress styles became an important consideration for most isicathamiya choirs. These changes, as we saw, expressed not only certain overall shifts over several decades in the fashion system with its ever-accelerating cycles of popularity. More fundamentally, these variations in themselves signaled a greater incorporation of migrant workers into the Fordist regime and the increasing ramification of their life worlds and patterns of consumption within the overarching economic system. Within the same logic perhaps, dress competitions, called "swanking competitions" were increasingly becoming popular as parts of isicathamiya competitions from at least the late 1960s. Organized along similar lines to the musical competitions proper, swanking events provide the *oswenka*, as the swankers are called, with a forum in which to act out the inherently competitive nature of capitalist consumption and the fashion system.

Before we take a closer look at the meanings of these post-1970 dress styles, it is important to examine the switch from one code to another as a performative strategy which in itself indicates (and effectuates) certain movements in social space. The transformations that occur between the two main phases of an isicathamiya night, *prakthisa* and *kompithi*, are the most significant arenas in which to observe these code switches. More than by the subtle shifts of musical repertoires, the two phases are distinguished from each other by two sartorial modes of presenting the body. As the night progresses and choirs gear themselves for the final contest, a strangely inverted movement into style takes place, a transition symbolizing in situ the passage from the contradictory world of industrial rationality to the pure realm of aesthetic beauty. Street clothes, coats, and other wear connected with the workplace give way to stylish outfits. In a similar manner, uniforms replace the unsystematic assortment of individual garments worn during *prakthisa*, and cleanliness and tidiness supersede drabness and grime. At times, these transformations even occur while the choirs are on stage: during *ukureka* many singers carry their jackets, neatly folded, and only put on their full uniform, momentarily turning their backs to the audience, after they have properly positioned themselves on the stage. It is obvious that these journeys across the fashion landscape and between different states of being affected, even contaminated, by the environment, represent a move toward social advancement and construct a narrative about the wearer's own social history, real and imagined.

Paradoxically, this move, from the apparel of the factory to that of a world of choice and opportunity, proceeds in the opposite direction from the bodily movements which prevail in *prakthisa* and *kompithi*. During *prakthisa*, it will be recalled, allowance was made for an enormously wide

range of bodily activities. But this freedom of corporeal expression contrasts sharply with the competition section in which the body seems almost
absent and becomes a mere tool of vocal production, a voice with a body
attached to it. In other words, while the body's role as an appendix to the
machine is compensated in a rich choreography which defiantly negates its
submission on the factory floor, in the streets and homes of the white city,
its encasement of textile still ties the body to the spatial regime of the dominant order. Conversely, in *kompithi* the subdued movements recall the
logic of the "proper" proclaimed by the mission, the school, and the other
institutions of power. The flamboyant ties, sports jackets, and polished
shoes in turn speak of the desire to escape, if only in the fantasy realm of
commodity consumption, from the world of regimented labor to which
the bodies they cover remain chained all the same.

Having discussed the dialectics of agency and bodily consumption, of
signifying and signified body, we must now turn to the different items of
clothing and their combination. As I have suggested, until the 1970s the
principal accoutrements donned were the suit and the sports jacket—both
of them icons of respectability and achievement at a time when "dressed
natives" were still considered somewhat ambiguously as evidence of "civilization" and a threat to that very order, and when, in the South African
countryside, Western formal dress not seldom earned the wearer the scorn-
ful, racist label "black Englishman." In this sense, isicathamiya uniforms, at
least until the 1950s, signaled protest. Today, some choirs such as the King
Star Brothers continue to stick to formal, executive-style dress, but most
choirs have developed highly idiosyncratic uniforms that suggest different,
potentially counterhegemonic and probably more polysemic schemes of
self-fashioning.

It appears that in the most prevalent of these current styles, a more conscious effort is being made at setting isicathamiya performers apart from
the constrained codes of the dominant culture by foregrounding designs
and fabrics emblematic of African indigenous cultures. The most important of these items are shirts, long robes, and ties embroidered in a certain
manner. Short-sleeved shirts such as those printed with *dashiki*-style patterns (fig. 10), although they are not indigenous to South Africa alone,
have come to signify a generic Africanness of sorts all over the world, and
in the context of isicathamiya identify the wearers as Africans rather than
Zulus. Somewhat more typical locally, South African connotations are
likely to be intended in one of Ladysmith Black Mambazo's outfits, featured during the *Graceland* tour. Here the group was wearing bright or-

Figure 10. Kwa Nquza Home Defenders. Courtesy Veit Erlmann.

ange shirts with colorful triangular patterns reminiscent of so-called Ndebele wall paintings. Although these paintings were essentially invented by
the tourist industry, they have come to signify the resilience of African tradition in South Africa (Schneider 1989). In a similar vein, Joseph Shabalala's group has been performing in the leopard-skin loincloths of *ingoma*
dance troupes which, too, were introduced by the Durban tourist association in the 1930s (Thomas 1988, 198 ff.). By contrast, long robes and
coats such as those worn by the Ladysmith Naughty Boys (fig. 11) and
Black Angels have a rather fuzzier semantic content. In shape and design,
some evoke the cloaks worn by Zionists, even though the standard white
considered to be a sacred color by Zionists is, of course, taboo in the secular context of all-night music competitions. Certain types of self-made ties,
finally, are noteworthy as indexes of Zuluness. They often display the name
of the choir and thus recall the bead letters with their bright colorful patterns and words written into them, and, at the same time, suggest the
power and social value of literacy.

Yet, isicathamiya uniforms also appropriate select symbols of dominance
and Western class structure. Sashes, for instance, that display the name of
the choir, index military power and have been part of numerous forms of
African organizations from brass bands to women's *manyano* prayer groups
from the start. Other accessories that incorporate elements of the iconog-

Figure 11. Ladysmith Naughty Boys. Courtesy Veit Erlmann.

raphy of capitalist society include briefcases carried by the conductors and name tags such as are used in some companies. On one occasion, I also saw a choir sporting in the pocket of their jackets pens with battery-lit tops. And to complete the list of insignia of the dominant system appropriated by isicathamiya practitioners, we finally have to mention white gloves, perhaps the most telling and most frequently employed sign of social advancement and refinement. Often dramatically highlighting carefully choreographed movements of the hands, these gloves express the freedom from the menial forms of manual labor to which the majority of migrants are condemned and underscore the playful character of isicathamiya performance.

Above all, the extravagant patchwork of these accessories, colors, and forms is in itself a way of signifying the intermediate social space occupied by migrants. It patently recalls an earlier, familiar figure of the black stage in South Africa and even the minstrel theater in the United States: the coon. But the dandylike, eccentric appearance of many choirs, modeled as it is on these older clothing patterns of the black urbanite of North America, is more than a mere masquerade cynically camouflaging a profound despair. The image of the urban swell, it will be recalled, introduced to black South Africans through the minstrel show and the street parades of the "Cape Coloreds," and its musical equivalent—the vaudeville tunes of the 1920s—together formed an indivisible whole which early isicathamiya performers called *isikhunzi*. Therefore the outlandish, "overdressed" costumes speak of the refusal of marginalized individuals to fashion themselves according to the balanced, measured designs dictated by the center. By overdoing, consciously or subconsciously, the ordered and one-dimensional assemblage of Western formal dress, by subverting "good taste," isicathamiya dress negates the law of the proper. At the same time, this aesthetic of splendor and wasteful generosity reaffirms fundamental indigenous principles of artistic production, for the creation of dense textures and multilayered, crowded surfaces in a great many African traditions of visual arts and performance engender a surplus, an excess of meanings which invite multiple, intersecting readings and, hence, ensure the permanent reconstruction of a multistranded yet unified web of social relations.

The dilemma, which has become apparent in my account of dance and dress in isicathamiya performance, of symbolically transcending a given order of things, not only marks, ontologically speaking, all performance qua mode of symbolic action, therefore frequently giving rise to Western views of performance as the sole, seemingly apolitical form of voicing dissent available under constrained circumstances. Rather, this paradox—Professor Krug's dilemma—emerges in and is symptomatic of a specific historical moment in which the capitalist instrumentalist logic and the attendant mass production of images of reality increasingly undercut the agency of the body and the formation of a personal identity by other means than the consumption of these same images of the body. Thus, the contradictory relationship in isicathamiya between the acting body represented by the dancer of *ukureka* and *istep* and the consuming body symbolized by the dedicated follower of fashion betrays the real obstacles to undoing the dichotomies of the modern world between production and consumption, to reconnecting the individual with the holistic web of economic, religious, and social ties of the precolonial world.

7　Praise and Prayer:

The Rhetoric of Isicathamiya

The argument which I presented in the previous chapters—that the construction of spaces for the imagination of alternative social practice is a multidimensional process cutting across numerous layers of meaning—called for a methodology that locates meaning not only in verbal texts such as song lyrics and their relationship to a "world outside the song" (Caraveli 1982, 130), and that transcends the divisions between different academic disciplines devoted to speech, song, and poetry (Seeger 1987, 50). Such a methodology, as I hope to have demonstrated, extracts meaning not from a set of abstract linkages between different sorts of texts, but rather views meaning as being produced by the conjuncture of verbal, kinesic, and musical elements in performance.

Africanists seem to have been in the vanguard in recognizing the interdependence of different forms of discursive praxis such as music and ordinary speech.[1] In southern African studies, for instance, this has produced some of the most advanced insights into the inter-discursiveness of performance genres.[2] Thus, as David Rycroft has asserted (1985), a number of vocal styles ranging from ordinary speech to some form of *Sprechstimme*, in Zulu thought are classified within the same category as other genres that are more readily recognized as song in Western terms. *Ukuhlabelela* (singing), for instance, is used to refer to fully melodic song and, at the same time, denotes certain nonmelodic vocal genres such as those accompanying certain *isigekle* dances. By contrast, the performance of *izibongo* praises, although they display certain melodic features, is never referred to by the verb *ukuhlabelela*, but by *ukubonga*.

Despite the impracticability, then, of analytically separating different modes of communication that, in African thinking, form an indivisible entity, some more concentrated attention to the verbal component of isicathamiya performance is in order. At first sight, though, the lyrics of isicathamiya songs, lacking the eloquence and metaphoric richness of Nguni mainstream verbal arts, do not appear as a likely object of sophisticated poetic analysis. At least, so popular prejudice has had it since 1948, when Hugh Tracey declared that *mbube* songs "are composed upon the slightest of lyrics" (Tracey 1948, x). But Karin Barber, discussing the popular arts in Africa, is, of course, right that traditional poetry is no absolute aesthetic norm from which criteria of evaluation for emergent literary forms can be derived. And thus, shifting the focus from a neoevolutionist perspective to an analysis of poetic style as an effective means of "authoring selves" (Geertz 1986), I argue that forms of popular poetry such as isicathamiya lyrics are not merely the immature, hybrid product of culture contact with the West, "the initial stages of a new phase" (Lestrade 1937, 291). Isicathamiya song texts have to be considered as a form of discursive praxis whose style reveals more than an analysis of topical content about the processes whereby socially located performers construct poetic structures in which different experiential domains are mediated and brought into meaningful relation with one another.

But these poetic structures can only be understood as emergent, processual, and performed. The repetitive, cyclical character of those "slightest of lyrics," the juxtaposition of unconnected, often seemingly obdurate, phrases and images in many isicathamiya songs is a case in point. Thus, when I sought to enlist the performers' assistance in clarifying one or another obscure word or line, some singers reacted defensively, suggesting that they did not fully understand the meaning themselves, and that they were not accomplished poets. It only occured to me much later that no other answer was possible to my inquiries. For what my questioning failed to elicit was not the semantic content of an obscure verbal utterance, but the meaning of poetic obscurity itself, of incessantly repeated cryptic phrases.

Migrant performers, as J. Clegg has made clear, are not interested in communicating fixed meanings. Rather, their minds are set on communicating an "ability to *give* meaning." This endeavor, Clegg suggests, is owing to a deeply social and, at the same time, formalist approach to performances and social practice. The typical migrant performer juxtaposes "multiple meanings, or tensions, in images and in references. It's these tensions which are being communicated, not the actual words or images. . . . His playing is not repetitive, because every time it comes around, it's new. . . . Every time it comes around, it's building up significance for him" (Coplan 1993, 323).

Clegg's insights are important, because they provide a powerful critique of one of the most enduring stereotypes about African verbal arts as formulaic. In particular, Clegg emphasizes the fact that since for migrant performers meaning does not reside in a word, a phrase, or a whole sequence, a repetition or seemingly formulaic use of such units is not seen as dimin-

ishing its symbolic impact. Since the significance of a performance does not
lie in the narrative linearity of discrete and unique elements, the meaning
of a performance is not fundamentally affected if parts of it are rearranged
or removed (Barber 1991, 23).

One of the principal means by which these processes of building up
significance can be elucidated is through examining the interdependence
of genres of verbal discourse in performance. Bearing in mind the fact that
performance, by its very nature, "is intertextual by virtue of the embodied
practices of the performers" (Drewal 1992, 3) who "rebehave" patterns
of social interactions, I shall examine three of the most important interdependent genres presently incorporated in isicathamiya: praise-poetry,
proverbs, and the Christian hymn. All three genres, as we shall see, are
centrally concerned with power in that they organize, in different ways,
migrant performers' quest for protected zones in which a meaningful social
life can be lived.

"They Are Praising Us"

In his book *The Poetics of Manhood* (1985), Michael Herzfeld has
shown how being a Cretan man involves the performative display of excellence, the ability to "foreground manhood by means of deeds that strik-
ingly 'speak for themselves'" (Herzfeld 1985, 16). "Being a good man"
in Crete means the same as "being *good at* being a man." The performance
of positive selfhood, then, requires the ability to direct the attention of an
audience on the performance itself. Instead of noticing *what* men do, Cre-
tans focus their attention on *how* they do it. This "stylistic transfiguration
of action," as Herzfeld calls it (16), also entails the skillful framing of the
self in a context of heightened significance. The self, Herzfeld writes, "is
not presented within everyday life so much as in front of it" (11). Style
becomes an indicator of identity and of meaningful being in the social
world.

Herzfeld's description of a Cretan mountain village provides striking
parallels with the way in which men and women throughout southern Africa engage in a "poetics of social interaction" that is constructed from
rhetorical eloquence and the performative management of heroic self-
images. In other words, the definition of selfhood in Crete as much as in
southern African societies is at root a question of metaphoric predication
in everyday verbal communication and forms of poetic language. The transcending of the bounds of the everyday, the creation of an image that alters
given, culturally codified meanings, links enacted social practice with one

of the core expressive genres of Southern African performance: praise-poetry (Alverson 1978, 195).

As Ruth Finnegan rightfully suspected in her classic overview of oral literature in Africa, praise-poems or, *izibongo,* as they are commonly called in isiZulu, are the master genre of southern African verbal arts (Finnegan 1970, 121–46). An enormously elastic body of performance practice displaying a striking wealth of styles and thematic subjects, *izibongo* have emerged and been remolded in contexts as diverse as African Christianity (Gunner 1988) and black working-class organizations (Gunner 1986). Complementing these studies, I shall examine in this chapter the appropriation in isicathamiya of some of the stylistic conventions of praise-poetry. Although it is true that form and content dialectically constitute each other and can never be separated, for the purposes of analysis I will focus here on poetic style as the chief instrument of isicathamiya practitioners' rhetorical strategy and formation of self-identity. A discussion of the imagery of praise-poetry will be offered in the following chapter.

The patrilineal homestead as the ultimate emotional, spiritual, and social center of gravity of South Africa's black peasant-proletarians—regardless of how fractured a reality it may have become for the majority of the poor and powerless—is intimately linked with a man's dignity and name. To build oneself, one's standing, and reputation in a community is to acquire a name that reflects as it creates experience, transcending the givenness of the here and now (Alverson 1978, 195). A name, or better still, a praise-name (*isibongo*) constitutes "moral and affective meaning structures for thinking about the self" (193). Often eloquent and compelling compositions fashioned from the skillful "play of tropes" (Fernandez 1986), praise-names objectify the subjective experiences of an individual and transform them into objects of shared knowledge. The self, even though made to stand apart, is thus inserted into the web of words that make up its social world.

Isicathamiya song texts clearly indicate that, in addition to lamenting the lost homestead, performers spend a great deal of time praising themselves in an effort to accumulate prestige and build up their names. In migrant guitar players' thinking, for instance, as J. Clegg has pointed out, the mark of skillfulness in performance (*ubugagu*) is the ability to introduce a song with an introduction (*izihlabo*) displaying virtuoso runs, to create original musical and textual material, and to engage in elaborate and fast praising (*ukubonga*). The way in which the latter flawlessly combines with the instrumental introduction in building up a tension between musical flow and speech rhythm, is particularly crucial in establishing a performer's reputation (Clegg 1981, 4–5). It is interesting to note that the origins of *ukubonga* in music may quite possibly rest in the very social context from which migrant performers seek to escape. Speaking about the poetry of *maskanda* musicians—guitar and concertina players—D. B. Ntuli has suggested that the introduction of the rapidly delivered self-praises was the result of the anonymity of the performance contexts migrant musicians encountered in town. "Since the musician was a complete stranger to some of the members of his audience, he felt obliged to introduce himself" (Ntuli 1990, 302).

Although isicathamiya performers, with very few notable exceptions such as Joseph Shabalala, do not intersperse their songs with these rapidly declaimed *izibongo,* certain elements of the nightsongs and some of the basic poetic techniques of *izibongo* and *maskanda* are interconnected, both stylistically and genetically. For while the recorded evidence of *maskanda* music and poetry prior to the 1950s is scanty, it appears that the introduction of *ukubonga* in guitar music coincides with the emergence of John 'Phuzushukela' Bhengu's two-finger picking style (*ukupika*) in the late 1950s. It is interesting to note that about the same time, or a few years later, isicathamiya groups such as Ladysmith Black Mambazo and King Star Brothers began adopting basic *izibongo* formulas from the *izihlobo* section of *maskanda* music.

Examples of such formulas are "khuluma Nkosi kimi" (talk to me, Lord) or "khuluma isinsizwa" (talk, gentlemen) in numerous King Star Brothers and Ladysmith Black Mambazo songs, and "awuzwe" (listen) or "awuzwe ma" (listen, mother) in songs by the Crocodiles and the K-Team.[3] In "Wena Ntombi" (You, Girl) by the Easy Walkers (SABC LT 16 258, A4), the "awuzwe" leads directly into a phrase such as "Yangen' imbhokodo yamagayise" (We are a stone that crushes everything). As Ntuli points out, in *maskanda* such introductory formulas are always directed at a second person, and only then does the performer switch to a subtle focus on himself in first-person mode (Ntuli 1990, 304). Surprisingly, this sequence, whose meaning we cannot explore further here, is practically reversed in isicathamiya. For reasons that I have been unable to determine, phrases such as those of the King Star Brothers and Ladysmith Black Mambazo have been appended at the end of each song!

In its most basic form, self-praise is expressed in statements in which some sign of excellence and social achievement ("famous," "popular,"

etc.) is predicated upon a personal pronoun, as in the following extract
from a song by the Empangeni Home Tigers (Mavuthela BL 22):

Leader: *Yith' abafana.*
              We are the boys.
Chorus: *Yith' abafana bogazi.*
              We are the famous boys.

In the following example, the identity of a choir—the Evening Birds in this
case—is established by contiguity, an inventory of the members of the
group, together with a sprinkling of other forms of metaphor ("That is
fire") (GE 800):

Zasho kumnyama eBantu Sport.
        They sang at night at Bantu Sport
Mfo ka Linda.
        Son of Linda.
Zath' ulalele mama ulalele uLinda.
        They said: listen, mama, listen to Linda.
Zasho ingane zika Linda.
        Linda's children were singing.
Zenithule bakithi ngizanitshela indaba zika Linda.
        Listen people, I am going to tell you about Linda.
uLinda nguye owama Evening Birds.
        Linda is the leader of the Evening Birds.
Washo umlilo.
        That is fire.
Yibo laba abafana bama Evening Birds.
        These are the boys of the Evening Birds:
Nguye lo umfo ka Mboma,
        This is Mboma,
Nguye lo umfo ka Mkhize,
        This is Mkhize,
Nguye lo umfo ka Khoza,
        This is Khoza,
Nguye lo umfo ka Sibiya,
        This is Sibiya,
Nguye lo umfo ka Madondo.
        This is Madondo.
Aba kwalama bawela ngelinzima.
        [Praises]

Nguye lo umfo ka Linda.
        This is Linda.

The next example, "Hamba Mfana" by the King Star Brothers (SABC LT 9476, B6), is based on what one might call inverted metonymy. Here, the name is built from images of what, as it were, the group is not.

Bass: *Emampondweni bayasazi thina.*
                In Pondoland they know us.
Leader: *Bayasaba bayasazi.*
                They are afraid, they know us.
Chorus: *Bayamazi umfoka Mfiso.*
                They know Mfiso.
        Ekhuluma ngathi besizonda lonke izwe.
                Talking about us and they hated us in this region.

Another feature that isicathamiya shares with *izibongo* is the use of certain standard phrases frequently used in everyday verbal communication. One example of this is Solomon Linda's song "Bashaye Evening Birds" (Beat them, Evening Birds) of 1939 (GE 876). Here the expression "jiki tshoba" is one that is commonly used to praise excellence in performance:

Choir: *We jiki tshoba!*
                You, expert dancers!
        We jiki tshoba!
                You, expert dancers!
        Abafana be Evening Birds.
                Boys of the Evening Birds.
        Mbub' ezimakhala.
                Big lions.

Somewhat more elaborate strategies of name building encountered in the nightsongs are through what Paul Friedrich calls "analogical tropes" (Friedrich 1991, 37–39). Metaphors in this category, as Friedrich points out, include aesthetically effective and culturally appropriate similarities between different domains and prepare some "golden middle-ground" (38). "Big lions" in the song quoted above, is a case in point. Tropes such as this, in which things are not too far apart and not nearly identical, either, have a particularly rich potential for engendering social action in that they facilitate the transition of persuasion into performance. A good example of this type of trope is "Baleka Mfana," a song by the King Star Brothers (L4 BOL EO 313, B2):

Choir: *Baleka mfana ngoba nampa okhukhulangoqo.*
          Run, boy, because here comes the tornado.
    Sebezokunyathela, sithi baleka mfana.
          They are now going to trample you down. We say, "Run, boy."

This passage is also interesting because the analogical trope is only one element in a more developed rhetorical figure. The "boy" in this passage is of course a member of a rival choir. The link between the first line and the imperative in the second (a "modal trope" in Friedrich's terminology) is pragmatically particularly effective—that is, in scaring the other choir into retreat—because it works from the "middle-ground" assumption made in the simple analogy between the King Star Brothers and a tornado: only a fool would not seek cover from a tornado.

Even more compelling is the coupling of tropes in "Noma Kumnyama," a song by the Dundee Wandering Singers recorded in 1941 (GE 883):

Noma kumnyama thina asikhathali.
    Although it is dark, we don't care.
Ngoba sesiqedile nomfo-kaMkhize.
    Because we have finished off with the son of Mkhize.
Ihwanqa seziphelele izinsizwa.
    The whiskered man, all men have now arrived.
Elemikhuba, ihwanqa lemikhuba.
    The cunning one, the whiskered man of trickery.[4]

Commenting on this song, Hugh Tracey maintains that it describes an isi-cathamiya competition in which the lights had gone out. This, however, did not worry the Dundee Wandering Singers because they had already won the competition (Tracey 1948, 61). The song draws together images of darkness, fearlessness, and masculinity in a densely textured argument about the superiority of the choir. The choir's success is attributed to Alson Mkhize's leadership symbolized by his beard, itself a sign of seniority, wisdom, and resourcefulness. Couched in the style of *izibongo,* this trope must be read "backward," as it were: foregrounding the description of an unfortunate situation that would have disheartened the other choirs taking part in the competition, and only at the end dealing the trump card of their lead singer.

Another rhetorical strategy is the metonymic inclusion of the self in an imagined collectivity distant from the chaos and isolation of the here and now. In addition to noting the use of extracts from traditional praise-poetry about Shaka, Dingane, and Cetshwayo in the introductory song he calls *ukubingelela,* Elkin Sithole offers the following passage from a song from northern Natal in which the singers praise their own lineages:

> Leader (half-spoken, half-sung): Tell them where you come from, boys. *Kwela!* [Attack].
>
> Choir (sung): We come from across Mzinyathi river Kwelakithi eDundee [from our home near Dundee]. If you ever come to Mzinyathi, inquire or ask about us *izinyoni exidla ezinye* [birds which feed on other birds].
>
> Leader (sung): Now I want to tell you who my colleagues are. This is the young man from Sibiya clan, who milk the cow in the mountain cliffs; if they milk it in the barn, it has been stolen" (Sithole 1979, 280)

Though a telling expression of migrant performers' concern with the re-definition of social space in images of home and family, a song such as the one quoted appears to be exceptional. For my own evidence, as I shall demonstrate in the following chapter, does not support Sithole's view that the collectivity metonymically encompassing the singers, for the most part, is their own lineage.

In any event, some songs feature intricate combinations of metaphor and metonymy, as in this brief excerpt from "Sanibonani Nonke" by the Winter Roses (SABC T 5634):

> Choir: *Nants' ikwaya eyethu.*
>   Here is our choir.
>   *Thina makhunzi aseThekwini.*
>   We are coons from Durban.
>   *Ukwanda kwaliwa umthakathi yedwa.*
>   Only a witch does not appreciate prosperity.
>   *Yen' ozond' iWinter Rose.*
>   He who hates the Winter Roses.
>   *Iyathuthuka iWinter Rose.*
>   They are prospering, the Winter Roses.

The argument here moves from a metonymic inclusion of the self in broader entities (we—coons—Durban) in the first two lines to a form of discontinuous analogy in the remaining three lines. By identifying them-selves as "coons" and citizens of Durban (again, rather than members of a lineage), the Winter Roses (the name in itself connotes victory over adver-sity) predicate upon themselves attributes of the allegedly superior urban culture: in black South African performance, "coons" have long repre-sented the adroit, prosperous black city dweller (Erlmann 1991, 62–63). This assertion of superiority is then set off against the argument that he who hates a choir so prosperous must be an enemy of prosperity per se and hence must be an evil witch, the line "ukwanda . . . yedwa" being a common proverb.

Self-praise and name building in isicathamiya clearly work on poetic principles similar to those in *izibongo*. What distinguishes both genres of heroic self-fashioning is the fact that in the former the addressee is always a group of individuals. As a result, rather than emphasizing individual eloquence, the "play of tropes" in isicathamiya sets a stage on which the creation of a positive collective identity is enacted in a particularly stark poetic structure.

What I have said about the persuasive power of poetic structure derived from *izibongo* can be extended to proverbs, the second genre of "orature" woven into isicathamiya lyrics. As a genre within a genre, a discursive frame inserted into larger frames of discourse, proverbs play a far less significant role in isicathamiya than in other forms of communicative praxis. True, a small number of choirs that are particularly able, poetically, such as the Empangeni Home Tigers, King Star Brothers, or Ladysmith Black Mambazo, use proverbs more frequently than other, perhaps verbally less proficient, choirs—a fact which greatly enhances their popularity and prestige. But these examples of exceptional poetic ability set apart, it remains a suprising fact that a performance genre so deeply concerned with the competitive construction and display of collective identity, places so little emphasis on the rich rhetoric potential of proverbial lore. The reasons for this abstinence, I suggest, are not solely to be found in different degrees of poetic excellence among different choirs. The structural features of proverbs and competitive performance, and the heterogeneity of themes in isicathamiya lyrics also make proverbs a less practicable poetic technique.

But first, let me offer three examples—all by the Empangeni Home Tigers—of the use of proverbs in isicathamiya song. The first example comes from a song about witchcraft (Motella MO 481) in which the proverb serves as a reminder that misfortune needs to be confronted through solidarity.[5]

. . . .

Leader: *Sawubamb' utikoloshe bo!*
       We caught a dwarf.
    Sas'bamb' is'lwanyana.
       We caught the little animal.
Chorus: *Sam'bamb' utikoloshe.*
       We caught the dwarf.

     Wayehamba nemfane.
       He was together with a baboon.
Leader: *Sam'bamba thina.*
       We caught him.
Chorus: *Sam'bamba, wakhuluma wathi uphuma kumakhelwana.*
       We caught him, he said he was from next door.
Leader: *Yini lena futhi-ke madoda?*
       What is this again, gentlemen?
Chorus: *Yini lok'?*
       What is this?
     Nawubona.
       You saw it.
Leader: *Awibheke umkhovu.*
       Look, a zombie.

. . . .

Leader: *Wakhumbula wethu,*
       Remember, brother,
Chorus: *wakhumbula ukuthi awumbhiwa ndawonye.*
       remember that it (medecine) is not dug up in one place.

The second example is a song by the Empangeni Home Tigers about the onerous task of bringing up children in a time of waning parental authority (Mavuthela BL 22):

Leader: *Sengibathe ngishona lapha nangalena,*
       Although I have been searching high and low
     ngifuna lendaba,
       for this story,
     abantu bayabhidliza.
       people are destroying.
Chorus: *Ngishona le nangalena ngifuna lendaba.*
       I have been searching high and low for this story.
     Angiyitholi.
       I did not find it.
Leader: *Madoda ngiphinde ngibuye mina.*
       Gentlemen, I am trying again.
Chorus: *Ngifike lapha, ngithatha lapha, ngibeke lapha, ngithe ngiyabuya.*
       I came here, took this and that, saying I was coming back.
     Kodwa kuyabhidlika.
       But all my efforts are being destroyed.
Leader: *Kuyafan' okwami.*
       All my efforts are in vain.

Chorus: *Kuyafananje noma usina edwaleni.*
    It is like dancing on a rock:
akushunqi uthuli kuyafan nje.
    there is no dust, it is purposeless.
Noma uthela amanzi emhlana wedada.
    It is like pouring water on the back of a turkey.
Leader: *Lengan' isingehlule bo.*
    This child has troubled me.
Chorus: *Inqaba le maZulu.*
    It is a problem, people.
Leader: *Lengane iyedelela bo.*
    This child is too disobedient.
Chorus: *Inkinga le maZulu.*
    This is a problem, people.
Yeqa yonk' imiyalo yami.
    He flouts all my rules.
Kodwa ukuzala kuhle, ukuzilula amathambo.
    Yet it is nice to have children; it means to stretch one's bones.

The above song uses three different sayings ("dancing on a rock," "pouring water on the back of a turkey," and "stretching one's bones") in which the problems of child raising are metaphorically linked to two images of futility that are particularly resonant in Zulu thought: a dance that does not raise dust cannot reveal all the dancer's vigor and effort, in much the same way as all education will be wasted that does not succeed in bringing a disobedient child to his or her senses. This description of an impossible situation is eventually contrasted with a familiar proverb ("it is nice to have children") that reaffirms the close links commonly perceived between a numerous progeny and prosperity.

The third and last example, excerpted from another song by the Empangeni Home Tigers (Motella MO 479), is that of a proverb inserted into, or attached to, a string of self-praises.

Leader: *Ngiboniselen' udoorkeeper.*
    Show me the doorkeeper.
Sesizongena.
    We are about to enter.
Chorus: *Sesizongena ngaphakathi enkundleni.*
    We are about to take the stage.
Leader: *Manjena.*
    Now.

Chorus: *Sondela nawe baba, nawe mama.*
            Come nearer father, mother.
        Nizolalela ukudla kwendlebe.
            Come and feed your ears.
Leader: *Ngikhalel' ongekho lapha.*
            I pity the person who is not present today.
Chorus: *Ngikhalel' ongekho.*
            I pity the person who is not present.
        Ngikhalel' ongabonanga.
            I pity the one who did not see,
        ngoba amehlo awaphathelwana.
            because you cannot borrow somebody's eyes.[6]

Examples such as these clearly demonstrate the fact that proverbs as "tools of persuasion" (Penfield 1983, 6) work particularly well in more explicitly traditionalist types of discourse about the "roots," the need to return to the old ways, and so on—the kind of themes that groups like Empangeni Home Tigers have been wont to address in their repertoire. More important, however, they work in types of communication in which the object lies outside the act of communication. Proverbs, then, by virtue of being less explicitly self-referential than *izibongo,* belong to a type of poetic strategy aimed at a movement in quality space, as J. Fernandez might say, that includes the addressee in a wider community with a shared body of cultural knowledge. In other words, I understand the functionality of proverbs here primarily in their activating, rhetorical efficacy in a given interactional setting. Following Jan Mukarovsky's seminal study, "The Proverb as a Part of Context," a certain dramatic element is always introduced in the use of proverbial lore through the intrusion of a third party who speaks through the mouth of the speaker (Penfield 1983). Adding a further element of dramatic transformation to an already highly persuasive performance frame, the third-party voice endows the speaker's attempts to persuade the listener with the authority of *isiZulu,* Zulu tradition.

"I Am Following the Zionists"

The formation through self-praise and proverbial wisdom of a viable self-identity as a foundation for autonomous action in an alien social environment is probably the most powerful force at the source of isicathamiya poetic creativity. As sources, isicathamiya practitioners appropriated not only traditions like *izibongo* but also other genres of no lesser importance. The most pervasive of these models are the hymns of the Christian churches.

In the most general sense, the solemn and dignified tone of many isica-thamiya songs cannot but strike the ear, and as I have shown in chapter 3, the musical components of Christian hymnody have had a profound impact on the nightsongs from the start. In addition, since the 1960s, a growing number of vocal ensembles singing sacred music of all descriptions have been participating in isicathamiya competitions, not without causing, it is worth noting, some dismay among isicathamiya choirs proper. But in the essentially fluid milieu of migrant expressive culture, such boundaries are difficult to maintain. Given the fact that some of the five thousand gospel and nonorthodox church choirs in South Africa, of whom many are affiliated with Zionist churches, count among South Africa's biggest-selling recording artists, a great deal of overlap in religious and secular music would thus seem less surprising.[7] In fact, many a choir such as the Kings Boys has built up a considerable repertoire containing strong admixtures of African American spirituals, Methodist hymns, and Sankey and Moody hymns.

It is not possible here to enter into an extended textual exegesis of such hymn-based songs, let along to embark on an in-depth comparative analysis between South African Christian hymnody and isicathamiya lyrics of a religious content. I shall return to the subject at the end of this study where I discuss the music of Joseph Shabalala, arguably the foremost exponent not only of isicathamiya, but of religious choral music as such. Instead, in this section I shall briefly examine the intertextuality of religious song lyrics with the other textual elements discussed earlier. In doing so, I shall dwell at some length on Zionist ritual practice, for, as the words of the following song by the Morning Light Choir, recorded in 1941 (1727, Unissued), suggest, Zionism has found numerous followers among isicathamiya practitioners:

> *Uyababona abafundisi bagqoke ezimhlophe?*
> > Do you see the ministers wearing white robes?
> *Ngilandela iZiyoni.*
> > I am following the Zionists.

Independent African Christianity, as some of the most interesting historical and anthropological research of the recent past has shown, is one of the most resilient and important modes of collective resistance to white hegemony (Campbell 1989; Comaroff 1985; Kiernan 1974; Sundkler 1961).

Zionism in particular, which seems to have received the most sustained scholarly treatment, is seen by social scientists as one of the most complex and culturally salient forms of everyday black opposition to white minority rule (Schutte 1974; West 1975). While all these studies are helpful in illuminating the tremendous potential for autonomous social action inherent in African Christianity, there has been a marked lack of attention to ritual performance as a crucial component of such broadly oppositional practice, and an even greater dearth of systematic studies devoted to the verbal, musical, or kinesic expressions of African ecclesiastical practice.[8] Despite these shortcomings, all these authors stress the fact that, while the sacred rituals incorporate numerous elements from the contested social order, many at the same time draw on the rich body of African cultural knowledge to resist the alien structure. Independent African Christianity, at the level of ritual practice, is both a statement of denial and estrangement and an act of mediation between orthodox Christian liturgy and African conceptions of the sacred and forms of embodied spirituality.

Thus Elizabeth Gunner, in a study of Isaiah Shembe's Nazareth Baptist Church, contends that the appropriation of *izibongo* in the liturgical practice of this predominantly Zulu church expressed "opposition to the kind of control over movement, mind and identity that official authority and the mission churches seemed to demand" (Gunner 1988, 222). Venda Zionists, by contrast, while clinging to the Western hymnals, insisted that their performances were superior to the versions taught at the missions, because the freedom of execution and bodily involvement in Zionist services furthered a greater degree of collective spiritual commitment. Thus, the crucial feature of the hymns was not their verbal content, but the "*way* in which they were sung, the systematic treatment that was given to all hymn melodies of European origin" (Blacking 1987, 197). David Dargie concurs with this view in suggesting that Xhosa Zionist music distinguishes itself from Methodist songs, Pentecostal choruses, and other religious songs which it commonly uses, by the "way the songs are performed" (Dargie 1987, 17).

Zulu Zionist ritual songs, finally, as several authors have pointed out, are based for the most part on the American Board Hymnal (Kiernan 1990, 189), and as Musa Xulu's examination of the reemergence of *amahubo* in Zionist performance exemplifies, are unique not so much in musical material or textual substance as in their "synchronization of theological issues which mainline church leaders usually consider to be irreconcilable" (Xulu 1992, 319). The intertextuality of such genres of moral imagination as *amahubo,* compositions of the Sankey school, and Methodist hymns and their synchronization in a mode of performance held to be indigenous, is considered by performers to be a hallmark of both Zionist ritual practice and isicathamiya performance. Evidence of this is found, of course, in those instances where isicathamiya performers directly incorporate entire Zionist hymns into their stage repertoire as did the Harding Boys with "Amagugu Alelizwe" in the competition described in chapter 2. Conversely, many Zionist hymns display a remarkable affinity with those isicathamiya songs that are based on the more solemn *amahubo.*[9]

Beyond this, as Caesar Ndlovu, whose own research devoted considerable attention to the parallels between Zionist ritual and isicathamiya choir practice, argues, these parallels can also be observed at other levels. Thus, for one, when performers speak of the preparatory *prakthisa* phase as *umlindelo* or *emlindelweni,* waiting time, they symbolically link this phase to the Zionist night vigils of the same name. Similarly, Zionists and isicathamiya performers prefer high-pitched and loud singing. "*Simemeza njengabo,* we shout just like them," Robert Thwala of the Natal Try Singers told Ndlovu. "Singing loud and fast songs shows *umdlandla,* power." Furthermore, as Ndlovu observes, the circling around in fast walking steps performed by Zionist believers and by most choirs at the beginning (and sometimes end) of each appearance on stage are both directly linked to the *isifekezeli* style discussed earlier (chap. 6). Last but not least, the themes of many Zionist hymns, like the lyrics and choreographic components of numerous nightsongs, emphasize the notion of "home" as a sanctuary and anchor amid the chaos of urban life (Kiernan 1990, 190 ff.).

Clearly, Zionist choral singing and the nightsongs share a common rhetorical strategy. Rather than presenting narratives cut from one cloth, both types of performances juxtapose praises, proverbs, and Western hymnody. From a functional perspective, such layering unifies choir competitions as much as it stitches "into an unbroken whole the multiple activities" of a Zionist service (203). But it also does more. By speaking to some of the oppositions engendered by the white system—oppositions between the sacred and the worldly, between revelation and participation—and by seeking to transcend them in a form of poetry that in itself bears the scars of a society in which these once-contingent realms of social experience are being forcibly kept apart, the "synchronization" of disparate meanings and expressive means, as Musa Xulu says, enables people to acquire the power essential for correct living (Xulu 1992, 307).

In its most basic form, this bridging across secular and sacred genres can be observed in the cadenzas with which many choirs conclude their songs. The King Star Brothers, for instance, use the following closing formula:

> Chorus: *He! Khuluma Nkosi kimi.*
>   He! Talk to me, Lord.

Commenting on the meaning of this line, the singers said, "We are trying to signal the end of the message and we also remember our Creator and conclude the song in a prayer. Instead of saying Amen, we would sing our cadenza. It is the late Masina and Mbatha who introduced this idea. Both these people were Zionist preachers. As preachers they frequently used to say Amen which may have influenced the final cadence in isicathamiya songs."

Earlier in my account, I related a discussion I had with a conductor about the Mendi, Shaka Zulu, and apartheid. The conversation, I said there, illustrated the way in which isicathamiya performers recast historical experience in a religious idiom, forging emotionally powerful connections between the past and black South Africans' modern predicament. In a similar vein, but speaking to more recent manifestations of oppressive white politics, I offer below the words of a song by the K-Team, a choir affiliated to the Congress of South African Trade Unions (COSATU), that demonstrates the deep links in black consciousness between heaven and earth (Shifty 24L4, A1):

> Leader: *Yilokhuya kwaqal' umzabalazo,*
>   Since the revolution began,
>   *yilokhu . . .*
>   since . . .
> Chorus: *Yilokhu kwaqal' umzabalazo,*
>   Since the revolution began,
>   *siyazabalaza.*
>   we are in revolt.
> Leader: *Thina . . .*
>   We . . .
> Chorus: *EDuduza*
>   in Duduza
>   *nase Tsakane.*
>   and in Tsakane.
>   *Yethel' eSprings,*
>   Springs caught on,
>   *la kwaphel' izingane zika baba.*
>   where my father's children died.

> *Zibulaw' amabhunu.*
> > At the hands of Boers.
> Leader: *Lokhuya . . .*
> > Since . . .
> Chorus: *Kodwa kogcina thina,*
> > But we will win,
> > *sizwe esiNtsundu.*
> > we, the black nation.
> Leader: *O Somandla.*
> > Oh, Almighty.
> Chorus: *Kuhamba ngerey.*
> > Everyone has his turn.
> Leader: *USomandla uyasithanda nathi.*
> > The Almighty loves us, too.
> > *Uyasithombisa kancane ukuthi sophumelela thina.*
> > He shows us little by little that we will conquer.
> Leader: *MaComrades.*
> > Comrades.
> Chorus: *MaComrades, phambili ngomzabalazo.*
> > Comrades, forward with the revolution.

On the surface, it would seem that songs such as the one cited are part of a long tradition of black political song based on contrafactum, the setting of new words to an old tune (Erlmann 1985). Most of these protest songs, couched in the stolid structures of the mission *makwaya* repertoire, protested not so much by verbally articulating opposition but by appropriating the key symbols of the very order into which the majority of black South Africans had been drawn economically, but to which most were completely denied political access (Blacking 1980b, 198). In the K-Team song, by contrast, protest does not seek to transcend the hegemonic order by embracing its central codes but by bringing into temporal alliance, in an unruly bricolage, the seemingly disparate voices of revolt and reverence.

Another fascinating example of this kind of rhetorical journey across genres was provided by the Danger Stars during the competition on 15 March 1984, described in chapter 2, Below I reproduce selected segments from what was an extended performance sequence in which one song seamlessly led into the next.

> *Kuwona lonyaka ophelile kwenzeka isimanga sokuthi sebengishonele*
> *bonke abakithi ekhaya.*
> > Last year, a sad thing happened, namely that everybody at home had
> > passed away.

Lomhlaba unjenjenje ukufa kulinuku ngokuthatha abazali bethu sisasele
siyizintandane.
> The world is like this. Death is a dirty thing, taking away our parents
> and leaving us behind as orphans.
Sesithembele kuyena umholi wethu uGatsha Buthelezi nengonyama
uZwelithini.
> Our faith is now in our leader Gatsha Buthelezi and our king
> Zwelithini.
Gatsha, Zwelithini, thina sibhekisa kini eniphethi isizwe etimnyama.
> Gatsha, Zwelithini, we say to you: leaders of the black nation.
Njalo nje baphuma emaphepheni.
> Their names appear in the newspapers all the time.
Njalo nje baphuma emsakazweni kumaFM ukuthi baphelile abantu
abansundu yonke indawo.
> Their names appear on FM radio every time we hear that black people
> are dying all over.
Webaba, we mama wami, bhuti wam, sisi wami kunzima lapho ngikhona.
> Father, mother, brother, sister, I am in difficulty.
Sebethi uQueen usawela adabule amanzi.
> They say Queen Victoria is crossing the sea.
Siwutholile umbiko ovela kuye usabela uthi yebo baba.
> We received a message from her saying, yes, father.
Mayebizwa amagama ngothi yebo nkosi nangu mina la.
> When the roll is called up yonder, I'll say, yes, Lord, here I am.

Like other songs quoted earlier, this passage plays with a whole number of
culturally sentient tropes and genres. Stock phrases from Methodist hymnody ("When the roll is called up yonder") appear side by side with descriptions of the political turmoil of the 1980s, praises of the Zulu king and
the Chief Minister of the KwaZulu "homeland," Gatsha Buthelezi, and
the familiar image of Queen Victoria's arrival in South Africa. Taken together, this string of tropes forms an emotionally charged and culturally
meaningful narrative about the personal misfortune of one migrant. By
combining authoritative and popular genres, by refusing to adhere to orthodox Christian imagery and textual conventions, isicathamiya songs of a
religious nature, though ostensibly setting up a dialogue with a haven beyond the thisness of the world, place themselves in a mediating position
between the dominant structure and marginality. Ultimately, of course, the
ability to recompose in words the pieces produced by a fragmented social
universe, constitutes an assertion of power. But this quest does not simply
amount to a return to some putative state of grace, to the acceptance of

monologic representations of the world, or an escape into an otherworldly realm of harmony. Rather, it involves a subtle attempt to find centers among the margins, as it were, to recognize and explain the fractured conditions of migrant existence by seizing on its dispersed elements and by bringing these into a multistranded dialogue with each other.

8   Attacking with Song: The Aesthetics of Power and Competition

Asigadli ngazagila, sigadla ngengoma.
We not attacking with assegais, but with song.

Empangeni Home Tigers, "Tntselelo"

Competition is perhaps the predominant mode of social interaction in modern capitalist societies. For Georg Simmel, conflict even formed the essential agent of socialization in modern society (1903). In many ways, one might argue, the experience of competition for employment and wages constituted perhaps the most crucial element of a new kind of social practice among migrant workers in the industrializing South Africa. In particular, the accumulation of wealth and the production of surplus on the basis of individual property were the main features distinguishing the new colonial order from the ways in which people in the precolonial Zulu kingdom structured their social practice. In precolonial society, the patrilineal and, to a large extent, self-sufficient homestead was the main unit of production. This is not to suggest, however, that competition was absent in this rural world. Quite to the contrary, it existed at various levels and between different categories of social actors. Herd-boys fought out *ubungqwele,* leadership among their fellow herd-boys. Brothers competed among each other over their paternal heritage, and women competed for the protection of men. In fact, life itself was conceived of as a constant struggle between opposing forces. By far the most important type of competition, however, arose from the independence of the self-reproducing homesteads and their organization in potentially opposing larger units, districts. But this "horizontal" territorial structure with its susceptibility to tensions from the time of Shaka had also become subject to a "vertical" system of age regimentation and loyalty to the king. While this system could not prevent the outbreak of territorial conflict, it was able to mitigate such competition to a certain degree. In other words, the combination of interlineage and interdistrict opposition with "vertical" hierarchy ultimately fostered precolonial social cohesion.[1] In fact, as we shall see below, the kind of competition that formed the very essence of this political order is one, albeit extremely remote, source of isicathamiya competitions.

One important concept that arose from this social system and one that was crucial to its functioning, was the idea of heroism (*ubuqhawe*). As we have seen in the previous chapter, praises and self-praises are the princi-pal poetic form in which the fashioning of the hero, in fact the individual, takes place. Foregrounding himself through words, a hero defines his self-identity primarily in relation to others. It is through the deeds of a hero who overcomes obstacles and defeats his adversaries that the good estab-lishes itself in the world. Even though a hero—whether a warrior, a hard-working miner, or a successful performer—satisfies his own needs, he will ultimately contribute to the well-being of others. In short, the hero is a builder of communities, a profoundly social being.

This notion of selfhood and the system on which it was based differed radically from the kind of competition (and the attendant notions of the bourgeois ego) black people in Natal increasingly came to experience as they were drawn deeper and deeper into the capitalist social order. But the emerging class of large landowners responded to this situation under con-ditions different from those facing the landless and impoverished masses. The first had become acquainted with the new property relations on the mission stations. There the gospel was preached in tandem with the idea that individual land tenure and the Protestant work ethic were the keys to improvement and progress, if not pure and simple salvation. These core elements of mid-Victorian bourgeois liberalism were seen as the very foun-dations of economic success, enhanced social status, and the eventual in-corporation of blacks into the dominant social order. Only those who had demonstrated the complete assimilation of these values through private en-terprise and economic competition, the "exempted Natives," were deemed sufficiently equipped to be admitted to the new society. But by the time this new social order was firmly in place, growing numbers of Africans had to realize that they were increasingly prevented from reaping the fruits of their labor and from enjoying the promised "civilization."[2]

The reconfiguration of the social dynamics and the meaning of pre-colonial competition in bourgeois society is at the heart of isicathamiya singing contests. As I shall argue in this chapter, the definition of a positive self-image and its anchorage in imagined spaces of collective cohesion is achieved through the competitive display of physical and symbolic attri-butes of power and manhood. The link that I am establishing here between power and competition, we should remind ourselves, is first and foremost grounded in the very nature of social interaction. Power is never simply stated. It has to be wrested from the hands of others; it is essentially a contested capacity of doing things. Beyond this, a view of power relations as a field of conflicting forces is crucial for our understanding of the historical dynamics of social practice as it intertwines with performance. As was seen in the previous chapter, in isicathamiya, this definition of the self involved a "poetics of social interaction" (Herzfeld 1985), an attention to the performance itself, in which it is the way things are done, rather than the things themselves, which are foregrounded. Self-praise and its intertextuality with other speech genres were the main elements of this poetics. It is now time to consider in more detail how the presentation of the self in performance always involves some exaggerated violation of the quotidian framed in self-referential terms. The skilled social actor does not want his words to be measured against his deeds but against other actors' words. Competition, in other words, the demonstration of difference, is the very condition of social practice as performance.

With this in mind, we have to return briefly to the point made at the beginning of this chapter and to follow the strangely bicausal genesis of isicathamiya competitions. Given the limited opportunities for economic competition that, it will be recalled, reduced them to low-paid and heavily policed laborers or frustrated white-collar workers with stunted prospects for upward mobility, Africans in Natal and elsewhere in South Africa developed new arenas in which to accumulate "symbolic capital." Choral competitions were among the most marked compensatory strategies. Thus, for turn-of-the-century *amakholwa* communities, choral music was the supreme manifestation of improvement and progress. In fact, choral music contained, as one correspondent to the black Durban newspaper *Ilanga Lase Natal* wrote in 1911, "an assurance of civilized advancement."[3] Proof of how far these communities had advanced toward this goal was to be found in the precision with which early church and school choirs imitated English turn-of-the-century musical events, down to such subtleties as the *ankori* (encore).[4] Other signals of assimilation, apart from the song repertoire itself which was characteristically called *imusic* or *makwaya* (choir), were stiff body postures and the presence of a conductor.

The apotheosis of "civilized advancement" were the national *eisteddfodau* that had been organized by black intellectuals, white welfare departments, and a host of other liberal institutions from 1931. As its chief promoter, Columbia talent scout Mark Radebe wrote, these events, through stimulating contest "should, in the first place, do something to lessen the implacable barriers of tribalism."[5] While much of this elite ethos of improvement through institutionalized, "friendly rivalry" still informs the ideology of present-day isicathamiya associations (as we shall see in chap. 10), Radebe's reference to the "barriers of tribalism" points to one of the more fundamental structural transformations of preindustrial society: the lateral opposition between lineages and territorial units in so-called faction fights. And it is the ideology and symbolic expression of faction fighting that forms the second, and possibly more powerful, model of competitive social interaction on which isicathamiya performance is based.

Yet where Radebe and other black intellectuals have tended to bemoan tribalism as a burden of the past and almost seemed to ontologize it as the black man's nature, recent scholarship now considers the creation of tribalism in more instrumentalist terms, as a product of modern society rather than its antithesis. As Leroy Vail has pointed out, the production of ethnic consciousness in southern Africa proceeded as much from the class-based interests of powerful brokers—tribal chiefs, missionaries, intellectuals black and white—as it enabled migrant workers to exercise the control that was necessary for them to protect their position in rural society (Vail 1989, 15). The Natal countryside—the area that interests us most in the context of isicathamiya history—is one of the terrains in which the construction of tribalism can be seen at work with remarkable clarity during the earlier decades of the twentieth century. Here, ethnic consciousness was anything but a leftover from an earlier historical moment. Rather, as Carolyn Hamilton and John Wright have pointed out, the rapid growth of migrant labor at this time was beginning to foster the development of a "broad collective identity among African male migrants from the Natal-Zululand region" (Hamilton and Wright 1993, 44). And thus, at the bottom end of the social spectrum among the landless and poor, the migrants and small peasants, the brutal social, economic, and cultural transformations that swept across the region led to an existential crisis that expressed itself in considerably less urbane practices than the "civilized advancement" of choirs, encores, and conductors. The individual freedom propagated by the missions and other agents of the dominant order had little appeal to migrants once they realized that freedom for them meant more the wrenching from the ancestral land, the dissolution of kin ties and secure domestic relations and, as a result of all of this, the atomization as isolated labor units. And thus, in Natal perhaps more than elsewhere, the competition for land, employment, better pay, and accommodation—all increasingly rare commodities—frequently took violent forms. It is in an attempt to contain rather than to eliminate these conflicts that some rural reserve dwellers developed practices such as stick-fighting, *ingoma* dancing and, eventually, isicathamiya competitions.

In a fascinating study on faction fighting and the ideology of vengeance in the Msinga reserve, Jonathan Clegg (1981b) has shown how these oppositions and emerging cultural responses to dispossession and poverty are interwoven. Clegg makes the following argument: When the Zulu kingdom was destroyed in 1879, the system of age regiments lost its former function to counteract "horizontal" oppositions and territorial conflicts. With increasing dispossession and scarcity of land, what had once been an element of precapitalist political cohesion could no longer be expressed and contained in legitimate ways. The precolonial territorial tensions spilled over into so-called faction fights which pitted families and clans against each other in grim battles. Consequently, in parts of Zululand a mechanism was developed whereby this interdistrict tension was defused and channeled into a form of ritual expression called *umgangela,* an interdistrict competition of playful stick-fighting (*ukudlala ngenduku*). These events were staged by returning migrants and were governed by a strict set of rules that, inter alia, prohibited stabbing and other lethal war techniques.[6]

In the white farm areas adjoining the Msinga reserve, the situation was similar, except that here the newly drawn territorial boundaries in no way respected those of the traditional districts. The latter only survived as phantom districts in the minds of reserve dwellers who now derived certain rights such as grazing or simply employment on white farms, from their erstwhile occupation of one of these phantom districts. As a result, ferocious armed conflicts were not uncommon between the workers on a farm which overlay two or more of these opposing phantom districts. In this situation, a self-policing institution such as *umgangela* increasingly turned into an occasion for serious confrontation. And, as Clegg argues, it was in yet another attempt to mitigate such conflicts, that *ingoma* dance competitions arose (Clegg 1982, 9). Stick-fighting and *ingoma* were, of course, the creation of migrant workers. And it was migrant workers who transported these ritualized conflicts into the cities and transformed them into expressions of competition between rural territorial units for urban resources.

Other competitive rituals, not directly related to faction fighting but that equally form models of isicathamiya contests, include *ukuqhatha,* a playful contest among herd-boys. The terminology and imagery of these youthful tests of strength—*inkunzi* (bull) for a powerful leader and *izingqwele* for boys who defeat their rivals—are often transferred directly to isicathamiya choirs.

Taking Clegg's argument to its logical conclusion, isicathamiya competitions, as I have indeed said, have to be seen as possibly the most recent form through which migrants give ritual expression to these conflicts. Thus, the notion of competition in isicathamiya harks back more to pre-colonial notions of social relations than to Christian models; more than in a vision of "civilized advancement," isicathamiya competition seems to be embedded in an aesthetics of power that has its roots in the "political economy of tribal animosity" (Phimister and van Onselen 1979) and ritualized regional conflict. Perhaps better than any ethnographic account, the words of a song by the Empangeni Home Tigers quoted in the epigraph to this chapter lucidly point to the links between faction-fighting, stick-fighting, and isicathamiya competitions (Mavuthela BL 22):

> Chorus: *Nants' intsele lo.*
> Here is a challenge.
> Basses: *Awuviki!*
> Shield yourself!
> . . . .
> Leader: *Asigadli ngazagela baba.*
> We are not attacking with assegais, father.
> *Asigadli ngazagila, sigadla ngengoma.*
> We are not attacking with assegais, but with song.

When isicathamiya began to be performed in competitions is not clear. But from the recollections of Enoch Mzobe, Gilbert Madondo, and other veterans we can conclude that in the early phases of isicathamiya history competitions were much less frequent than today and that early groups such as the Crocodiles and the Evening Birds were mainly occupied with concerts and wedding parties. Although the examples of present-day song texts quoted previously do not differ fundamentally from earlier songs of the 1930s and 1940s, the very structure of competitions and the ways in which conflict and opposition were ritualized in performance changed markedly over time. In fact, it seems that much of the course of isicathamiya history was influenced by an uneasy balance between the two models of competitive performance: the urban middle-class concert and the rural stick-fight. For the first was essentially denuded of all immediate material and social causes for violent conflict and stemmed from the desire to overcome social and political divisions. In the second, rural model, the urge to act out such conflicts was built into its very constitution and therefore, perhaps less surprisingly, could easily slip into a confrontation involving the use of physical force (fig. 12).

Although the linkages between more militant forms of ethnic conflict

Figure 12. Program of an isicathamiya competition, Johannesburg, 1968. Courtesy David Marks.

and isicathamiya are undeniable, we must be careful not to downplay the role of symbolic mediation in social practice by opposing symbolic and instrumental practice or by granting the pragmatic dimension priority over the semantic aspects of social action. The problem with Clegg's analysis as with other studies that see competitions as compensatory activities replacing violent conflict (Jones 1980; Spencer 1985, 3–8) is that the practices of the subordinate are reduced to a substitute for real action, to a role as a mere safety valve. But, as James Scott (1990) has cogently argued, hidden forms of resistance are not merely an explanation of political action; they are a "condition of practical resistance" (Scott 1990, 191). The less overt forms of resistance are social actions, and the quest for power is deeply inscribed into them. Resistance, Scott insists, does not generate powerless realms of social interaction. The arts of resistance not only consist in the creation of a social realm insulated from control and surveillance, but this space is socially constructed and formulated in the sense that it imposes a disciplined form on these acts of opposition. For if the articulation of protest is to become the property of a subordinate group, it must be further disciplined by the shared experiences and power relations within that group. It must carry meaning for them and reflect the meanings and distribution of power among them (119). Thus, it seems futile to separate practical resistance from the symbolic interrogation of power or to consider the hidden transcript as a mere prologue to or substitute for public opposition. The meaning of a given action is socially constructed from different ends of the power spectrum (205).

Clearly, then, in analyzing the dynamics and aesthetics of competitive performance we have to be aware of the underlying power strategies as the driving forces of the construction of alternative social space. As Jean Comaroff has written (1985, 263), the demystification of resistance and its (often ethnocentric) privileging in anthropology and performance studies as a unified, explicit, and conscious mode of social action calls for a methodology different from the mode of social inquiry that freezes the social practice and culture of the powerless into cut-and-dried categories such as resistance, subordination, and so on. If the study of performance can lay any claims to offering a particularly rewarding avenue for treating social process as a dialectic, it is because the polysemy of performance provides an effective base for a relatively autonomous realm of discursive freedom.

Metaphor, then, as I have said throughout, is at the root of the construction of power relations. Metaphoric predication is a means of "entitlement," as Kenneth Burke called it, that is, a means of creating identity, of defining situations and the place of the self in time and space (Burke 1966, 359–79). With this in mind, I shall be concerned in the remainder of this chapter with the examination of metaphor as the chief vehicle of regional identification. Following James Fernandez's observation that in nineteenth-century Andalusian poetic duels a figurative way of speaking about a place becomes transformed into a part of that place (Fernandez 1988), I shall examine the construction of metonymy in isicathamiya performance through attention to the processes of metaphoric association. In other words, I am suggesting that the singing about the "home" transforms the nightsong performers into parts of that imagined space. In doing so, I shall concentrate, as I have attempted in previous chapters, on a variety of symbolic parameters, both verbal and nonverbal, such as choir names, song texts, and sound texture. For, much like the reconstruction of the "home" is prefigured in the social organization of isicathamiya choirs, in choir names, and in song texts, these same symbolic layers also provide ready clues to the power dynamics in isicathamiya competitions.

To begin with the names of choirs, many of these express strength and power through what appear to be three types of key tropes. The first type contains names that seem to convey a general idea of force, potency, danger, and fearlessness such as in Amavuthela (Strong Ones), Nsimbi Kayigobi (Iron Does Not Bend), Danger Stars, Fear No Harm Choir or, rather more ominously, Heavy Violence. Other names give more direct clues to the instruments of such power as in Ladysmith Black Mambazo or Zulu Assegai. Yet others like Danger Express elaborate on any one of these images by adding another superior quality. The second group of names draws on symbols of social hierarchy. The term "king" as in Durban King Express, Kings Boys, and many others is, of course, the first name that catches the eye here, but unlike the role of Kingi dance associations in East African *beni* this term is not necessarily thought of as a reference to English royalty. Rather the meaning is understood in a more general sense as "ruler," "leader," and only occasionally does a direct reference to traditional Zulu royalty or local chieftaincy seem to be intended as in Mavukela Chiefs. The third category of choir names, finally, is perhaps the largest and the most telling. It consists of the names of semiwild animals such as bulls (Black Bull), the smaller and sometimes dangerous species such as Scorpions and Vultures. Above all, this category of tropes includes the much-feared wild creatures of the southeast African fauna, and the heroes of so much of Zulu lore: snakes (Green Mamba), crocodiles (Izingwenya Zasenkuthu), tigers (Black Tigers, Empangeni Home Tigers), and lions (Brave Lion Singers).

Many of these names belong to a common repertoire and are therefore not specific to isicathamiya choirs alone. As we have seen, some names, like Vultures or Royals, have also been appropriated by football clubs and criminal gangs. But in some cases, these names also tell a story. As Enoch Mzobe, for instance, explained, during the 1920s some members of the Crocodiles were living on the banks of the Umgeni river "like crocodiles." And like crocodiles that threaten those who cross the river, the choir would devour other choirs.

A more unusual way of expressing their self-confidence by means of the accoutrements examined more fully in chapter 6 is the badge which the Kings Boys sport on their blazers. It shows a pelican crouched on a map of the African continent against a red background. While the map identifies the singers, so choir leader Thomas Mtshali stated, as Africans who sing African music, the pelican is an animal which is difficult to catch and therefore stands for a choir which "other choirs can't catch."

In a similar manner, the lyrics of the nightsongs are also important components in encoding assertions of power. As I explained in chapter 7, the majority of isicathamiya songs are adaptations of heroic poetry. There, I pointed to the formal properties of song lyrics as elements of a rhetorical strategy aimed at the redefinition of a positive group and self-identity. In this chapter we have to look briefly at the poetic imagery used in these songs to express ideas of power and manhood and their acquisition in social contest. A few examples from more recent songs may illustrate this. A standard phrase, for instance, that is repeated in many songs, such as the following song by CTC, almost ontologizes the idea of competition by evoking the familiar metaphor of wild animals fighting:[7]

> *Sekudiben' ingwe nengonyama.*
>> Now a tiger meets a lion.
> *Akuziyeke zishayane.*
>> Let's watch them fight.

In a similar manner, some choirs use other primordial metaphors of strength such as wind and fire, as in the opening lines of the following song by the King Star Brothers (L4 BOL EO 313, A1):

> Leader: *Yash' imizi webafana es'khotheni kwaMamlambo*
>> Burning are the homesteads, boys, and the veld fires are threatening Mamlambo's place.

Bass: *Yash'imizi es'khotheni kwaMamlambo.*
                Burning are the homesteads and veld fires are threatening Mam-
                lambo's place.
Chorus: *Lelizwe lesithembiso.*
                This is the promised land.
Leader: *Yizo lezintsizwa ndoda*
                These are the gentlemen, man,
Chorus: *eze King Stars ezaziholwa uMasina.*
                of the King Stars led by Masina.

The link in this song from the album *Yashimizi* between the veld fire and
the King Star Brothers is illustrated even more vividly on the album cover
which shows composer and manager Herman Pelo with a container eject-
ing flames and the King Star Brothers clustering behind him pointing to
the fire (fig. 13).

By far the most frequent type of image, however, is drawn from the
realm of performance itself and the interaction it generates between performers and their audiences, thus reflecting the key African conception of
power as a socially engendered and maintained form of practice. In other
words, the ability to attract big captive audiences and to speak to the experiences of a listenership of diverse social, regional, and historical backgrounds is a crucial mark of distinction for migrant performers. Or, as the
following song by Solomon Linda's Evening Birds puts it with an ironic
twist (GE 1051):

Basibiza lonk'ilizwe.
      We are invited all over the country.
Sizokufa yindlala.
      We'll die of starvation.
Ngoba lapho basibiza khona asazi bantu.
      Because where we are invited to, we don't know anybody.[8]

The reference to the relatives is significant not only because it bemoans
the alienation and insecurity of migrant life, but in that it alludes to the
deracination of traditional performance from a communal, lineage-based
context. One of the many paradoxes of migrant life, the singing of *amahubo*—conceivable only in and for situations connected with the ancestral
lineage—is depicted here as an assertion of ancestral filiation and simultaneously an act of estrangement producing celebrity. Clearly, in the land
of displacement and great racial divides, a price is to be paid for fame. The

Figure 13. Album jacket, *Yashimizi*. Courtesy Reamusic.

image of starvation, then, beneath all the irony would also appear to hide a tone of despair and frustration.

Entirely in the same vein, albeit playing on images of empire and the glittery world of international stardom, is the following excerpt from Ladysmith Black Mambazo's song "Homeless":

> *Yith' omanqoba.*
>> We are the winners.
> *Abayibamba phakath'eLandani.*
>> We fought the (musical) battle in the center of London.

In the next example, sung by the Kings Boys in the competition described in chapter 2, the same idea is turned inside out. Here it is the inability to compose original songs that is seen as a mark of cowardice which provokes the Kings Boys to seek a confrontation with the imposters.

> *Siya le eMgungundlovu eSobantu.*
>> We are going to Sobantu in Pietermaritzburg.
> *Bathi kukhona amavukana asecula amagoma ethu.*
>> They say that there are some cowards (young bulls) who sing our
>> songs.

Excellence in performance, as I have stressed time and again, is not sought for its own sake. A skilled performer, an *umgagu,* and an *umqhawe* are men whose moral qualities and ability to build alliances of people bound by common values and experiences earn them a name and—the two mutually enforce each other—a network of supportive social relations. The song "Sengihamba Ngedwa" ("I am traveling alone") by the Evening Birds (1799, Unissued) expresses this quite ingeniously by evoking a beer party, one of the most symbolically charged and culturally central domains for the formation of masculine identity.

> *Yibo laba abahamba bekhuluma ngathi ematshwaleni.*
>> These are the ones who talk about us in drinking sessions.
> *Bedla ngathi utshwala.*
>> While drinking beer, discussing us.
> *Webaba nomama sengihamba ngedwa.*
>> Father and mother, I am traveling alone.

The textural quality of musical sound, as I have suggested, also serves as an important element in the aesthetics of power. The metaphoric forging of correspondences between musical and social order, as Christopher Waterman rightly points out, is often more a matter of expressive "qualities" (timbre, texture, rhythmic flow) than of the abstracted musical structures so privileged in Western analytical thought (Waterman 1990, 220). Indeed, as I have indicated in chapter 3, for isicathamiya practitioners distinctions between different levels of volume and pitch are among the most meaningful criteria for determining genre boundaries and aesthetic value. Terms such as *isikhwela Jo* and *'mbombing* illustrate this quite clearly.

What distinguishes the principle of "as loud as your voice can take" (as the *Ilanga* correspondent characterized *isikhwela Jo* in 1956) from choir names and song texts is that the production of these vocal sounds belongs primarily to the realm of metonymic association. By singing in a loud voice and in high-pitched registers, choirs demonstrate that they are part of a wider entity of people who can make themselves heard. Although the stylistic conventions of singing "as loud as your voice can take it" may be taken as a metaphor for exploding bombs or a physical attack, the performance itself of these songs as a form of social action operates through a metonymic ordering of social relationships that challenges the dominant order. As is well known, this order, taken here as the totality of speakers in South Africa, consists of very rigid hierarchies between the rulers, who may express themselves at any time, in whatever language and intonation they please, and the ruled, whose style and content of speaking, indeed, whose whole demeanor, are dictated by those in power. By rejecting a subdued tone in their performances, migrant workers reconfigure the metonymic hierarchy between oppressors and oppressed in which different voice registers signal positions of social dominance and subordination. The imagery of protest, as Deborah Durham and James Fernandez have indeed written with regard to the 1976 Soweto uprising, may lie in a new metaphoric assertion—as, in fact, the song lyrics quoted above amply demonstrate. But as the two authors go on to say, it may also lie in "metonymic reworkings of metaphoric assertions, reworkings that challenge conventional, culturally specific structurings of the social order implied in conventional metaphor" (Durham and Fernandez 1991, 209ff.).

This is not to deny, of course, that a loud voice signaling social power is also a metaphoric image. In point of fact, the constant shifts between metaphor and metonymy make performance become a form of social action and a symbol for such action at the same time. It is interesting in this regard to examine the constellation of metonymy and metaphor and its refiguration in the aesthetics of power since Ladysmith Black Mambazo. As we have seen, it was Ladysmith Black Mambazo who first departed from the principle of "as loud as your voice can take it." But in his desire to relinquish the conventional vocal signals of strength, Joseph Shabalala has created other effects that convey the idea of power and superiority. Commenting on the glides and the short, gruff interjections that punctuate the even, mellow flow of vocal harmonies in his songs, he said,

> This "grr, grr" stuff you hear on the records, is something I contrived in taking it from a white farmer's ox which was huge and had big horns. So when you wanted to tie a rope around the ox's neck you wouldn't do it while he was standing, because the neck is straight. The best way was to touch the forehead and call "grr, grr Mpotshongo" [name of a cow]. Then it would tilt its head, then you can put the rope around its neck. Now this came to my mind that since we're singing we're competing. And I thought that in the silent passages we could fit the "drr, drr" or "grr, grr." In fact, the sound made for the ox was "drr," but I converted it to "grr." But I thought it would also weaken my counterparts so that they would obey me a little bit, or move away at a distance. Because this sound was for telling the ox to move further. In fact, any cow, when you said "drr," it would move further. Now this then came to my mind that I could put it into the silent passages, it would embellish the song, although I didn't know whether it was going to sound nice. But to my surprise, the community accepted it. To say "grr" is just an embellishment, but the actual sound is "drr," it's just an addition. Just like saying "grr bhu heyi wethu." The addition of "heyi wethu" means that you are nailing the other guys in music.

To conclude this discussion of the aesthetics of power we will briefly have to consider witchcraft accusations, one of the most frequently employed idioms of discursive praxis in situations of conflict today. Misfortune, in Zulu thinking, is considered to be caused by evil forces exercising witchcraft (*ubuthakathi*). Failure at the workplace, poverty, disrupted family relations, and similar ruptures that make migrants' lives miserable are frequently attributed to the working of such evil forces. In the insecure environment of the migrant labor system, as a survey conducted in the early 1980s indicates, witchcraft was one of the major sources of worry among migrant workers, more than half of the hostel dwellers interviewed expressing anxiety regarding witches (Møller and Schlemmer 1982, 141).

Regrettably, the existing literature on the subject offers little help in deepening our understanding of the symbolic dimension of witchcraft and magic and their appropriation within the context of South African industrial society. Earlier studies have primarily been concerned with Max Gluckman's dictum that the multiplication of situations of conflict in the urban environment corresponds to an increase in witchcraft accusations (Scotch 1970, 249). Others have debated the question whether "the secularization of urban life finds its counterpart in the secularization of worldview" and, hence, a decline in witchcraft (Hammond-Tooke 1970, 38). Even so, as Hammond-Tooke's findings for Grahamstown and Khalana usefully show, the frequency of witchcraft and sorcery cases dropped markedly in these towns. Moreover, the existing accusations were expressed in nonpersonal, nonkin terms (33), and urban-generated causes were mostly explained in nonmystical terms (38).

With virtually no personal experience of my own of the techniques of *ubuthakathi* and how to counter them, I have to limit my discussion of witchcraft in isicathamiya to a few remarks about witchcraft as a topic of isicathamiya song texts. In the most general sense, witchcraft as a source of evil and misfortune is the topic of a great number of songs. Given migrant performers' preoccupation with the homestead we should not be surprised that witchcraft, as in fact the song "Sambamb' Utikoloshe" (SABC LT 15 099, A2) by the Newcastle Five Roses shows, is perceived as a threat to the integrity and involateness of the home and, with it, of the ancestral lineage.

Leader: *Sam' bamb' utikoloshe thina.*
        We caught the dwarf.
        Thina samfak' emgodlweni.
        We put him in a bag.
        Kodwa kwathukuthel' amadoda.
        But men got angry.
        Sam'bamb' utikoloshe thina bo!
        We caught the dwarf.
Chorus: *Sambamba utikoloshe.*
        We caught the dwarf.
Leader: *Tikoloshe.*
        The dwarf.
        Ngabe kwenzenjani kangaka?
        What could be the problem?
        Awu, awu kwenzenjani, mfana?
        Awu, awu, what happened, boy?
Bass: *Obaba, mama.*
        Oh father, mother.

Leader: *Obaba, mama.*
        Oh father, mother.
Chorus: *Webaba thina asisazi lutho.*
        Father, we don't know anything.
        Kwathukuthel' amadoda.
        Men are angry.
Leader: *Mbambheni nina-ke,*
        Catch him,
        kodwa mbambheni ngezandla.
        but catch him with both hands.
Chorus: *Mbambheni madoda, huy' oqed' abant' abam'.*
        Catch him, men, he killed my children.
Leader: *Haye.*
        He.
Chorus: *Bakubhekil' abakithi.*
        The ancestors are keeping an eye on you.

By contrast, the use of magic in performance is sung about much less often. The following song by the New Home Brothers was recorded in the competition of March 1984 described in chapter 2. Given the secret nature of witchcraft, the choir obviously boasts of its power "in the negative," as it were, by denying the use of witchcraft and by claiming that the singers' success is based solely on musical skill.

Yini lena engiyizwayo?
        What is this that I am hearing?
Benzani lababantu? Bazifunani izingoma zami. Babophe, bafake izinsimbi.
        What are these people doing? What are they doing with my songs?
        Arrest them, handcuff them!
Wo he bayeke zingane, bayafunda bafundela kimi.
        Ho, take no note of them, they are novices trying to copy from me.
Wozani zinsizwa nizocela ingoma asenzi ngamuthi nangamlingo.
        Come and ask for our advice, gentlemen! We do not do it by herbs or
        magic.
Hhayi ukushela ngathi, musani ukushela ngathi izintombi.
        Do not use our name in trying to win girls, do not use our name in
        trying to win girls.
Asiyithandi lento eniyenzayo, musani
ukushela ngathi izintombi.
        We dislike what you are doing, don't use our name when accosting
        girls.

Similarly, the following song by the King Star Brothers (SABC LT 9477, A2) does not admit to the use of countermagic. Instead, the singers use the familiar image of the sea killing its own waves to signal the fact that a powerful performance prevails over the use of magic.

Leader: *Awubheke wendod' emnyama.*
        Look, you sorcerer.
        Yekel' izikhwana zakho.
        Leave your bags behind.
        Nant' ulwandle seluyaqubuda.
        Here is the sea, overwhelming.
        Awubheke wendod' emnyama.
        Look, you sorcerer.
Chorus: *Awubheke wendod' emnyama.*
        Look, you sorcerer.
        Yekel' izikhwana zakho.
        Leave your bags behind.
        Nant' ulwandle seluyaqubuda.
        Here is the sea, overwhelming.
        Awubheke wendod' emnyama.
        Look, you sorcerer.
Bass: *Seluyaqubud'* . . .
        It is overwhelming . . .
Chorus: *Seluyaqubud' ulwandle amagagasi alo.*
        The sea is overwhelming its waves.
Leader: *Thalala.*
        Thalala.
Chorus: *He! Khuluma Nkosi kimi.*
        He! Speak to me, Lord.

In conclusion, isicathamiya performance, like other forms of social practice among South African migrants, intensely queries the dominant power relations in a profoundly antagonistic and oppressive social and political order. But as this chapter has demonstrated, in confronting the alien system, isicathamiya performers not only counterpose a different idea of social order. They also engage with the hegemonic system in numerous ways and often, almost mimetically, do so on the terms and in the figurative language set by the system itself. Opposition and dissent are not some better, purer form of social practice but frequently a variant of the prevailing mode of social interaction. At the same time, the attempts by the nightsong practitioners and their audiences to combat an aggressively competitive world meant to replicate, in a different guise, its very competitive logic. And thus the aesthetics of power and competition that emerges from this oppositional practice as a form of human consciousness and popular culture does not merely respond to or reflect society. It is, in itself, a form of "realistic praxis" (Fabian 1990, 19) that asks questions about society.

9   "Strengthening Native Home Life":

Isicathamiya and Hegemony

In the previous chapter I have shown how isicathamiya, through the anchorage in the home-people system and by dint of the ethos of competition, has been directed at the internal negotiation of power relations among male migrants. The definition of social space—the search for spheres of autonomous social and political action in the face of ever-decreasing choices for South Africa's laboring population and slum dwellers—and the diverse economic and cultural resources to underpin this space, have clearly emerged as the key objectives of isicathamiya performance. This is not to suggest, however, that the nightsongs exist in a social vacuum, untouched by forces outside the narrow perimeter of the migrant world. Quite to the contrary, powerful mechanisms beyond the control of migrants have always had a profound impact on isicathamiya. Two of these we will now have to consider in more detail: the commodification of isicathamiya through concert agents and the recording industry and its political instrumentalization by the media.

Although neither of these forces was in any direct way involved in the processes mediating isicathamiya and the grim world of land shortage, faction fighting, or shabby "hostels," the recording industry and the media, each in its own way, sought to exploit for its own ends the multiple, unpredictable, symbolic, and pragmatic dimensions that make, as we have seen, isicathamiya such a vital form of social practice. This implies, of necessity, that the manipulation of isicathamiya by the forces of domination was never simply a matter of coercion or downright oppression. As we shall see, the commodification of isicathamiya and its appropriation as an instrument of social control depended to a considerable degree on participation and acceptance from its practitioners. Like all forms of popular culture, isicathamiya is an arena in which the dialectic of opposition and consent, structure and agency, is constantly reenacted.

Isicathamiya and the Recording Industry

It was the astute observer of black urban popular culture, Herbert Dhlomo, who first attributed the rise of isicathamiya to the growth of the South African recording industry. The origin of *jazibantshi* music, he wrote in an article, "Evolution of Bantu Entertainments," was a "curious by-product" of the recording companies "that found a huge, profitable market in Bantu music (and) brought about the birth of a national (but undirected and almost unconscious) revival in Bantu forms of art, drama and music."[1] The point has since been reiterated in similar form by a number of other authors (Huskisson 1968, 5). Isicathamiya choirs, as we have seen, have, of course, been in existence since long before the explosive expansion of the local recording industry during the mid-1930s. The point that Dhlomo seemed to be making, however, was not so much that isicathamiya owed its origin to the recording industry. Rather, Dhlomo's account alluded to two more fundamental processes in the further growth of this genre. First, the growing commercial interest in an already flourishing migrant workers' music led to the rise of isicathamiya as the first mass-produced performance style. Second, the undirected nature of this transformation reflected the fragmentary situation in the nascent black entertainment market at the beginning of the 1930s and the uncertain beginnings of a business policy which sought to mold black musical preferences in accordance with the profit interests of private enterprise.

South Africa's recording industry had been producing records for the black listenership from as early as 1908. But until the late 1920s these products were little more than a motley omnium-gatherum of styles, artists, and traditions without any recognizable policy line. Within this assortment migrant workers' rural-traditional genres constituted some of the major categories of recorded material. By the 1930s this kind of music made for probably the largest category in the African catalogues of HMV, Columbia, Gallo, and other labels. Other categories included vaudeville and "coon songs," hymns, and traditional praise-singing by members of the westernized elite. The new, city-born styles, however, such as *marabi* were largely ignored. The reasons for this neglect are not without relevance to the early rise of isicathamiya as a commercial genre. As David Coplan argues, early black producers such as Mark Radebe of Columbia and Griffith Motsieloa of Gallo were members of the black elite who held that *marabi* and other "lowly" shebeen and slumyard types of music did not merit preservation on wax. Moreover, some urban musicians might have been unwilling to compete for their established audience with the gramophone that was increasingly replacing live performances in shebeens (Coplan 1979, 144). It is conceivable that in this situation the industry's interest in migrant performance genres such as isicathamiya represented something of a compromise. Isicathamiya was neither as "lowly" as *marabi* nor quite as traditional as *izibongo* or Chopi *timbila* orchestras that found far fewer buyers than recordings by elite choirs.

Lindi Makhanya who toured extensively with the elite vaudeville troupe Pitch Black Follies under Motsieloa's direction during the 1930s, recalled that the group had to record songs which it considered decidedly declassé and inappropriate for live shows, because Gallo managers saw them as a potential base for profitable mass production. "And it's quite true," she added, "Motsieloa didn't like this, this primitive, these primitive songs, you see. He liked, he went for high class music. But for living, you see, for his living, you see. Like I say the money that came from Gallo had to augment the salaries. They want the music to sell the record and make money. Because the rank and file . . . this music is rank and file."

Thus the early history of recorded isicathamiya seems to be marked by a paradox. While Motsieloa's reservations about "primitive" songs did not exactly further the popularity of isicathamiya, the pressure from the company to sell the music of the "rank and file" in turn failed to produce the desired recognition for the genre. As a glance at the early catalogues of HMV and Gallo reveals, it is this uncertainty of recording policy coupled with the inadequate knowledge of the African market and Motsieloa's elitist views that are responsible for the hesitant attitude until the late 1930s toward more urbanized forms of working-class music such as isicathamiya. In 1930, HMV and Gallo had both sent Reuben T. Caluza and Motsieloa to London to record a series of several hundred records with sacred hymns, *makwaya* material, and traditional songs. These were released in the Yellow Series (with the prefix GU) of His Master's Voice and on the green label (GE) of Gallo. In 1932, HMV followed with a further batch of vaudeville tunes, "coon songs," and traditional material performed by mission-educated choirs like the Bantu Glee Singers, William Mseleku's vaudeville company Amanzimtoti Royal Entertainers, the Aliwal North Sesotho Choir, and the Hope Fountain Native Girls Choir. Gallo expanded its catalogue by further releases of elite vaudeville items by the African's Own Entertainers, John Mavimbela, Lot Dube, Dan Twala and Company, Daniel Marivate, and others. Until 1935, the only more working-class-oriented music featured on this list of high-class music was a series of *ingoma* dance songs performed by the leading *ingoma* team of the time under Mameyiguda Zungu, and a number of concertina pieces played by an unnamed "Zulu Minstrel," both on the HMV label.

Eventually, in 1935, the first commercially recorded example of isicathamiya was released by Gallo as GE 100. The record featured the Humming Bees with "Uya Memeza Umama" and "Itambole Nyoka." The Humming Bees, by present-day criteria, would probably not be regarded as an isicathamiya group or, at best, as a group that sang *isikhunzi*. But in discussions with some of the older nightsong performers, the Humming Bees were regularly named as one of the earliest isicathamiya choirs. After GE100 and the Humming Bees, Gallo issued a small number of discs featuring two of the best known choirs of the time, the Durban Evening Birds and Maktshwa's Choir, but it was not until 1938 that the industry appeared to have undergone a major policy shift. The three major labels, Gallo, Columbia and HMV, released a whole series of recordings featuring the most popular isicathamiya choirs of the time:

Columbia
YE18   Durban Humming Bees
YE40   Philip Msimanga's Zulu Choir
YE42   E. Mkize and his Singing Birds
YE43   E. Mkize and his Singing Birds
YE48   Phillip Msimanga's Zulu Choir
YE51   E. Mkize and his Singing Birds
YE52   Phillip Msimanga's Zulu Choir

Gallo
GE143   Mkatshwa's Choir with the Merry Blackbirds
GE185   Mkatshwa's Choir and Merry Blackbirds
GE186   Cape to Cairo Choir
GE187   Cape to Cairo Choir
GE800   Linda's Evening Birds
GE801   Linda's Evening Birds
GE829   Linda's Evening Birds
GE830   Orlando Flying Birds
GE874   Linda's Evening Birds

HMV
JP4   Durban Humming Bees
JP5   Durban Evening Birds
JP9   Durban Humming Bees
JP10   Durban Evening Birds
JP21   Durban Evening Birds
JP23   Shooting Stars
JP27   Shooting Stars Zulu Choir with Kuzwayo's Band
JP28   Durban Evening Birds

One thing is striking about this list of recorded choirs of 1938. The majority of the Gallo releases feature a choir backed by either an anonymous orchestra or the Merry Blackbirds. JP 27 has the Shooting Stars accompanied by Kuzwayo's Band and—what the rest of the labels do not tell—most of the remaining choirs appear with some kind of instrumental backing of either piano or banjo or both.

The instrumental backing on record of a strictly a cappella genre constituted the most pronounced intervention into performers' autonomy in the
early history of commercial isicathamiya. This practice had started with the
"Uya Memeza Umama" recording of 1935 by the Humming Bees that
featured an unobtrusive backing of piano, guitar, and saxophone. All veteran performers agreed quite unanimously that this practice was an invention of studio engineers and talent scouts that had little to do with their
own concepts of an ideal recording.

These interventions have a great deal to tell us about the marketing
strategies of the companies. Most of the 1938 Gallo releases, as we have
seen, feature an isicathamiya choir backed by the Merry Blackbirds, far and
away the most polished black dance orchestra of the 1930s. Led by saxo-
phonist Peter Rezant this five-piece ensemble included as one of its prominent members the classically trained pianist Emily Motsieloa, the wife of
Griffith Motsieloa (Ballantine 1993, 95–96). Clearly, Gallo's black marketing strategies, Motsieloa's own business acumen, and his role as a high
priest of "high-class music" formed one indivisible whole. The peculiar
marriage of elite dance band sounds with migrant workers' robust songs
about the beauty of rural life was intended to bring isicathamiya music
to financially potent middle-class consumers by making the crusty choral
idiom sound more polished and urbane. At the same time, as David Coplan
points out, members of the black elite hoped that such enterprises would
help to close the widening gap between themselves and the laboring masses
(Coplan 1979, 142).

The 1938 releases must have proved so successful that the major companies soon decided to produce more records of isicathamiya music and to
widen their range of recording artists by adding other choirs to their catalogues. The best known of these novices on the record market were the
Naughty Boys and the Morning Stars, both of which recorded for Decca,
a newcomer on the commercial isicathamiya circuit. Another newcomer,
Better, recorded Isaac Mzobe's well-established Crocodiles (XU 12–14)
and the lesser-known Hamlet's Male Voice Choir (XU 16). But it was
Gallo that took the largest slice. The company released no less than nine
records of Solomon Lind's Evening Birds of which "Mbube" (GE 829)
became by far the greatest success. GE 829 sold so well, indeed, that the
year 1940 saw even more isicathamiya releases. Decca now added the Natal
Champions to its catalogue with at least three records, while Gallo, for
its part, produced further Evening Birds recordings, and in 1940, at least

five records with the Dundee Wandering Singers, as well as a number of records with the Union Express Company and the Orlando Flying Birds. In 1941 record production somewhat ebbed away, and by the end of 1943 war restrictions eventually brought the production of records in South Africa to a complete halt. Production picked up again in 1947, but although in that year and until the late 1940s the number of isicathamiya releases remained at a fairly constant level, the artists were mostly those of the early war years.

How can this gradual stagnation of isicathamiya record sales until the late 1940s be explained? One reason may, of course, have been the industry's relative inability or unwillingness to update its recording personnel and thereby to introduce more novelty into its output. Another, and probably more likely, cause is suggested by the number of releases as compared to unpublished matrixes. In 1939, Gallo probably had only five unreleased recordings on its shelves, but between 1940 and 1942 this figure had risen to twenty-four. Most of these were recordings of the relatively unknown Morning Light Choir which appears never to have recorded again afterward. Clearly, Gallo's sales managers must have been reluctant to increase the production of isicathamiya records, because the market for this type of music was largely saturated.

Another reason for the stagnation was the competition isicathamiya was increasingly experiencing from American swing. The late 1930s, in the opinion of a substantial portion of South Africa's most urbanized black populace, was a period in which cities like Johannesburg were about to develop a Harlem of their own, with their own South African pendants to Fats Waller, Duke Ellington, and Coleman Hawkins (Ballantine 1993). The audiences of these South African Nicholas Brothers and Mills Brothers—jazzmen like Solomon "Zuluboy" Cele, Wilfred Sentso, the vocal quartet Manhattan Brothers—were by no means restricted to the urban elite alone. For even migrants, as we have seen in the report by the Manhattan Brothers' Dambuza Mdledle, were perfectly au fait with a tune such as "Walking My Baby Back Home." Furthermore, the overall similarity in musical sound was enhanced by parallel song topics. To the young buck fresh from the countryside there was probably no real difference between walking one's baby home and "waiting for Dudu at the station."

It is this convergence of styles which probably accounts for yet another attempt by the recording industry to fuse isicathamiya with some of the more up-tempo urban genres. Sometime around 1953, Decca studio staff began experimenting with ways to back the Danger Express Choir by adding percussive effects. The surviving twelve matrixes (ABC. 10287–10297, 10299) of this session show the choir singing in typical *'mbombing* fashion. On some of these (ABC 10287), the Danger Express Choir is accompanied by a set of rattles and claves providing, among others, standard swing patterns. The Decca test recordings were, however, never released and although audiences continued to relish the related qualities of both male vocal swing ensembles and isicathamiya choirs, the latter stubbornly refused to admit instrumental accompaniment into their music. And, as we have seen in chapter 3, it was not until the late 1960s that the first successful fusion of isicathamiya singing and electric guitar backing led to the emergence of a genre in its own right: *umgqashiyo*.

All of this raises, of course, the question of how popular this type of music really was and how its commercial success intertwined with marketing strategies, artistic quality, and listeners' tastes. Unfortunately, no concrete sales figures for this early period are available, but an idea of the tremendous popularity of these discs can perhaps be gained from the advertising strategies adopted by Gallo. Thus the release of "Mbube" in 1939 was not only remembered by most of the older interviewees as having happened during the first year of the "Hitler war." Gallo was also remembered for having installed a loudspeaker on a truck that patrolled the townships, blaring "Mbube" and other hits of the day into the streets. And Lindi Makhanya sneeringly related that Gallo-sponsored concerts by the Pitch Black Follies had to feature renderings of Linda's "Mbube" in order to boost the company's sales figures of that record. And, finally, even more curiously, the skit "T.B." recorded by the Dundee Wandering Singers in 1941 featured "Mbube" which was played from a gramophone in the rear of the studio (1757, Unissued). The massive campaign for Linda's group initiated a pattern which continues to characterize commercial sales strategies as well as the preferences of the isicathamiya-record-buying public up to the present.

From 1950, things started to look considerably brighter for isicathamiya recording artists. More and more recordings appeared, new labels emerged, and younger choirs began replacing the big ones of the prewar isicathamiya scene like Linda's Evening Birds. But this increase has to be seen in proportion to the growing numbers of migrants in the cities after the war and the relative rise of wage levels. It does not reflect a growing popularity of isicathamiya as such. The general decline of nonelectric, vocal music continued unabated, and by the late 1950s and early 1960s, isicathamiya, as Joseph Shabalala phrased it, had "nearly died."

The reasons for this slow death can only be sought for in the more complex interplay of broader socioeconomic forces with the development of the recording industry, the growth of broadcasting, and other factors. Regrettably, we do not as yet possess any quantifiable data on the basis of which these processes might be evaluated. One of the factors, however, to which the declining popularity of recorded isicathamiya can be attributed, is the absence of any sustained promotion after the late 1950s. Up to that date, isicathamiya records had benefited from the same promotional strategies as the other major genres of recorded music.

But if the attraction of isicathamiya as a mass-produced genre began to fade during the 1960s, it survived largely because of the confluence of two factors: Ladysmith Black Mambazo and the South African Broadcasting Corporation (SABC). The enormous influence of Ladysmith Black Mambazo, as I have suggested in chapter 3, was based on Joseph Shabalala's skillful manipulation of the stylistic conventions of the genre by merging it with elements from other traditions. The heightened intertextuality in his songs was made possible by and in turn fostered the explosive growth of broadcasting for black audiences in the 1960s. It is to this process, to the history and politics of Radio Bantu, that we must now turn.

Isicathamiya and the Media

In chapter 8 I attempted to show how the construction of alternative spaces of social action did not eliminate conflict and inequity from migrant performers' practice. Rather, I described performance as an important arena in which models of social reality are developed which, while being opposed to the prevailing system of power relations, nevertheless are not free from domination as such. In this section I shall explore how this dialectic of consent and dissent intersects with the South African state-controlled media's attempts at manufacturing popular consent with the policies of oppression and apartheid.

Media construct images of reality. Produced and tightly controlled from above as they clearly are in South Africa, such images mostly reveal something about how the ruling class wishes the oppressed to perceive the world. A brief glance at the history of the SABC confirms this quite clearly.[2]

From the information available about the early years of African broadcast-ing, it appears that the ideological rationale behind these broadcasts was to "strengthen Native home life and to keep at home young Natives living in towns, who, for want of entertainment in the evenings, wander about the streets in search of some form of diversion and thus get into mischief." In addition, these programs were designed "to counteract the warped and dangerous doctrines which are being propagated assiduously by agitators among Natives throughout the country and particularly in urban areas."[3] Significantly, although a rediffusion service had been inaugurated from the early 1940s, it was only available to compound and "hostel" residents. Transmitted via the English and Afrikaans channels, short programs in isiZulu, Xhosa, and Sesotho were broadcast on three mornings of the week. Little is known about the contents of these programs and in 1945, in any case, the entire service was suspended (Hayman and Tomaselli 1989, 39). It only resumed in 1947, by which time there were two "African pro-grammes" per week, broadcast on Tuesday and Thursday mornings from 9:45 to 10:15 A.M. Two typical half-hour programs involving isicathamiya choirs were a "Zulu Marabi Programme" on 18 November 1947 with the Evening Birds and the Sons of Zululand and a "Programme of Zulu Songs (Marabi-Mbube-Traditional)" on 2 December 1947, featuring the Natal Junior Champions under Solomon Ngcobo, accompanied by Merry Black-birds pianist Emily Motsieloa. The items in the program as listed by the weekly *Bantu World*, were as follows:

1. "Ilizwe," Zulu (traditional)
2. "Singabalap'eskalweni" (Here we are), Euro-Zulu (traditional)
3. "Balekani" (Flee), Zulu (traditional)
4. "Ngo ngo ngo" (Knock knock) Zulu (traditional)
5. "Mbube" (The lion), Zulu (traditional)
6. "Ingwenyama" (The crocodile), Zulu (traditional)
7. "Bonani" (Look), Zulu (traditional)[4]

Other programs, broadcast daily from the Durban studios under their di-rector Hugh Tracey, featured a similar blend of traditional material and *makwaya* music. In addition to live transmissions by the Dundee Wander-ing Singers, the Crocodiles, the Humming Bees, and other lesser Dur-ban choirs, regular use was made of commercial 78 rpm discs, including the following isicathamiya titles: "Yetulisigqoko" (GE 887) and "Sangena Mama" (GE 877) by Solomon Linda and the Evening Birds, and "Bash-obha Upickup" (GE 883) by the Dundee Wandering Singers (Tracey

1948, 6). In addition to such commercial recordings, transcription records had been in use since the days of the African Broadcasting Corporation (ABC), but it was only in 1948 that the SABC began pressing multiple copies of original program material (Hayman and Tomaselli 1989, 33ff.). Surviving discs from this era, for example, recordings made in 1947 of Nontombi Dhlamini's Opera Stars (M12089) singing Zulu songs such as "Ngangithi Uyangithanda" and "Nkonyana Ye Ndhlovu" show that the SABC had selected predominantly traditional material for its black listenership.

Eventually, by 1952, the total air time for isiZulu, Xhosa, and Sesotho had risen to sixteen hours a day and by the late 1950s, more than sixty thousand rediffusion systems had been installed in Soweto households (Hayman and Tomaselli 1989, 51, 80), too small a number for the successful expansion of the system. Although some experiments with AM broadcasts were made, it was not until 1960 that a nationwide FM service was introduced. In the following year, full-blown services in the major African languages were finally inaugurated. Radio Bantu, as the collective services were called, started operating on 1 January 1962, and within less than a decade had grown into one of the most powerful radio stations on the African continent. By 1974 it was estimated that 97.7 percent of South Africa's black population had access to a radio and listened to Radio Bantu.

Throughout the 1960s and 1970s, as Keyan and Ruth Tomaselli point out, Radio Bantu set itself the task of imbuing black South Africans with the belief in the homelands as viable repositories of communal development. At the same time, the apartheid radio sought to socialize a smaller sector of the urban population into a work ethic compatible with the demands of capital for skilled manpower.[5] Traditional music, as Charles Hamm notes in a brilliant discussion of black broadcasting, seemed ideal for these ideological imperatives of Radio Bantu. "Theoretically," he writes, "no music could emphasize the separate identity of each 'tribe' more emphatically than a repertory dating from a time when, according to the mythology of Separate Development, each 'tribal' group formed a discrete cultural and political entity" (Hamm 1991, 160–61). Accordingly, as the SABC's annual reports of the early 1960s show, immense efforts were being made to record traditional music both in the studios and through mobile recording units. Thus, close on ten thousand recordings had been accumulated by 1964, and if the serial matrix numbers of SABC transcription records offer any viable indication of the quantity of items recorded, the number of recordings realized up to the late 1960s and early 1970s, in a conservative estimate, can be put at more than one hundred thousand. Of course, the vast majority of these were items of traditional and choral music (fig. 14). As for their needs in the category of "light Bantu music," as it was called, the SABC program makers relied on the commercially available repertoire. And this need intensified proportionally with the realization that more was required to persuade the black urban listenership of the benefits of Separate Development than the sounds and lore of the country-side. Thus, by the late 1960s, the bulk of Radio Bantu air time devoted to music consisted of popular music of every description, provided it succeeded in attracting as many listeners as possible and did not subvert, in content or association, the goals of Separate Development.[6]

Much, if not all, of the music policy of the Radio Bantu era was formulated by two highly influential broadcasters: Yvonne Huskisson and Alexius Buthelezi. The former had received training of sorts in ethnomusicology—her Ph.D. dissertation, "Social and Ceremonial Music of the Pedi," was written before she rose to the position of an organizer for the music programs of Radio Bantu in 1962. Among her published work is a peculiar compendium, *The Bantu Composers of Southern Africa* (Huskisson 1969), in which she compiled detailed biographical information predominantly on the composers of *makwaya* choral music. A self-styled "musical mentor" and "pivot of Black music in South Africa," who made a "contribution towards preserving the identity of the Black peoples whilst helping to ease their transition to a White civilization," Huskisson's influence was enormous.[7] And as a kind of Hendrik Verwoerd of music, she cultivated a peculiar pseudophilosophical blend of patronizing traditionalism and apartheid ideology, claiming that "each nation . . . finds its aesthetic satisfaction in musical sounds which differ, more or less, from those of other nations." The growing urbanization of black South Africans notwithstanding, she concluded, "sooner or later the innate must manifest itself, finding much lacking in music based on other people's thoughts" (Huskisson 1969, xxii).

Alexius Buthelezi had been appointed announcer in the Zulu Service in Johannesburg in 1961. He was a Vryheid-born man who had spent most of his childhood at Pomeroy in the Msinga district. It is here that he also came into contact with Solomon Linda and his music when the latter returned to his home over the Christmas holidays and organized major isicathamiya competitions. One of the most successful programs started by Buthelezi at the SABC and one that he is best remembered for even today, was called "Cothoza Mfana." Starting in 1961, the weekly show was

Figure 14. SABC transcription record. Courtesy Veit Erlmann.

broadcast at first from the Johannesburg studios only. However, the show proved immensely popular, and so by 1970 two additional programs, broadcast from Durban, were added. The term "Cothoza Mfana" had been coined by Buthelezi himself and described the catlike movements performed by the choirs on stage. Although dubs of these early broadcasts could not be located, older isicathamiya practitioners fondly recall the mixture of music, concert announcements, and quizzes about the history of isicathamiya that made up the show. As a signature tune, Buthelezi had chosen "Cothoza Mfana," a tune composed by Gershon Mcanyana and his Scorpions (fig. 15) that describes the atmosphere in the SABC recording studio (SABC LT 6765, A4, reissued on Rounder Records CO 5025, track 14).

Bass: *Cothoza mfana.*
     Tiptoe, boy!
Chorus: *Cothoza mfana siyanisakazela.*
     Tiptoe, boy, we are broadcasting.
Bass: *Thela wayeka.*
     Music is galore.
Chorus: *Thela wayek'.*
     Music is galore.
     Yek' ungahleka siyanisakazela.
     Don't laugh, we are broadcasting.

In 1976, television was introduced in South Africa, with a black channel, called TV2/3, being added in 1982. Although not a "Radio Bantu with pictures," as Keyan Tomaselli and others argue, TV2/3 nevertheless in its serials followed a "back to the homelands" policy, while the magazine/documentary programs concentrated on the self-development of the black urban middle classes.[8] In the beginning, a fair amount of air time was devoted to traditional performance, including isicathamiya choirs, but the corporation had to reduce the amount of time allotted to such material following unfavorable opinion polls and critical press reports. Thus, only 1 percent of the Soweto viewers of TV2/3 favored classical/traditional music programs, while *mbube* shows were castigated as a monumental bore. Isicathamiya choirs were said to perform for thirty minutes solid without a break, using the same stage and lighting design. In addition, there was criticism that many choirs were given unnecessary repeats, and although the groups changed their uniforms, they could not change their voices and faces.[9]

Figure 15. Scorpions. Courtesy Veit Erlmann.

There can be little doubt, then, that isicathamiya, during the 1960s and 1970s at least, enjoyed disproportionately privileged attention from SABC broadcasters. But how did the performers themselves and their audiences respond to the SABC's interest in their art? From all accounts, it appears that in the studio, the SABC's ideological straitjackets translated into a rigid censoring practice and a patronizing style of interaction between studio staff and the choirs. The first and biggest target of SABC censorship was language, the linguistic purity of the Zulu language in particular. English and Afrikaans borrowed words, themselves the products of more than a century of contact between precolonial and urban industrial society, were replaced by invented, more traditional sounding terms: a deliberately constructed vernacular lexicon mediating apartheid through tribal imagery.[10]

An example of such contorted perspectives on everyday township linguistic practice and the SABC's attempts to correct it, is provided by Crocodiles leader Enoch Mzobe. Discussing his song "Uyaphi" (Where are you going) (SABC LT 8765, B4) Mzobe recalled with acrimony how SABC studio staff objected to the use of the term "emashebeen." The song is about a shebeen near the Wemmer "hostel" in Johannesburg called *Ilangamo*. But although Mzobe's song, in line with apartheid liquor laws, warns his fellow workers about the risk of being arrested at the illegal drinking site, he was asked to replace "emashebeen" with "etshwaleni" (beer hall).

Another area to which SABC broadcasters responded with particular fastidiousness, was that of their own status and practices. Thus, again, Enoch Mzobe recalled one of his compositions in which he sang about radio announcers. "At that time I was still in Johannesburg," he explained. "I thought I was praising myself. The song started by greeting announcers and calling them by their names. Then in the middle of the song I would say I greet the Johannesburg radio announcers and I'm leaving the greetings of Durban announcers to those isicathamiya groups in Durban. The SABC didn't like that. They asked me why I didn't extend greetings to those in Durban and I said I'm leaving it to groups in Durban. In a way I was trying to encourage Durban groups to compose and record a song praising and greeting Durban announcers." On a similar issue, Scorpions leader Gershon Mcanyana had to find out that his song "Bayajabula" (SABC LT 10 247, B4) was objectionable, because it quoted broadcaster Maqhawe Mkhize with one of his favorite expressions of joy and gratitude: "Ngizokuhlabela inkawu!" (I would give you monkey meat). "He was a comedian," said Mcanyana. "So in the song I wanted to say 'I will give you monkey meat, says Maqhawe.' Because I had a lot of followers. So when I arrived at the competition hall, I would be well applauded and gain many fans. As a result it came to my mind one day that I wished I could give my fans something in return, like 'killing a monkey for them' (killing a beast) as a thanksgiving gesture to my fans. But they censored that line. They said it wouldn't sound right and suggested that I say 'I would slaughter a goat for them.'"

By far the most cutting intervention, however, into the lyric fabric of studio-recorded isicathamiya songs aimed at the very heart of the night-song tradition: the attainment of *ubuqhawe* through the expression of competitive elan and fighting spirit. The recorded version of Enoch Mzobe's song "Bavimbeni" (SABC LT 10 157, A1), for instance, shows how astute the censors were in picking up the associations with stick-fighting that the song plays upon. "The initial title of the song was 'Catch them, stop them,'" Mzobe commented on the genesis of the song. "But the SABC suggested that we say 'keep them away, keep them away'" and now the meaning is lost. I would say to my group 'let us catch them,' meaning that they shouldn't surpass us in singing. Then later one would say 'no let's have them,' meaning 'let's have them, they are dangerous.' You know, in the farms there was a game we used to play. Men would be sitting inside the house and suddenly we would chase the women. Then there would be stick-fighting, as a game and also to teach young boys how to fight with the sticks. Now it is 'keep them away, keep them away.' We don't know how we should keep them away. The meaning is lost. You see when making a record like at Gallo records we didn't have problems of censorship. We sang anything."

The most annoying aspect of SABC censorship, however, was the fact that all the changes requested had to be made on the spot. As Gershon Mcanyana remarked, "You know, I would have preferred it if they had told us to attend to mistakes they had pointed out and record that song some other day. But they wanted us to change it on the spot and that was hard to do. This is what put us off with the SABC. Instead of saying we should go rectify the mistakes and keep the song for future recording they will want us to change it on the spot. And that really put us off. This embittered me very much, because it would come as a surprise to me."

From the examples quoted it should be equally clear that behind these autocratic and seemingly capricious interventions stood, in fact, a calculated policy of emphasizing the alleged communal nature of black society.

What in SABC parlance was proclaimed as a "rendering of service to the community," in practice meant that the lives and cultural practices of black South Africans were to be portrayed as being harmoniously embedded in integrated, self-contained, and content "communities"—a world in and unto itself, scrupulously to be sequestered from white civilization. Any hint of internal dissent, even if it was expressed in the most innocuous form such as in isicathamiya competitive lyrics, was to be scrupulously avoided.

But for all the staff interference and censoring, isicathamiya performers for the most part identified with the SABC and eagerly sought to obtain studio bookings and air time. Alison Gumbi's Easy Walkers even changed their name to SABC Easy Walkers. Other choirs composed songs in praise of particular radio announcers, such as the King Star Brothers in their song "Kwaphinda Kwenzeka" (It has happened again) (L4 BOL (EO)313, A3):

Leader: *Yeh! We baba hey!*
        Yeh! Father, hey!
Chorus: *Yeh! We baba hey!*
        Yeh! Father, hey!
Leader: *Mfana wami, mfowethu, yeh, wendoda.*
        My boy, brother, yeh, man!
Chorus: *Kwaphinda kwenzeka.*
        It has happened again.
Leader: *Kodwa nje . . .*
        But now . . .
Chorus: *Kungasaqali wemfo ka Nzimande.*
        It is not the first time you have done it, Mr. Nzimande.
        Sisho kuwe mfo ka Nzimande.
        We are talking to you, Mr. Nzimande.
        Sithi bheka emoyeni.
        We say: Look in the air!
        Sakazela abalaleli.
        Broadcast for the listeners!
Bass: *Wi-wi-wi.*
        Wi-wi-wi.
Chorus: *Yeh! Khuluma Nkosi kimi.*
        Yeh! Speak to me, Lord!

At present, isicathamiya has all but disappeared from radio and TV. Only "Ezodumo" (The hits), a weekly TV show hosted by Welcome Nzi-

mande on what is now called the CCV channel, was still devoted to traditional music of various kinds, including isicathamiya. Similarly, isicathamiya
sounds have recently also been used as background music in TV commer-
cials for sorghum beer and other products targeted at predominantly rural
consumers.

10   Things Will Come Right: The Political
Economy of Noncommercial Performance

Ukuhlabelela kuyamthokozisa odabukileyo.
Singing brings joy to the distressed.

Cup and Saucer

My treatment of isicathamiya performance in the last five chapters has shown how migrant workers have devised an extraordinary range of alternative spaces that connect them in multiple ways with the dominant structure and, at the same time, enable them to disengage themselves from the oppressive effects of the alien order. From choir uniforms and song texts to choreography and the internal organization of choirs, the symbolics and pragmatics of performance were shown to be equally driven by the desire to invest the elements of the hegemonic society with positive meaning and agency as well as by an attempt to mobilize the meanings of the past as a protective shield against the invading forces of the present. It is now time to conclude this section by exploring a domain of space building that only recently began to play a prominent role in the politics of isicathamiya: the organization of choirs in regional associations.

This discussion will return us to an aspect of the social organization of isicathamiya performance that was discussed in chapter 5. There I argued that the social relationships at work inside many choirs had much in common with the networks of "home people" that structure numerous aspects of migrant life throughout southern Africa. But, I added, these networks were not a grid that could be superimposed on all choirs without distinction. In this chapter I pursue this argument by showing that these new associations are not simply modern extensions of the home-people-based choirs, but rather represent an attempt to maintain the autonomy of isicathamiya in the face of the growing commodification of social relations and, hence, of a declining popularity of noncommercial forms of expressive culture. Most of all, these associations provide conviviality and sociability among migrant workers and secure a stable financial basis for ongoing performance activities through the raising of capital on a rotating credit basis.

Although performers insisted that it was "love of music" rather than monetary interest that made them sing isicathamiya, the proper functioning of a choir requires an extraordinary expenditure not only of time and energy, but, above all, of money. The uniforms have to be purchased, dry-cleaned, and kept in mint condition throughout the year. Choirs travel to and from competition venues, membership fees have to be paid, and at times individual members need to be supported. Unlike top groups such as Ladysmith Black Mambazo, King Star Brothers, and Empangeni Home Tigers, few if any of the lesser-known choirs are in a position to generate these funds from performing in concerts alone. And, to be sure, not one of the choirs that have recorded commercially, Ladysmith Black Mambazo again being the exception, has been known for receiving fees or royalties of any kind. This situation has, of course, been the dominant practice in the South African entertainment industry for much of its existence since the early 1920s. It was, however, aggravated by the general decline in popularity of isicathamiya. Moreover, as alternative sources of income such as concerts began to dry up, most choirs had to think of other means of keeping themselves afloat. It is thus that isicathamiya associations came into being.

My hypothesis is indebted in part, of course, to some of the interesting work on African social transformation that emerged in the 1950s from the British school of social anthropology. Among the more invigorating theoretical insights of such classic studies as Michael Banton's work on Free-town (1957), Kenneth Little's article on West African voluntary associations (1957), and J. Clyde Mitchell's seminal *Kalela Dance* (1956) was the argument that the cultural practices and institutions of migrants—the dance clubs, saving clubs, burial societies, and similar voluntary associations—are to be seen as modifications of African traditional institutions and form part of frameworks in which to resolve the dilemmas or urban life. This line of thought was pursued, in the South African context, by Brian Du Toit (1969), Kuper and Kaplan in their studies of *stokvel* and *mahodisana* (1944), and by Martin West in his book on Soweto independent churches (1975).[1]

Where Banton, Little, and others were primarily concerned with the types and functions of voluntary associations, some social historians, for their part, have been inclined to overemphasize the oppositional ideologies of such communal practices. William Beinart and Philip Bonner, to name but two recent examples, have discovered in various forms of migrants' associations the resilient and richly expressive strategies of resistance against proletarianization (Beinart 1987, 1991; Bonner 1990; Mayer 1980). Both theoretical models complement each other and need to be taken into consideration if we are to understand the working of voluntary associations in the 1980s.

Stokvels, in particular, as a recent study by Khehla Lukhele shows (1990), have become a vibrant form of voluntary association and a major factor of the South African economy. A National Stokvels Association of South Africa was formed in 1988 representing the interests of more than twenty-four thousand credit associations in the metropolitan areas of the country, with monthly contributions averaging R 52 million. Thus, far from being the survival strategies and sites of proletarian resistance they used to be, informal savings schemes have grown into powerful agents—to use the rhetoric of "black economic empowerment"—of black entrepreneurship and black purchasing power.

In this chapter I shall shift the focus of analysis and concentrate on the pragmatic and expressive dimensions of the migrants' politics of self-fashioning and self-representation. In particular, I shall examine the origin, concept, and the politics of three choral associations and suggest explanations for their links with other types of voluntary associations in South African society. To round off my account, a fourth association, the South African Traditional Music Association (SATMA) will be discussed at the end of this chapter.

Three Isicathamiya Associations

Two of the associations I shall discuss on the following pages are based in Durban—one at the Dalton Road "hostel," the other at the Glebe "hostel"—while the third association operates on the East Rand. There exist many more associations on the Witwatersrand such as the Benoni Association as well as smaller associations based at Durban's YMCA hall and the Promotion Hall in downtown Johannesburg. The association at Dalton Road does not have a name, but its origins reach back to at least 1976 when its present chairman, Paulos Mfuphe, withdrew from active performance to take care of the competitions that had been taking place at this venue for a long time. The Mfuphes are graybeards of isicathamiya, Paulos's father having performed with the Morning Stars as early as 1928. The association is a small organization with only eleven member choirs: the King of Mountain; Royal Messengers; City Walkers; Home Rovers; New Morning Stars; Heavy Stars; Greytown Evening Birds; Mtwalume Young Aces; Natal Express; High Stars; and Easy Walkers. The Glebe association, for its part, was founded in the early 1980s by Solomon Ndlovu, a shopkeeper and hairdresser. Its member choirs in 1988 were the Nongoma Morning Stars;

Kings Boys; Cup and Saucer; Jabula Home Defenders *A;* Jabula Home Defenders *B;* Assembly of God; White Water; Harding Morning Stars; Natal Universal; and Durban City Boys. The East Rand Cothoza Music Association, finally, is the youngest and the largest of the three associations. It was formed in 1978 in Thokoza, a township south of Johannesburg, under the name Thokoza Cothoza Mfana Music Association. Its founder, chairman, and, in fact, its very soul from the start has been Henry Mdladla, a full-time organizer of Inkatha's trade union UWUSA. The Magogo-born Mdladla (Nkandla District) had been an ardent isicathamiya performer from as early as 1954 when he lived in Johannesburg's Wemmer "hostel" and attended weekend shows at the Bantu Sports recreation grounds. When the Thokoza township was built in 1960, Mdladla gained access to the hall on Khumalo Street and began organizing regular competitions that attracted even such audience favorites as King Star Brothers and Ladysmith Black Mambazo. In the 1980s the association was divided into branches, each of which controlled a particular performance venue. The following halls, each with their own member choirs, were affiliated with the Thokoza Cothoza Mfana Music Association: Benoni Hall, Phokwe Hall, Church Hall, Mavimbela Hall, Tsolo Hall, Mahasaba Hall, Kjwesine Hall and D. H. Williams Hall. During the early 1980s the number of registered member choirs rose steadily from forty-eight to eighty-six, but in 1985 some fifteen choirs seceded from the parent body to form the Benoni Association. The remaining seventy choirs regrouped themselves as the East Rand Cothoza Music Association and continued to participate in a multitude of competitions, concerts, and training courses until Henry Mdladla suffered a serious car accident in 1987. Although he has since recovered, the association never really overcame the prolonged absence of its chairman and has since been lingering in a vacuum.

Organizations like the East Rand Cothoza Music Association, as I have indicated, provide shielded zones of interaction between migrants that are highly structured and yet unrestrained by the law of the here and now. Such associations construct spaces that, while being unhinged from the control of the dominant order, nevertheless reflect its logic. To understand this, we will now have to examine the functioning of these associations. It appears that at least in the three associations considered here, the activities center on the raising of capital and income for the member choirs, on the control of venues and the maintenance of a certain order within them, on the provision of support and solidarity, and on the links with the wider community.

As is well known, voluntary associations work on a rotating credit principle. During each cycle, each member becomes a creditor once and a debtor as many times as there are members. In other words, the funds a host obtains are only a loan which he must return by eventually becoming a creditor himself. All three isicathamiya associations, with minor variations, are based on this principle. The East Rand Cothoza Music Association, for instance, has adopted a rotating principle whereby member choirs take turns as beneficiaries of a competition's total cash income. For every competition each choir pays a joining fee or member fee (*imali yamaqembu*) of R 30 and an additional R 2 per singer. Together with the spectators' entrance fee, the gate (*imali yasemnyango*), and after all expenses such as prizes, transport (*imali yemoto*), and adjudicators' honoraria (*imali yejaji*) have been deducted, this money is paid out to the hosting choir.

The Glebe association under its chairman Solomon Ndlovu and the Dalton association chaired by Paulos Mfuphe have adopted a similar, if slightly more complicated, system. Upon entry for the competition, each choir pays a joining fee (*imali wejoyini*) of R 2 and R 15 respectively, but each time a choir wishes to take the stage during the more informal *prakthisa* section of the evening, extra money, the request fee, is payable. In the case of the Glebe association the request fee ranges from R .50 to R 20 depending on the length of time spent on stage, while at Dalton a lump sum of R 25 must be paid. The request fee is designed to enable the fans in the audience to see their favorite choir onstage and is reminiscent of the *khonsati* procedure described in the Msane-Kambule sketch "Ikoňsati eBantu Sport" quoted in chapter 3. More often than not, however, the request fee is paid by members of the choirs themselves. To this are added the returns from the gate as well as the revenue from a small restaurant that operates in a room next to the hall. After the expenses for the restaurant, hire of the hall, and especially the prizes have been deducted from this gross income, the net profit is paid out to the hosting choir. The extra revenue from the gate and requests is, at the same time, the only way of raising extra capital. In addition to the funds that circulate on a weekly basis, the associations also raise annual subscription fees and penalties which are used for advertising and other purposes.

Table 2 shows the financial transactions of the Glebe association from 9 June 1984 to 8 June 1985. During this twelve-month period competitions had been organized on most weekends except during January and parts of December and February. These are the months when most migrants take their annual leave and return to their families. There were five

Table 2 Financial Transactions, Glebe Association, 1984–85

Record	Gate	Kitchen	Request	Joining	1984 Total	Expense	Prizes	Net	Part
June:									
Chairman	110	185	244	...	539	...	535	...	15
Natal Universal	96	189	228	30	543	...	97	446	15
Hall	35	81	27	...	143	76	67	67	9
July:									
Kings Boys	115	389	70	40	614	...	135	479	20
Cup and Saucer	66	310	209	34	619	25	109	485	17
Heavy Violence	64	202	114	24	404	25	78	301	13
Harding Morning Stars	62	177	197	26	462	25	74	363	13
August:									
Durban City	74	172	139	20	405	35	65	305	10
Chairman	45	120	44	12	221	25	39	157	6
Jabula Home Defenders	112	92	128	28	360	25	91	244	14
Natal Universal	59	131	145	20	355	25	65	265	10
September:									
Cup and Saucer	81	188	146	16	431	25	52	354	8
Kings Boys	192	107	146	24	469	25	78	366	11
Jabula Home Defenders	70	118	115	14	317	...	78	239	8
Heavy Violence	63	148	151	20	382	...	65	317	10
October:									
Chairman	74	135	109	26	344	25	84	235	13
Owenhlangano [Assembly]	62	100	80	24	266	...	78	188	12
Harding Morning Stars	68	...	166	24	258	78	13	167	?
Durban City	82	190	165	24	461	25	75	361	12

November:									
Natal Universal	68	161	103	10	342	35	26	281	4
Kings Boys	177	188	137	22	524	...	71	453	11
Cus and Saucer	71	162	129	16	378	...	52	326	8
Jabula Home Defenders	88	145	284	517	...	170	347	...	?
December:									
Harding Morning Stars	73	206	134	28	441	...	91	350	14
Indiva	110	142	96	26	374	...	84	290	13
					1985				
February:									
Chairman	47	86	61	23	217	48	27	142	?
Chairman	68	150	158	...	376	52	324	...	9
March:									
Cup and Saucer	101	237	103	95	536	35	84	417	13
Kings Boys	81	174	165	24	444	35	81	328	12
Jabula Home Defenders A	45	216	190	28	479	35	97	349	16
Harding Morning Stars	89	202	212	30	533	...	97	436	15
White Water	72	178	156	32	438	...	104	334	17
April:									
Umfolosi	66	154	172	22	414	...	71	343	11
Assembly of God	100	207	167	24	498	...	78	420	12
Nongoma Morning Stars	96	207	167	24	494	...	78	416	12
May:									
Chairman	123	213	262	...	598	...	97	501	15
Cup and Saucer	22	225	171	22	440	...	71	369	11
Wendiva	56	87	56	...	199	64	44	91	6
Jabula Home Defenders A	84	229	218	28	559	...	91	468	14
June:									
Nongoma Morning Stars	134	223	189	24	570	...	78	492	12

Figure 16. Membership card, East Rand Cothoza Music Association. Courtesy Veit Erlmann.

"rounds," as the cycles are called that all member choirs have to run through as creditors before reaching another chance of getting a "record," as a choir's turn as debtor is called. Apart from documenting the substantial sums circulating within what after all appears to be a fairly small body, these figures are impressive as a testimony to the communal spirit that unites isicathamiya performers. Like the motto "Koye Kulunge" (Things will come right) and the rising sun in the logo of the East Rand Cothoza Music Association (fig. 16), the figures speak of a sustained desire to transcend the divisions that are so endemic in the competitive environment labor migrants are forced to live in.

Further evidence of this communal ethos is provided by the constitutions which all three associations have given themselves. One representative example of this, the one adopted by the East Rand Cothoza Music Association, is reproduced in its entirety.

> East Rand Cothoza Music Association
> SECOND AMENDMENT
> 1. The name of the Association shall be known as East Rand Cothoza Music.
> 2. The Head-Office shall be situated at no. 54 Khumalo Street, THOKOZA.

3. The Executive shall be constituted as follows:
   i)   President.
   ii)   Chairman.
   iii) Vice-Chairman.
   iv)   Secretary General.
   v)   Assistant Secretary.
   vi)   Treasurer.
   vii) Vice-Treasurer.
   viii) Chairman in charge of Halls.
   ix)   Secretaries in charge of Halls.
4. AIMS AND OBJECTS OF THE ASSOCIATION:
   i)   To promote Love, and the development of Mbube Classic among Black Nations
   ii)   To maintain and enhance this type of National Music as to last for generations
   iii) To defend and protect the interest of the Musicians partaking in this type of Music, who are Foreigners.
5. THE REGISTRATION AND AFFILIATION OF MEMBERSHIP:
   i)   Each Choir shall contribute a sum of R 5.00 (Five Rand), as a Registration Fee, at the beginning of each Year (Payable at the beginning of every year).
   ii)   At the beginning of each and every year, choirs that are registered may or are entitled to open or use the Hall under which they are registered. The Hall shall be open for use, when all choirs have renewed their Registration, as well as new affiliates.
   iii) Whenever the Competitions are staged the choirs shall contribute a fee amounting to R 5.00 (Five Rand).
         N.B. It shall be increased to R 30.00 on condition that it is a Special Competition, or the Prize money is set at R 300.00 (Three Hundred Rand).
   iv)   Only Registered choirs shall participate and perform at Associate Halls.
   v)   Choirs other than those from the East Rand could participate after obtaining permission from the Chairman of the Hall concerned. Alternatively when a choir is invited to participate, all prior preparations shall be done by the Hosts.
   vi)   East Rand Choirs shall participate in competition with cash reward or prize money only.
6. An entry of R 2.00 shall be payable per individual on all daily per-

formances and, on special performances, R 3.00 shall become payable per individual.

7. All groups shall pay a joining fee prior to their entry at the Hall where they are expected to perform.

8. In the event of a dispute, discontent, fight, all groups shall be refunded. But if one of the contestants is the cause of the fighting, dispute, discontent, the choir he represents shall forfeit their funds. The individual or individuals shall face a Disciplinary Committee. He will neither represent his choir nor partake in any other contest, until he has faced and resulted in his not being found guilty by the Disciplinary Committee.

9. PRIZES:

Prizes by the Association shall be defined as follows:

Groups from One (1) up to Ten (10) shall be eligible for 1st Prizes, in the event of their participation at any given competition.

Groups shall be eligible for Second Prize from group Eleven (11) up to Fifteen (15). Groups from Sixteen up to Twenty-Four (24) shall qualify for the 3rd. prizes, groups from Twenty-Five upward will qualify for Fourth Prizes.

10. MEETINGS AND ELECTIONS:
    i)   The Executive Meetings shall be convened once quarterly (Per Three Months).
    ii) General Meetings shall be held three times annually, i.e. February, May and October.
    iii) Emergency Meetings:
         An emergency meeting can if necessary be convened either by the Executive or General
    iv) Annual General Elections:
         An Annual General Meeting to elect the Officers shall be held once a year.

11. FINES/PENALTIES AFFECTING REGISTERED MEMBERS:
    11:1. A choir that behaves in an unbecoming, or violent manner that might lead to bloodshed, will be banned from all Competitions, until it faces the disciplinary Committee, which shall then decide on the matter.
    11:2. Fines or Penalties depend on the merits of the case.
    11:3. From Fifty Rand (R 50.00) to Four Hundred Rand (R 400.00) or more, these penalties are decided by the Executive.
    11:4. The S.A.P. [South African Police] shall with the co-operation of the Association/Executive do their duty, should violence take place.

11:5. A penalty of R 2.00 will be payable should a choir or choirs arrive late, i.e. (per choir).

11:6. It is the duty of the Chairman in charge of the Hall as well as choirs partaking in the competition to prepare contestants for the occasion.

11:7. Official in charge of the halls may accommodate a choir registered at a Hall other than theirs.

11:8. The Chairman of the Hall has no permission to allow a choir to contest without having registered. An infringement shall lead to a fine of One Hundred Rand (R 100.00).

11:9. A Chairman can be dismissed, asked to resign, in the event or proof of his Dishonesty. Before this is done, grievances by individual choirs would have to be submitted in a written form signed by Officials in charge of choirs, to the Executive.

Unless we take every form of public discourse at face value, a document such as the constitution reproduced above not only reflects principles of rational accounting but would equally appear to signal the appropriation of core practices of modern capitalist society. One might even speculate whether there is not a deliberate attempt here on the part of migrants to turn the instruments and intricacies of bureaucratic state power around and use them to their own advantage. Be this as it may, in most associations the letter of the constitution is animated by a spirited practice of mutual support. The Dalton association, for instance, in 1989 agreed on an impressive set of regulations stipulating, among other things, that a "club" pay R 60 to the family of a deceased member and R 30 to a member who loses a relative. Furthermore, R 40 must be paid when a choir loses its conductor, while a member who gets married receives R 60. A similar example is the case of Jabu Dlamini, a prominent isicathamiya organizer, who narrowly escaped death in a car accident in 1987. To express their sympathy with the victim of the accident, the East Rand Association promptly organized a benefit concert that was sponsored by member choir African Music. In addition, amicable relations are maintained with fellow associations. Regular participation of visiting choirs in competitions is encouraged to provide for a wider range of competitors against whom member teams might measure themselves. As a result of this, some more mobile groups such as the Easy Walkers register at two or even three competitions in one night. Beyond this, some choral associations also display an interest in forging links with the wider community. In contrast to what has previously been assumed about the deep social and political divides between migrant workers and township residents, choirs of the East Rand Cothozá Music Association have entertained spectators at tournaments of the National Soccer League and participated in fund-raising activities of the South African National Tuberculosis Association and a day child care center in Alrode.

Solidarity and the principle of revolving credit can only work efficiently when two conditions are met: complete control over the performance venue and over the circulation of cash during the performance. Basic principles of accountancy and executive powers to enforce these rules through fines and other punitive measures are therefore important components of the everyday practice of the associations. We have seen how one of these principles works, at least in practice. Table 2 was established on the basis of the very detailed books kept by the chairman of the Glebe association. The basic fine, and probably the most important of all fines, is the sum a choir has to pay when it fails to attend a competition. In the Glebe association, this fine amounts to R 20, but other choirs may fill in for an absent choir on payment of a small fee. Other fees, as the constitution quoted above shows, are imposed for late arrival and violent behavior.

But constitutions and bookkeeping are one thing, the lived practice and conflicting interests of migrant performers quite another. For, as I argued in chapter 6, the aesthetics of isicathamiya rests on the display of physical and artistic superiority over competing performers and on the construction of a positive self-image and group identity through the symbolic demarcation of territorial boundaries. On the following pages, we shall see how this aesthetics of power clashes with the communal ideology as I outlined it. The first factor to be taken into consideration—and here we need to return briefly to table 2—is the incentive for each choir to gain considerable amounts of cash in the course of a "round." In other words, it may pay to be a member of an association. A look at the balance sheet of the Glebe association in the table and the situation of a more successful choir such as Cup and Saucer, for instance, reveals that this choir had five "records" during the 1984–85 period. During this time, the group had a net intake of R 1,951 for gate, kitchen profits, and joining fees. An additional R 458 was received for prizes won. The total of R 2,409 stood against R 828 the choir had spent on request fees and thus this choir was able to net the proud sum of R 1,581 in one year. For a less successful group, by contrast, things look considerably less bright. The Durban City Boys, for example, had only two records during the 1984–85 period, because the group decided to withdraw from the association by the end of 1984. As a result these two records netted them only R 425, while the joining fees and request fees cost the group R 707.

Again, as we have seen in chapter 6, there are many ways in which choirs seek to increase their prestige and share of the cake, one of the most prevalent methods being the use of magic and the bribing of judges. It is around the latter issue, and charges of corruption, mismanagement, and the embezzlement of funds by association officials in general that most of the disputes within the associations ignite. A few examples may illustrate this. The remarkable success of Cup and Saucer, for instance, is not based on chance and excellence in performance alone. As table 3 shows, Cup and Saucer carried away the first prize no fewer than seven times during the 1984–85 period and came second and third five times each. The explanation for this

Table 3 Prizes Awarded to Choirs by Glebe Association, 1984–85

Choir	1st	2d	3d
Jabula Home Defenders	9	5	7
Cup and Saucer	7	5	5
Harding Morning Stars	6	6	2
Kings Boys	5	4	4
Easy Walkers	3	4	1
GMC	3	1	2
Greytown	3	1	2
Natal Universal	2	1	1
Daily News	1	...	...
Danger Stars	1	...	...
Durban City	...	2	1
Ngaba	...	1	2
White Water	...	1	2
Assembly of God	...	1	1
Nongoma Morning Stars	...	1	1
Danger Boys	...	1	...
Happy Brothers	...	1	...
Heavy Violence	...	1	...
Manekwane Red Stars	...	1	...
Pietermaritzburg Young Fiders	...	1	...
Warriors Quartet	...	1	...
Young Stars	...	1	...
Green Mamba	...	...	3
Five Roses	...	...	2
Clermont Home Defenders	...	...	1
Nconyama Christ	...	...	1

unusual success is that the choir concluded a secret agreement with Solomon Ndlovu, chairman of the Glebe association, whereby he bribed the adjudicators in return for a share in the group's prize money. This system had worked well for both parties. But although the chairman had carefully avoided arousing suspicion by sometimes placing his partners second or third, he frequently found himself reproached by members and the executive committee for enriching himself. Thus during an executive meeting in April 1985, a number of members accused the chairman of having financed his second-hand truck with association funds and demanded that his petrol allowance for transporting adjudicators be reduced from R 1.50 to R 1.00. As the minutes of this heady meeting document, Ndlovu defended himself with these words:

> The committee members are actually wrong when they think I was going to be rich out of their own pockets. That is why they always maintain that I should not be given money that comes from the hall, and they even scandalize my name. . . . I would like to emphasize the fact that the car that I have, I did not buy it with the money that I obtained from the hall. I have a business to manage and I am also paying those people who work for me. The business that I have, I am not doing it out of the money that I receive from the hall.[2]

Adopting a more threatening tone, Ndlovu concluded his speech by confronting the committee with the following question: "How would it be, if I explain to the organizer of a particular competition that I am not in a position to pick up the adjudicator with my own car, because it is too expensive?" This final remark must have calmed down the indignant committee, for it touched a nerve center of competitions.

Other conflicts arise from the imposition of fines. How severe such conflicts can be on occasion is demonstrated by a dispute over the Abahambi Bezwe choir, a member of the East Rand Cothoza Music Association, that preoccupied the association for several months. In October 1987, Mandla Mthalane, the leader of the choir, had provocatively asked Mdladla to return some money to him that his choir had paid to the association. When Mdladla refused this, Mthalane followed him to his house, insulted him, and threatened to kill him. Subsequently, Skebe Mlotshwa, a member of the Abahambi Bezwe, confronted Mthalane and asked him why he got the choir into difficulties. Mthalane refused to backtrack from his threat, and a week later, the choir was barred from the competition until such a day as it appeared before the disciplinary committee.

SATMA: The Politics of Reform

The gradual decline in popularity of isicathamiya at home and the strangely paradoxical, cometlike rise of Ladysmith Black Mambazo to international fame not only led to the formation of regional associations such as the East Rand Cothoza Association. Especially after Paul Simon's *Graceland* and Black Mambazo's Grammy Award–winning album *Shaka,* the first serious effort was made to form a national isicathamiya association: SATMA, the South African Traditional Music Association.

The beginnings of SATMA go back to May 1986, when Joseph Shabalala met with S. D. Ngcobo, a prominent Durban politician, to discuss the foundation of a South African Cothoza Music Association (SACMA). It was decided to convene a meeting of all chairmen of isicathamiya associations in Shabalala's church in KwaMashu on 16 August. This meeting in turn initiated a string of activities, including contacts with Radio Zulu announcer Welcome "Bhodloza" Nzimande who helped to publicize the aims of the association over the radio. By February 1988, its name changed to SATMA, the association had been formally established and a steering committee consisting of music educators and isicathamiya organizers had been elected. The whole was chaired by Professor James E. B. Msomi, a former inspector of music, graduate of Syracuse University, and presently director of the Umbumbulu College of Education. By the end of 1988, more than one hundred choirs had joined the association, several chapters and branches having been formed throughout Natal and in the Transvaal. Soon thereafter, nationwide competitions were held which culminated in a final contest in Durban in July 1989.[3] By 1993, the hopes raised in the immediate post-*Graceland* euphoria had sunk somewhat and SATMA, now under the presidency of S. D. Ngcobo, had practically ceased to function as a national body. Individual local organizers, however, such as Ladysmith-based Simon Hletshwayo—a brother of King Star Brothers leader Bernard Hletshwayo—and Paulos Msimanga in Durban continue to stage regional contests and to mobilize financial support from private companies.

The rational behind these activities, the original aim of SATMA, according to Msomi, was and continues to be, to "seek means and ways to better the standard of Cothoza music, so that it will grow and be popular." Ladysmith Black Mambazo, he told a meeting of SATMA supporters in Ladysmith's Steadville Community Hall, "had made isicathamiya music famous worldwide. Internationally this music is enjoyed and liked by both the educated and the uneducated people. . . . Isicathamiya also forms our roots of being and also paves the way to our national liberation for all South Africans. This music is our pride and wealth—a wealth that has to be kept intact for the generations to come. We pray that this celebrated music of ours will generate and progress in the face of the whole world."[4]

There are several points in the above passage that require further explanation. For one, it is obvious that an attempt is being made here to forge new alliances by collectively redirecting and making disparate audiences—"the educated and the uneducated"—coalesce around a core performance tradition. As such, SATMA's discourse is clearly informed by the language of nationalism with its Janus-faced ideology of originality on one side and the more universalist, homogenizing image of linear progress on the other side. Clearly, the canon is to be reshaped primarily from the outside, the "whole world." Or, as Joseph Shabalala put it, "That's why there are now many isicathamiya groups in South Africa, although so far they are all imitating Black Mambazo. But I trust that one day they will get their own thing. This is the beginning. It makes people to know that we can do something, our own thing, we can create our own thing. Because all along, people they thought that we've got nothing, we must wait for those foreign musics, foreign ideas, that's all. But now each and everyone knows that we've got something. Even those who are playing instruments, saxophones, they all come back."

It is interesting to note how this narrative of homing, renewal, and cultural revalorization informs the attempts by SATMA officials to develop aesthetic standards by which to measure the "own thing." To use the terms proposed by its president, James Msomi, SATMA intended to improve isicathamiya in four major areas: musical performance, song texts, education, and the selection of adjudicators. For this purpose, the association sought the advice of the country's leading black music educators, whose recommendations, given the century-long inculcation of the black elite with Western values, reflected more the precepts of the Western musical grammar than of Zulu aesthetic categories. As a good example of this kind of benign intervention, I offer here a passage from a letter of advice written to SATMA by the late Bongani Mthethwa, lecturer in ethnomusicology at the University of Natal, in October 1987. "It is clear to me," Mthethwa writes, "that this music is following certain patterns which make it famous, but I think that these patterns will have to change if we are looking forward to selling it to outside countries." With this in mind, Mthethwa suggested that competitions should be held during the day and that choirs should be structured according to areas of residence. And he went on to state, "If we want this music to progress so that it is accepted in other communities, the following steps will have to be followed:

—The choirs should sing the words clearly. They should not mumble the words when singing.
—The sound of the choir should come out round and combined. No part should be heard louder than the others. This needs good supervision.
—Another fault I have discovered is that when the tenor and alto are weak, the choir will not perform well. If the leaders of the choirs could correct this, the choirs could perform well.[5]

It is instructive to compare some of Mthethwa's suggestions with the criteria that the East Rand Cothoza Music Association, for instance, has sought to implement in its own competitions. To help judges in their evaluation of choirs, the association drew up a list of criteria, an "Adjudicating Sheet," that is worth reproducing here in full.

UMCULO WEZINSIZWA ZEMBUBE
ADJUDICATING SHEET IPHEPHA LOMEHLULELI

Choir No: _____   Date: _____

Item	Max.	Marks	Remarks
1. The Choir: Appearance/Ukubukeka	10		
2. The Conductor: Igosa: Smartness: - Ubunono Artistry: - Ubugiko _____	10		
3. Music: - Umculo Ingoma: - Suitable Song Ukugasela: - Attack Nokuphethwa: - Ending _____	5		
4. Balance of Parts and Volume: Ukuzwakala Kwezindlela: Isigqi Sengoma: _____	10		
5. Melody - Harmony - Smoothness & Voices: Ubumnandi Ukucoyiseka Nobuhle: Bamazwi: _____	10		
6. Interpretation - Phrasing, etc. Ingoma Nendaba Eyixoxayo: _____	30		

7. Flexibility - Accuracy -
   Rhythm, etc.
   Ubulula - Umculo Ongabhimbi
   Nomnyakazo Omuhle: _____   25
TOTAL   100

This Choir Comes to Position: _____
Adjudicator: _____
Date: _____

Similar score sheets are being used by SATMA's regional branches, although local representatives who lack formal Western musical training are known to have faced considerable difficulties in understanding such criteria as "tone quality" and "smartness."

Song texts, as I have stated, are the second area of isicathamiya composition singled out for "improvement" in the SATMA discourse about preservation and progress. Thus, pointing to the high degree of intertextuality and the complex overlay of different narrative elements in isicathamiya song texts, James Msomi complained, "You get two or three messages in one song, which is incorrect." By contrast, the songs of Ladysmith Black Mambazo, he argued, were "solid and compact" and had a "message." The assumption that is being made here is based on the (Western) notion of a song as a microcosmic encapsulation and delineation in time of an idea, a truth. This logic of a one-stranded narrative and of linear textual progression, as implied in Msomi's notion of a "compact message," stands in opposition to the aesthetic principles of the nightsongs. For isicathamiya, as I have argued, is a deliberate attempt on the part of migrant performers to wrench themselves from the "proper" spatiotemporal logic of the oppressive order and to capture the paradoxical experience in their fractured lives of, as Ernst Bloch put it, the "simultaneity of the nonsimultaneous." Like the Basotho poets of *lifela*, isicathamiya performers reject a sequential relationship between textual segments, constantly crossing and redrawing boundaries in space, time, and expressive means, as do indeed all unhomed people transcending the boundaries of the proper.

Both these changes, "improved" musical performance and song texts with a "message," according to J. Msomi, were to be achieved through the training of conductors and choirs and a wider dissemination of isicathamiya in schools. Both issues—training and the incorporation of isicathamiya into the curriculum—had been on the agenda of a number of associations for some time. Thus, extensive lecture series had been organized by the

East Rand Association in which choirs were instructed on topics such as
the following:

> 1. Tone: Music must be pleasant to the ear. It must be rich; voices
> clear and free; no nasal and throat music. Keep your music as natural as
> possible and not too much vibration.
> 2. Diction: Correct pronunciation; purity of vowels, consonants,
> etc.
> 3. Rhythm: Blacks are known throughout the world for their rhyth-
> mical music. Keep your music up. . . .
> 4. Phrasing: Group your music into comprehensive phrases or sen-
> tences. Do not cut words, phrases or sentences by breathing wrongly.
> Try uniformity whenever you do such exercises.

As for a wider dissemination of isicathamiya in schools, I have no further
information about present SATMA activities in this area. At the time of
writing (1993) Joseph Shabalala had been appointed a professor in the Department of Music at the University of Natal, and the city of Colenso had
ceded him a plot on which to erect a music school.

Adjudicators, finally, have always been a sore spot in isicathamiya performance. As we have seen, the selection of judges has for decades been
both the arena of intense disputes and subject to a wide range of tactics.
True, the realization of SATMA's stated aim to give preference to black
adjudicators over judges who cannot speak isiZulu will be crucial if performers are to be as successful as Shabalala's group. But whether all choirs
will agree to such important changes and whether the other proposed measures discussed earlier will eventually produce the desired effect, remains to
be seen. When I discussed SATMA's aims with some choristers in Durban,
they criticized the lack of stakes and the lack of accountability of the officers
as the main impediments to further development. Other choirs, on the
other hand, have expressed support for these reform moves. Thus, in a
series of meetings of the East Rand Association, held in preparation for a
training course in 1987, a lively debate arose about "the changing times of
mbube music." For instance, NTU Brothers leader Zulu, suggested that
mbube shows should be staged during the day. This, the meeting agreed,
would bring back older choirs like the Dlamini Home Defenders. Similarly,
the standard of people chosen as judges should be higher. Judges should
be people who really understand music and who are proficient in black
languages. Furthermore, all songs to be sung at competitions should have

an introduction, content, and an ending. Mr. Mazibuko of the Babazani Boys, for his part, emphasized that all choirs should be on time, before the competition starts, because the audience would like to listen to all the songs sung by each competing choir. This was important, he argued, because people were paying an admission fee. Mr. Sithole of the Buhle Bethelezi choir then added that the leaders of the choirs should be given intensive training, because they are the producers of songs. Finally, Mr. Buthelezi demanded that the choirs should perform actions when singing *mbube*. They should not sing gospel or classical music, because they wished to revive *mbube* as an African idiom. Along the same lines were further suggestions made by the chairman of the association. The choirs, he said, "should be distinguished according to the 'tunes' (*shuni*) they are singing. That is to say, there should be a category for those singers who sing high-pitched music (*phezulu*), a category for those who sing in low range (*phansi*), and another one for those singing in medium range (*phakathi*)."

In conclusion, the emergence of choral associations from the mid-1970s marks an important strategic move through which performers, in the face of the growing commodification of culture and the concurrent marginalization of alternative modes of expression, are struggling to maintain isicathamiya as a viable alternative. At the same time, these very organizations represent an attempt at anchoring migrant performance in the widening international commercial networks on which the future of South African music so vitally depends.

PART III SELF

My account of the nightsongs has reached its conclusion. In the past ten chapters I have submitted a range of texts, explored the spatial strategies of migrant workers, unraveled the complex symbolic mesh of a genre—all this, to be sure, with a gaze that was directed at the collective, the body politic as an organized, coherent, albeit dialectically structured, realm of social practice. Now the word is returned to Joseph Shabalala, South African musician extraordinaire and godfather of isicathamiya. One last text remains to be considered, one that will return us to the beginning of this book. For chapter 11, a biographical sketch of the leader of Ladysmith Black Mambazo, will restate some of the issues and questions raised throughout this study; questions about performance, metaphor, creativity, power, and practice. But the chapter will also refocus these slightly. For if, as I have argued, isicathamiya performance is as much about the symbolic reversal of hegemonic power relations as about the constitution of self-identity, it must equally be shown how these processes are based on and simultaneously uphold individual action and notions of personhood. Self-identity, after all, is what people think makes other people into people.

The formation of a self, as I demonstrate in chapter 11, is, of course, every bit as multifaceted and polysemic as the symbols performers handle as part of their social practice. But is this process of self-fashioning also to be compared to writing? Are we dealing, as Clifford Geertz has suggested, with the "authoring" of selves (Geertz 1986) and are, consequently, the lives that accumulate through individual action and structural constraint to be considered—and read—as texts? Or is the constitution of the self among South Africa's marginalized more like the desperate attempt to separate truth from illusion, to anchor stable meanings amid a sea of ceaselessly reshuffled texts, commodities, and images? And how, finally, do individual practice and artistic imagination condition each other in the creation of such spaces of the self?

Such, then, are some of the questions raised by a narrative as rich and compelling as that of Joseph Shabalala talking about his life, his visions and dreams, and, most important of all, his music.

11 "Two Worlds, One Heart": Joseph Shabalala and Ladysmith Black Mambazo

> By "two worlds" we mean your world and our world, but we also mean heaven and earth.
> By "one heart" we mean the power which rises above all of us, for it is this power that guides the unity and peace among people everywhere.

With these words from Ladysmith Black Mambazo's album *Two Worlds, One Heart,* released in the summer of 1990, my account of isicathamiya reaches its conclusion. And as record titles—like book titles—at times seem to translate richly ambiguous worlds of experience into compact and yet fractured apothegms, "Two Worlds, One Heart" evokes the creative core of the isicathamiya tradition while at the same time it bemoans its unredeemable predicament. Unlike any other image in Joseph Shabalala's entire work, the phrase also captures the innermost experience of a man whose entire life has been profoundly shaped by his attempts to reconcile increasingly contingent and yet separate worlds. Joseph Shabalala has always been an *umhlaba wonke,* a world traveler, a wanderer between a world of affluence and power ("your world"?) and a world of poverty and powerlessness ("our world"?); a migrant, in other words, a broker, a peacemaker, and a builder of communities. And Shabalala has been a mediator between the here, the past, and the future; a poet, a dreamer, and an interpreter of dreams.

How to write about such a life and the music from which it is inseparable, is the subject of this chapter. By examining more personalized and intersubjectively produced accounts of reality such as autobiographical self-portrayals, biographies, and life histories, I wish to bring the anthropology of performance more firmly within the purview of a psychology of individual creativity. By situating the object of musical analysis at the juncture between individual experience, stylistic constraint, and depersonalized patterns of mass cultural production, I seek to add a perspective to the emergent literature discussed in chapter 1 that highlights the role of performance as a potential subversion of synecdochic master narratives.

Harmony (1941–1957)

Joseph Shabalala was born 28 August 1941 on a white farm called Tugela near Ladysmith. His father, Mluwane Jonathan Shabalala, called his son Bekhizizwe, Look-after-the-Nation. He and his wife Nomandla Elina, née Zondo, were born on the same farm—a family of farm laborers, then, whose roots probably reach back deep into the long history of dispossession and exploitation of Natal's black peasantry. But like all poverty-stricken farm hands, Jonathan Shabalala was not going to leave it at that. He wanted his children to go to school. And so, in 1945, in order to free his children from farm labor and to raise more money, Jonathan purchased a piece of land near Kikontalok. But before he could reap the benefits of his new property, Jonathan Shabalala died and the whole family moved back to Tugela farm.

I had told Joseph that I wanted to write a biography of him, a book, or a chapter in a book. But he is reluctant to talk about his childhood days. His thoughts seem to trail off into the distance and his expression changes to a sudden introverted sadness when he talks about the poverty on the farm, his father. I try a number of other topics, to find entry points into the remote parts of his memory. Where and when did he become interested in music, I ask. "All the time," he says. "Even when I was at home I heard my mother just praising me, 'Oh my son is singing!' And I realize that I am singing, I just sing. Although the place where I grew, people were singing every Saturday. When you finish working, there are workshops: singing, dancing. They teach you to sing and dance. And then we don't collect the music to the records, we don't listen to the record and then we make the music. The music is in me all the time."

"And what about church?"

"Ja, there was churches there. When we saw those churches we just think about, we thought church is only for the women, because there we always carry our stick to fight. When people are going to church we don't care of the church, we want to go there and sing at Christmas time just to enjoy, not going for church. We thought that the church is for the women and then all those other boys who go to church, we called them cowards. Because they are afraid to fight and they are going to church."

"So that was not your thing?"

"Nothing, nothing. Even my mother, she told me that she used to follow her grandmother going to church. The church was Methodist, ja, she told me that when I asked her about church. But she didn't know well about church. That's why when she grew up and married my father and she changed to be a diviner. We don't know nothing about church. Even at school, I remember when I was at school, there's a place called St. Hilda day school in Roosboom. There other guys used to tell the teacher that I always do funny things instead of praying. Because they told us, they taught us, before we left we must go to where there's a church. We must go there and kneel and pray."

Shabalala chuckles. "But I just get in there and hit those statues again. What's going on? I'm not going to pray to you! And then I go out and then other guys, when we come back on the following day and then tell the teacher that, 'Oh this guy was doing a bad thing there,' and then they hit me. I don't want to pray, I said no. Praying for what? God is in heaven, has his angels there and he is staying very well. But here there are many troubles here. Now we are going to worship him when we arrive that's all, not now."

And the conversation comes to a halt here. I had hoped to hear something more startling, revealing. Assuming that much of the course of a musician's life is set at a very early stage, I was looking for key childhood experiences, important teachers—origins, in other words. As though individual lives were scripted like a Bildungsroman. But for Joseph Shabalala, as much as for any performer, musical talent was more something that was innate. "It was in me all the time," he said, and before I could probe deeper, he changed the subject and started to tell a story.

"This region where we grew up was our region, our district. There were other districts nearby. Our district was called emaHlutshini, land of the Hlubis. The Hlubis had another name in addition; they were called amaNgelengele, the Ngelengeles. Then there were neighbors called ama-Nteshe. The Nteshes also had another name in addition; they were called amaPhumuza, the Phumuzas. Now these two districts were fighting; every time there would be beatings, stabbings, shootings. Then I recalled this thing that I have not told you about.

"As I grew up, when I started singing, there was a type of music called *umculo womshado,* wedding music. Through this wedding music I stopped the quarrel between these two districts. Because one day there was a wedding where one boy from our district from the Ngcobo family was in love with a girl from the other district. Now normally in such a case only the elderly women would go over to the other district to wed the two, and the men would not go there, because it was the men who were fighting.

"And when the wedding ceremony was over it would come to our district and again only the elderly women would come over to our district. Now then, when I was given the responsibility for the wedding, to conduct the music at this wedding, I asked the people we practiced with, with whom we prepared the music and dance for weddings, and I said: It seems to me that we should go to the other district in peace, all of us, young men, young women, old women. Those in charge of the district, the leaders, felt uncomfortable that I was doing something which is not done. And, frankly, I also knew this is not done, but I had this thing in my mind that we should go to the other district in peace. Not to fight or to carry spears, but just to go there and to conduct the wedding ceremony.

"And, true enough, we went there, although we were sorry after going there when we heard the young men chanting outside, 'Baphakathi!! They are inside!!' Oh, we realized that, truly, things were bad. But luckily, only the old respected men of the district came out, who were the leaders of the district. There were four of them and they came to the house we were in. They asked, 'Who is the leader of the group?' The others pointed at me and there were two elderly men in our group, one with the surname Hlatshwayo. Then they came to me and said, 'You, why do you bring people here, because you know there is fighting? We are not on friendly terms with this district.' Then I said, 'No, we have come here in peace, we have come as friends, we have come to fetch the bride. Let this fighting come to an end; we have not come to war, we have not come to fight. The only request I have is that this fighting ends, because now we are becoming relatives.' Then they went to the elderly men (of our group) and asked them. Then they answered, 'Yes, we are older, but he leads the wedding party. He is the head today and we have to listen to him.' And then these men went out of the house and gathered all those outside to report to them.

"What transpired then, was like magic, a miracle. Because while they met outside to discuss, I just started a wedding song in the house. The singing filtered outside, stopped the meeting and they came in to listen. Now something was removed from their minds, because as this fighting had been going on, their minds were filled with the notion that a Nteshe is a Nteshe, a Hlubi is a Hlubi. You see, it's just like talking about animals which should be slaughtered. Because while they listened to our singing I overheard someone saying, 'Oh, so the Hlubis are also living human beings. You know, we thought they were animals!'"

Shabalala laughs, and continues, "By then the mothers were ululating: 'hi hi hi hi hi hi hi hi.' Ku, they were now ululating next to us, saying, 'Jealous down! My child is getting married to gifted musicians!' And then they returned one by one to come into the house to listen to the music. And that is how the fighting stopped.

"What makes me happy is that, as you can see, I am reflecting about this matter. I was going to make a documentary in the same district. And one boy who was young then said to me, 'Oh, here is this person who brought the fighting to an end.' Since then it has been over. I think it was between 1962 and 1963. That fighting has stopped since, until this day. My emphasis is the power of music. If music develops that power, it is the only thing in the world that can bring peace."

Later on that same day, I saw Joseph Shabalala close a concert in a church with a moving appeal for peace. With one fist raised high in the air, he stood alone for minutes, repeating on a high, drawn out note: p–e–a–c–e, p–e–a–c–e, p–e–a–c–e. I had to think again about the episode he related earlier in his hotel room. "Music is something like peace," he said. This was a powerful, compelling idea in a genre so deeply concerned with the ritualized enactment of opposition and dissent. The mediation of conflict through music, how to bring about mutual comprehension between two separate and antagonistic domains, was a radically novel concept. And it is an immensely political concept resonating with Shabalala's and many black South Africans' desire for unity: unity between African Americans and Africans, between feuding tribal factions, and—most pressingly ever since our conversation in 1990—between Gatsha Buthelezi's Inkatha Freedom Party and the ANC under Nelson Mandela.

But most of all, the music-peace allegory stands for Joseph Shabalala himself and how he fashions his own life. The harmony that the young Joseph's powerful singing generated at the wedding is the same unifying principle that holds his own self and its creative powers in place. The songs for peace and the desire to fashion this self as a coherent subject, as a life that almost logically and fatefully unfolds and arranges itself into a narrative sequence, stem from one and the same source.

Self (1958–1974)

A few years prior to the encounter just related, I met Joseph Shabalala at his home in Clermont, a township of Durban. In the course of this meeting Shabalala, interrupted only by a few questions, presented a far-reaching account of his life, an "oral autobiography" proper.

"After some time, in 1958," he started his carefully rehearsed story, "when I was still a young boy at home, I was asked by some other boys of my age to commence singing with them, or rather they sang with me. In fact, they admired my voice, since I was singing a solo with guitar accompaniment, these home-made guitars. So they asked me to come and join them. Their group was called the Durban Choir. When I was with them, I discovered that they were singing quite beautifully, nice tunes, which they called 'D tunes.' I don't know what this *D* stands for, but they called it 'D tune.'

"Now, when I came to them, as a person who is used to tuning guitar strings before playing, I discovered that their singing was not congruent. Harmonically speaking, that is. Then I said, 'Gentlemen, I think this voice should sing like this, and the other voice the other way round.' Meaning that the voice parts were not right, so I had to put them right by changing them to achieve better harmony. But it posed problems for me to teach older people, and what I was teaching them appeared difficult to them. They couldn't grasp it with ease. Then it was difficult, and I found that I couldn't change their singing. Then I left them just like that.

"But I was not in a jovial mood; such that when one day I attended a concert with them, I said after listening to other groups, 'Gentlemen, let's not sing, because we are not ready.' But they insisted to sing since they couldn't bear the thought that they were not right. They forced me to sing, but I dodged them and hid myself outside. By then I was singing bass. People laughed at them when they were performing and they had to stop and go outside. When I met them outside I reminded them that I had warned them that our singing was not yet ripe. That's when they realized it. We must also take into consideration that it was a farm setting and the standard of music was not high.

"Then on December 31, 1959, or we can say, January 1960, I first came to Durban. I found a group called Highlanders. My father's younger brother was in that group. This is where and when I discovered that when you sit down and arrange music critically, it sounds good. But I also saw that you need people who are going to listen to you. Then I thought that people who could listen to me would be people who are younger than I am. Then I decided that when I go home I would take my younger brothers and teach them what I feel inside me and see how it goes. Then at Christmas time in 1960 I gathered my brothers. They listened to me and I gave them what I want and feel, which is what inspires me every time I sing. The boys blended well, thereafter. You will remember that where we lived was at the *plaas,* the Boers' farm. You live there and work on the *plaas.* Singing was just to while away time, to remove the tedium of work, and it happened once or twice a year, during Christmas or an occasional concert. So it wasn't a frequent event such that we would only practice when there was going to be a concert. When it was going to be Christmas season, we would start practicing shortly before Christmas.

"But in 1964, or from 1960, –61, –62, –63 to 1964, I was playing guitar and as for singing, I had neglected it. But in 1964 when I went to Durban again, I was overwhelmed by zeal and the power of singing such that I wished that I could have a teacher every night. Because now music came by a dream visitation where I saw children singing for me. These kids would just float in the sky, singing on some stage platform, but the stage is always floating. Every time I sleep I would have this dream. It was like a disease—every time these children singing for me. But to me, going to sleep was so pleasant, because I knew that I would see a show. Watching those kids, I discovered that I had learned everything there was to be learnt about singing.

"This is when I started again singing, when my younger brothers came to Durban to work. I told them that we should start singing again, and that I'll teach them. They didn't ask me where I had got it from since I said I was going to teach them. They just took what I said and accepted it from person who at home has been an *umqhawe,* a hero in charge of weddings, conducting, playing guitar. I'm sure that since I was someone who was known in music circles, my brothers felt that I had a knowledge of music. They didn't know that I had developed a new style. I then started to form this group.

"The name Black Mambazo is a name that I had been using at home, because where I come from, it is a place of music and musicians are called oxen. I'm sure you know that oxen on a white man's farm are called span, sixteen of them. Now singers in our district are called oxen. Now coming to the word *black,* it is like this: a span of black oxen, among other spans which are black, red, white, and colored, being three types of spans—the black span was very strong. This is why I decided to call my span Black. Then I called the group Black Mambazo. Now coming to the word *Mambazo.* The word *Mambazo* in fact depicts an *imbazo,* an axe, because when we went home from Durban at Christmas in 1964, people were shocked. We started to axe them, axing them on their head, meaning chopping all groups we came across and winning all competitions. Then I said to people, 'That's because I have an axe, a black axe.' That's how the name Black Mambazo came into being.

"Now coming to 1965, I usually say every time I am talking about my history when they ask me when I formed Black Mambazo, that I formed it in 1965. This is because it was in 1965 when I felt that no hell would bar my way, since I love music so much. In 1964, 1960, 1961, it was merely whiling away time. But in 1965 I decided that now we must really sing, sing for flourishing.

"In 1966 was the year when we first went to the hall for performances. During the years 1964–1965 we just practiced after work, but we were not engaged in performances. Even then, going to the halls, I did it because my groupmates were constantly begging me since they wanted to test and measure their capabilities, since they have been practicing for so long, that we should also go to other people and also enter for competitions to test ourselves.

"Eventually we went to the halls and encountered problems. What I am referring to is that when there are competitions, the organizers take anyone from the road, be it a white man, or an Indian. Whether drunk or sober was immaterial, they just take anyone. This really didn't please me, because I saw that the standard of music was not going to be known, and also because the organizers would say to the adjudicator, 'Oh, you'll just pick out any group that pleases you, or the group that appeals to you, or a group that you feel has a good song. Anyone you like, you'll give him number 1, 2, 3 as you desire.' So this was a spoiler, but nevertheless we entered the competitions, won, and received those prizes: goats, blankets.

"It was a difficult job, because we sang the whole night, just for pleasure, for music's sake. Then at dawn, at a psychological hour, a judge would be seen. A joining fee would normally be R 5. Suppose you win and come out number 3, third position, and win R 10 when your joining fee was R 5. Sometimes the joining fee is R 10 and you come out third again and win R 10. What I want to emphasize is that it was just like a game. But when you win the first prize you get a goat if the stake was a goat. If the stake is a blanket, you'll win that as first prize, maybe with an extra of say one pound or one pound ten.

"It's at Greenacre Contraction as a mechanic assistant where I began to create my music. I remember the white guy there who I was working with, he would always encourage me and tell me about the contracts. I must watch out for a contract. I said: What is that? He said, 'No, all the time when I'm listening to your voice I discover that you are arranging the voices. All the time alone. I'm sure if you had a choir you're going to sing very well. Now you're going to sell the record.' 'I don't know nothing about records,' I said, 'I'm not going to sell records. I'm teaching my group that's all. I want them to sing in a perfect harmony.' He said, 'No, don't tell me, you are going to sign a contract somewhere.' ,

"There was a conflict because I wanted to go and record. My appointment was at one o'clock. I said, 'I'm going to record now.' They said, 'No you are not going there.' I said, 'No I'm going.' Then I take my clothes and go, that's all and then they fired me. I remember it was 1972. And then from 1972, I was just working on music, that's all.

"As time went on, they decided to leave us out of the competitions. I remember that when I first met choirs from Johannesburg, it was 1973. By then we had released our first LP entitled *Amabutho* [Warriors, Motella BL 14]. When we met with these choirs in Johannesburg, we were left out of the competition, the reason being that we were no match for those choirs and the audiences loved us so much. We had the largest following. They so much loved us, that after each rendition people would applaud and the rule was that people should not applaud. The first time our performance was cancelled. Then during the second performance it was announced to the audience that they were allowed to applaud all groups entering the stage and also applaud when the group leaves the stage after singing. This, obviously, was an attempt to prevent people to give us the loudest applause. Nevertheless the audience responded as requested. But when we entered there was a difference in the applause which was putting us ahead of other groups.

"Now I remember that during that day there were fifty-seven choirs, the whole of Johannesburg had assembled in the hall. Benoni, Alexandra, Pretoria, Thokoza, the whole of Johannesburg who had heard that we were around, and who had also heard that the last time we were here, we had won. People had come in their scores to hear for themselves, whether this time we would be able to make it or not. We were billed as number 7 and we won and got first prize. Thereafter I was summoned by the organizers of the *cothoza* competitions who said, 'Son, we don't want you to die. You have got tremendous power. You are a person that is supposed to entertain people with your singing, and not for competitive purposes. If you continue to compete, your counterparts will be jealous of you, and hate you, and perhaps even kill you. But we as organizers are supposed to protect you. So tell your agents or promoters that they should arrange shows for you, where you'll be hired at a flat fee and that the other choirs should compete alone so that there is time for entertainment and time for competitions. Because people who come here when you are around, do not come when only these other choirs are performing. Now that is a problem, because there are scores of your followers.' That was how I was taken out of the competition circles.

"I then continued to make recordings and stage performances, and when our counterparts wanted to make public appearances with us, we gave them a chance. But the audiences complained and said that if some people share the stage with us, they are deprived of some pieces because we have given time to other groups. So this created problems such that we were forced to perform alone and when these groups, our rivals, wanted to see us perform, they would come, but as part of the audience. The only time when we would accommodate other people onstage was when we needed guitar accompaniment. That outfit was greatly appreciated by the audience because the guitar players had their own patrons, too. Therefore both parties were satisfied. This was how we left the competitions.

"But I can tell you that from that time when we were going to be full-time in music, many of the guys they go back to work. Because we got a notice from the factories, from the factories where they work. They said, "Now, you have been absent many times. Now, if you are going to be absent again, the law here, it says we must fire you.' And then all the other guys come to me and tell me that, no, we are not going to sing anymore. Except when we are singing around here, not going to Johannesburg, because we always come late on Monday. I remember when they invited us in Johannesburg, we were only five. We toured the whole of southern Africa, only five. And people were very happy, until my guys came back one by one, because they discovered that our life is okay.

"The older groups you people are talking about, honestly I recall, we met for a short period. I met groups like the Crocodiles in Durban for a very short time, also groups like Inqaba Yabesuthu [Sotho Castle] and other numerous choirs I'm sure I know, but I've forgotten their names. Also groups from Clermont and at Wemmer and in Johannesburg at Thokoza and Boksburg. There are many groups whose names I unfortunately forgot, but we know these groups intimately.

"Now coming to the time of *ibombing*. I say I wouldn't be able to sing it, because my veins were telling me that it was a mammoth task for me. But I knew that those who had good voices were tailor made for it. Then I decided to sing the style that I'm singing now and it ended there. Besides that, we would rather say that our first record *Amabutho* was released in 1971 and it earned us a gold disc.[1] Thereafter, although I wouldn't be able to give you the correct order, I would say that I was able to produce three LPs each year. Or two, or one when my producers said that I shouldn't record more that year since the ones already recorded were selling quite fast and then I was supposed to push them. According to record producers, especially at Gallo, there hasn't been a record by Black Mambazo that never struck gold. Or sometimes they would pick up a record that made the best sales and then made that one the title of the album and they would register, say, one hundred forty thousand sales. That would mean that these sales figures included the sales of other records. But the record that shocked them the most was the sacred one, *Ukusindiswa* [Be Blessed, Motella BL 86]. That one, they say, made double gold discs within three weeks.

"In other words, the SABC is where we started to record. Then by so doing it made these songs so famous that people were craving for our records so that when you got to these big record shops in Johannesburg like Mallets, you discovered that the order of the record was equivalent to a gold disc. Now the same record made a platinum disc, double platinum, followed by another one entitled *Phansi Emgodini* [In The Mines, Mavuthela/Ezomdabu BL 321] which also made a gold disc in no time. Another one that shocked them was *Ibhayibheli Liyindlela* [The Bible Is the Road, Mavuthela/Ezomdabu BL 472] which made a double gold, platinum, another gold, another double gold, such that they were confused and didn't know what awards to give. Then it was quite evident that our style was a style that was much appreciated by people.

"Let me say what I started from my veins told me that there should be a better way of voice placement. It occurred to me that one voice would be placed here, another voice there, another there and so on. And then the majority of the parts [i.e., bass parts]. Now when I listened to *ibombing* I could feel that, no, the parts were not alright, not well placed, as if it required anyone who had a beautiful voice to sing anyhow. But I felt that, no, it must be alright for them. Maybe it's because they had beautiful voices, maybe their voices were self-sufficient, they could therefore use their voices anyhow. But I personally felt it would be better for me to arrange the voices, since it was in me when one voice was singing like this, the other one had to sing this way—as I said, when I was in the Durban Choir I tried to shift the voices such that there was good tonal blending. So to me, the voice parts were not right and I felt that I should rearrange them in the manner that rings in my head and see what comes out. But the driving force behind my vocal arrangement was the dream that made me realize that this is what I want. I wouldn't say there is anyone I was trying to emulate except the dream. It was already in me, but I didn't know how I was going to do it. Then came the dream.

"It means that the older choirs you are referring to, I would say, I do sing those styles, those songs even now, but I place the key conveniently so that it is easy to fit in the voice parts in a way that I think would be pleasant to the ear. Songs during those times, say in 1958, that were sung by my uncles, I rearranged them. In fact I wish to point out that when you listen to these songs they give you a vague idea of the text, the composer's intention. I don't know which one I can quote to demonstrate this phenomenon. But the language used in the songs was not quite right. For instance, when talking to a person who is sitting next to you, you don't have to shout. But softly, nicely. When you shout he may even turn around and think that you are talking to someone else sitting behind you. So there were things like that I was trying to get rid of.

"In other words, the *cothoza mfana* that I'm singing is still the same old *cothoza mfana*, but now, because it's something I grew up with, I have been wishing to rearrange it. This is why earlier I resorted to playing the guitar. But when I got the energy to teach people the right way to sing, I decided to reveal the way of singing I had long been wishing to impart. But I can still say that there were quite nice songs in that style. But the problem was range. They were high! Even some of Solomon Linda's songs, his Evening Birds had this problem.

"I think most of these *ibombing* groups were each boasting of their voices' range. They were not competing on the beauty of songs, but on shouting, wanting to find out who can shout the loudest, the furthest. They didn't care if it's beautiful. But even then you could hear that there were some groups who were striving for beauty, but hadn't succeeded sufficiently. Because when you listen to some older records, like those by Mngadi with his A Natal, singing songs like 'Wobheka Enzantsi Uma Ugibele Imfene Ka Baba' (You must look down when riding father's baboon). In this song you can hear that they had come down in range. But even then, it still had a trace of 'bombing.' In performances they were singing high, but on records they thought that they had to record them low so people could appreciate the songs. According to me, isicathamiya nearly became a useless style because of noise. Even when narrating a story to a person next to you, you shout. It really nearly died.

"Another aspect contributing to the preservation of isicathamiya until the present was because of some radio personalities who very much liked the style. Although they were aware that most of the educated people did not appreciate it, they tried to preserve it since it was an original, traditional genre. They stored it until we came across it in the music scene. Groups like the King Star Brothers are credited for bringing back the style, straightened it out, such that people could hear that these are the guys that are really singing for us. Now groups started coming back to this style so that now there are so many groups, they are innumerable and they sing quite alright.

"But the real old groups, no, I really don't know them because when I first came to live here in Durban, from 1960 singing with the Highlanders, meeting Ocean Blues, we hadn't been going much to the halls. Even our manager had been an old man who would say that he was old and wouldn't like to sing frequently and that we should sing at home this weekend and the following weekend again, and we wouldn't go to the hall. So it stands to reason that I don't have the history of the old groups.

"This style just came to me, although the feeling was also there. In fact, I wasn't quite sure that this style was alright, and that composing was permissible, because we were always told to sing songs that were already in existence, as if composing was not encouraged, not right. So that in 1970 when I first started to make recordings at the SABC in Durban, Dr. Huskisson said, 'We have tapes of songs we really don't know what songs they are.' Then I decided to present myself in another recording session. Then this coincided with our recording. Now even the songs that I heard, I wasn't really sure of them. But I was teaching these songs privately. Now in the halls there were remarks that although I was singing the same songs that everybody else was singing, my rendition was a bit different from other people's. Now when I was going to record, this is where I got encouragement. We first recorded the known tunes, then Dr. Huskisson said, 'No. Sing your own tunes, this is not your tune!' This surprised me and I was shocked. How could she know this? Then she finally said, 'Leader, sing songs of your own, songs that you composed.' There I was overjoyed. It was the first time to hear a person say that I must sing my own compositions.

"By then I had only four compositions that I had taught the group. Then she told us instantly that those four songs have been passed—we could then record them. The first one was 'Nomathemba' which is the one that made the LP famous [*Amabutho*, the first LP]. 'Amabutho,' another one, 'Isitimela' (Train), 'Sasuka Sithandana Sawela uThukela Salala' (We left, in love, crossed the Tugela river and slept). I remember clearly that

there were four songs. Then she requested us to sing a Zulu traditional
male courting song. We sang 'Unkanka Odla Amacembe' (A buck that
preys on tree leaves). They recorded it, too. Then she said, 'Go and compose your own songs and forget about all the other songs.' As you say that
some songs are reminiscent of other composers, she had seen that our aim
was performances at the halls and she took me out of that and put me in
my own compositions and recording them. This is what I had been praying
for, but I hadn't come across a person to encourage me until I met her.
This is how I got encouragement for composition. She said to me that
when I compose I must pay attention to the following: (*a*) I shouldn't be
sarcastic. (*b*) Don't be sarcastic about the country. (*c*) Don't swear at anyone. And then compose songs, she said. I then went home and composed
more songs and came back with eight songs, singing my own thing. At the
recording session at the SABC I was going to sing these songs last, because
I was shy and uncertain about them. I first sang the songs that were locally
famous, sung by every *cothoza* group. Even in Johannesburg when I was
there I found people singing the same songs. I thought these songs were
going to succeed at the SABC hoping that at the end I would put my four
compositions, not knowing that my own compositions were going to make
me succeed. Now, what made me continue to compose and be brave with
my songs, was really the encouragement by this lady, who knew music.
Coming from Johannesburg, a white doctor.

"Another thing. I'd like to conclude with my personal history. When I
recall how I started singing and so on, I discover five stages. Say, when I
first started Black Mambazo, I took some boys that I met here in Durban,
taught them and even took them home so that when I sang with them on
Christmas, the other guys I had left at home were quite shocked to hear
them. After that I was quiet for some time. Then in 1964 I formed another
group. In 1968 this group disbanded and I started afresh and formed a
fourth group. What made me fed up with most of these groups was their
drinking habits. I told them that I didn't tolerate it. Therefore in 1968 I
formed another group. That is the only group that stayed for quite a long
time until we decided to record. The members were coming and going,
but the group remained. Then there was the one I sang with here in Durban, the Highlanders, and the other one in 1958 that I sang with at Ladysmith called Durban Choir. I usually say to myself, yes, I am Ladysmith
Black Mambazo today. But I have had my ups and downs to such an extent
that if I look at the members, I recall that I once sang with so-and-so, and
again with so-and-so, and there I remained only with so-and-so and the

two of us until I came to Durban. I put this into six stages if I also count my group at home. Where we played guitars, because we were five, playing very well. That's the only thing I used to think about."

(Auto)biography

Upon closer reading, Joseph Shabalala's self-portrait, apart from being the result of a masterful performance, seems to be indebted to two genres of biographic literature closely akin to ethnography: the literary biography as such and the anthropological life story. Both ways of describing a life are, of course, highly problematic. For one, the presentation of the self as a sequential, almost teleological, unfolding of a destiny, or the "biographical illusion," as Pierre Bourdieu (1987) calls it, is a time-honored convention of biographical writing and nineteenth-century historicism (Weintraub 1975), focusing predominantly as it does on the lives of the great men of Western history, politics, and (mostly classical) arts. In examples of the latter, in the portraits of writers, composers, and painters, that is, life and art are constructed as two fundamentally cross-referential domains: the meaning of a life is seen as being contained in the core of the work of art, while, conversely, every work of art has traces of its creator's life written into it.

This and the seemingly egoistic focus of the biography and the autobiography have led anthropologists to shy away from accepting such texts as part of the discipline's methodology. But as Judith Okely points out, these hesitations rest on deeply entrenched Western ethnocentric traditions (Okely 1992, 4). Other peoples not only have varying notions of self and ways of describing them, but an anthropological perspective is, first and foremost, concerned with the "process of autobiographical construction." Unlike literary studies, which have primarily been preoccupied with integrating the analysis of others' autobiographies into the literary canon, anthropologists should desist from critiquing others' existing texts (8).

In practice, however, biographical accounts constructed by anthropologists have been no less allegorical than those produced in the Western Great Man tradition. As Renato Rosaldo has observed, such life histories have tended to depict more "the passage of generic persons through the life cycle as a means of understanding the institutional arrangements of a society" (Rosaldo 1976, 145). Much of this rhetorical stance survives even in the more recent ethnographic literature where the presentation of individual life experiences in continuous narratives and neatly bounded life phases seem to be the most pervasive strategy. In both subgenres of biographic literature, then, lives that arrange themselves into life stories or life cycles are the products of an imagination that conceives of the individual as a coherent self.[2]

Moreover, the construction of coherent selves from fragments in the production of biographical and autobiographical fiction is also essentially an act of performance. To write and to narrate such accounts as images of a life is to engage in a process that does not differ fundamentally from other modes of performance, other types of "performative utterances." Life histories and performance both enact processes of self-fashioning; they are all autobiography, constructed in different symbolic modes. Hence, questions of genre, intertextuality, frame, and so on are of no lesser relevance for the understanding of such culturally controlled fictions of life than they are in the interpretation of ritual or song. What discursive genres are available in isiZulu to communicate individual experience? How do these blend with the prefabricated rosters—interviews, stories, gossip columns, and so on—of the entertainment industry? Do these genres emphasize the same things, such as narrative sequence and the heroic self, as do some traditional genres of self-portrayal such as *izibongo* praise-poems? Conversely, it is impossible, of course, to grasp the meaning of an individual's creative work without paying attention to the ways in which a person arranges his or her life into a shape. Both are modalities of the same process.

Joseph Shabalala, the performer and showman, is also a powerful narrator who has gained considerable experience in accommodating the demands of stardom by presenting scrupulously crafted life histories. And like a biographer, Shabalala divides his life into distinct phases which he makes contingent on key events, major works. But like the ethnographer who seeks to condense the repetitive and uneventful, the "empty" passages, into meaningful, culturally relevant events, Shabalala concentrates on particularly telling moments, avoiding redundance and parentheses, bringing order into events by putting events in order.

The shaping of a life, then, like the performance of a play or a dance, is ultimately a matter of metaphoric predication. Metaphor, as James Olney states in his study *Metaphors of Self: The Meaning of Autobiography,* says very little about the world but a great deal about what I am, or am like, and about what I am becoming. It is by means of the metaphors the self creates that we come to know the self, in art as much as in autobiography (Olney 1972, 32–35). Performance, as I have said throughout, links migrant workers to their rural home and thereby transforms a song into a kind of autobiography. Conversely, through its metaphoric impulse, every act of self-portrayal becomes a performance.

But the writing of biography is not only the making of a subject, it is also its unmaking. The biography seeks to expose the seams and fissures which the crafting of the self in narrative performance tries to conceal. If life has a pattern—and no biographer can afford to deny that—it seldom is a rounded one. The lives that ever-increasing numbers of individuals are living in the interstices of the two worlds described by Shabalala resemble more a patchwork of episodes, interwoven with numerous other stories—world segments—than a continuous trajectory. If modern life is not of one piece, biographical events, as Bourdieu (1987) writes, become mere "positions and shifts in social space." Therefore, to account as an anthropologist for such a disjointed experience as we call life is to become acutely aware of one of the central predicaments of ethnography. The writing of biography, while potentially undermining the objectivist, synecdochic stance in anthropology, is deeply caught up in the dialectic of identity and distance that marks all acts of representation. As Georg Simmel, writing at the threshold of the twentieth century and with the one-dimensional man of the societies of the industrialized North in mind, has poignantly remarked about the impossibility of a sociology of the individual: every human being has in himself a core of individuality which cannot be re-created by anybody else whose core differs qualitatively from his own. Because the challenge to re-create is incompatible with the distance and objectivity on which the representation of the Other equally rests, we cannot know completely the individuality of another. "We are all fragments," Simmel concludes, "not only of man in general, but also of our own selves. It is this fragment which the gaze of the other adds to that which we can never purely and completely be. Not only can he not see the given fragments next to each other, but as we complete the blind spot in our vision without being aware of its existence, so we form of the fragment his completed individuality" (Simmel 1908, 25).[3]

Dreams (1975–1986)

"Late in 1975, when I was in Durban, then the dream explained this to me. I was very afraid of this. And then that day I was sleeping and then I heard a voice, it said, 'You must fast for four days. Don't eat. By doing that you'll defeat your enemy.' That voice used to help me all the time. But that voice from my childhood, that voice used to talk with me while I was not sleeping. It used to talk with me and tell me when and what happened, what I did. Wrong things, this is wrong, this is good. But that day I said, this is the right voice, but talking about not eating? What is this? Four days? When I wake up I tell myself to do this because the result is to defeat my enemy. And I said, this is good. I did it. Four days I didn't eat. There was something funny. On the first day before I sleep, I put my food next to me. I said, maybe if I feel that at night I'm going to die, I'm going to eat quickly. Because I was just thinking about . . . I never did this before. I was just doubting, the voice was the voice which I know, but maybe there's somebody imitating the voice. Certainly, he wants me to die and I said, alright let me put my food next to me. When I discover at night that I want to eat, I can wake up and eat quickly before I die. But I just lived and I'd wake up early and go to work, doing some job and come back late and I'd discover that now after two days I feel more strength! I said, oh this is good. And then I carried on, finish those four days.

"And then after that among the group there are two guys who are very seriously ill and then I take them to the Zulu doctors. They fail to heal them. I take them to the doctors, they fail to heal them and I discover that now they are going to die. And then there are the men who came in my room and said, we heard that there are people who are sick here. Even my wife was sick. Now we are coming here to pray for them. God is wonderful, and look at this. And then I agreed and said okay, let's pray. They prayed for them. I remember that one of them was in hospital because the doctors discovered that he has TB and I left him back with my wife and with my brother Headman, the one who I began the group with. And then they came there and pray for that, pray for them. I listened to their prayer. I said, they have confidence, they talk like people who have seen God and talked to him and he gave them a promise. I said, no, this is not right. But when they wake up—because I'm a person who has a vision all the time—when they finish to pray to my wife, I saw something: a black shadow coming out of my wife, move away from my wife. I said, oh, what is this? And then they said to me, 'Don't worry, they will be OK.' At the same time, I said, oh, they know how to pray. But they don't know how to see that my wife is OK now. And then after that they get healed and I tell myself that, no, I must go to worship God. That was my first day to know that God can help you here, in this world.

"And then I began to follow those people and ask them, 'Do you have a church?'

"They said: 'Yes, we have a church.'

" 'I'd like to join you.'

"They said: 'Right, you can join us.'

"And then I joined them. But I remember that it was October, 1975, but I took three months reading the Bible before I dedicated myself. I remember that December 16th I dedicate myself to God. And then I tell them that now I'm going to worship God with you, after reading Bible."

*

Dreams have accompanied Joseph Shabalala all his life. As we have seen, three of these nocturnal visitations in particular have marked the three most crucial turning points of his life. The singing children in the sky taught him a new style. The black shadow coming out of his wife was the decisive event that led to his conversion to Christianity. And, finally, the dreams about flying with wings, which Joseph began to have from the early 1980s, were the first omen of his later worldwide success.

Without dreams, informants told Axel-Ivar Berglund, "true and uninterrupted living is not possible." Nights without dreams, as one of Berglund's interviewees suggested, are like sitting in a prison, not knowing when the court case will be. In dreams, the shades reveal themselves to the living, becoming real, intimate, and concrete. Diviners in particular are said to be profuse dreamers whose calling frequently originates in a dream visitation by the shades. Dreams also continue to play a significant role in the lives of individuals whose loyalty to the ancestor religion remains strong while they also organize their religious practices within the so-called Zionist churches. Thus, as Bengt Sundkler has asserted, it is at the "dream level of life" that a great many black South Africans of varying religious orientations "experience their deepest conflicts and somehow try to come to terms with them" (Sundkler 1976, 265ff.).[4]

Dreams are also a major source of musical composition. Music is thought to be a product of the ancestors which they communicate, through dreams, to those whom they like. Consequently, there is not much difference in Zulu thinking between a musician who communicates with his ancestors in his sleep and receives songs, a diviner who derives his power from dreams, or a homestead head who relies on dreams to run the affairs of his homestead.

Dreams, then, and their interpretation are always culturally patterned, in much the same way as the relationship between dream and reality is a projection that differs from one cultural context to another. At the same time, as conventional Western dream analysis tells us, dreaming in African societies transcends "stereotyped symbolism and interpretation" (Sundkler 1961, 268). Like the individual life experience of which they form an integral part, they are inherently idiosyncratic. And like all self-descriptive accounts, dreams seek to render more choate the subconscious by making images available to post facto rationalization and metaphoric predication.

By contrast, another view on dreaming in a variety of non-Western contexts suggests that dreams, like the construction of autobiographical narrative, may be regarded as a strategy of self-fashioning, a kind of performed fiction that bridges the space between the fragmentary self and the other. The shift toward dreaming as a form of communication, as Barbara Tedlock reminds us, refocuses the attention on dreams as performative acts in the sense that dreaming becomes a part of the doing of something and not merely a description of the doing of something.[5] If we understand dreams in this way, that is, as an emergent reality and a dynamic means of communication rather than, as psychologists have been wont to do, as passive mirror images of the subconscious, as texts whose meaning is to be extracted through careful interpretation, we might begin to understand the enormous role of dreaming as a source of inspiration for composers and musicians in a wide range of cultural settings.

With this in mind, it becomes clear why for Joseph Shabalala dreaming and composing, by virtue of the children-in-the-sky dreams, are overlapping experiences. The reality of the composition, its text, so to speak, merges with the act of composing in the dream. But because in Zulu thinking all dreams are ultimately encounters with the ancestors, composition by analogy becomes a means of integrating the self in the overarching entity of the ancestral lineage. To dream and to compose isicathamiya songs are thus parallel strategies at creating continuity with the past.

In addition to the performative power of dreams, several details in Shabalala's dreams are particularly noteworthy. The first is the striking role of children in the first dream that does not entirely match the social position of children and their significance in dreams. Although children frequently appear in dreams and are said by dreamers to be *amadlozi* (ancestor spirits), it is emphatically denied that a "shade of a child can either give advice or exercise influence of any kind" (Berglund 1976, 119). The contrast between normative dream interpretation and Shabalala's own reading and creative practice is made all the more poignant by his earlier insistence on instructing his juniors only. Comparing his own position as a student in the dreams with that of a leader of his own choir, and not without authenticating, in passing, his narrative by invoking Shaka's own didactics, Shabalala remarked, "When I think about my father telling me about Shaka Zulu.

Shaka Zulu, he just came in this world, there was people who are fighting all the time. And when he began to take over, he had his strategy to fight, he had his technique to fight, but with the same spear. He arranged not to throw your spear, no, you must keep your spear, work with that spear, come back with it. I trained the group, because they gave me a chance. The first group failed, the second group failed, and then the third group I tell them before I work together with them, I said, 'I'm not going to carry on with you if you don't want to listen. If you have something, you must give me.' But I want something, and I tell them. I train even their mouth, even their tongue, even their face, even the way to walk, even on the street. Just sit down with them and talk with them before we sing. Just train them and tell them to use your voice like this and like this, how to breathe in and out.

"Nobody taught me that, but from the dream I was just watching and listening. Sometime they used to talk to me, sometime those children used to thank me before they leave. They said, 'It was nice to be with you. We'll be with you every day.' And there was a voice, always talking to me, 'Alright, I'm going to help you to be patient. I'm glad that you love music.' And then disappeared. That was the end of the show. All the time, before they leave me. Now, I train them. I was very happy that they were small at that time, that they were very happy with my teaching. They sit down and they'd laugh, they were very happy with teaching, they asked me, where did you get this. I said, it's in me, I feel it. They said, no, maybe you're mad. I said, yes, it's in me, I am mad of this music, I want to create this music, I want to present our music to the people. I sometimes even sing that we're going to fly with this music."

Thus it seems that in the dreams, the human social order with its hierarchies and principles of authority and seniority, is inverted. Whereas in real life juniors are the learners and receivers, in Shabalala's dreams children are the instructors. True, there is a strong sense here of the appropriation of a number of key Christian images. The children in the sky are clearly reminiscent of angels, an association made all the more plausible by the fact that the children are singing. Furthermore, in Zulu Zionist thought angels are conceived of as channels by which the Spirit reveals itself. Like the ancestors, angels appear mostly in dreams, criticizing misbehavior and showing the way out of an impasse (Sundkler 1961, 249).

More to the point, however, of the constitution of social power through the power of performance, the strangely mirrored, paradoxical relationship in Joseph Shabalala's dream between the production of authoritative cultural knowledge and the social position of an individual can also be interpreted as a strategy of self-fashioning through which, as I have said, the individual mediates between his own fragmentary self and culturally constituted social reality. In Joseph Shabalala's case, his extraordinary success and persuasive power are cast as being simultaneously received from the outside and created from within his own subjectivity. The wellsprings of this performer's moral imagination lie in realms beyond the reach of direct human agency, in the past of a lived collective experience symbolized by the impenetrable but contingent world of the shades, and in the unknown and yet deeply felt inner recesses of the self. Children, the weakest and most powerless members of society and, at the same time, the symbols of unbridled imagination, are perhaps among the most irresistible and enchanting mediators between these two parts of the human psyche. Perhaps the covers of *Phezulu Emafini* (fig. 17) and *Inkazimulo* (Mavuthela BL 504)

Figure 17. Album jacket, *Phezulu Emafini.* Courtesy Gallo (Africa), Johannesburg.

should be read as parallel visual attempts to capture the power of performance in mediating the two worlds, heaven and earth, even if the position of the children here is taken by Ladysmith Black Mambazo themselves.

Prophecy and Preaching

From the foregoing account, it seems undeniable, then, that Joseph Shabalala's music is endowed with a special power. It is clear that through Shabalala's special kinds of nightsongs speaks a voice of revelation. His is a music, nay, a moral discourse about truthful living, about finding the center in a world that has lost its bearings. "Music is like a book," Shabalala once told me. "Telling the people . . . This is us, we feel it in our blood. But this is like preaching, because it just reminds us that we are people, we are human beings, we must come together, we can do something." Elaborating on this point Shabalala talked about his famous song "Nomathemba." "Even my lyrics, it's just preaching. Ja. When I am talking about Nomathemba, talking about that lady, I was just encouraging the people. How can I help the people to love each other, those who sometimes used to fight each other? And I just write this song. Nomathemba who went to Johannesburg. The man go to look for her, and he apologize to her, said, come back. Something like that, I thought maybe I am going to bring the people together to forgive each other." Bekhizizwe, Look-after-the-Nation.

The creation of togetherness and conviviality in the face of uncontrollable alien forces, I have argued, animates isicathamiya performers' social organization in choirs and choral associations modeled on home-people structures and *stokvel*. But this process of male bonding was constructed through and reflected in intensely antagonistic relations and power-laden images. By extracting himself from the competitive contexts of migrant performance, Shabalala opened himself up for a more comprehensive, almost universal, modernist vision of peace and social harmony hitherto unavailable in isicathamiya ideology and performance practice. The model for this scheme proper of all-encompassing salvation, I argue, is rooted in the social role of diviners in preindustrial society. In the precolonial societies of southern Africa, divination was an essential social regulative addressing both personal and social ills. In modern South Africa the role of divination, in modified form, has increased considerably due to the "ever increasing search for security against all threatening dangers" of industrial society (Sundkler 1961, 255). In fact, as Bengt Sundkler has roundly asserted, witch finding has largely been replaced by Zionist prophecy (256). Like divination, Zionist prophecy diagnoses the ailment afflicting the individual and locates the invisible evil force that causes it.

We have seen that the articulation of Shabalala's prophetic gifts, with the entitling power of performance to revive the past, act upon the present, and to imagine another future is deeply inscribed into his biography and even that of his family. Jonathan Shabalala was a *nyanga,* an herbalist, while Joseph's mother elected to become a diviner (*sangoma*). Joseph Shabalala's own life trajectory, as he made abundantly clear, took a dramatic turn in 1975 when he decided to join a church, and again in 1981, when he was ordained a minister of the Church of God of Prophecy in Southern Africa. Coinciding with these changes, Shabalala issued several sacred albums during the mid-1980s that feature Methodist hymns and what, for want of a better term, might be called sacred isicathamiya. Although Shabalala's beliefs are quite distinct from those of the Zionist churches, his work as a performer enriches his double role as prophet and preacher, in itself "an essential partnership in the work of Zion" (Kiernan 1976). As with a number of well-known isicathamiya performers such as Zephania Mzolo of the Mzolo Mbube Group and Robert Mkhize of the Colenso Abafana Benkokhelo, both of whom are active *sangoma,* Joseph Shabalala's integration of prophecy, preaching, and performance forms the spiritual foundation of a moral imagination that seeks renewal from the reproduction of conventional meanings and that salvages the old by setting the course of future action on the correct path.

"The Way We Look to Us All"

I have portrayed isicathamiya not as a timeless, isolated rural tradition transformed by urbanization and industrialization. The making of isicathamiya, I argued, involved a much more indeterminate conglomerate of forces—both impersonal and grounded in individual agency—interacting with each other on a stage of much larger dimensions. In shaping migrants' social practice and consciousness, isicathamiya performance, in fact, was itself history in the making. It was a form of practice that from the start enabled migrant workers to connect their individual experiences with a world beyond the village, the factory, and the "hostel." In other words, the history of Ladysmith Black Mambazo as I have presented it here is grounded in a microcosm of personal choice and local culture. But it is also part of a much wider process of the modernization of isicathamiya and its articulation with the modern world system.

Both these, however, the modern world system (the "two worlds") and the creative individual, are but imperfectly known phenomena in anthropology and ethnomusicology. Both disciplines have traditionally construed their objects within well-bounded, small-scale communities such as tribes, cultures, and villages that leave little room for individuality and dissent (Barber 1987; Nettl 1983, 239–40). Although the growing articulation of the world's cultures through large-scale labor migration and massive intercontinental waves of refugees is commanding increased scholarly attention, this process is mostly being portrayed as the result of a juncture of abstract forces, as a phenomenon of the masses, of markets, apparatuses, and industries manipulating the needs of an amorphous urban population. Few and far between are the attempts that explore the dialectic of individual creativity and cultural constraint by linking intensely studied individual and local performance practices with global networks. Only a handful of studies is available that seek to uncover the working of macro-systems—worldbeat, ethno-pop, and so on—in ways that assign a greater role to local cultures than mere colorful illustrations of the global picture.[6]

In this final section of my account of the nightsong tradition, I attempt to bring the individual and the global system more firmly within the purview of ethnography as interdependent yet conflicting realities. Both constitute each other. Markets, media, the role of technology in the production of music, have left deep traces in the lives and creative work of generations of black performers in South Africa. In turn, the fate of South African musicians—from the international tours of the South African Choir and the Zulu Choir in the 1890s and the emergence of Solomon Linda's "Mbube" on U.S. pop charts in the 1960s, to the rise of Miriam Makeba to international stardom—has been osmotically bound up with the cyclic up and down swings of the world entertainment industry. By far the most central project, however, of the internationalization of South African music was to materialize only in 1986 with the release of Paul Simon's seminal album *Graceland*.

A wide-ranging roster of musicians participated in the making of the album, but most notably a number of well-known South African acts, including Ladysmith Black Mambazo. The group has since participated in a number of other international ventures, including an album containing a Rudyard Kipling story read by actor Danny Glover, joint stage appearances with the Cologne-based rock and folk group Bläck Föss, and more recently the collaboration with Andreas Vollenweider on his 1991 album *Book of Roses*.[7] To complete this list, Shabalala's choir also appeared in Michael Jackson's movie *Smooth Criminal* and in Spike Lee's music documentary

Do It a Capella. Graceland, however, remains the single most creative and controversial collaborative effort Joseph Shabalala engaged himself in to date.

Paul Simon has been variously praised and criticized for involving these South African musicians in the making of his LP, and much of the debate following the release of *Graceland* concentrated on political issues such as the UN-proclaimed cultural boycott of South Africa, the economic plight of black musicians in South Africa, and so forth.[8] Going beyond these debates, Louise Meintjes, in one of the most trenchant analyses to date of *Graceland,* has pointed out that the plural authorship in many of the tracks is, in fact, a celebration of the social collaboration and dialogue between center and periphery. At a deeper level, however, Meintjes observes, highly power-laden images of the other are involved in this conjunction between global economic and political systems and the local lived experience of specific creators and interpreters (Meintjes 1990, 37, 69). Critiques such as Meintjes's are indispensable if we are to understand the very real power processes at stake in the production of transnational musical styles. However, one important fact seems to have been largely overlooked in the debate on *Graceland,* worldbeat, and postmodern cultural production. For unlike any other project involving musicians from such disparate sociocultural realities, Simon's multimillion-dollar enterprise probably represents one of the most powerful expressions to date of the modern world system, one that has far-reaching implications for the aesthetics of popular music in the postmodern era.

This aesthetics, beneath all the celebration of universal ecumene, is fundamentally an aesthetics of difference and local identity (Erlmann 1993; Guilbault 1993). Thus, following Paul Simon's biographer Patrick Humphries, the songs on *Graceland,* at the broadest level, represent a search for some kind of truth, locally rooted and culturally shaped. For Simon, Humphries claims, the *Graceland* songs had "a very similar theme: acceptance, aiming at some state of peace, looking for some state of redemption or grace" (Humphries 1989, 131). After two decades during which *Graceland,* Elvis Presley's Tennessee retreat, had symbolized "the first lost promise of rock and roll," the name *Graceland* on the Simon album once again "offered the possibility of the dream being reborn" (132). By appropriating isicathamiya and other South African music, Humphries argues, Paul Simon sought to introduce to the world "Black African music . . . in a purer and more recognizable form" than the one that Elvis Presley wove into rock and roll in the 1950s (156). But Simon's quest for redemption does not lead him back to a center. On first hearing the music of the South African townships in 1984, he was reminded of the 1950s rock and roll out of the Atlantic Records school, of Zydeco music. What bridged the South African material and the more familiar down-home sounds was that it was "Third World music," music that "really is just outside the mainstream." It is here, at the margins, Simon confesses, "outside the mainstream . . . where I always enjoyed being."[9]

Clearly, then, although *Graceland* is about the fashioning of an authentic identity from the margins, from the position of the subaltern, the more likely reading of the album by First World consumers such as Humphries is that of a new frontier opening up between the saturated West and some other space before time. At the same time, the attempt on *Graceland* to construct an authentic identity is informed by a semiotic traffic back and forth across this frontier. In trying to bring to the fore the voices of difference while at the same time recognizing the universal in the local, in other words by finding a "common bond," *Graceland* partakes of what Arjun Appadurai has called a certain kind of cannibalism: the "politics of the mutual effort of sameness and difference to cannibalize one another and thus to proclaim their successful hijacking of the twin Enlightenment ideas of the triumphantly universal and the resiliently particular" (Appadurai 1990, 308). This becomes perhaps nowhere clearer than in "Diamonds on the Soles of Her Shoes," one of the two songs on the album performed jointly by Paul Simon and Ladysmith Black Mambazo.

What is striking about the juncture between Simon's Manhattan and Black Mambazo's Zululand in "Diamonds" is the degree to which this cannibalism is encoded at the level of sound texture—itself to a large extent the product of far-reaching developments in sound-recording technology—and onstage presentation. The seamless, blurred, and almost contourless cross-referencing that is achieved in the vocal parts, between call-and-response, English and isiZulu, is accentuated by the onstage positioning of Black Mambazo and Simon, most vividly perhaps in live performances such as the famous "African Concert" in Harare, Zimbabwe, in 1987.[10] Here the group, like all isicathamiya choirs, stands in a straight line with the lead singer Joseph Shabalala moving about freely in front of the choir. Simon, for his part, stands on the side at a little distance, almost extending the line formed by the choir. While the choir sings the overture, Simon watches them silently, later unobtrusively blending in on the same E-major chord with Shabalala on "She's a rich girl." Following this, a subtle, low-key pattern of call-and-response establishes itself between Shabalala, the choir, and Simon, each taking turns in singing either the solo vocal line or the chorus.

All of this suggests, as Louise Meintjes correctly points out, that the collaboration celebrated in *Graceland* is metaphorically configured in structurally integrated rather than merely juxtaposed musical styles (Meintjes 1990, 43). At a deeper level, however, *Graceland* might be used as an exemplary text to interrogate the ability of the postmodern, global aesthetics to capture an identity, to offer redemption. A brief look at the lyrics of "Diamonds" may demonstrate this. The track is really two songs in one, loosely strung together: a brief introduction in isiZulu, followed by Simon's eerie story about the rich girl and the poor boy floating—disembodied and physically forgotten—through the somewhat unearthly space that could be New York City. At the end of the track, elements of the first section ("Ta na na") resurface.

> *Awa awa,*
>> Awa awa,
> *akucwayele kile kanjalo.*
>> it is usually not like that.
> *O kodwa ezinsukwini uzongenelisa namhlanje.*
>> Oh, but in the days ahead, she is going to satisfy me, today.
> *Zanamuhla sibona kwenzeka kanjalo amantombazane ayazondla.*
>> Today we are witnessing that the girls are self-reliant.
> *Awa awa sibona.*
>> Awa, awa, we see.
> *Kwenzeka kanjani?*
>> How does it happen?
> *Awa, awa amantombazane ayeza.*
>> Awa, awa, the girls are self-reliant.
>
>> *She's a rich girl*
>> *She don't try to hide it*
>> *Diamonds on the soles of her shoes*
>>
>> *He's a poor boy*
>> *Empty as a pocket*
>> *Empty as a pocket with nothing to lose*
>> *Sing Ta na na*
>> *Ta na na na*
>> *She got diamonds on the soles of her shoes*
>>
>> *People say she's crazy*
>> *She got diamonds on the soles of her shoes*

Well that's one way to lose these
Walking blues
Diamonds on the soles of her shoes

She was physically forgotten
Then she slipped into my pocket
With my car keys
She said you've taken me for granted
Because I please you
Wearing these diamonds

And I could say Oo oo oo
As if everybody knows
What I'm talking about
As if everybody here would know
Exactly what I was talking about
Talking about diamonds on the soles of her shoes

She makes the sign of a teaspoon
He makes the sign of a wave
The poor boy changes clothes
And puts on after-shave
To compensate for his ordinary shoes

And she said honey take me dancing
But they ended up by sleeping
In a doorway
By the bodegas and the lights on
Upper Broadway
Wearing diamonds on the soles of their shoes

And I could say Oo oo oo
As if everybody here would know
What I was talking about
I mean everybody here would know exactly
What I was talking about
Talking about diamonds

People say I'm crazy
I got diamonds on the soles of my shoes
Well that's one way to lose
These walking blues
Diamonds on the soles of my shoes

Ta na na.

The introduction in isiZulu is based on a wedding song, a genre which, as I have persistently argued, symbolically reconstructs a vanished world of regional identity, domestic cohesion, and specific gender hierarchies. Thus, in the opening lines we hear a voice deploring the growing independence of young women. Written by Joseph Shabalala as a comment in response to Simon's lyrics—"awa, awa" expressing amazement at the unusual Manhattan story—the introduction in reality echoes some of the patriarchical concerns of migrant workers over the growing independence of women in South African society. At the same time, isicathamiya, like most other South African music, is a genre in which traces of the American minstrel show, the Methodist hymn, and doo-wop have become the signs and vehicles of a long and irrevocable entanglement of local performance practice and modern world system. The historical moment that produced isicathamiya and, within the wider genre, the music of Ladysmith Black Mambazo, is therefore anything but a beginning, a primordial juncture "where it all began" (Humphries 1989, 156). Labor migration, in other words, the growing encroachment of the forces of global commodity exchange on black South Africans' lives, is the pivotal context in which these opening lines have to be read, and not some pure Black African identity.

The contrast between this intensely laden personal response to a particular historical disjuncture between the world of custom and habitus—"it usually is not like that"—and the present moment of growing female autonomy might, of course, suggest a whole number of possible readings. Without wanting to forestall any of these, the most obvious interpretive option would be that we are dealing here with a bricolage of sorts between two different types of gender relations in two radically different times and places. Ultimately, of course, stylistic bricolage—even in the most integrated fashion—cannot recapture the experience of a local world, firmly framed by the clear-cut binary relation between signifier and signified. Nor does a bricolage such as that in "Diamonds" necessarily disrupt the hegemony of the First World (Comaroff 1985; Hebidge 1979). *Graceland*, in the final analysis, seems to have dissolved any concrete historical referential frame. The album, and the Black Mambazo tracks in particular, represent a global soundscape in which the boundaries between the symbols, perspectives, and interpretations of culturally distinct spheres have become almost seamlessly enmeshed with each other to produce a postmodern space littered with semiotic debris without any referent to authenticity; a sonic scenery without actors, pulverized into gazes, copies of copies, a world filled with ubiquitous role models. Or, as "The Boy in the

Bubble," another track on the album, says, with "cameras that follow us in slow mo; a distant constellation that's dying in the corner of the sky, a loose affiliation of millionaires and billionaires, the way we look to us all." *Graceland*, despite all the outstanding musicianship, resembles what Jean Baudrillard, the master thinker of simulation, has called a "melodrama of difference." In the melodrama of the interface, Baudrillard claims, we simulate and dramatize, in an acrobatic act, the absence of the Other that has been swept away by the universal triumph of the sign. In the interaction that results from this artificial dramaturgy, the subject becomes the Other of nobody. Fashioned in this manner, the interactive, transversal subject is not the product of some new form of exchange, but of the wholesale disappearance of the social and otherness as such (Baudrillard 1993, 125–26).

Postscript, 1994

"When we say 'war dance songs,' it is not all for war. Some *amahubo* are for worshipping, others are for the homestead or the lineage." Joseph Shabalala met me in his new office at the University of Natal, where he is now a professor of African music. After having been away from South Africa for several years during which I wrote this book, I returned to Durban and Johannesburg in 1993 to discuss my manuscript with friends, colleagues, and performers. It was a different South Africa I encountered then, in the spring of 1993. Not quite the new South Africa, but not exactly the old one either. More than fifteen thousand people had lost their lives since the mid-1980s, and every week dozens more were falling victim to political violence and ordinary crime. On the other hand, the ANC had been unbanned, most of the old restrictions of apartheid—the Group Areas Act, the Registration Act, and many others—had disappeared. And in May 1994 Nelson Mandela was elected the first black president of South Africa.

"Not all for war," Joseph Shabalala said. He was examining my manuscript, and especially reconsidering his own introduction. In particular it was the list of a dozen or so genres making up isicathamiya that caught his attention. *Amahubo empi,* war dance songs, it said there. "I should revise that," Shabalala pondered over his text. "Because I am planning to sing these songs. There were knives in the past, there were spears. But people saw that knives do not get rid of stubbornness, and the gun does not get rid of stubbornness. But with the stick the fighters are capable of fighting until they are satisfied. And in this way stubbornness disappears and the fighters end up loving each other. In other words, what the saying *Inkani iqedwa yinduku,* stubbornness is stopped by a stick, really means is peace. We could have stopped stubbornness, but because the whites have come with guns, there is no way of stopping it. By introducing guns, the whites have spoiled everything. That is to say, white people are killers."

Clearly, what Shabalala was expounding here amounted to a complete revision, a decolonization of all the received images of Zuluness, African collective identity, and warfare. Violence, he insists, is not innate in people; it is an expression of social conflict and a means of dealing with it. There may be many causes of violence, but ultimately, armed conflict is a reality in an inescapably political world. Never is it an end in itself, let alone a mindless slaughter of the kind brought by the white man. The ultima ratio of violence, Shabalala seems to suggest, is the construction of alliances, of a profoundly social world, not its destruction. Such a perspective may seem romantic, especially at a time when a great deal of social conflict in South Africa is fought out with automatic weapons and grenades. But Shabalala's view is also at odds with those proselytes of ethnic purity who can only conceive of Zulus as "brothers born out of Zulu warrior stock" (Maré 1992, 68).

Parallel with the demystification of notions of belligerent Zulus, the corresponding, quintessential, musical image of Zuluness, too, is to be de-colonized. In other words, the cliches of skin-clad, stamping regiments shouting war songs, have to be revised. To illustrate his point, Joseph Shabalala started to sing an *ihubo:*

> *Siyoshintsh' upond' enduden'.*
>> We are going to change a pound at the chief's place.
> *Ningasishayi, siyoshintsha upond' enduden'.*
>> Do not hit us, we are going to change a pound at the chief's
>> place.

"This song," he then commented, "puts it quite clearly that the people you are fighting with, you will fight at a specific time. You are in full armory, shields, spears, because you are traveling in the veld. There you approach, singing the *amahubo* and the children are scared. They leave the cattle and run away. When they reach home they report that there is a war. The people at home come out with their sticks and hear the song. Then they realize that the warriors are just passing. Actually, you sing this song when you are asking for a path, when you are passing a village."

What will become of the isicathamiya performers and their songs in a new South Africa, only the future will tell. The "hostels," to be sure, in some modified or even upgraded form will remain an important domain of housing for millions of underprivileged South Africans. Poverty, too, will not disappear overnight. And so it is to be expected, woefully or blissfully, that the nightsongs, too, will continue to be performed. Born from the experience of deprivation and humiliation and an essential form of social practice and everyday consciousness, the songs and dances of the migrant performers will subject the new social order to critical scrutiny. They will go on to record the suffering. They will keep alive the past and give direc-tions for the future. But, above all, the nightsongs will continue to ask questions about this society and how to best live in it.

Notes

Preface

1. See also Asad (1986); Crapanzano (1986): 51–53.

Chapter One

1. Bauman and Briggs (1990): 68.
2. Other important texts that have been written in the essay format and that experiment with life histories and issues of authority and fieldwork are Lortat-Jacob (1990a); Chernoff (1984); and Yotamu (1979).
3. See also Grenier and Guilbault (1990).
4. See also Werbner (1990).
5. Along the same lines, see Frank (1991).
6. For a useful survey of music and gender see Sarkissian (1992) and the collection "Women and Music in Cross-Cultural Perspective" edited by Elen Koskoff (1987).

Chapter Two

1. A recording of this song is available on Heritage HT 313, side B, track 2.
2. Ibid., track 3.

Chapter Three

1. For similar perspectives on ethnicity among isiZulu-speaking migrants see Sitas (n.d.); la Hausse (1987, 1990); and Marks (1989b).
3. *Ilanga,* 13 October 1956.
3. Amy Bridgman-Cowles: *Annual Report of Umzumbe Station,* 19 May 1918, American Board Commission of Foreign Missions (hereafter ABCFM), South African Mission, Zulu Branch 1910–19, Documents 1:7 (Harvard University).
4. For a detailed portrait of Caluza see Erlmann (1991): 112–55.
5. Elkin Sithole who was an active isicathamiya performer in Newcastle during the 1940s maintains that *isikhunzi* is derived from "grumbling" (Sithole [1979]: 278). Later, in a private communication to me, he suggested that the correct term was *izikunzi* (pl. of *inkunzi* [bull]) and signified the deep, bull-like bass parts of isicathamiya.
6. *Bantu World,* 12 February 1938.
7. Compare Rounder Records 5025, side A, track 2.
8. *Umteteli wa Bantu,* 11 July 1936, 5 April 1941.
9. For an SABC transcription record of an early Crocodiles tune recorded in 1968, see Rounder Records 5025, side B, track 4. As for Mkhize's Evening Birds, both the label and Columbia catalogues incorrectly list Mkhize's choir as Singing Birds. For the words of two of his songs see Tracey (1948): 56.
10. Recordings of the Cape to Cairo Choir are Gallo GE 186–87, 1316–1317, and Bantu Batho BB 521. For recordings by the Morning Stars see Decca DC 7, 24–25, 40, and ABC 401, 404.

11. Supplement to *Bantu World*, 1 May 1954.

12. F. Bridgman: *Annual Report*, Durban, 1901–2, ABCFM, South African Mission, Zulu and Rhodesia Branches 1900–1909, Documents 3:2.

13. *Ilanga*, 12 January 1917.

14. *Bantu World*, 22 February 1941.

15. An alternative spelling of this term is *ibombing*, but this does not conform with the way most isicathamiya veterans pronounce the term.

16. *Bona* (April 1965): 41.

Chapter Four

1. For four sensitive portraits of South African peasant migrants see Keegan (1988).

2. See also the many useful studies on alcohol, mine labor, and migration in Crush and Ambler (1992).

3. See also Breckenridge (1990).

4. But see, in this regard, Bradford (1987); Breckenridge (1990); Hemson (1979); and la Hausse (1990).

5. See their album on Gramma Records/Ndiza NDLP 15.

6. See, e.g., "Ngoanyana" and "Aja Apepa," both on the album *Umama Lo!* (Mavuthela BL 23).

7. It is interesting that the Ngoni in Malawi have not developed an idiom similar to isicathamiya, although they are related to the Zulu and have been migrating to the Witwatersrand for many decades.

8. N. W. O. Shepstone to Town Clerk, 12 June 1935, Town Clerk Files, 467c, Durban.

9. See, e.g., the SABC transcription recording by the CTC Mbube Choir (SABC T 5041). See also "Sikheshekheshe" (Prostitute) by the King Star Brothers (SABC LT 9477, A3).

Chapter Five

1. Mavuthela BL 22, *Ufakazi Yibheshu*. The complete lyrics of the song are as follows:

Leader: *Niyilizwa yini maZulu akithi KwaZulu*
        Do you hear, all you Zulu people
        umthetho wakwa Phindangene?
        the law of the Zulu kingdom?
        Niyezwa yini?
        Do you hear?

Chorus: *Nina nonke maZulu* . . .
        All the Zulus . . .

Leader: *ukuthi* . . .
        that . . .

Chorus: *mas' buyele kwezomdabu.*
        we should go back to our roots.

Leader: *Kusho bani lokho?*
        Who is saying that?

Chorus: *Kush' umntwana wakwa Phindangene.*
   The word comes from the king.
Leader: *Kusho bani na?*
   Who is saying that?
Chorus: *Kush' ingonyama yamaZulu.*
   The word comes from the lion of the Zulus.
   Ubhejane aphume esiqiwini.
   The bull should escape from the game reserve.
Leader: *Awu! Yini kodwa?*
   Oh, where is the problem?
Bass: *Awu, ayi, yini kuzo 'nyama Zulu*
   Oh no, says the king of the Zulus:
   Mas' buyele kwezomdabu.
   Let's go back to our roots.
Leader: *KwaNongoma lena,*
   There at Nongoma,
Chorus: *Kwa Nongoma le, enale,*
   at Nongoma, and there,
   emzini wengonyama yamaZulu,
   in the house of the lion of the Zulus,
Leader: *Kuthiwa madoda*
   they say: Gentlemen,
Chorus: *Mas' buyele kwezomdabu.*
   let's go back to our roots.

2. Comaroff (1985); Vail and White (1991).

3. For the words of the Mendi Memorial Anthem as it was sung during the 1930s, see the program of the Mendi Memorial Anniversary, 1933, in Forman Papers, BC 581 D3.3, University of Cape Town Libraries.

4. For a useful discussion of the Mpondo homestead, see Kuckertz (1990).

5. Recorded in Durban, 10 March 1984. See also "Ikhaya Lami" by the Scorpions (SABC LT 10 247, B2).

6. This line refers to an incident that took place in Durban in the 1970s. An old man, trying to demonstrate his bravery had imitated the "staffriders"—young men riding on the outer steps of railway cars—and in the process was run over by another train.

7. The correct spelling would be *eSandlwana*.

8. See, e.g., "Mangosuthu" on Ladysmith Black Mambazo's album *Induku Zethu* (Mavuthela/Ezomdabu BL 393, side A, track 1).

9. See "For Music Action—Call the 'K Team.'" *South African Labour Bulletin,* 10, no. 8 (1985): 75.

Chapter Six

1. For a more detailed discussion of this point see Comaroff and Comaroff (1991): 86–125.

2. Engard (1989); Fernandez (1974–75); Spencer (1985).

3. Blacking (1985): 68; Cowan (1990): 18.

4. Caraveli (1985): 277; Cowan (1990): 24, Comaroff (1985): 5ff.

5. See, however, Blacking (1955).

Chapter Seven

1. But see also Seeger (1987).

2. See, e.g., Coplan (1988).

3. The songs are "Uyaphi" (SABC LT 8765, B4), "Akeniphume" (SABC LT 10 158, B5), "uCosatu Ulwa Nabalwa Naye" (Shifty 24L4, side A, track 3).

4. For a slightly different translation see Tracey (1948): 61.

5. See Nyembezi (1963): 78.

6. The image is repeated in another song by the Empangeni Home Tigers (Motella MO 479).

7. *Jive* (May 1989): 44–45.

8. Blacking (1980a), Dargie (1987); Gunner (1988); Pewa (1984); Xulu (1992).

9. An example of this is "Yizwa Imithandazo" by Inthethelelo Yabazalwane (C&G Records CRS (C) 197, side A, track 1).

Chapter Eight

1. This paragraph largely follows Guy (1980) and Clegg (1981b).

2. For parallel notions of the individual among the Tswana and missionary concepts of selfhood see Comaroff and Comaroff (1991): 142–43.

3. *Ilanga Lase Natal,* 12 June 1911.

4. *Ipepa Lo Hlanga,* 26 June 1903.

5. *Umteteli wa Bantu,* 11 November 1933.

6. Regrettably, Clegg's argument is informed by Evans-Pritchard's rather dated model of the segmentary society. But this shortcoming does not impair the validity of Clegg's other findings.

7. See also "Ngqo Ngqongo Vula" by Solomon Linda and the Evening Birds (Gallo GE 801).

8. See also "Babanza Abantu" (1797, Unissued) by the Evening Birds:

> *Bayasibabaza abantu bayasibabaza.*
> They are praising us, people are praising us.

Chapter Nine

1. H. I. E. Dhlomo: Evolution of Bantu Entertainments. Durban: Killie Campbell Africana Library (n.d.) KCM 8290 Z, MS DHL 1.08, D 58–280.

2. Most of the information in this paragraph relies on Tomaselli et al. (1989), Hamm (1991), an interview with SABC broadcaster Patrick Buthelezi, and my own research in the SABC "black music discotheque."

3. SABC Annual Report, quoted in Hayman and Tomaselli (1989): 45.

4. *Bantu World,* 15 and 29 November 1947.

5. Tomaselli and Tomaselli (1989): 100ff.

6. Hamm (1991): 163; Hayman and Tomaselli (1989): 72ff.

7. *Bantu Education Journal* (April 1971): 7.

8. Tomaselli et al. (1989): 168.

9. *Black TV Monitor* 1, (1982), no. 4, p. 4, no. 6, p. 6.
10. Tomaselli and Tomaselli (1989): 101.

Chapter Ten

1. See also Coplan (1982); Koetting (1975), 31.
2. Minutes of Glebelands association. In author's possession.
3. *Ilanga Lase Natal,* 24–26 October 1988, 26–28 June 1989.
4. Speech by James E. B. Msomi delivered at Steadville Community Hall, 26 March 1988. I am grateful to Professor Msomi for providing me with a copy of his speech.
5. Bongani Mthethwa to SATMA officials, 31 October 1987.

Chapter Eleven

1. *Amabutho* was released in 1973.
2. See Clifford (1986): 106. Also Crapanzano (1980); Rosaldo (1976); and Shostak (1981).
3. My translation here differs slightly from that of K. H. Wolff in Simmel (1965): 343.
4. See also Berglund (1976): 97ff; Kiernan (1985); Sundkler (1961): 265–75; and the critique by Charsley (1992): 170ff.
5. Tedlock (1987): 7.
6. See, however, Wallis and Malm (1984); Waterman (1990).
7. Danny Glover reads "How the leopard got his spots" (Windham Hill Records WD-0715); "Passage to promise" on Andreas Vollenweider's *Book of Roses* (Columbia COL 468827 2).
8. The debate is usefully summarized in Denselow (1989); and Humphries (1989).
9. Warner Brothers, "Media information. Paul Simon talks about *Graceland,* accordion jive, and 'life outside the mainstream'" (p. 5). I am indebted to Louise Meintjes for this and other sources from her files.
10. Paul Simon: *Graceland: The African Concert,* Peregrine/Zenith Productions (938136-3), 1987, videotape.

A Select Discography of Isicathamiya

Rob Allingham and Veit Erlmann

The following discography lists every known *mbube, isikhwela Jo, cothoza mfana,* and isicathamiya recording up to and including 1990. A few recordings of isicathamiya precursor styles are also selectively listed (Humming Bees, for example).

Regrettably, this discography must be regarded as a preliminary effort. Despite the fact that a large number of different sources were used in its compilation—statutory notices, composers' deeds of assignment, recording logs, payment sheets, engineers'/producers' notations on master tape boxes, record catalogues, newspaper and magazine advertisements, and, of course, the records themselves; this listing is far from complete. Probably only 85%–90% of the total number of commercial isicathamiya recordings and a considerably smaller percentage from the South African Broadcasting Corporation's vast transcription catalogue are listed. Time did not permit the necessary extensive research required to separate probably hundreds of isicathamiya items from an overall total of some 26,000 SABC transcription discs recorded from 1953 up to the present. The completeness of the commercial listings largely depends on the particular label and just how far research into its history has progressed.

The masters produced by Gallo's studio have now been extensively catalogued from the studio's inception in 1934 up to about 1951, hence the citing of those that are untraced (almost all of which are unissued items with no surviving test pressings). In contrast, the output of Lafayette's Better label of the 1939–45 period, a prime source of early isicathamiya, is far less well researched; less than half of the total issued catalogue has been identified. Almost nothing is known concerning the catalogue and history of the Manzini label, another interesting source of Zulu material of all types, while Troubadour's BZ prefix "ethnic" series which comprised almost 800 issues between 1951 and about 1967 is also largely untraced.

Also missing are many of the details concerning each particular recording: dates, personnel, etc. Much of this information is probably lost forever, although some might be retrieved by tracing and interviewing the musicians involved. Further details might also emerge from a careful aural review of the material. Unfortunately, in the compilation of this discography, it was not possible to listen to every single recording listed.

Nevertheless, without the assistance of several organizations, this discography would be vastly more incomplete. The International Library of African Music's catalogue of their 78 holdings, particularly their unissued test pressings, was an invaluable source of information. Both the Durban and Johannesburg record libraries of the SABC generously made their extensive holdings and facilities available for research, while the Johannesburg transcription library provided the dates which accompany those transcription discs listed. Last, the resources of Gallo Music Publishers and the Gallo Archive were utilized extensively. Albert Ralulimi assisted with many queries, while typist Karen Lepora struggled through a mass of paperwork to assemble the discography in its finished form.

The format of this discography is modeled after Brian Rust's *Jazz Records 1897–1942* and R. M. W. Dixon and J. Godrich's *Blues and Gospel Records 1902–1943*. The groups/artists are arranged alphabetically. Then, within each group heading, the recordings are arranged chronologically. With the paucity of available information on certain groups and recordings, it has sometimes been difficult to determine correct chronological sequences, particularly where there are several undated recordings on different labels. An even more critical problem arises because isicathamiya groups have such a marked propensity for using the same or similar names. In the absence of complete personnel listings, it is often difficult to determine whether a number of different recordings issued under the same name were indeed produced by one group (which may have existed over a long period albeit with gradual personnel changes) or were recorded by two or more entirely different groups. Decisions in these instances have sometimes been purely arbitrary and/or based on "educated" guesswork.

Underneath the group heading, the known personnel is listed. If only one or two names are cited, they have probably been taken from a composer's deed of assignment. (The composers of the material recorded by isicathamiya groups are almost always members of that group. A sole composer is usually the leader.) If a full personnel listing is given, the source is almost always the payment sheet for the session. These names are arranged as follows: first the leader, if known; then, listed alphabetically, the names of the musicians being paid royalties, as these were almost certainly the regular members of the group; then, last and also listed alphabetically, the names of the musicians being paid flat fees, as these were probably added to the lineup only for the recording session.

Underneath the personnel, the recording location and date, if known, are listed. Underneath the date and location comes the information regarding each individual title. From left to right, this includes:

1. Matrix number(s). These are only cited when they are true matrix numbers, that is, in a totally independent series from the catalogue numbers.

2. Track title.

3. Catalogue number(s). Only shellac and vinyl records are listed, not parallel issues on other formats: 8-track tapes, cassette tapes, or compact discs. However, after vinyl formats began to decline in popularity in favor of cassette tapes in the 1980s, many albums were only pressed on vinyl in limited numbers for radio promotion. South African issues are listed by catalogue prefix and number only. This saves space, especially where one 78-rpm coupling remained in print for an extended period with the same prefix and number but was re-pressed using newer labels. (Some issues, for example, first appeared on Decca, then Trek, and then still later on Tropik.) Foreign issues are shown by listing both the label and catalogue number. A key to South African catalogue prefixes follows, showing the record speeds and labels where they appeared, together with their corporate owners where known.

Underneath the track listings, the following information appears in parentheses:

1. Name changes/pseudonyms on individual issues where different from that listed on the alphabetical heading.

2. Untraced masters which may have been recorded at the same session. This listing only appears where the overall master sequences have been researched.

3. Groups appearing on the reverse side of an issued recording if different from the group concerned.

4. The title of any LP/cassette albums appearing in the listing.

Catalogue Prefixes

AB 78/45: CBS (GRC)

ABRL 33: HEART OF AFRICA

B 78: INTOKOZO

BB 78: BANTU BATHO (RECORD INDUSTRIES), BB (RECORD INDUSTRIES, TRUTONE)

BFM 45: FAST MOVE (RPM)

BH 45: BLACK HI-LIGHTS (MAVUTHELA-GALLO)

BL 33: BUS STOP, EZOMDABU, GALLO GRC, GRC, MOTELLA, SMANJE MANJE, ZEBRA (MAVUTHELA-GALLO, GALLO)

BOL 33: BOOTS (REAMUSIC)

BRM 78: BRM

BS 45: BRANDS

BSLP 33: MOTELLA (MAVUTHELA-GALLO)

BSLP 33: THOKOZA (WEA)

BSMC 33: RAP

BZ 78: AUDION (INTERNATIONAL TRANSCRIPTIONS), TROUBADOUR (TROUBADOUR)

CB 45: EMDUBANE (GRC)

CEL 33: CHOCOLATE CITY (RAINBOW)

CNH 33: CHOCOLATE CITY (RAINBOW)

CRS 33: C & G (C & G)

CT 33: CTV (CTV)

CYL 33: MAJAVAJAVA (TEAL)

DC 78: DECCA, TREK, TROPIK (GRC)

DMP 33: DMP

DLPL 33: MOTELLA (MAVUTHELA-GALLO)

GAL 33: GUDLA GUDLA (ANNIC)

GB 78/45: GALLOTONE (GALLO)

GE 78: SINGER, SINGER-GALLOTONE, GALLOTONE-SINGER, GALLOTONE (GALLO)

GL 33: GALLO (GALLO)

GOL 33: GOLI (EMI)

HB 45: HOT BEAT (RPM)

HBL 33: HOT BEAT (RPM)

HITL 33: KNOCK OUT (RPM)

H-PIC 78: HMV (EMI)

HUL 33: EZOMDABU, GALLO GRC, GRC (GALLO)

IAL 33: Soul Soul (Teal)
IGH 33: Ingwenya (Rainbow)
JML 33: Jamloti (EMI)
JP 78/45: HMV (EMI)
JUL 33: Jaguar (Reamusic)
KA 78: Chaka (Radio Record Company)
KT 78/45: Tempo (GRC)
LAB 33: CBS (GRC)
LCH 33: Church (GRC)
LIH 33: Lindela
LJD 33: Umjondolo (GRC)
LT 33: SABC Transcription
LZG 33: Imbongi (GRC)
MAB 45: Mama (Teal)
MAL 33: Mama (Teal)
MBT 33: Midnight Beat (Dephon)
MFB 45: Mafutha (Teal)
MFB 33: Mafutha (Teal)
MFL 33: Mafutha (Teal)
MGG 78/45: Gumba Gumba (Mavuthela-Gallo)
MKB 45: Radio Zulu (Trutone)
MO 78/45: Motella (Mavuthela)
MOU 33: Mountain (Mountain)
MPL 33: Mpumelelo (David Gresham)
MRP 45: Meropa
MXH 33: Soul Brothers (Tusk)
NB 78: Better (Lafayette)
NOISE 45: Noise (Shifty)
NTL 33: NTU (David Gresham)
NV 78: Envee (Trutone)
NZL 33: HVN (GRC)
OK 78/45: Winner (Trutone)
OSA 33: Osishayo
PDM 33: Paradise
PK 45: Phillips (Trutone)
PKLP 33: Phillips (Trutone)
RB 78: Rayma (Raymond & Marshall)
RL 33: Star Rays (Mavuthela-Gallo)
RLLP 33: Red Label (CTV-Music Team)
RPM 45/33: RPM (RPM)
SEH 33: Supertune
SHIFT 33: Shifty (Shifty)
SHINE 33: Shine (RPM)
SJH 33: Diamond Spiritual
SJM 78/45: Smanje Manje (Mavuthela)
SK 33: Skyline

SLB 45: Sondela (WEA)
SMC 33: Motella (Mavuthela)
SML 33: Six Mabone (Teal)
SONOR 33: Sonovision (Sonovision)
SRLP 33: RAP
SSL 33: Sondela (WEA)
SYK 33: Siyakha (CSR)
T 33: SABC Transcription
TBH 33: Themba
TEL 33: Indumezulu (Teal)
TJ 78/45: Quality (Trutone)
TMA 33: Music Team (Music Team)
TR 33: African Music Afrique (International Library of African
    Music)
TRAD 45: TRAD
TV 78/45: Zonk (GRC)
VUH 33: Vuka Afrika (Priority)
WZLP 33: World Ilizwe (Meteor)
XED 45: Ezom Dabu (Mavuthela-Gallo)
XU 78: Better (Lafayette), Trutone (Trutone)
XWI 33: Ezomdabu (Mavuthela-Gallo)
YE 78/45: Columbia (EMI)
YELP 33: Columbia, EMI (EMI)
YMA 45: Vuma
ZZ 78: Manzini

Abasindisi Black Singers
vocals: P. Mbikwana, others unknown
Johannesburg

Siyanimema Bazali
Wenzenjalo Uthixo
Masithandazeni
Bawowam
Wakrazulwa
Lomhlaba Uyahlaba   } MOU45
Ndomlandelauyesu
Intlizioyam
Siyanibona Thina
Ind'Indlela

(All titles released on MOU45, *Lomhlaba Uyahlaba*.)

Abathandazi
vocals: Moses Ntuli (leader), Elliot Buthelezi, others unknown

1974

ABC33101, ABC5800	Lalela Ndoda	MO502, DLPL291/2
ABC33102, ABC5801	Umosi Loyo	MO502, DLPL291/2

ABC33103, ABC5800   Ikhond'Indaba   MO503, DLPL291/2
ABC33104, ABC5801   Induna Lena   MO503, DLPL291/2
ABC33105   Kikizela Mama   MO504
ABC33106   Emhlabeni   MO504
VOCALS: Elliot Buthelezi, Moses Ntuli, others unknown
Johannesburg   *c 25 Sept 1975*
ABC33673   Tshela Lomuntu Ahambe   MO635
ABC33674   Shenge   MO635

ABATHANDAZI ZULU CHOIR
VOCALS: A. Dnego, others unknown
Johannesburg   *1978*
     Zimyama   TRAD332
     Ibonakala Ngani   TRAD332

ABYSSINIAN EIGHT
Johannesburg   *1937*
XYZX1   Seueleule   GE184
XYZX2   Me Le Ntate   GE184
XYZX3   Re Sentse Linako   GE183
XYZX4   Naledi   GE183
XYZX5   Hamang Lipoli   GE182
XYZX6   Mala Mabeli   GE182

AFRICAN PRIDE SINGERS
VOCALS: J. Z. Maseko (leader), others unknown; BANJO (1): unknown; PIANO (2):
Emily Motsieloa
Johannesburg   *c 1940*
1676 Egemara   Unissued
1677 Amanzi Aweko (1)   GE878
1678 Wee Mfann   Unissued
1679 Sifikile Tina   Unissued
1680 Tela We Ma   GE888
1681 Abafana (1, 2)   GE878
(1675 untraced.)

AFRICAN ZULU MALE VOICE CHOIR
VOCALS: unknown; PIANO: Sid Meyer (1) or Mark S. Radebe (2); BANJO: Johnny
Souris
Johannesburg   *1933*
WEA1542-1   Sivela Kuleli Lase J.G.   AE34
WEA1543-1   Cry Cough! (1, 3)   AE38
WEA1544-1   Akuko Ntombi Ezala Tina   AE36
WEA1545-1   Kuyekelini Kukule (2)   AE86, Rounder 5025

WEA1546-1	Lusapo Lwe-Africa (2)	AE86
WEA1547-1	Isandhla Esavela Sabhala (2)	AE77
WEA1548-1	Sesibuya Kona Lena (2)	AE35
WEA1549-1	Bakupuke Izwe Lonke (2)	AE77
WEA1550-1	Kukona Izindaba Ezinkulu	AE36
WEA1551-1	Wosabenz' Ubuye Mntaka	
	Baba (2)	AE35
WEA1552-1	We Sishimane! (2)	AE98
WEA1553-1	Bayadonsa Donsa (2)	AE38
WEA1554-1	Ufufunyana Use-Tekweni	AE99

(AE34, AE38/WEA1543-1 issued as African Zulu Male Voice Choir, Accompanied by Jazz Revellers Band. AE35 issued as African Zulu Male Voice Choir; Piano
Accompaniment: M. S. Radebe. Rounder 5025 entitled *Mbube Roots*. WEA1516–
41, 1555–64 untraced.)

Johannesburg   1938

CEA2105-1	Ezintsukwini Zo Tshaka	YE12
CEA2106-1	Bengini Zono	YE12
CEA2107-1	Into Iya Ngidumaza	YE13
CEA2108-1	Ntombi Mgangi Yeshela	YE13

(YE12, 13 issued as African Male Voice Choir. CEA2087–2104 untraced.)

ALENHOME (see LADYSMITH ALLEN HOME)

ALEXANDRIANS (see MAKTSHWA'S CHOIR)

ALL NATIONS MALE VOICE CHOIR
VOCALS: unknown; CONCERTINA: unknown; GUITAR: unknown
Johannesburg   c 1942
| Sabela Mfana | XU63 |
| Uy'Ngogw'E Malina | XU63 |

AMABHUNGU AMNYAMA
VOCALS: M. Manyaka (leader), others unknown
Johannesburg   1976
Ngithi Uyakhumbula	
Silindele Imoto	
Yathutha Yaphelezela	LT15685
Thula Thandiwe	
Siyanibingelela	

AMANZIMTOTI MALE VOICE CHOIR
VOCALS: Maseko (conductor), others unknown; CONCERTINA (1): unknown;
GUITAR (2): unknown; BANJO (3): unknown
Johannesburg   c 1941
Khelina	XU32
Sobalindela	XU32
Amafufuyani (1,4)	XU33

Ayilwanga (3,4)	XU33
Ekuda Leni	XU38
S'telela Ama Kanda	XU38
Vula Muyango	XU41
Talaza	XU41
Basixoshile (1,2)	XU42
Laza Lashona (2)	XU42

AMAZULU AMNYAMA
Johannesburg   *1974*
 Ngaliwa Yentombi
 Kwezwakakala Umuntu   LT14335
 Abafana Basentshongweni

A NATAL TRY SINGERS (see TRY SINGERS)

ARNOT HOME SINGERS
VOCALS: G. Mambane, others unknown
Johannesburg   *8 May 1980*
 Babazani   NTL7001
 Ingulube   NTB721, NTL7001
 Makhosazana   NTL7001
 Glory Glory   NTB721, NTL7001
 Yini Umlomo
 Disco
 Makwaya
 Ezulwini
 Bongi Wami   NTL7001
 Uze Ube Nami Nkosi
 Ama Ndebele
 Kahleni Uku Khuluma
(All titles released on NTL7001, *Babazani.*)
Johannesburg   *1983*
 Kwakhetha Omthandayo
 Zanele
 Makwery
 Umtwana Waka Phindangene
 Baba Nomama
 Umona   CT52
 Izembe
 Noanyana
 Amabhubesi
 Inthiliziyo Ayiphakelwa
(All titles released on CT52, *Umtwana Waka Phindangene.*)

BERGVILLE GOLDEN STARS
Johannesburg   *20 July 1987*

    Ekanana
    Egolgotha
    Bayazivuma Bayazishiya
    Kingdom Of Lord
    Ivangeli
    Oh! Samaritan   RPM7123
    Ngangilahlekile
    Simenyiwe
    Nantigazi
    Ihubolentokozo

(All titles released on RPM7123, *Ihubo Lentokozo*.)

BERGVILLE NGWADI NDUKUZIBOMVU
Johannesburg   *1 Apr 1982*

    Babasibusisiwe
    Sihubela U Jehova
    Ngiphakamisela Mehlo
    U Jesu U Yasibiza
    Jehova Singabakho
    Nathikwaba Ncono
    Kosibaba Sihlangene   RPM7070
    Thina Bantu Balom Hlaba
    Wena Uyamthanda Na?
    Bafana Bengwadi Guqani
    Singa Buswa Ngu Jesu
    Balekani Niyocasha

(All titles released on RPM7070, *Iqili Lamqili*.)

BLACK BUSH BUCKS
VOCALS: Victor Mzimela, others unknown
Durban   *1984*

    Ibuya
    Thina Sibiziwe
    Ngixolele
    Ntombi Eyonakele
    Umhlaba Usahlule
    Sibezwile   RPM7099
    Lizoduma
    Jesu Msindisi
    Sesifikile
    Indiza

(All titles released on RPM7099, *Sibezwile*.)

Johannesburg   *11 Aug 1987*
    Limnandi Evangeli
    Indlela Sa Singayazi
    Ufunayo Uzo Fumana
    Thina Sithandaza Kuwe
    Indandazo
    Kuwe Jesu Wami   RPM7119
    Liyate Isoko Lakho
    Jesus Is My Plea
    O Umthwalo Osobokweni
    Zantlantlatha
(All titles released on RPM7119, *Limnandi Evangeli*.)

BLUE HAMS CHOIR
Johannesburg   *Early 1942*
2012   Umfazi Maweni
2013   Ekuqaleni
2014   Salibamba   Unissued
2015   Sikuzwile
(This may not be an isicathamiya group.)

BOILING WATERS CHOIR
VOCALS: A. Dhlamini, others unknown
Johannesburg   *7 Oct 1961*
ABC20763   Siyanimema   Unissued
ABC20764   Amathishela   GB3252
ABC20765   Dali Sohlangano   GB3252
ABC20766   Wangibuka Waklala   Unissued
(According to the original file cards, ABC20765 should be titled *Dali Sohlangano*, but on GB3252 it was labeled *Wangibuka Waklala*. Neither title, however, correlates with the lyrical content of the performance!)

BRAKPAN YOUNG STARS
VOCALS: Simanga Dube, Bafana Hlongwane, Oupa Phillip Madonsela, Jacob Khelha Nhlapo, Phillip Khelha Nhlapo
Johannesburg   *June 1983*
          Thokozile
          Siyabonga Bhodloza
GRC8343   Ngishayelwani Kangaka
          Thina Sizingwenya
          Yibo Lab Abasizi Bethu
          Sicela Amandla   LJD102
          Usawule
GRC8344   Siyabonga Nokubonga
          Wonkumhlaba Jikelele
          Ujesu Uliqhawe
(All titles released on LJD102, *Thokozile*.)

BRAVE LIONS SINGERS
VOCALS: J. M. Chili, others unknown
Johannesburg   *1952*
CEA2568-1 Shwele Mtakwethu   YE57
CEA2569-2 Ngahamba   YE57
CEA2570-1 Nganginomfazi   YE58
CEA2571-1 Webaba Sabela   YE58
Johannesburg   *1952*
CEA2614-1 Ndikhumbula Evantini   YE67
CEA2615-1 Sabela Brave Lion   YE67
CEA2616-1 Balekani   YE71
CEA2617-1 Kukona Indaba   YE71
Johannesburg   *Feb 1960*
           Sengi Besathalaza   T5528
           We Dudu Lavi Uthangithini T5528
           Okunjanokwe Bhula Thina T5529
           Sodlula Kanjane Majuba   T5529
           Okuncono Siponono   T5530
           Bayakhala Ngenkunzi   T5530
           Ntombi Ziya Buluka   T5531
           Wayeshelelwa Ngubani   T5531
(T5528-31 issued as Brave Lions Mbube Choir.)

CAPE TO CAIRO CHOIR
VOCALS: unknown; PIANO: Emily Motsieloa; BANJO: unknown
Johannesburg   *c 1938*
1316 Bapi Abafundisi   Unissued
1317 Intombi Ngayi Tshela   Unissued
1318 Mlamlankunzi   GE187
1319 Zilandelana   GE187
1320 Sipuma Le   GE186
1321 Bayi Dontsa E Tekweni   GE186
(1315 untraced.)

C.C.X. ZULU MALE VOICE CHOIR
VOCALS: Benjamin Mkhondweni (leader), others unknown
Johannesburg   *1959*
OAS1062 Impolompolo   JP2146
OAS1063 Baby Ngane   JP2146
Johannesburg   *1974*
      Mazulu Masilalele Umthetho ⎫
      Azibuyi |
      Jabula Mfana   ⎬ LT14314
      Sawubona Sithando Sami |
      Izwe Lasegoli |
      Intombi   ⎭
(LT141314 issued as CCX Brothers.)

CHAMPION NAUGHTY BOYS
VOCALS: Seth Shembe, others unknown
Johannesburg   *1959*
OAS1180   Yangi Qcomekuseni?   JP507
OAS1181   E Benoni?   JP507

CLERMONT HOME DEFENDERS
Johannesburg   *1974*
    Iyashalaza
    Ngeke Ngishele Kulomuzi
    Uxolo Ntombi   } LT14310
    Aziphelele Mfana

CLOVER CHOIR
Durban   *June 1985*
    Sibingelela uFOSATU   SHIFT 6, Rounder 5020
    Sicela Indlela FOSATU   SHIFT 6, Rounder 5020
(SHIFT 6 entitled FOSATU *Workers Choirs*. Rounder 5020 entitled *South African Trade Workers Choirs*.)

COLENSO ABAFANA BENKOKHELO
Johannesburg
    Njengamankentshane
    Zemuka
    Thula Gaxekile
    Uthi Uyagula?
    Kade Ngizulazula
    Kumnyama Sikhona   } CRS185
    Ngaxoshwa Izinduku
    Ngezwa Ngisemncane
    Musuyishela Intombi Yami
    Izulu Lami
(All titles released on CRS185, *Njengamankentshane*.)
Johannesburg   *1987*
    Sanibona
    Nala Labantu Bengisukela
    Imnandi Lengoma
    Sibashaye Sabaqeda
    Ngake Ngahamba Izwe
    Awungisindisi   } CRS192
    Size Ngodumo
    Kuxabene Omakhuba
    Nantithuba Lami
    Ngasala Kanjalo
(All titles released on CRS192, *Udumo Lwenkosazane*.)
VOCALS: V. Mkhize, others unknown

Johannesburg
- Usiko Lwesizulu
- Wothina Silapha
- Kwathi Ngingenamali
- Yibo Laba
- Amanqe A Yohla Bani   } MBT227
- Usathane
- Akusenani Ubuhle Bayo
- Intombi Ihamba
- Ngenkomo Zikababa
- Ngeneme

(All titles released on MBT227, *Usiko Lwesizulu.*)
VOCALS: V. Mkhize, others unknown

Johannesburg
- Heyi Heyi
- Ubaba Nomama
- Uya Khathaza
- Nansi Lensizwa
- Libalele   } MXH26
- Mabulalekheka
- Sehla Senyuka
- Ngiyamathanda
- Hayi Wemfana
- Wemhlaba

(All titles released on MHX26, *Inhlanhla.*)
VOCALS: V. Mkhize, others unknown

Johannesburg
- Umkhulumeli Wethu
- Sengizohlukana Nawe
- Ngikhuzeleni Labantu
- Wobheka Kusemhlabeni
- Induku Ebandla   } DMP2
- Kade Ngihamba
- Thina Siyahamba
- Umalume
- Hawu: Khuzanimadoda
- Ujesu Usemafini

(All titles released on DMP2, *Ukuthula Ezweni.*)
VOCALS: V. Mkhize, others unknown

Johannesburg
    Indaba
    Izangoma
    Behlulekile
    Sithando Sami
    Zibiza Ama Thousand (1 000)
    Umuntu Onenhlanhla   DMP8
    Wemakoti
    Inhlekelele
    Usathane Wenzani
    Indabazabantu
(All titles released on DMP8, *Indaba*.)

CROCODILE MALE VOICE CHOIR
VOCALS: Isaac Mzobe (conductor), others unknown
Johannesburg   *1939*

Ingubu Yami	XU12
Umpati (Chairman)	XU12
Umfana Akaloboli	XU13
Sasingaxabene	XU13
Mzobe	XU14
Intoyami	XU14

VOCALS: Isaac Mzobe (conductor), others unknown; CONCERTINA (1): unknown
Johannesburg   *c 1941*

Safa Indhlala	XU30
Inecala Intombi (1)	XU30

VOCALS: unknown; ALTO SAX: unknown; ACCORDION: unknown; GUITAR: unknown; BASS: unknown; DRUMS: unknown
Johannesburg (?)   *c 1948*

Shimane	NB21, XU160

VOCALS: Enoch Mzobe (leader), others unknown
Durban   *3 Dec 1958*

ABC17316	Emaweni	GB2916
ABC17317	Dali Angishongo	GB2916
ABC17318	Bafuna Thina	GB2914
ABC17319	Ziyu Buya	GB2914
ABC17320	Unknown	Unknown
ABC17321	Unknown	Unknown

(ABC17316-21 as The Crocodiles.)
Johannesburg   *13 Nov 1959*

ABC18171	George	Unknown
ABC18172	Ezulwini	Unknown
ABC18173	Natal vs Transvaal Part 1 (Take 1)	GB3015
ABC18173	Natal vs Transvaal Part 1 (Take 2)	Unissued
ABC18174	Natal vs Transvaal Part 2	GB3015

ABC18175 Noseyishayile
ABC18176 Umfundisi
ABC18177 Kulungile
ABC18178 Bayeza
        } Unknown

(ABC18171-76 as The Crocodiles.)

Johannesburg   *1962*
ABC22336 Uthwala   GB3403
ABC22337 Amorqatha Amangane GB3403
ABC22338 Baleka
ABC22339 Qagela (Take 1)
ABC22340 Izinceku   } Unissued
ABC22341 Masimdumisi
ABC22339 Qagela (Take 2)
(ABC22336-41 as The Crocodiles.)

Johannesburg   *1967*
 Masimdumise
 Amanzenze
 Imithwalo   } LT8764
 Akukho Soka Lahlala
 Dali Angizange Ngisho
 Zingelosi Ze Zulu
 Hei Malomei
 Vula Wesdudla   } LT8765
 Ngikhumbula Usizi
 Uyaphi
(LT8764-65 as Crocodiles.)

Johannesburg   *1968*
 Nhloyile
 Umshado   } LT10034, Rounder 5025
 Akasangibhaleli
 Thula Mntwana
(LT10034 as the Durban Crocodiles. Rounder 5025 entitled *Mbube Roots.*)

Johannesburg   *1968*
 Bavimbeni   LT10157
 Asigoduke   LT10157, Rounder 5025
 Basakazi
 Ntombi Yo Mthakathi } LT10157
 Uhambo Lwami
 Awutinyikithi
 Hloyile
 ETekhwini
 Impolompolo   } LT10158
 Kudala Sihamba
 Isistimela Samampondo
 Akeniphume
(LT10157-58 as Crocodiles. Rounder 5025 entitled *Mbube Roots.*)

CROCODILE SINGERS
Paulpietersburg   *Nov 1985*
    Hewu: Kwaqaqamba Amathambo   Rounder 5025
(Rounder 5025 entitled *Mbube Roots.*)
(The Crocodiles who recorded for RPM in 1975 were not an iscathamiya group.)

CROWDVILLE OLYMPICS
VOCALS: Alpheus Mtalame (conductor), others unknown
Johannesburg   *c Oct 1950*
N1202 Noma Kumnyama   BB514
N1203 Imbuzi   BB514
N1205 Wena Ndhlovu   BB531
(N1204 untraced. Reverse of BB531 by Morning Shine Choir.)

C.T.C. CHOIR
VOCALS: Isaac Ndhlovu (leader), others unknown
Johannesburg   *c 30 July 1951*
N1310 Ngeke Ngipinde   BB521
N1311 Bengine Kulalami   BB521
N1312 Sani Bona   BB?
N1313 Ngizoreka Kanjani   BB?
Johannesburg   *5 Feb 1952*
N1398 Beka E Mnyango   NV3315
N1399 Nga Zula'Mpela   NV3315
N1400 Guga Mzimba   BB?
N1401 Amarabi   BB?
(NV3315 as C.T.C. Zulu Choir.)

CTC MBUBE CHOIR
Johannesburg   *1959*
    Sanibonan Boma   T5041
    Intombi Zasi Parktown   T5041

C.T.L. MBUBE CHOIR, VOLKSRUST
Johannesburg   *1970*
    Safika Emasimini
    Ukate   }   LT12087
    Sambamba Umnumzane
    Siyayidabula Lengoma
    Kungcono Ngihambe
    Unokuzula   }   LT12088
    Irisha Lami
    Sifike Izolo

C TO C ZULU CHOIR
VOCALS: Jafta Mtshali (leader), others unknown

Durban   *1961*
ABC20356   Izwalase Natal   KT3004
ABC20457   Tshelu Mama   KT3004
ABC20358   Wemama Ngiyagiya   DC823
ABC20359   Molo Zihobo   DC823
Johannesburg   *19 Oct 1961*
ABC20783   Thamkohemjoka   Unissued
ABC20784   Uyamame Zumama   Unissued
Johannesburg   *c 1961*
ADB484   C To C   BZ1639
ADB485   Ncola   BZ1639

CUP AND SAUCER
Durban   *10 March 1984*
   Akasangibhaleli   Heritage HT313
Durban   *24 Nov 1985*
   Hamba Ntombi   Heritage HT313
   Uhlekani Emzini   Heritage HT313
(Heritage HT313 entitled *Iscathamiya.*)

DANGER EXPRESS
Johannesburg   *1983*
   Sanibonani Bantu Bakithi
   Ntaba Exikude
   Salli'Suthula Mama
   Siwuhambile Wonke Umhlaba
   Uthando Lwami
   Hambani Sihambe   IGH1011
   Sakesahamba Thina
   Oh Josina
   Sana Lami Ungishiyelani
   Uma Liduma Izulu
   Noma Bekhuluma
   Isikhalo Samadoda
(All titles released on IGH1011, *Sanibonani Bantu Bakithi.*)

DANGER EXPRESS CHOIR
VOCALS: unknown   *c 1953*
ABC10287
ABC10288
ABC10289
ABC10290
ABC10291   Unknown   Unknown
ABC10292
ABC10294
ABC10295
(ABC10293 untraced.)

c 1953

ABC10696 ⎫
ABC10697 ⎬   Unknown   ⎫   Unknown
ABC10699 ⎭   ⎬
(ABC10698 untraced.)

DANNHAUSER FLYING STARS
VOCALS: Sehla Hlatswayo (leader), others unknown
Johannesburg   1976
    Wendoda Egawula Lapha   ⎫
    Ngiyayithanda Lentombi   ⎬   LT15859
    Bambizinja Zakho   ⎭

DECCA WANDERING MINSTRELS (see **UNION EXPRESS COMPANY**)

DECCA ZULU SONG BIRDS (see **SOLOMON LINDA'S ORIGINAL EVENING BIRDS**)

DHLAMINI HOME DEFENDERS
Johannesburg   1966
    Yehla Moses   ⎫
    Yithi Abanini Somuzi   ⎬
    Selikude Ikhaya Lami   ⎬   LT4737
    Maye Ubuhle Belanga   ⎭
    Mbube Ahi   ⎫
    Sanibonani Nina Bakhuti ⎬   LT4738
    Tennessee Blues   ⎬
    Hamba Mfana Ka Baba   ⎭

DIEPKLOOF MESSENGERS
Johannesburg   *c 23 Aug 1981*
    Heyi Madoda   ⎫
    Bavimbeni   ⎪
    Nda Famba   ⎪
    Iyedelela Lentombi   ⎪
    Bahoualo   ⎪
    Ingilube   ⎬   RPM7059
    Mkhuewami   ⎪
    Ntombazane   ⎪
    Asambeni Bafowetho   ⎪
    Kwabhca   ⎪
    Hambani Sihambe   ⎭
(All titles released on RPM7059, *Bavimbeni*.)

DUNDEE TRY SINGERS
Johannesburg   *8 Nov 1952*
N1536   Yekani Abantu   ⎫
N1537   Hop Sabela   ⎬   BB?
N1538   Sikalela   ⎬
N1539   Babuyile   ⎭

Dundee Wandering Singers
VOCALS: unknown; BANJO (1): ——Gumede; PIANO (2): Emily Motsieloa
Johannesburg   *c 1941*
1737 Zimajuma (1,2)   DC13
1738 Ulele Ezweni   DC14
1741 Noma Kumnyama   GE883, London LPB431
1742 Bashobha Upickup   GE883
1743 Namtini Kathi Wemakaya (2)   DC13
1744 Yithi Abafana   Unissued
1745 Wemarabeni (1,2)   GE882
1747 Balambile Abafana   DC14
1748 Akuyisete (1,2)   GE882
1749 Darlie No-Mama   Unissued
1750 Poll Tax   Unissued
1751 Zulu Laduma Emdubane (2)   GE888
1753 Yizwa Mngoma   GE887
1757 T.B.   Unissued
1761 Sekuyiti   GE941
1766 Wangi Bamba Seliyoshona (1,2)   DC27
1767 Eloff Street   GE902
1768 Obaba Sabashiya (1,2)   DC27
1769 Washo Umfana Wami (1,2)   GE902
(DC13, DC14, DC27 issued as Natal Champions. 1739–40, 1746, 1754–56,
1758–60, 1762–65 untraced. Reverse of GE887 by Solomon Linda's Original
Evening Birds. Reverse of GE888 by African Pride Singers. London LPB431
entitled *Zulu Music And Songs*.)
VOCALS: unknown; PIANO: unknown; BANJO: unknown
Johannesburg   *Late 1941*
1811 Ngi'E Kaya   Rounder 5025
1813 Hamba Sitemela   GE941
1814 Kwamaye Maye   DC44
1815 Ngasuke' Kaya   DC44
1816 Akasabhati   Unissued
(DC44, Rounder 5025 issued as Natal Champions. 1809–10, 1812, 1817 untraced. 1818–24 by Snowy Radebe and Company. Rounder 5025 entitled *Mbube
Roots*.)
VOCALS: unknown; PIANO (1): unknown
Johannesburg   *Late 1941*
1828 Bonke Abantu   Unissued
1829 Yiniloku (1)   DC46
1833 Ricksha (1)   DC46
1834 High Court   Unissued
1835 Witch Doctor   DC43
1836 Boyabamba   DC43
(DC43, DC46 issued as Natal Champions. 1825–27, 1830–32 untraced.)
VOCALS: unknown; BANJO (1): ——Gumede, PIANO (2): Emily Motsieloa

Johannesburg   *Early 1942*
1907 Izono (1,2)   DC42
1908 Basopa (1,2)   GE923
1909 Eku Mlangana   Unissued
1910 Leta   Unissued
1911 Kini Mazula (1,2)   DC42
1913 Sakala (1,2)   GB1049
1914 Usedululu   DC45
1915 E-Gemara   Unissued
1916 Tembi Lami   DC45
1917 Vula Imbobo (1,2)   GE923
(GE923 as Zulu Wandering Singers. GE1049, DC42, DC45 as Junior Natal
Champions. 1897–1906, 1912 untraced. Reverse of GE1049 by Solomon Linda's
Original Evening Birds.)
VOCALS: unknown; BANJO (1): unknown; PIANO (2): Emily Motsieloa

Johannesburg   *1942*
2016 Tina Siboshiwe   GE952
2017 Sengibathalaza   Unissued
2018 Wangi Ponsa (1,2)   GE952
2019 Kwe Lakithi   Unissued
2020 Ngeke Wayi Tola   Unissued
(2021–24 untraced.)
VOCALS: unknown; GUITAR (1): unknown

Johannesburg   *c 1942*
2156 Arungixolele (1)   GB999
2157 Maye!   GE989
2158 Stimela Baleka   GE989
2159 Mqombothi   DC70
2161 Hamba Nawe (1)   GE946
2167 Nqakamazinyo (1)   GE945
2168 Zindunduma (1)   GB946, London LPB431
2169 Khulumani Nonke   DC70
2170 Champion (1)   GE945
2172 Wemahlasela (1)   GE999
2174 Ba Mbopa U Lavi   GE966
2175 Mzimba Uza Pheka   Unissued
2176 Ayi Kwazi Ukupheka   GE966
2177 Ngi Saba Ulenwalwa   Unissued
(GE945, GB946, GE989 issued as Zulu Champions. DC70 issued as Natal
Champions. 2155, 2158, 2160, 2162–66, 2171, 2173, 2178–82 untraced. London LPB431 entitled *Zulu Music and Songs*.)
VOCALS: unknown

Johannesburg   *c 1947*
ABC3014   Hamba Stutubaker   GE990, Rounder 5025
(ABC3000–13, 3015–16 untraced. Reverse of GE990 by Herzon Ngobese with
Morning Light Choir. Rounder 5025 entitled *Mbube Roots*.)

DUNDEE WANDERERS
Johannesburg   *4 Aug 1961*
ABC20398   Magweqwana
ABC20399   Ngihamba Ngedwa
ABC20340   Inhliziyo Yami
ABC20341   Zisethe Miss Makeba
ABC20342   Sizinyoni   } Unknown
ABC20343   Emarabeni
ABC20344   Umfazi Wami
ABC20345   Thatha Uteba

DURBAN CITY BROTHERS
VOCALS: Gravis Cele (leader), others unknown
Johannesburg   *1974*
    Dolly
    Sabela Mfoka Chili
    Esikhaleni Kwanobamba   } LT14315
    Izulu Lizoduma

DURBAN CITY CHOIR
Johannesburg   *1965*
    Likude Ikhaya Lam
    Eshukumayo Ukufa Kuliwala
    Mayemaye Umntakababa   } LT7941
    Sakubona Sithando Sam
    Akeni Phumeni Bekemnyango

DURBAN C TO C
Johannesburg   *1970*
    Bethal   LT12097

DURBAN EVENING BIRDS
The group led by A. W. Mthembu who recorded under this name on Envee is
choral rather than *mbube* in style. See also Evening Birds.

DURBAN HIGH STARS
Durban   *18 Nov 1984*
    Awungangi Dluli Jesu   Rounder 5023
(Rounder 5023 entitled *Mbube!*)
Durban   *28 Apr 1985*
    Lapha eSandlwana   Heritage HT313
    Siyolila Sonke   Heritage HT313
(Heritage HT313 entitled *Iscathamiya*.)

DURBAN HUMMING BEES
VOCALS: unknown; CONCERTINA: unknown; GUITARS: unknown; TAMBOURINE:
unknown

Johannesburg   *1938*
OAS41-1   Wo Ngi Hambha Ngi
         Ngedwa   YE18
OAS42-1   Emarabini   JP4
VOCALS: unknown; CLARINET: unknown; VIOLIN: unknown; CONCERTINA: un-
known; GUITARS: unknown; TAMBOURINE: unknown
Johannesburg   *1938*
OAS65-1   Ngo Mtshel! Ubaba No
         Mame   YE18
OAS67-1   So Hambi No Bani Na   JP4
OAS68-1   Omame Ba Ya Sikalela   JP9
         E'Makaya
(The lead vocalist of the Durban Humming Bees is definitely a different singer to
the lead vocalist of the Humming Bees who recorded for Gallo a few years earlier.
OAS60-64 untraced. OAS66 by Kuzwayo's Band.)

DURBAN HUMMING BEES
Johannesburg   *1974*
   Umfoka Baba
   Nyonini Leyo
   Emahlathini Amnyama
   Benginehashi   } LT14329
   Ngiyamthanda Usimelane
   Phesheya Kwalezontaba
   Uhleka Mina Nje   } LT14330
   Sengiya Ekhaya
(This is almost certainly a different group from the one which recorded as the Dur-
ban Humming Bees for EMI in 1938.)

DURBAN KING EXPRESS
VOCALS: Samuel Zulu (leader), others unknown
Johannesburg   *1976*
   Amakehla   LT15858

DURBAN LETTER STARS
Johannesburg   *1966*
   Khwela
   Sakubona
   Uyeza Umama   } LT6983
   Thina Siyambonga
   Animkhuzeni

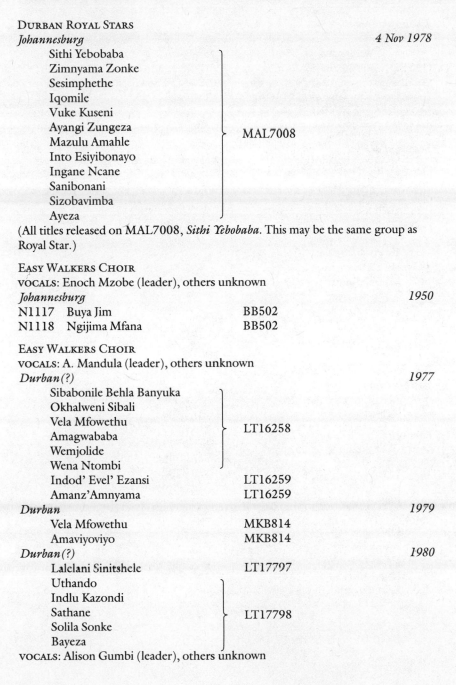

DURBAN ROYAL STARS
Johannesburg   *4 Nov 1978*

> Sithi Yebobaba
> Zimnyama Zonke
> Sesimphethe
> Iqomile
> Vuke Kuseni
> Ayangi Zungeza   MAL7008
> Mazulu Amahle
> Into Esiyibonayo
> Ingane Ncane
> Sanibonani
> Sizobavimba
> Ayeza

(All titles released on MAL7008, *Sithi Yebobaba*. This may be the same group as Royal Star.)

EASY WALKERS CHOIR
VOCALS: Enoch Mzobe (leader), others unknown
Johannesburg   *1950*
N1117   Buya Jim   BB502
N1118   Ngijima Mfana   BB502

EASY WALKERS CHOIR
VOCALS: A. Mandula (leader), others unknown
Durban(?)   *1977*

> Sibabonile Behla Banyuka
> Okhalweni Sibali
> Vela Mfowethu
> Amagwababa   LT16258
> Wemjolide
> Wena Ntombi
> Indod' Evel' Ezansi   LT16259
> Amanz'Amnyama   LT16259

Durban   *1979*
> Vela Mfowethu   MKB814
> Amaviyoviyo   MKB814

Durban(?)   *1980*
> Lalelani Sinitshele   LT17797
> Uthando
> Indlu Kazondi
> Sathane   LT17798
> Solila Sonke
> Bayeza

VOCALS: Alison Gumbi (leader), others unknown

Durban   *10 Mar 1984*
    Imbube   Heritage HT313
    Sawubona Baba   Heritage HT313
(Heritage HT313 entitled *Iscathamiya*.)
Durban   *18 Nov 1984*
    Oh Yes Is Coming   Rounder 5023
(Rounder 5023 entitled *Mbube!*)

EMDENI IMTUTHUKO
Johannesburg   *2 April 1976*
    Zivulele Mfo Ka Mcunu
    Bayede
    Mgonothi
    Iyangi Delela
    Ophe O Selina Wami   HBL5501
    Thina Intuthuko
    Ngeke Nise Hlule Thina
    Wa Thengi Impepha
    Asi Funeke Isidakwa

EMPANGENI FLYING STARS
VOCALS: E. Cebekhulu (leader), others unknown
Durban(?)   *1976*
    Ikhona Indaba   LT15684

EMPANGENI HOME TIGERS
Johannesburg   *12 Oct 1973*
    Akenithule   MAL7002
    Gwinyitshe   MAL7002
    Unokuthula   MAB729, MAL7002
    Khulumezako   MAB729, MAL7002
    Yini Lena   MAL7002
    Siyamazi Ushaka   MAB730, MAL7002
    Enkwezela   MAB730, MAL7002
    Liphendule
    Selethwese
    Umshado   MAL7002
    Kwezomdabu
    Mfokambambo
(All titles released on MAL7002, *Empangeni Home Tigers*.)
VOCALS: Milton Mbhambho, others unknown

Johannesburg(?)   *c 8 Jan 1974*

ABC32783, ABC5016	Intselelo	MGG619	
ABC32784, ABC5017	Selethwese	MGG619	
ABC32785, ABC5016	Ufakazi Yibheshu	MGG620	
ABC32786, ABC5017	Lwasuka Usinga	MGG620	BSLP22, BL22
ABC32787, ABC5016	Liphendule	MGG621	
ABC32788, ABC5017	Ihlongandlebe	MGG621	
ABC32789, ABC5016	Encome	MGG622	
ABC32790, ABC5017	Niyezwa Yini?	MGG622	

(BSLP22, BL22 entitled *Ufakazi Yibheshu*.)

Johannesburg(?)   *c 24 June 1974*

ABC33019, ABC5410	Waqala Ngokuwendlala	MO479	
ABC33020, ABC5411	Nqonqonqo Emnyango	MO479	
ABC33021, ABC5410	Angina Mali	MO480	DLPL291/2
ABC33022, ABC5411	Khulum' Ezakho Izindaba	MO480	
ABC33023, ABC5410	Yini Lena?	MO481	
ABC33024, ABC5411	Uthikoloshe	MO481	

(DLPL291/2 entitled *Cothoza Mfana*.)

Durban   *1979*

| Zinsizwa Zomdabu | MKB818 |
| Phansi Imikhonto | MKB818 |

EMPANGENI MESSENGERS
VOCALS: Linus Mkhize (conductor), others unknown

Durban(?)   *1976*

Molweni Zinsizwa	
Ngixolele Mfowethu	LT15686
Maye Babo	
Wathatha Intombi Yami	

EMPANGENI MESSENGERS: DURBAN

Durban(?)   *1977*

Sengiyazisa	
Nixolele Mfowethu	LT16259
Webaba Vula	
Sibali Wami	

ESCORT C TO C ZULU CHOIR
VOCALS: unknown

Johannesburg   *19 Oct 1967*
ABC20783   Thambo Lenyoka   ⎫
ABC20784   Uyameme Zumama   ⎬   Unissued
ABC20785   Guga Mzimba   ⎪
ABC20786   Amampondo   ⎭

EVENING BIRDS
VOCALS: Alson Mkhize "Bomvu" (leader), Alphas Mkhize, Edwin Mkhize, Josiah
Mkhize, ——Msibi; CONCERTINA: unknown; BANJO: unknown; GUITAR: un-
known; PIANO: unknown
Johannesburg   *1937*
1180 Itye   GE144
1181 Igama La Le Ntombi   GE145
1183 Intombi Nezintsizwa   GE144, London LPB431
(1177–79, 1182, 1184 untraced. Reverse of GE145 by Maktshwa's Choir with
Merry Blackbirds. London LPB431 entitled *Zulu Music and Songs*.)
VOCALS: Edwin Mkhize, others unknown
Johannesburg   *1938*
OAS43-1   Yiwo Ama Evening Birds   JP10
(JP10 issued as Durban Evening Birds. OAS44 untraced. Reverse of JP10 by Kuz-
wayo's Band.)
Johannesburg   *1938*
OAS81-1   A Ka Sa Ngi Bhaleli   JP5
OAS82-1   Yenz'Inqab'Intombi   JP5
(JP5 issued as The Evening Birds. OAS77–80 untraced.)
VOCALS: as above; PIANO: unknown
Johannesburg   *1938*
OAS254-1 Jabula Mfana   JP21, H-PIC-2
OAS255-1 Ntombi Ngi Ngi Ye Shela   JP21, H-PIC-2
(JP21, H-PIC-2 issued as Durban Evening Birds. H-PIC-2 was a picture disc is-
sued in 1951. OAS253, 256–58 untraced.)
Johannesburg   *1938*
OAS261-1 Woza Lapha 'Sitandwa
              Sa Mi   JP28
OAS264-1 Se Hla Nyuka Si Ya
              Embhotsheni   JP28
(OAS260, 262–63, 265–68 untraced. JP28 issued as Durban Evening Birds.)
Johannesburg   *1938*
CEA2330-1 Sa Mbambha   YE42
CEA2331-1 Vi Bo La 'Bafana A Ba
               Diliza Utayini Wo Lo YE42
CEA2332   Ya M Qom Ekuseni   YE51
CEA2333   Si Phuma Lena E Dundee   YE51
CEA2334-1 Wo Sa Ngena   YE43
CEA2337-1 Wa Kal' U Mama   YE43
(YE42, YE43, YE51 issued as E Mkize and His Singing Birds. CEA2335, 2336
untraced.)
VOCALS: Edwin Mkize (conductor), others unknown

Johannesburg			*1950*
N1117	Buya Jim	BB502	
N1118	Ngijima Mfana	BB502	
N1119-D	Naba Bengibiza	BB503	
N1120-D	Tela Amanzi	BB503	

FEAR NO HARM CHOIR
VOCALS: unknown; PIANO: Emily Motsieloa; BANJO: ——Gumede

Johannesburg			*c 1936*
357	Mombiza Lo Nyaka	GE121	
358	U George	GE121	
359	Ina Ma Wala	GE120, Rounder 5025	
360	Nga Bona Islmanga	GE120	

(356, 361–63 untraced. Rounder 5025 entitled *Mbube Roots.*)

FLYING STARS

Johannesburg		*1942*
2043	Wangi Kolisa	
2044	Isono Sami	
2045	Wafa Flying Stars	Unissued
2046	Leta Into Your	
2047	Tula Mama	

(2026–42, 2048–57 untraced. This may not be an *mbube* group.)

FRAME CHOIR

Durban		*1984*
	Bayasichaphaza	SHIFT 6, Rounder 5020

(SHIFT 6 entitled *FOSATU Workers Choirs.* Rounder 5020 entitled *South African Trade Workers Choirs.*)

FUNNY VOICE MBUBE CHOIR

Johannesburg		*1970*
	Yini Loku	LT12353
	Sengikhumbule Ikhaya Lika Baba	
	Ngangiyozingela Amakhowa	LT12354
	Ngizulazula Nje	

Johannesburg		*1970*
	Angizange Ngisho	
	Siponono	
	Ithemba Lami	LT12477
	Intombi Yami	
	Fulela	

(LT12477 issued as Funny Voices.)

GEE GEE'S BROTHERS
VOCALS: Obed Shangase, others unknown

1975

ABC33634	Mangisele Ngedwa	MO628
ABC33636	Ngivulele	MO628
ABC33637	Abazali Bethu	MO629
ABC33638	Thokozile	MO629

G.M.C. CHOIR
VOCALS: Kleinbooi Lukhele (leader), others unknown
Johannesburg   *c 1965*

OAS2146	Bhula	JP862
OAS2147	G.M.C.	JP862
	Siyambongo	JP826
	Ikhaya Lam	JP826

Johannesburg   *c 1965*

OAS2233	Vulanamasango	JP904
OAS2234	Yithabaninibomuzi	JP904
	Eluthela	JP934
	Ezola	JP934
	Sobabamba	JP962
	Lashomlanga	JP962
	I Qololibuhlungu	JP964
	Mayoyo	JP964

GMC GOOD BOYS
Durban   *21 Feb 1982*

Walala Uphenduka
    Njengesangoma   Heritage HT313
(Heritage HT313 entitled *Iscathamiya*.)

G.M.C. MBUBE CHOIR
VOCALS: Wilson Mbele (leader), others unknown
Johannesburg   *1977*

Eyi! Wethu
Uqamb' Amanga   } LT16344
O, Dela Wena

(The G.M.C. Choir under Kleinbooi Lukhele and the G.M.C. Mbube Choir under Wilton Mbele may be the same or largely the same group.)

GREEN MAMBAS
Johannesburg(?)   *1976*

OSA102

(OSA102 entitled *Nansimali*. No information on individual track titles.)

GREYTOWN EVENING BIRDS
Durban   *18 Nov 1984*

Nisibona Silapha Siphuma
    Siphuma Kude   Rounder 5023
(Rounder 5023 entitled *Mbube!*)

HAMLET'S MALE VOICE CHOIR
VOCALS: unknown
Johannesburg   *c 1939*
    Indaba   XU16
    Isitimela   XU16

HAMMARSDALE RED HEARTS
VOCALS: Solomon Mazibuko, Moses Bhekukwenza, Shadrack Khanyile, Vincent
Khomo, Jabulani Mpanza, Alpheus Shoba, Elmon Zondi
Durban   *20 Feb 1981*

ABC10294	Ntomb'Futhi Thuleleni Dumazile Eminyakeni Engaka Oshibham Unyak'Omusha Usibongile Ngiyamthanda Sibingelel'Umndeni	BL298
ABC10295	Wezwa Ngobani U Thuleleni Ungiphoxile Mntanomuntu Masibiya Ninhlakanhlaka Nje	

(All titles released on BL298, *Ntomb'Futhi*. The recording sheet lists the name of
the group as the Hammarsdale Choppers.)

HAPPY BOYS MALE VOICE CHOIR
VOCALS: unknown; CONCERTINA: unknown; GUITARS: unknown
Johannesburg   *c 1941*
    Ayi Lwanga   XU43
    Siyakwesaba   XU43
    Ulele   XU44
    Suka Emvakwami   XU44

HAPPY BOYS MBUBE CHOIR
                                                         1966
    Unknown   T4722

HAPPY HEARTS
VOCALS: M. Mathobela, others unknown
Johannesburg   *c 1952*
OAS460   Intombi Eziphamibile   JP114
OAS461   Asambe Magoduka   JP114

HARDING LUCKY STARS
Johannesburg   *1974*

	Sizonibona Intombe Eduduza Mina Kwelakithi Thandiwe Sanibonani Zihlobo Thandiwe	LT14418

HARDING MORNING STARS
Durban   *18 Nov 1984*
    Ithemba Lami   Rounder 5023
(Rounder 5023 entitled *Mbube!*)

HARRISMITH BOYS
VOCALS: David Tshabalala, others unknown
Johannesburg   *1958*
OAS1049   Zimbili Bili   JP2101
OAS1050   Entombe Zingi Yale Zile   JP2101

HARRISMITH CHOIR
                                         1975
                             SML7003
(No further details available for this item.)

HARRISMITH FLAMINGO BOYS
VOCALS: Hilton Shabalala (leader), E. Sithole, J. Mthembu, others unknown
Johannesburg   *1990*
    Inxeba (Nansi Lendoda)
    Angibaboni
    Commando
    Sanibonani
    Themba Likababa
    Thathumese
    Impi   SYKL106
    Thula Mama
    Intombi Yami
    Uphi Umfo Ka Mshengu
    Isangoma
    Intandane
All titles released on SYKL106 *Inxeba.*)

HARRISMITH SINGERS
Johannesburg   *19 July 1952*
N1452   Maye'Nkosi   BB?
N1453   Kone Kele   BB?

HARRISMITH TWIN BROTHERS
VOCALS: Thomas Selepe (leader), others unknown
Johannesburg   *1976*
    Ikhona Into Engiyizwayo
    Woza Kimi Wesithando
    Siphuma Entabazwe   LT15684
    Bayebuwa (in Sesutho)

HLABISA HAPPY STARS
VOCALS: T. Mtshali, others unknown

Johannesburg   *1984*
   Ziyanqonqotha
   Asizibeki Phambili
   Ngidibene Nentobmbi
   Hayi! Igama Lethu
   Bophanis Sihambe
   Umfoka Mtshali
   Lowonthombo Ka Jesu   CT59, TMA1007
   Sizwe Sakithi
   Thum' Imvuselelo
   Nkosi Yethu
   Thina Laph'Emhlabeni
   Khawulani Ukudakwa
(All titles released on CT59, TMA1007, *Ngidibene Nentombi.*)

HOME DEFENDERS CHOIR
VOCALS: unknown; CONCERTINA: unknown, GUITARS: unknown
Johannesburg   *c 1943*
   Let'I Nto Yami   XU65, XU408
   Bati U Dhlulile   XU65, XU408
(XU65, XU408 issued as Durban Home Defenders.)
VOCALS: unknown; BANJO: unknown; GUITARS: unknown
Johannesburg   *c 1950*
ABC3738   Boph'Imithwala   DC116
ABC3741   Safa Saphela   DC116
(ABC3739–40, 3742–45 untraced.)
Johannesburg   *1959*
   Sesibancane
   Bopha Imithwala   T5052
   Se
Johannesburg   *August 1959*
   Wo Balele Ekhaya   T5141
   Thokozile   T5131
   Yekelani Ukuhuluma   T5132
   Idhlozi Wethu   T5135

HOME SWEEPERS
Johannesburg(?)   *c early 1960s*
NA10105   Intaba   ZZ50
NA10106   eKhaya   ZZ50

HOME TIGERS
VOCALS: L. Ngoba, others unknown
Durban   *1956*
ABC15340   Phikisanini   DC651
ABC15341   Indoda   DC651
VOCALS: Sampson Ntombela, others unknown

Durban(?)   *1967*
16162   Thula Gaxekile   TJ957
16164   Izingilosi   TJ957
Durban(?)   *1967*
         Asambeni ⎫
         Ngafik'Egoli ⎪
         Sabel'Uyabizwa ⎪
         Kwath'Ebusuku   ⎬   LT9080
         Thula Wena Gaxekile ⎪
         Impevana ⎭
         Mayoyo   LT9081
         Intombi Engithandayo   LT9081

HUMMING BEES
Johannesburg   *c 1935*
204   Uya Memeza Umama   GE100
205   Itambole Nyoka   GE100
(200–203 untraced. This is almost certainly a different group from the Durban
Humming Bees who recorded for EMI a few years later.)

HUMMING BEES
Johannesburg   *1974*
         Baphi Abakithi ⎫
         S'Dudla Phuma Endlini ⎬   LT14257
         Ubani Ongqongqothayo ⎭
(It is unlikely that this group is the same as that which recorded for Gallo in
1935.)

IMFUME MALE VOICE CHOIR
Johannesburg   *August 1959*
         Omabizwa Basabela   T5041
         Namhla Sine Ngoma Enkulu   T5041
         Unomvuyo Wami   T5440
         Inqaba Yamakholwa   T5440
         Silaphanje Siphuma Ekhaya   T5441
         Ngilandela Ubaba   T5441
         Dlungwane   T5442
         Noma Kumnyama   T5442

IMI ZWILILI CHOIR
Johannesburg   *1951*
         Basombo Upikapu   BZ26
         Sekusile   BZ26
         Genke Ngiye   BZ28
         Nansi Ioaba   BZ28

INALA LADYSMITH
Johannesburg *31 July 1973*

Wozasambe Siyemendweni
Ngizonitshela Indaba Enkulu
Ndoda Ukhalelani
Kwashumana Eyala Unitanakhe
Sehibuya Eswanzini
Ngaliwa Intombi Kwaduma Izwe } MAL7001
Tkhalakabuhlungu Inyoni
Cothoza Infana Sidhile
Molo Molo Madoda
Sasuka Ezathukweni

(All titles released on MAL7001, *Inala Ladysmith.*)

INGQONGQO AMA ALLEN HOME (see LADYSMITH ALLEN HOME)

INHLABA BOYS
VOCALS: Enock Sibiya, Maichel Mungwe, Joseph Mtungwa, Patrick Zamisa, others
unknown
Johannesburg *1981*

Mabi Amanga
Uxolo Makhwaya
Mngani Wami
Izindaba
Khulumani Madoda
Amabheshu } IGH1005
Umfundisi
Thokozile
Tsidi
Sheri Yaka

(All titles released on IGH1005, *Umfundisi.*)
Johannesburg *1982*

Ngiya Buza
Zinsizwa
Mfana
Mntanami Ulidela
Sanibona Madoda
Thembekile } IGH1009
Ngangikuthanda
Ingoduso
Nkunzini
Anibosala Kahle

(All titles released on IGH1009, *Ngiya Buza.*)

Johannesburg   *13 Aug 1984*
 · Themba Lami
 · Lalel'Amagama Ami
 · Phuthuma Sohna
 · Woyishada Intombi
 · Yakho
 · Zinsizwa Asambeni Siye
 ·   Sontweni   IGH1014
 · Amapantsula
 · Otsotsi
 · Sizo Bhekhaphi
 · Thula Sengibuyile
 · Msindisi
(All titles released on IGH1014, *Otsotsi*.)

INKANDLA COTHOZA STARS
Johannesburg   *1976*
 · Aba Semzini   MRP71
 · Sifikile   MRP71
 · Enufini   MRP72
 · Khethe Yakho   MRP72

INQABA YABESOTHO
VOCALS: S. Mkhize, others unknown
Johannesburg   *16 Apr 1973*
ABC4162   Indulu Ka Zondi   CB4050
ABC4163   Kwakhala Insingizi   CB4050
ABC4164   Nansi Impi   CB4051
ABC4165   Into Engidinayo   CB4051
ABC4176   Umathenga Umuthi   CB4055
ABC4177   Indoda Isegoli   CB4055
Durban   *1979*
 · Nangu Jesu Uyeza   MKB813
 · Usathan'Ungilandele   MKB813

INTETHELELO YABAZALWANE
VOCALS: P. Ngcobo, others unknown
Johannesburg
 · Yizwa Imithandazo
 · Ungangilahli Baba
 · Ngangiboshiwe
 · Bayozisola
 · Ngizomphilela Yena
 · Thumela Abefundi   CRS197
 · Ngalithatha Ivangeli
 · Limnandi Igama
 · Singancedwa Ngubani
 · Khaye Lihle
(All titles released on CRS197, *Yizwa Imithandazo*.)

INTHUTHUKO BROTHERS
Johannesburg   *1981*
    Intombi   RPM7863
    Nomvula   RPM7863
    Thembekile   RPM7864
    Nomvusa   RPM7864

INTOKOZO YAMASWAZI
VOCALS: I. Yamaswazi, others unknown
Johannesburg   *1983*
    Hlomani
    Ngaphosengafa
    Ukwenzelani
    Khathazile
    Ufunani   YELP5006
    Ngiyamthanda Ujesu
    Ngizibonele
    Nasemanzini
    Indluyamandla
(All titles released on YELP5006, *Makabongwe Ujesu.*)

INTOMBI ZEPHEPHA
Johannesburg   *Jan 1978*
    Hlanganani   MAB765
    Masisuke   MAB765
Johannesburg   *July 1978*
    Elundi   MAB768
    Izintombi   MAB768

INTUTHUKO YAMASWATI
VOCALS: Robert Malinga, others unknown
Johannesburg   *8 Sept 1977*
    Mfo Kamalinga
    Umthakathi
    Ucarolina
    Unomcebo
    Isishimane
    Okomhlaba
    Ibhuluko Lokugqoka   MAL7007
    Amathende
    Indodana Yolahleko
    Ingama Lenkosi
    Intombi Yami
    Ngikhokhele Jehova
(All titles released on MAL7007, *Ibhuluko Lokugqoka.*)

INYANDA YE-ZIZWE
VOCALS: Simon Ngubane, others unknown
Johannesburg   *c June 1979*

Jabulani-Nonke
U Jesu-Uyangazi
Ubuhle-Bentombi
Oh! Nkosi-Yami
Siyeza   HITL500
Nkosi-Siha'Ukele
Dumisani-U Jehova
Amaqola
Ngifunga-Abakhwekazi
Nangu-U-Tikoloshe

(All titles released on HITL500, *Ukuphuma-Kwe-Langa*.)

IZINGILOZI EZIMNYAMA
VOCALS: William Tobakale, Mthandani S. Hadebe, Mvunyelwa Hadebe, Hyland
Mabaso, Samuel Mdluli, Richard Mnculwane, Sipho Ndlovu, Canson Nyoka, Isaac
Zikode; ORGAN AND BASS GUITAR: David Mzwandile
Johannesburg   *30 April 1982*

              Mamdubane
              Abafazi Babantu
              Heyi Nina Maswati
ABC10776   U Lizi
              Gobondela
              Thekwane
                                   BL369
              Sanibonani
              Mahlalela
              Ntandane
ABC10777   Kudala Sinitshela
              Mapule
              Mfo Ka Mabaso

(All titles released on BL369, *Mamdubane*.)

IZINGWENYA ZASENKUTHU
Johannesburg   *1977*
Ingane Eyismanga   BFM127
Khumbulu   BFM127

JABULA HOME DEFENDERS
Durban   *18 Nov 1984*
Obaba Bafun'Imali   Rounder 5023
(Rounder 5023 entitled *Mbube!*)
Durban   *28 Apr 1985*
Ngithole Indaba   Heritage HT313
Ngifuna Imali   Heritage HT313
Durban   *24 Nov 1985*
Where You Come From?   Heritage HT313
(Heritage HT313 entitled *Iscathamiya*.)

JUNIOR NATAL CHAMPIONS (see DUNDEE WANDERING SINGERS)

K. C. CHOIR
VOCALS: unknown
Johannesburg   *1955*
ABC13966   Intombi Iqome Kude   DC705
ABC13967   Sehle Entabeni   DC705

KHANYI-SANI
VOCALS: N. T. Mncwango, H. Mazibuko, others unknown
Johannesburg   *c Apr 1982*
   Ungishiyelani Dumazile
   Uthando Lwethu
   Yangihlek'Intombi
   Nginikeni Umkami
   Masiyobatshela
   Ngiqonywe Intombi   IAL3023
   Kwazulu
   Thina Sahamba
   Ngangithandwa
   Sinethemba
(All titles released on IAL3023, *Ungishiyelani Dumazile.*)
VOCALS: N. T. Mncwango, others unknown
Johannesburg   *c Apr 1982*
   Ngiyamthanda Ujesu
   Siphetho Seqiniso
   Banenhlanhla Labobantu
   Kuyayiwa Ezulwini
   Abane Zondo
   Bahlala Bekhululekile   IAL3024
   Lezo Zono
   Sicel'Indlela Bazalwane
   Ujesu Wasifela
   Kuhle Ukukholwa
(All titles released on IAL3024, *Ngiyamthanda Ujesu.*)
VOCALS: T. Mncwango, others unknown
Johannesburg   *7 Oct 1987*
   Onozindaba
   Eyami Ayikho
   Ingane Yami Iyogana
   Yakhala Lengane
   Ulindiwe
   Mngani Wami   BL622
   Ishayile Madoda
   Usuthu Lukhandaba
   Bafana Bama Soul Brothers
   Izwe Lesethembiso
(All titles released on BL622, *Onozindaba,* as Khanyisane Mbube Choir.)

KINGS BOYS
Durban   *10 Mar 1984*
    Just A Closer Walk With Thee   Heritage HT313
    Thula Sithandwa Sami   Heritage HT313
Durban   *24 Nov 1985*
    Sawubona Ntombazane   Heritage HT313
(Heritage HT313 entitled *Iscathamiya*.)

KING STAR BROTHERS
Johannesburg   *April 1963*

Asinqonajwa	
Khubalo Lami	
Sati Umasihamba	LT4565
Asishayi Ingoma Yomuntu	
Gew Gew	
Baba No Mama	
Ezinsukwini Zawo Chaka	LT4566
Gabi Gabi	

Johannesburg   *1967*

Umfana	
U Khu La	
Ngaliwa Yintombi	
Sanibonani	LT7900
Uirene	

Johannesburg   *1968*

Hamba Njalo Wena	LT9476
Hamba Mfana	LT9476
Sikheshekheshe	LT9477
Isitimela Sasembabane	LT9477
Mus'Ukuqubuda	LT9477, Rounder 5025
Ithemba Lami	LT9477
Awubheke Ndod'Emnyama	LT9477
Nqaliwa Intombi	
Nampa Besibiza	
Nqaliwa Intombi	LT9478
Wangibiz'Umama	

(Rounder 5025 entitled *Mbube Roots*.)
VOCALS: Enoch Masina, others unknown
Johannesburg   *Nov 1967*

ABC27110	Khubalo Lami	AB3005	
ABC27111	Wogawula Lapha Mfana	AB3005	LAB4024
ABC27112	Gewu Gewu	AB3006	
ABC27113	Leth' Ibeshu Lami	AB3006	

Johannesburg   *Feb 1969*

ABC28006	Isitimela Sase Mbabane	AB3028
ABC28007	Sathi Uma Sihamba	AB3028

ABC28008	Skheshekheshe	AB3030	
ABC28009	Asiqonywa Nje	AB3030	
ABC28010	Maqondana	AB3031	
ABC28011	Ihashi Elimhlophe	AB3031	
ABC28012	Mfo Ka Buthelezi	AB3032	LAB4024
ABC28013	Musukuqubuda	AB3032	
ABC28014	Iyedelela Lentombi	AB3033	
ABC28015	Hamba Mfana	AB3033	

Johannesburg   *13 Aug 1970*

ABC29593	Umahamba Nendlwana	AB3050
ABC29594	Silaphanje	AB3050
ABC29595	Ulithemba	AB3051
ABC29596	Ihashi Elimhlophe	AB3051
ABC29597	Amadoda Esakhe Nawo	AB3052
ABC29598	Ntombi Noma Ungangala	AB3052

Johannesburg   *20 Aug 1970*

ABC29629	Wamtshelelani Ubaba	AB3053
ABC29630	Ulizzie Ungalile	AB3053

Johannesburg   *27 Aug 1970*

ABC29631	Ingodosi	AB3054
ABC29632	Sambona Umfana	AB3054
ABC29633	Sabafica Begaya Imithi	AB3055
ABC29634	Badlala Ngomama	AB3055

Johannesburg   *Sept 1973*

ABC4644	Kawubeke Ndodemnyama	AB3087
ABC4645	Ngandinda	AB3087
ABC4646	Hayi Makhanda	AB3088
ABC4647	Nampa Bezibiza	AB3088
ABC4648	Bayosala Besibuza	AB3089
ABC4649	Wemshengu	AB3089
ABC4650	Isimanga	AB3090
ABC4651	Mfoka Mhayisa	AB3090
ABC4652	Wangilaya	AB3091
ABC4653	Thatha Konke Ntombi	AB3091

VOCALS: E. Masina, B. Hlatshwayo, E. Khumalo, S. Zulu, others unknown

Johannesburg

Izidumo Zase Ncome	
Koze Kubeninj	
Iwisa Lanamhlanje Imfundo	
Sanibonani	
Thembi	SJH117
Uzindlela	
Ingoma Yomuntu	
Basazozalwa	
Ingoduso	
Kunzima Ukuphila	

(All titles released on SJH117, *Izidumo Zase Ncome*.)
VOCALS: E. Masina, B. Hlatshwayo, A. Jwara, E. Khumalo, others unknown

Johannesburg

Akusekho Ukwethembana	
Ngubani Omdala	
Akesiguqeni Sonke	
Waquqha	
Intandane	
Angilali Imfene	SJH124
Gabi Gabi	
Induku	
Woza Sondela	
Senzekile	

(All titles released on SJH124, *Akusekho Ukwethembana*.)
(Note: In 1975, King Star leader/composer Enoch Masina changed his name to
Enoch Nhleko.)

Johannesburg   *2 May 1975*

ABC33435	Khawubheke	MO588	
ABC33436	Wangi Laya	MO588	
ABC33437	Madod'Emizi	MO589	
ABC22438	Babelibusa	MO589	
ABC33439	We, Mshengu	MO590	
ABC33440	Iqomel'Empondweni	MO590	
ABC33441	Ngiyayizonda Lendoda	MO591	BL48
ABC33442	Ngiyazizwa Izidumo	MO591	
ABC33443	Madoda Nithule Nje	MO592	
ABC33444	Thatha Konke Ntombi	MO592	
ABC33445	Ngaphesheya Komfula	MO593	
ABC33446	Yesala Kutshelwa	MO593	

(All titles released on BL48, *Khawubheke*.)
VOCALS: Enoch Nhleko, Benjamin Hadebe, Bernard Hlatshwayo, Doctor Hlatsh-
wayo, John Hlatshwayo, Phillip Mabizela, Hamilton Mbatha, Abel Mntambo,
Shadrack Tshabalala, Obed Twala

Johannesburg   *18 Mar 1976*

ABC33850, ABC6522	Khangelani Umsindisi	
ABC33851, ABC6523	Jerusalem Entle	
ABC33852, ABC6522	Ngiyamuzwa Umsindisi	
ABC33853, ABC6523	Nhlengiwe	
ABC33854, ABC6522	Amagugu	
ABC33855, ABC6523	Uthe Wena Baba Wethu	BL75
ABC33856, ABC6522	Nkosi Bheka	
ABC33857, ABC6523	Usizi	
ABC33858, ABC6523	Mfo Kamabizela	
ABC33859, ABC6522	Emabaceni	
ABC33860, ABC6523	U Irene	
ABC33861, ABC6522	Ngaliwe Yintombi	

(All titles released on BL75, *Amagugu*. ABC33855 'Uthe Wena Baba Wethu' and
ABC33861 'Ngaliwe Yintombi' only appeared on the tape cassette issue.)

VOCALS: Mlamlankunzi Bernard Hlatshwayo, Kula John Hlatshwayo, Mshiyeni
Phillip Mabizela, Mandla Mgaga, Mjazini Shadrack Shabalala, Thamsanqa Saul
Shongwe, Ntsimbini Johan Twala

Johannesburg   *13 Nov 1981*

GRC7683
- Umfana Omfishane
- Kukhona Ukuzula
- Amadoda Ayosebenza
- Mfana Unenhlahla
- Bafana Hambanini

GRC7684
- Mus'Ukuqubuda
- Amabhadi
- Kufa Siyakwesaba
- Yithi Imbumbulu
- Umamncane

LJD63

(All titles released on LJD63, *Umfana Omfishane.*)

Johannesburg   *1984*

- Yashimizi
- Bangithumela Ngomkhovu
- Kwaphinda Kqwenzeka
- Musudlala Ngami
- Lizzy
- Esanlwane
- Baleka Mfana
- Into Zalomhlaba
- Uxabana No Baba
- Mngani Wami

BOL313

(All titles released on BOL313, *Yashimizi.*)

VOCALS: B. Hlatshwayo, J. Hlatshwayo, M. Hlatshwayo, T. Mabizela, M. Mgaga,
V. Mtambo, J. Twala, J. Yende, R. Zungu, others unknown

Johannesburg   *1987*

- Bazoyikhotha Imbenge Yomile
- Lapho Ukhona Ungakhohlwa
- Ngisolela Kuwe Ndod'Emnyama
- Sathi Umasihamba
- Ngaphesheya Komfula
- Thathani Amabhantshi
- Uthando Luzawuphela
- Ijazi Etshwaleni
- Mhlaba Kawunoni
- Ukuhlupheka Kwami

RLLP034

(All titles released on RLLP034, *Bazoyikhotha Imbenge Yomile.*)

Johannesburg
    Amaqhawe
    Bantu Bakithi
    Nina Bantu Basemzini
    Iziwi Lokhokho
    Waqheketha Izindaba   } PDM307
    Inhlonipho
    Halala Zinsizwa
    Lashona Ilanga
    Baba Wethu

(All titles released on PDM307, *Amaqhawe.*)
VOCALS: B. Hlatshwayo, P. Mabizela, P. Nhlapo, N. Twala, others unknown

Johannesburg
    Amagoduka
    Ngaliwayintombi
    Hiloyenyoni
    We Enjelina
    Mabi Amanga   } LIH2000
    Amaqol'Emvelo
    Niyambona Lomakoti
    Izintombi Zami
    Madoda Kunzima

(All titles released on LIH2000, *Yithi Sodwa.*)

K TEAM
VOCALS: A. Xaba, others unknown
Johannesburg
    Ubaba Wabhubha
    Wamlumelani Omunye Esandleni
    Ngicela Ukubuza
    Sesiyamba
    Sanibonani
    Thembi   } MPL4027
    Imindindi Nemizwilileki
    Inkosi Yethu Yinye
    Wangishiya Ngedwa
    Wozani

(All titles released on MPL4027, *Wamelumelani.*)
Durban   *1985*
    Siyabonga FOSATU
    Andries Raditsela
    Umkulumeli uFOSATU   } SHIFT 6, Rounder 5020
    Sasol 2 & 3

(SHIFT 6 entitled *FOSATU Workers Choirs.* Rounder 5020 entitled *South African Trade Workers Choirs.*)
VOCALS: Agrippa Xaba, others unknown

Johannesburg
    Lokhu Kwaqala Lomzabalazo ⎤
    Usomandla
    Ucosatu Ulwa Nabalwa Naye
    Izwe Lakithi
    Asimbongeni Ucosatu
    Wawukhona Edurban   ⎬ SHIFT 24
    Izinduku Ezimbili
    Bonke Bambonile
    Bekufanele Ngibonge
    Siswele Imilomo   ⎦
VOCALS: Agrippa Xaba, others unknown

Johannesburg   *1990*
    Viva ANC ⎤
    Ukubonga Kumnwandi
    June 16
    Soccer City
    Usizi Nezenyembezi
    Senzeni Na   ⎬ SHIFT 40
    Phantsi Udlame
    Viva Swapo Viva Namibia
    Africa
    Uyeza Umandela
    Salute Namibia People
    Nkosi Sike'l I-Africa   ⎦
(All titles released on SHIFT 40, *Viva*.)

KWAITOS D
Johannesburg   *1984*
    Amakhosi Akwazulu ⎤
    Sasinawe Juliya
    Ngibongeleni Zinsizwa
    Abafana Bezibaya
    Abafokazana
    Thembekile
    Kudala Besiqhoshela   ⎬ IGH1013
    Sesifikile
    Ngiphelezele Mama
    Thulani Nkalele
    Abafokazana
    Ngikhumbul'Ubaba
    Makungelami   ⎦
(All titles released on IGH1013, *Amakhosi Akwazulu*.)

KWA THEMA HIGH JUMPERS

                                                        1982
                        GOL317
(GOL317 entitled *Izimbali*. No information on individual titles.)

LADYSMITH ALLEN HOME
VOCALS: Elykel Magubane, Epheus Sithole, D. Vilikazi, others unknown
Johannesburg   1977
    Iqhude   SLB191, SLL4009
    Akhona Amaphutha   SLB191, SLL4009
    Jabula Nsizwa   SLL4009
    Lindiwe   SLL4009
    Abahlahli Bezulu   SLB192, SLL4009
    Ngaliwa Intombi
    Manalapho Nsizwa   } SLL4009
    Isihlahla
    Sikiza   SLB192
(SLB191, SLB192 issued as Alenhome. SLL4009 entitled *Isihlahla*.)
VOCALS: Elykel Magubane, Epheus Sithole, others unknown
Johannesburg   1980
    Ukuhamba Ukubona Zinsizwa
    Langishiya 'Themba Lami
    Selokhu Kwavulwa Ugologo
    Wemfana Ongenankomo
    Ugogo Wami
    Ukujabula Emhlabeni
    Uma Singaqhamuka Lapha   } BSLP1120
    Ngithandwa Intombi Enhle
    Khuzani Izingane Enhle
    Khuzani Izingane Zobaba
    Uyedela Wena Ongaganwanga
    Lomhlaba Amakhosi Akwazulu
    Asihambeni Bafana
(All titles released on BSLP1120, *Ukuhamba Ukubona*.)
Johannesburg   1981
    Langa Lomphefumulo Wami
    Ezulwini Nginobaba
    Bonganini Nonke
    Umzuzu Egetsemane
    Nginezono Eziningi
    Imnandi Indaba Yaphezulu
    Woza Moni   } BSLP1122
    Soya Ngaphi
    Wozani Bazalwane
    Lapho Izivuvungu
    Jesu Kumnandi
    Uyangithanda Unkulunkulu
(All titles released on BSLP1122, *Ilanga Lomphefumulo Wami*. BSLP1122 issued
as Ingqongqo Ama Allen Home.)

Johannesburg

Langa Lomphefumulo Wami
Ezulwini Nginobaba
Bonganini Nonke
Umzuzu Egetsemane
Nginezono Eziningi
Imnandi Aindaba Yaphezulu
Woza Moni   BSLP1129
Soya Ngaphi
Jesu Kumandi
Uyangithanda Unkulunkulu
Wozani Bazalwane
Lapho Izivuvungu

(All titles released on BSLP1129, *Bonganini Nonke*.)

Johannesburg

Noma Bonke Behlubuka
Vukani Bandla Bo
Yeki Jerusalema
Onkulunkulu
Siyakubonana
Ungumngane   BSLP1146
Kuwe Jesu Wami
Woza Moya
Ngiyamuzwa Umzindisi
Ezulwini Wenyukela

(All titles released on BSLP1146, *Noma Bonke Behlubuka*.)
VOCALS: E. L. Magubane, E. V. Magubane, I. B. Magubane, S. C. Magubane,
E. T. Sithole, R. M. Sithole, others unknown

Johannesburg   1985

Gijima
Umhlaba Nezulu
Yibo Laba
Yithi
Wangidela   VUH44
Sebeyavuma
Iyona Lena
Intandane
Nkunzemnyama

(All titles released on VUH44, *Umhlaba Nezulu*.)

LADYSMITH BLACK BUTTERFLIES
VOCALS: David Mchunu, others unknown
Johannesburg   *6 Apr 1977*

GRC1447
- Sisebusweni Bakho
- Kudala Ngihamba
- Ezinsukwini
- Izwe Liyabhubha
- Gijima Mfoka Baba
- Khuphukani Nonke

LZG10

GRC1448
- Wohlala Usibheka
- Sasuk'Edlamini
- Benginethemba
- Lalelani Zinsizwa
- Zokhala Zonke
- Gijima Mfoka Khathide

(All titles released on LZG10, *Zokhala Zonke*.)

Johannesburg   *6 Apr 1977*

GRC1079		Sathi Uma Sihamba	CB4139
GRC1080		Mfoka Macingwana	CB4139
GRC1143	GRC1203	Qaphela Mfoka Nzima	CB4140
GRC1144		I Bambheni Zinsizwa	CB4140
GRC1271		Sasuka Len'Emakhaya	CB4141
GRC1272		Wena Mbhayimbhayi	CB4141
GRC1195		Shobane	CB4133
GRC1196		Ziph'Ezakithi Emnambithi?	CB4133
GRC1215	GRC1204	Ayi! We Madoda	CB4137
GRC1216		Woza We Wethu	CB4137
GRC1217		Uyavuth'Umlilo	CB4138
GRC1218		Obaba Nomama Sabashiya	CB4138

LZG11

(All titles released on LZG11, *Sathi Uma Sihamba*.)
VOCALS: S. Mazibuko, others unknown
Johannesburg   *1977*

GRC1449
- Abameli Benkululeko
- Yizwani Nginitshele
- Ngibheke
-   Esiphambanweni
- Thokozani Nonke
- Mangibe Qotho
- Hola Baba

LCH2

GRC1450
- Yahlala Imfama
- Kuwe Nkosi
- Mangivus'Ingoma Yami
- Dwala Lami
- Thina Abantu
-   Balomhlaba
- Ulithemba Lethu

(All titles released on LCH2, *Ngibheke Esiphambanweni*.)

LADYSMITH BLACK MAMBAZO
VOCALS: Joseph Shabalala, Walter Malinga, Albert Mazibuko, Joseph Mazibuko,
Milton Mazibuko, Enoch Shabalala, Headman Shabalala

Durban   *22 Aug 1972*

ABC32097, ABC9982	Igugu Lami	MO341, BL253
ABC32098, ABC2973, ABC9983	Nkosi Yamakhosi	MO341, BSLP14, BL14, BL253
ABC32099, ABC5018	Mama Lo	MO342, BSLP23, BL23
ABC32100, ABC5019	Lonyaka	MO342, BSLP23, BL23
ABC32101, ABC2972, ABC9983	Isigcino	MO343, BSLP14, BL14, BL253
ABC32102, ABC2973, ABC9982	Nqonqotha Mfana	MO343, BSLP14, BL14, BL253
ABC32103, ABC5017, ABC9983	Lindiwe	MO344, BSLP22, BL22, BL253
ABC32140, ABC5016, ABC9982	Bayosala Bekhala	MO344, BSLP22, BL22, BL253

(BSLP14, BL14 entitled *Amabutho*. BSLP22, BL22 entitled *Ufakazi Yibheshu*
featuring Empangeni Home Tigers. BSLP23, BL23 entitled *Umama Lo!* BL253
entitled *Nqonqotha Mfana*.)

Johannesburg   *16 Jan 1973*

ABC32394, ABC2973	Sivuya Sonke	MO392, BSLP14, BL14
ABC32350, ABC2972	Amabutho	MO392, BSLP14, BL14
ABC3251	Endlunkulu	MO393
ABC32352, ABC9983	Baleka Mfana	MO393, BL253
ABC32353, ABC2972, ABC9983	Yadla Yabeletha	MO394, BSLP14, BL14, BL253
ABC32354	Bayalobola	MO394
ABC32355, ABC2973	Ngelekelele	MO395, BSLP14, BL14
ABC32356, ABC2972	Awu! Wemadoda	MO395, BSLP14, BL14
ABC32357	Ushaka	MO396
ABC32358, ABC2973	Utugela	MO399, BSLP14, BL14
ABC32359, ABC2973, ABC9982	Nomathemba	MO397, BSLP14, BL14
ABC32360, ABC2972	Mlaba	MO397, BSLP14, BL14

(BSLP14, BL14 entitled *Amabutho*. BL253 entitled *Nqonqotha Mfana*.)

Johannesburg   *c July 1973*

ABC32575, ABC4380, ABC9982	Imbongi	BL414, BSLP18, BL18, BL253
ABC32576, ABC4380	Uthando	MO414, BSLP18, BL18
ABC32577, ABC4380	Abazali	MO415, BSLP18, BL18
ABC32578, ABC4380, ABC9983	Awu! Phathaphatha	MO415, BSLP18, BL18, BL253
ABC32579, ABC4380, ABC5380	Isimanga Sikathekwane	MO416, BSLP18, BL18, BSLP27, BL27
ABC32580, ABC4380, ABC5381	Izinkomo Zikababa	MO416, BSLP18, BL18, BSLP27, BL27

ABC32581, ABC4381	Mazulu Thandanani	MO417, BSLP18, BL18
ABC32582, ABC4381	Yithina Labo	MO417, BSLP18, BL18
ABC32583, ABC4381	Bhala Mabhalane	MO418, BSLP18, BL18
ABC32584, ABC4381	Ibhubesi Lase Nyakatho	MO418, BSLP18, BL18
ABC32585, ABC4381	Gijimani Wezintombi	MO419, BSLP18, BL18
ABC32586, ABC4381	Sengikhumbule Unomathemba	MO419, BSLP18, BL18

(BSLP18, BL18 entitled *Imbongi*. BSLP27, BL27 entitled *Isitimela*. BL253 entitled *Nqonqotha Mfana*.)

Johannesburg   *3 Nov 1973*

ABC32767,	ABC5018	Benzani	MO439
ABC32768,	ABC5019	Lalelani Masoka	MO439
ABC32769,	ABC5018	Lomhlaba	MO440
ABC32770,	ABC5019	Umtwana	MO440
ABC32771,	ABC5018	Ngoanyana	MO441
ABC32772		Aja Apepa	MO441
ABC32773	ABC5019	Isihlalo	MO442
ABC32774		Uyobunenhlanhla	MO442
ABC32775		Ithekisi	MO443
ABC32776,	ABC5018	Busisiwe	MO443

BSLP23, BL23

(MO442, MO443 issued as Joseph Shabalala. BSLP23, BL23 entitled *Umama Lo!*)

Durban   *21 May 1974*

ABC33013, ABC5380	Isitimela	MO476
ABC33014, ABC5381	Zithi Nqonqonqo	MO476
ABC33015, ABC5380	Jomba Mlaleli	MO477
ABC33016, ABC5381	Ikhaya Likababa	MO477
ABC33017, ABC5380	Wematshitshi	MO478
ABC33018, ABC5381	Thandiwe Wami	MO478

BSLP27, BL27

(BSLP27, BL27 entitled *Isitimela*.)

Johannesburg   *c Dec 1974*

ABC33285, ABC5956	We, Nhliziyo Yami	MO557
ABC33286, ABC5957	Ngxa Ngimbona Umsindisi	MO557, BL35
ABC33287, ABC5956	Yizwani Indaba	MO558
ABC33288, ABC34340, ABC5957	Wazithwal 'Zono Jesu	MO558, MO694, BL35
ABC33289, ABC5956	Uphi Umhlobo Onjengo Jesu	MO559
ABC33290, ABC5957	Ngingahlanzwa Ngani Na	MO559
ABC33291, ABC5956	Baba Wethu Singenile	MO560
ABC33292, ABC34341, ABC5957	Vuka Jona Sithandaze	MO560, MO694, BL35
ABC33293, ABC5956	Uboyekinyanga Yakho	MO561
ABC33294, ABC5957	Uhambho Lwamambazo	MO561
ABC33295, ABC5956	Jabula Mfana	MO562
ABC33296, ABC5957	Isimanga Salomhlaba	MO562

MO694, BL35

BL35

(BL35M entitled *Ukukhanya Kwelanga*.)

Johannesburg   *1975*

   Uthekwane
   Wawukhona Yini
   Wemfo Kamshengu   LT14319
   Zangihleka Izintombi
   Jabula Mfana

   Imbalala   LT14320
   Injobe Ithungelwa Ebandla   LT14320

   Baleka Mfana
   Lindiwe   LT14351
   Lomhlaba Wakithi

   Umama Lo   LT14351, Rounder 5025
   Nqonqotho Mfana   LT14351
   Liphi Igugu Lami   LT14352

(LT14319, 20, 51, 52 issued as Ladysmith Mambazo. Rounder 5025 entitled
Mbube Roots.)

Durban   *c May 1975*

ABC32975, ABC5380 Vulan'   MO462
                    Amasango
ABC32976, ABC5381 Khulekani   MO462
                    Zinsizwa   BSLP27, BL27
ABC32977, ABC5380 Sasuka   MO463
                    Lemakhaya
ABC32978, ABC5381 Sibezwile   MO463

(BSLP27, BL27 entitled *Isitimela.*)

Johannesburg   *c Aug 1975*

ABC33543,   ABC6238   Shintsha Sithothobala
ABC33544,   ABC6239   Ziyangibiza
ABC33545   Mawufunungenzenje
ABC33546   Kudala Ngizula
ABC33547 ABC6238   Bantu Radio
ABC33548   Makoti
ABC33549   Yinhle Lentombi   GL1798, BL54, BL91
ABC33550   Amalanda
ABC33551   Sicelumshado
ABC33552 ABC6239   Zangihlek'Intombi
ABC33553   Yayingangalanga
ABC33554   Ibhubezi

(BL91 entitled *Shintsha Sithothobala.*)
VOCALS: Joseph Shabalala, Albert Mazibuko, Milton Mazibuko, Ben Shabalala,
Enoch Shabalala, Headman Shabalala, Fikile G. Khumalo, Abednigo Mazibuko,
Albert F. Mazibuko, Ndoda Russel Mthembu, Jockey Tshabalala, Patric Zondo

Durban   *5 May 1976*

ABC6788 {
  Amaqhawe
  Sanibonani Maswati
  Nansi Incwadi
  Inkazimulo   } BL81
  Ngisele Ngedwa
  Ngi Boniseleni
ABC6789   Ngiyekeleni
ABC6789   Lapho Ezulwini }

(All titles released on BL86, *Ukusindiswa*.)

Johannesburg   *1977*
ABC34362   Zonke Lezizwe   MO697
ABC34363   Yalala Insizwa   MO697

VOCALS: Joseph Shabalala, Groonwell Khumalo, Albert Mazibuko, Funokwakhe
Mazibuko, Hilton Mazibuko, Russel Mthembu, Ben Shabalala, Olicent Madlala,
Abednigo Mazibuko, Jabulani Mwelase, Jockey Shabalala

Johannesburg   *30 Sept 1977*

ABC34512, ABC7462 {
  Ushaka
  Awu Wemadoda
  Hamba Nhliziyo Yam
  Intombi Mayiqoma
  Ukuthula Zinsizwa
  Lomhlaba Kawunoni
  Ayilwanga   } XED4002, BL129
  Zehla Entabeni
  Ikhaya Lagangcwele
ABC34513, ABC7463 {
  Yangiluma Inkukhu
  Ngeke Ngiphinde
  Iya Bhompa }

(All titles released on BL129, *Ushaka*.)

VOCALS: as per BL129 except add: Headman Shabalala, Albert F. Mazibuko, Patric
Zondo, Sandra Serne, and delete: Funokwakhe Mazibuko

Durban   *21 Aug 1978*

ABC7851 {
  Wozani Ku Jesu
  Uligugu Lami
  Woza Moni
  Izwi
  Uma Ngingena Esontweni
  Kukhona Zonkizinto
  Safa Thina   } BL153
  Igama Lenkosi
  Intando Ka Thixo
ABC7852 {
  Thatha Konke
  Woza Sambe
  Ngiyamthanda 'Ujesu }

(All titles released on BL153, *Indlela Yase Zulwini*.)

VOCALS: Joseph Shabalala, Groonwell Khumalo, Albert Mazibuko, Albert F. Mazibuko, Miton Mazibuko, Russel Mthembu, Ben Shabalala, Enoch Shabalala, Headman Shabalala, Abednigo Mazibuko, Jabulani Mwelase, Jockey Shabalala

Johannesburg *19 April 1979*

ABC9356	Bamnqobile	BL186
ABC34950, ABC9356	Hello My Baby	XED4028, BL186
ABC9356	Siyakhanya Isibane	BL186
ABC9356	Woza Sambe	BL186
ABC34952, ABC9356	Hamishaweta	XED4029, BL186
ABC9356	Amafutha Esibane	BL186
ABC9357	Jubilee	BL186
ABC34951, ABC9357	How Long Should I Wait	XED4028, BL186
ABC9357	{ Bayaslthanda We Dudu We Themba Lami Bhayi Bhayi Lindiwe }	BL186
ABC34953, ABC9357	Kura Gazankulu	XED4029, BL186

(All titles released on BL186, *Ezinkulu*.)
VOCALS: As per BL186

Johannesburg *16 Oct 1979*

ABC9688	{ Sikhonze Inkosi Ngomlandela Praise the Lord }	BL205
ABC35154, ABC9688	Tsamaya Pelo Yaka	XED4036, BL205
ABC9688	Bayede Nkosi Yami	BL205
ABC9688	Vela Somandla	BL205
ABC9689	Wonke Amehlo Azokumbona	BL186
ABC35158, ABC9689	Nearer My God	BH36, BL186
ABC35156, ABC9689	Tsamaya Sathane	XED4037, BL186
ABC9689	Awu Jerusalema	BL186
ABC35155, ABC9689	Re Betsa Batho Bohle	XED4036, BL186
ABC35157, ABC9689	Fall Rain Fall Rain	XED4037, BL186

(All titles released on BL205, *Intokozo*.)
VOCALS: As per BL186 but add: Steven Motaung, and delete: Enoch Shabalala

Durban *11 Feb 1981*

ABC10110	{ Izithembiso Zenkosi Limnandi Izulu Ulwandle Olungcwele Sishumayel' Ivangeli Siphum' Emnamlezweni Nkosi Yami Ngabusiswa }	
		BL300
ABC10111	{ Ayanqikaza Amagwala Baba No Mama Khayelihle Khaya Lami Lifikile Ivangeli Woza Emthonjeni Vukani Sihambe Zingelosi }	

(All titles released on BL300, *Ulwandle Oluncgwele*.)

VOCALS: Joseph Shabalala, Groonwell Khumalo, Abednigo Mazibuko, Albert Ma-
zibuko, Milton Mazibuko, Russel Mthembu, Jabulani Mwelase, Ben Shabalala,
Headman Shabalala, Jockey Shabalala, Albert Khumalo, Simon Sibiya, Sipho
Zunga
Johannesburg   *17 Aug 1981*

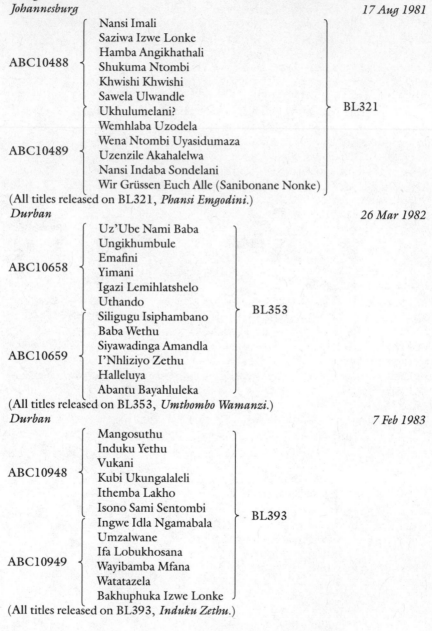

ABC10488
- Nansi Imali
- Saziwa Izwe Lonke
- Hamba Angikhathali
- Shukuma Ntombi
- Khwishi Khwishi
- Sawela Ulwandle
- Ukhulumelani?

ABC10489
- Wemhlaba Uzodela
- Wena Ntombi Uyasidumaza
- Uzenzile Akahalelwa
- Nansi Indaba Sondelani
- Wir Grüssen Euch Alle (Sanibonane Nonke)

BL321

(All titles released on BL321, *Phansi Emgodini.*)
Durban   *26 Mar 1982*

ABC10658
- Uz'Ube Nami Baba
- Ungikhumbule
- Emafini
- Yimani
- Igazi Lemihlatshelo
- Uthando

ABC10659
- Siligugu Isiphambano
- Baba Wethu
- Siyawadinga Amandla
- I'Nhliziyo Zethu
- Halleluya
- Abantu Bayahluleka

BL353

(All titles released on BL353, *Umthombo Wamanzi.*)
Durban   *7 Feb 1983*

ABC10948
- Mangosuthu
- Induku Yethu
- Vukani
- Kubi Ukungalaleli
- Ithemba Lakho
- Isono Sami Sentombi

ABC10949
- Ingwe Idla Ngamabala
- Umzalwane
- Ifa Lobukhosana
- Wayibamba Mfana
- Watatazela
- Bakhuphuka Izwe Lonke

BL393

(All titles released on BL393, *Induku Zethu.*)

Durban   *7 Mar 1984*

ABC11667	Kuzohlatshelelwa Ibhayibheli Lami Umthombo Wegazi Ngeke Ngiphinde U Jesu Wami Hlangabeza U Jesu	BL472
ABC11668	Ivangeli Labasha Waktazulwa Khaya Lami Vul'Inhliziyo Inyanga Enkulu Igama Elinje	

(All titles released on BL472, *Ibhayibheli Liyindlela.*)
VOCALS: Joseph Shabalala, Abednigo Mazibuko, Albert Mazibuko, Russel Mthembu, Jabulani Mwelase, Onos Phungula, Headman Shabalala, Jockey Shabalala, Keke Dlamini, Jeffrey Mdletshe

Johannesburg   *14 Feb 1985*

ABC12147	E Golgotha Izindlela Zimbili Saba Khuluma Izindaba I Love Jesus Umthetho	BL504
ABC12148	U Jesu Uyeza Makabongwe (Halleluya) Mathathu Lamadoda Vater Unser Uma Ngimbona	

(All titles released on BL504, *Inkazimulo.*)
VOCALS: As per BL504 except add: Daniel Mkhize, Philip Motha, and delete: Keke Dlamini

Johannesburg   *4 Sept 1985*

GRC9489	Buya Uz'Ekhaya That's Why I Choose You Wahlala Emnyango Ngothandaza Njalo Kulomhlaba (Thula)	BL531
GRC9490	Udla Nge'Nduku Zabanye Pauline Isala Kutshelwa Kwashintsh'Isthothobala Uthando Oluphelayo	

(All titles released on BL531, *Inala.*)

Johannesburg   *26 Feb 1986*

GRC9655 ⎧ Amagugu (Inkulu Lendaba)
⎪ King of Kings
⎪ Ngithunyiwe Kini
⎨ Ezulwini Siyakhona
⎪ Woza Ku Jesu   BL548
GRC9656 ⎪ Walk in the Light Of God
⎪ Dumisa Inkosi Yami
⎩ Buya Mntwana

(All titles released on BL548, *Ezulwini Siyakhona*.)

Johannesburg   *28 Feb 1986*

GRC9653   Kuyakhanya Madoda   XWI123
GRC9654   Mabahambe Abathakathi   XWI123

Johannesburg   *14 Oct 1987*

GRC89 ⎧ Emshadweni
⎪ Yekubuhle Bokukholwa
⎨ Asisho Ingoma
⎪ Ukubonga Kumnandi
⎪ Jabulani Sesingabantwana
⎪ Kanti Usasheba   BL613
⎪ Umzuzu Nay'Ujesu
GRC90 ⎨ Ngingenwe Emoyeni
⎪ Mhlangidinwa Ngikhathele
⎩ Shwele Baba

(All titles released on BL613, *Thandani*.)

Johannesburg   *20 Nov 1986*

Homeless
Inhle Lentombi
Namathemba
Isigcino
Nkosi Yama Khosi
Isitimela   HUL40131
Zintombi
Amabutho
Baleka Mfana
Vulani Amasango

(All titles released on HUL40131, *Zibuyinhlazane*.)

                                                                      1988

Unomathemba
Hello My Baby
At Golgotha
King of Kings
The Earth Is Never Satisfied
How Long?   Warner Bros 25582, HUL40157
Home of the Heroes
These Are the Guys
Rain, Rain, Beautiful Rain
Who Were You Talking To?

(All titles released on Warner Bros 25582, HUL40157, *Shaka Zulu*.)

1988

Umusa Kankulunkulu (Mercy of God)
Lindelani (Get Ready)
Ukhalangami (You Cry for Me)
Bavimb'Indlela (The Stumbling Block)
Bhasobha (Watch)
Nomakanjani (Dark or Blue)   Warner Bros 25753,
Hamba Dompasi (No More Passbook)   HUL40170
Ungayoni Into Enhle (Destroy Not This Beauty)
Amaphiko Okundiza (Wings to Fly)
Wayibambezela (Don't Waste Her Time)
Ungakhohlwa (Don't Forget)
Amazing Grace

(All titles released on Warner Bros 25753, HUL40170, *Journey of Dreams.*)

Durban   *1990*

Usema Yedwa (The Child Now Supports Himself)
Umuntu Uhlale Phenduka (One Who Is Always
     Indecisive)
Thatha Iseluleko Sami (Take My Piece of Advice)
Xhawula Mzalwana (Let Us Shake Hands My Brother
     in Christ)
Uthando (Love)   HUL40203
Lelilungelo Elakho (This Is Your Privilege)
Makabongwe (Let Us Sing Praises to God)
Liph'Ithemba Lakho (Where's Your Hope? Trust in God)
Guqa Uthandaze (Kneel and Pray)
Zama Ukuyezulwini (Try to Reach Heaven)
Lelilungelo Elakho (Percussion Remix)

(All titles released on Warner Bros, HUL40203, *Izigqi Zendoda.*)
VOCALS: Joseph Shabalala, Abednigo Mazibuko, Albert Mazibuko, Geoffrey
Mdletshe, Russel Mthembu, Jabulane Mwelase, Onos Phungula, Ben Shabalala,
Headman Shabalala, Jockey Shabalala

1990

Township Jive
Ofana Naye (Nobody Like Him)
Bala Ubhale (Count and Write)
Love Your Neighbour
Leaning on the Everlasting Arm
Rejoice   Warner Bros 26125,
Hayi Ngalesiskhathi (Not Right Now)   HUL40222
Emhlabeni (In This World)
Isikhathi Siyimali (Time Is Money)
Ngomnyango (By the Door)
Scatter the Fire
Cothoza Mfana (Tip Toe Guys)

(All titles released on Warner Bros 26125, HUL40222, *Scatter the Fire Spread the
Music.*)

LADYSMITH BLUEBIRDS
VOCALS: V. Magudulela, others unknown
Johannesburg

A Bantu
Mazulu
Ethekwini
Moses
Dladla
Intandane
Thunalami   } GOL310
Lalelani
Ntsimpi
Asazi
Ingola
U Baba

(All titles released on GOL310, *Mazula*.)

LADYSMITH FOUNTAIN BROTHERS
VOCALS: D. Cebekhulu, B. Khumalo, E. Kubheka, S. Kubheka, E. Langa,
H. Langa, J. Langa, W. Langa, S. Mbatha, A. Mvelase, U. Sibisi
Johannesburg   *1981*

Xawune Zono
Zinsizwa
Ubhanana
Zintombi
Lomhlaba
Umthakathi
Hloniphani   } IGH1006
Vukubaleke
Jabulani Bazalwane
Usithathathi
Who Can
Sibambene Nosathane

(All titles released on IGH1006, *Xawune Zono*.)
Johannesburg   *1984*

Inkatha
Siphuma Etholeni
Kuyaluza Abantu
Makhelwane
Sengicabanga Emnambithi
Dela Ntombazane
Sondela   } IGH1012
Gwinyitshe
Wuye Lomakoti
Lalelani Bomame
Lomunt'Ozonda Thina
Sanibona Bantu Bakithi

(All titles released on IGH1012, *Siphuma Etholeni*.)

LADYSMITH HERALDS
VOCALS: Shadrack Kunene, Queenie Bendile, Nicholas Khumalo, Johannes
Kunene, Sondile Kunene, Enoch Mabaso, Hamilton Mabaso, Obert Mazibuko,
Albert Jabulani Mvelase, Bhekuvise Sithole

Johannesburg *14 Feb 1977*

ABC7110
- Icilongo Malikhala
- Emfuleni Ebabiloni
- Njenge Bhadi Libhadula
- Ngalemihla Yokwenyuka
- Ukuvela Eziyoni
- Wafunga Ujehova

ABC7111
- Jerusalem Ikhaya Lam
- Ujesu Unamandla
- Igagu Lobukhosi
- Sayibona Inkanyezi
- Dumisani
- Umuzi Ka Tixo

BL112

(All titles released on BL112, *Sinelizwi Lika Tixo*.)

VOCALS: Shadrack Shabalala, Irene Mawela, Abednigo Mazibuko, Elliot Mncube,
Albert Jabulani Mvelase, Jockey Shabalala; ORGAN: Mac Mathunjwa

Johannesburg *27 June 1980*

ABC9954
- 'Indaba Zevangeli
- Jabulani
- Emnqamlezweni
- Sikuyo Indlela
- Lihle Izulu
- Singabahambayo Emhlabeni

ABC9955
- Buhle Ubukholwa
- Linamandla
- Kukhona Izwe'Lihle
- Emhlabeni Izinhlupheko
- Amen Alleluya
- Sihamba Naye

BL246

(All titles released on BL246, *I'Ndaba Zevangeli*.)

Johannesburg *28 July 1981*

ABC10654
- Wozani
- Umoya Wami
- Lalelani
- Inhliziyo Yami
- Nant'Uthando
- Sibon'Ujesu

ABC10655
- Yithi Amasoka
- Ngicela Uxola
- Ake Ugcine Isithembiso
- Isiphambano
- Yangiqom'Intombi
- Izintombi

BL352

(All titles released on BL352, *Sibon'Ujesu*.)

LADYSMITH LION CUBS
Johannesburg   *1975*
    Kwakhalu Thekwane
    Usisi Ndini
    Ebusuku Nasemini
    Ungalahli Wena
    Unama Uyajabula
    Ingonyama Yamazulu
    Ukhanjana   TBH2001
    Wozalapha Wenqola
    Bayakhalomama
    Dali Musukungala
    Nanka Lamakhwaya
    Inkungu
(All titles released on TBH2001, *Ladysmith Lion Cubs.*)

LADYSMITH NAUGHTY BOYS
Johannesburg   *1982*
    Ngilangazelela Lelo Khaya
    Ngikhumbula Leyo Mini
    Rosé My Girl
    Usamsoni
    Baba Wethu
    Mozisi
    Saluthe Madoda   CNH1025
    Sanibona Madoda
    Bantu Bakithi
    Bengine Ntombi
    Ibusisiwe Intombi
    Asi Hambe Mngani
(All titles released on CNH1025, *Ngilangazelela Lelo Khaya.*)

LADYSMITH RED LIONS
VOCALS: Abednigo Sibiya, others unknown
Johannesburg   *1979*
    Amazondo
    Egcomani
    Ngihamba Ngedwa
    Uyazi Ntizwa
    Asambeni Zintsizwa
    Kudala Singezwani
    Amazambane   WZLP504
    Okokaqala
    Siphuma-Lakuphuma-Ilanga
    Nomvula
    Thuba-Loku Thandaza
    Ngingu'Mhambi
(All titles released on WZLP504, *Ladysmith Red Lions.*)
VOCALS: Abednigo Sibiya, others unknown

Johannesburg   *May 1979*

ABC9288 { Ezulwini Lakho
Inkanyezi
Ngikhokhele
Umakhelwane
Mfo Ka Thusini
Asha Amazambane

BL183

ABC9289 { Abalandeli Bakhe
Emifuleni
Ilanga
Bathinta Amabhubhesi
Ngenzeni Na?
Selishonile

(All titles released on BL183, *Inkanyezi*.)

Johannesburg   *27 July 1981*

GRC7419 { Umbango Owani?
Bophani Imithwalo
Mina Nawe
Isizwe Sabantsundu
Ifa Lalomhlaba
Kwataphasi

LZG60

GRC7420 { Oh! My Brother
Jesu
I'm Looking
Nkosi Yami

(All titles released on LZG60, *Umbango Owani?*)
VOCALS: Abednigo Sibiya, others unknown

Johannesburg

Hamba Minyaka
Delisa Amabhungu
Ezingozini
Ngayaluza
Baba Wethu
Siyanibongela
Into Yakhe
Into Yakhe
Ilanga Liyakhanya
Amandla Ami
Ehla Ema

VUH5

(All titles released on VUH5, *Hamba Minyaka*.)
VOCALS: Abednigo Sibiya, others unknown

Johannesburg   *1987*
    Ezintaveni Zasezion ⎫
    Haleluyah
    Thokozani
    Ungabasiza
    Ujesu Ezelwe
    Nkosi Jesu   ⎬ CEL553
    Sengiyabaleka
    Ungakwenza Konke
    Iyamangalisa
    Jerusalema ⎭
(All titles released on CEL553, *Ezintabeni Zasezion*.)

LESLIE SHOOTING STARS
Johannesburg   *1970*
    Baleka Mfo Dhlamini ⎫
    Iyedelela Lentombi
    Dali Bopha   ⎬ LT12097
    Uma Liduma ⎭
    Sikhulekela Indawo   LT12098
    Ithemba Lami   LT12097
    Uthi Asigonane ⎫
    Hamba Mfana Kababa ⎬ LT12098
    Ihashi Elimhlope ⎭

SOLOMON LINDA'S ORIGINAL EVENING BIRDS
VOCALS: Solomon Linda (leader), Gilbert Madondo, Gideon Mkhize, Samuel Mlangeni, Boy Sibiya, Owen Sikhakhane; CONCERTINA (1): unknown; BANJO: unknown; PIANO: unknown
Johannesburg   *1938*
1424   Ngqo Ngqongo Vula (1)   GE801
1425   Ngi Boni Sebeni   GE801
1426-1 Ngi Hambile (1)   GB829
1427   Ntombi Ngangiyeshela (1) GE874
1428   Makasane   GE800, London LPB431
1429   Mfo Ka Linda   GE800
(GE800 issued as Linda's Evening Birds. 1940–43 untraced. London LPB431 entitled *Zulu Music And Songs*.)
VOCALS: as above; GUITAR (1): Peter Rezant; BANJO (2): ——Gumede; PIANO (3): Emily Motsieloa
Johannesburg   *1939*
1522   Yetulisigqoko   GE887
1526   Bashaye Evening Birds   GE876
1527   Mbube (1,2,3)   GE829
1527-1 Mbube (1,2,3)   GE829, Rounder 5025
(Rounder 5025 entitled *Mbube Roots*.)
VOCALS: as above; REED PIPES (1): unknown; PIANO (2): unknown; BANJO (3): unknown

Johannesburg *1939*

1531	Sengiyofela Pesheya (1)	GE850
1532	Hamba Pepa Lami (2, 3)	GE874
1533	Ziyekele Mama (1)	GE850
1534	Sangena Mama(2, 3)	GE877
1535	Ijuzibele (2, 3)	DC3
1536	Sigonde 'Mnambiti (2)	GE872

(GE887, 876, 877 issued as Solomon Linda's Evening Birds. DC3 issued as Decca Zulu Song Birds. 1523–25 untraced. 1528–30 by David de Lange Met Die Welgens Suikerbossie Orkes.)
VOCALS: as above

Johannesburg *c 1940*

1630	Zingango Kwela	Unissued
1631	Yehla Moses	GE876
1633	Bhamporo	GE872
1635	Sohlangana	GE877
1636	Jerusalema	GB1051
1637	Anoku Gonda	Rounder 5025
1638	Waze Wangi Bamba	DC3
1639	Zasho Ingane Zika Linda	Unissued
1639	E Jimara	Unissued

(GE872 issued as Linda's Original Evening Birds. GE876, GE877 issued as Solomon Linda's Evening Birds. DC3 issued as Decca Zulu Song Birds. 1629, 1632, 1634 untraced. Rounder 5025 entitled *Mbube Roots*. Matrix 1639 listed for two titles in ILAM catalogue.)
VOCALS: as above; BANJO: unknown; PIANO: Emily Motsieloa

Johannesburg *c 1941*

1795	Sabona Matambo	Unissued
1796	Ngazula Emagumeni	GB1050, Rounder 5025
1797	Babanza Abantu	Unissued
1799	Sengihamba Ngedwa	Unissued

(1786–94, 1798 untraced. Rounder 5025 entitled *Mbube Roots*.)
VOCALS: as above; BANJO: unknown; PIANO: Emily Motsieloa

Johannesburg *Early 1942*

1978	Gijima Mfana	GB1050
1979	Ndaba Zika Linda	GE929
1980	We Nobulangoma	Unissued
1981	Ngiyomutshel'Ubaba	GE929
1982	Savumelana	GB1049
1983	Bandibophe	Unissued
1984	Basibizalonkizwe	GB1051
1985	Zakulandela	Unissued

(1973–77 untraced. GE929 issued as Solomon Linda's Evening Birds. Reverse of GE1049 by Junior Natal Champions.)
VOCALS: as above

Johannesburg   *Late 1951*
ABC3952   We Dali Vuka   GB1285
ABC3953   Mfana Onmcane   GB1285
(ABC3942–52, 3954–56 untraced.)
VOCALS: as above(?); GUITAR (1): unknown
Johannesburg   *1954*
ABC12419   Yekela Uyenyeni   GB2024
ABC12420   One, Two, Three (1)   GB2024
Johannesburg
          Sakhe Sadliwe   GB3040
          Mayibuye Iafrika   GB3040

LUCKY BOYS CHOIR
VOCALS: Thomas Mngomezulu (leader), others unknown
Durban(?)   *1960*
ABC19464T   Ngikumbula Ubaba   GB3156
ABC19465T   Sanibonani   GB3156
ABC19466T   Ngikhumbul'Kaya   GB3157
ABC19467T   Dali Masigodukhe   GB3157
Durban
ABC20893   Kubuhlungu Ukulala
                Wedwa   GB3262
ABC20894   Ngekhe Ngishadi
                Nantombi   GB3262
(GB3262 issued as *Lucky Boys.*)

LUCKY STARS
VOCALS: Zebulon Dlamini (leader), others unknown
Johannesburg   *1974*
          Sangena Exuseni
          Saraphina   ⎫
          Uyothi Wabonani   ⎬   LT14316
          Uhambe Ntombi   ⎭
VOCALS: Zebulon Dlamini, others unknown

                                                                           1974
ABC33111, ABC5801   Zehla Zenyuka   MO512, DLPL291/2
ABC33112, ABC5800   Asambe Sponomo   MO512, DLPL291/2
ABC33113   Sesifikile   MO513
ABC33114   Hlanza Ngedela   MO513
(DLPL291/2 entitled *Cothoza Mfana.*)

MADIBA BROTHERS
VOCALS: David Madiba, others unknown
Johannesburg   *8 Nov 1973*
ABC32777   Yini Wena Dali   MO444
ABC32778   S'Thandwa Sami   MO444

MADIDI MESSENGERS
VOCALS: Frederick Phiri, Asiel Poo, Joseph Ramatlo, others unknown
Johannesburg   *5 Sept 1981*

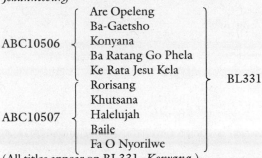

ABC10506
{
Are Opeleng
Ba-Gaetsho
Konyana
Ba Ratang Go Phela
Ke Rata Jesu Kela
}

BL331

ABC10507
{
Rorisang
Khutsana
Halelujah
Baile
Fa O Nyorilwe
}

(All titles appear on BL331, *Konyana*.)

MAHLABATINI BEKHIMBAZO BROTHERS
Johannesburg

Enhlambamasoka	NOISE 1
Bantubakithi	NOISE 1

(An album was released which included the two recordings listed above but the
details have not been traced.)

MAKTSHWA'S CHOIR
VOCALS: ——Maktshwa (leader), others unknown; TRUMPET: Enoch Matunjwa;
ALTO SAX: Peter Rezant; PIANO: Emily Motsieloa; DRUMS: Tommy Koza
Johannesburg   *1937*

1163	Arayi Ampoyisa	Unissued
1166	Isigebengu	Unissued

(The surviving test pressings of 1163 and 1166 are labeled as the Alexandrians
with the Merry Blackbirds. 1158–62, 1164–65 untraced.)
Johannesburg   *1937*

1173	Nanga A Ma Poyisa	GE145
1174-1	Leta Into Yani	GE185, Decca F40505
1175	Nase Mdubane	GE143
1176	Wangi Sha Ya U Baba	GE143

(GE143, GE145, GE185, Decca F40505 issued as Maktshwa's Choir with the
Merry Blackbirds. Decca F40505 entitled *Congo Calling*(!). Reverse of GE185,
Decca F40505 by the Merry Blackbirds. 1177–79 untraced.)

MARAPYANE HOME BROTHERS
Johannesburg
> Ntwa Ke Ena
> Bona Jaaka Ke Godile
> Mmapula
> Kemakaditswe Ke Mosadi
> Matshidiso
> Ausi Dikeledi
> Naga E Teng   } SRLPC18
> Sathane
> Papolo Ya Morena
> Jeso Morena Wa Rona
> Khutio Tse Nne
> Saulwe
(All titles released on SRLPC18, *Selelo*.)

MAVUKELA CHIEFS
Johannesburg   *1978*
> Reboni Kabanana   MFB533
> Likoe   MFB533
> Tlokoano   MFB534
> Jobolo   MFB534
> Bonnake   MFB535
> Mapetla   MFB535
> Mfana Uyosebenza
> Zenda Zonke
> Gida Gida
> Bayasibona
> Ngikhumbula Ng'Imcane
> Sambona Lonumzane   } MFL5300
> Amadoda Amabili
> Ntombi Ngikhumbula Nawe
> Uphondo Luka Bejane
> Ngangisethekwini
> Sibopha Umnthwalo
> Izwelakithi
(MFL5300 entitled, *Amadoda Amabili*.)

M.C.C. CHOIR
Johannesburg   *24 Mar 1952*
N1422   Sishimani
N1423   Bamshayile   } BB?
N1424   Sikala Ngo Pem
N4125   Thalitha
(N1422–25 as MCC Zulu Choir.)
VOCALS: unknown; PERCUSSION: unknown

Johannesburg			*1953*
ABC10286	Bathi Belele	GB2528	
ABC10287	Ayagula Amabutho	GB2528	
ABC10288	Mfana Onfushane	GB2529	
ABC10289	Ikula Lebokile	GB2529	
Johannesburg			*Feb 1960*
	Umfana Omtishana	T5524	
	Khonzani	T5524	
	Uyamazi Ubaba	T5525	
	Mbambathoni	T5525	
	Wawuthini	T5526	
	Awu Beke Ikhanda Lami	T5526	
	Ayi Abantu	T5527	
	Embotsheni Yamajuba	T5527	

(T5524, T5525, T5526, T5527 issued as M.C.C. Mbube Choir.)

MELODY MASTERS
VOCALS: O. L. P. Mbata (leader), others unknown

Johannesburg			*c 1965*
OAS2166	Babusisiwe	JP878	
OAS2167	Udumo	JP878	

MKHIZWANE HOME STARS

Durban			*18 Nov 1984*
	Sanibonani	Rounder 5023	

(Rounder 5023 entitled *Mbube!*)

E. MKIZE AND HIS SINGING BIRDS (see EVENING BIRDS)

MORNING LIGHT CHOIR
VOCALS: Herzon Ngobese, others unknown; CONCERTINA: unknown; GUITARS: unknown

Johannesburg			*1940*
ABC356	Kwa Zulu	GE912	
ABC357	Ndabeni	GE990	
ABC358	Ziyenda Souke		
ABC359	Uk'Waliwa	Unissued	
ABC360	Ngu Bani		
ABC361	I-Morning Light		

(GE912 issued as Herzon Ngobese Choir and Concertina Orchestra. GE990 issued as Herzon Ngobese with Morning Light Choir. Reverse of GE990 Dundee Wandering Singers.)

Johannesburg   *c 1941*
1723 We Mama ⎫
1724 Kweli Mtackiar ⎪
1725 Nga Zula ⎪
1726 Sabona Mathamba ⎬ Unissued
1727 Ngi Landel'i Zion ⎪
1728 Bayasi Babaza ⎭
VOCALS: unknown

Johannesburg   *1942*
2100 Kukude'E Goli   TV233
2101 Izindaba Ezinkulu Zika "Kawa"   DC59, Rounder 5025
2102 Amabele'Entombi   TV233
2103 Mamhla Siyash Adisa   DC59
(2104–13 untraced. Rounder 5025 entitled *Mbube Roots*.)

Johannesburg   *Late 1951*
ABC3911   Intombi Uboybamba   DC122
ABC3912   Intombi Ezinthanda Tina   TV246
ABC3913   Otsotsi Esophia   DC122
ABC3914   Kuwikalwa Emakhaya   TV246
ABC3915   Langa Lishonile   DC124
ABC3916   Yiwo La Ama   DC124
(ABC3903–10, ABC3917–20 untraced.)
VOCALS: V. Mbatha, others unknown

Johannesburg   *1955*
ABC11834   Utisha   DC649
ABC11835   Isono   DC550, TV272
ABC11836   Guga Mzimba   DC550, TV272
ABC11837   Unknown   Unknown
ABC11838   Unknown   Unknown
ABC11839   Intombi Engiyithandayo   DC649

Johannesburg   *10 Dec 1959*
ABC18261   Gijima Mfana ⎫
ABC18262   Sipumalena ⎪
ABC18263   Yakala Insingizi ⎪
ABC18264   Zikala Emahlangeni ⎪
ABC18265   Saubona Sbali ⎬ Unknown
ABC18266   Uelele Endumeni ⎪
ABC18267   Spononosami ⎪
ABC18268   Saubona Salafina ⎭

MORNING LIGHTS
VOCALS: Ephraim Hlatshwayo (conductor), others unknown
Johannesburg   *1949*
N1111   Ngaqonyana   BB500
N1112   Ilanga La Shona   BB500

Johannesburg   *1949*
N1149   Angisozengalawa   BB510
N1150   Wawutini Kimi   BB510
Johannesburg   *Feb 1952*
N1407   Vukani Bandla Bo   BB523
N1408   E Sizwe Se Mnyama   BB523

MORNING LIGHTS CHOIR
VOCALS: Absolom Vulani (conductor), others unknown
Johannesburg   *1950*
N1182   Ngazulu   BB517
N1183   Maye Safatina   BB517
(The Morning Lights conducted by Ephraim Hlatshwayo may be the same group
as the Morning Lights Choir conducted by Absolom Vulandi.)

MORNING LIGHTS CHOIR
VOCALS: C. Xaba, others unknown
Johannesburg   *Feb 1962*
ABC21260   Sitimela   DC833
ABC21261   Mayoyo   DC833

MORNING SHINE CHOIR
VOCALS: unknown
Johannesburg   *Feb 1952*
N1406   Bedlala Ngo Baba   BB531
(Reverse of BB531 by Crowdville Olympics.)
Johannesburg   *c Aug 1952*
N1448   Ungangi Ndluli Jesu   BB525
N1449   Ziyo Zela Ezithunywa   BB525
Johannesburg   *c early 1960s*
NA10091   Fulatela Intombi   ZZ43
NA10092   Shiela Gwai   ZZ43

MORNING STARS
VOCALS: S. Madakane (conductor), others unknown; PIANO: S. Madakane
Johannesburg   *1939*
1587 Ngangiye Pitoli   DC40
1588 Ba Kude O Baba   DC24
1589 Isi Timela Sase Mbabane   DC7
1590 Singe Kumbule Dolopini   DC7
1591 Se Kwhela   DC25
Johannesburg   *1941*
ABC401   Pendukani   Unissued
ABC402   Siye Orlando   DC24
ABC403   Into Zam   DC25
ABC404   We Manyenyeza   Unissued
ABC405   Ibatje   DC40
(ABC398–400 untraced.)

MORNING STARS
VOCALS: Philemon Betha Nkosi, Daniel Msisi, Walter Mozi Nhlangothi, Elias
Mbiba Pungwayo, Joseph Boy Radebe, William ——iele, Arron Zwane
Johannesburg   *7 Dec 1977*

ABC7596	Sicela Unkungena Thina Gijima Mfana Omcane Woyitshela Inyanga Mfana Yakhali Intombi Uthando Sengikhumbula Into Yami	BL141
ABC7597	Umahlalela Sibuza Kini Nonke Niyayibona Lendoda Lendaba Inkulu Emhlabeni Ithi Angifanele Sixoleleni Zinsizwa	

(All titles released on BL141, *Sibuza Kini Nonke*.)

MORNING STARS
VOCALS: J. Thabete, A. Zuma, T. Zuma, others unknown
Johannesburg   *1982*

Ziyakhala Izinsimbi Umntanomuntu Indaba Yakho Lova Lalibi Izwe Bantwanyana Solila Sonke Ngomusa Wakho Sesingofakazi Wahlupheka Umoses Nkosi Jeasu Hlala Nathi Ngizimisele Ukushada Nawe Into Yokuqala Lapho Simandla Khona	SHINE 3

(All titles released on SHINE 3, *Ngomusa Wakho Sesingofakazi*.)

MORNING TIGERS
VOCALS: A. Mbatha, others unknown
Johannesburg   *1951*
CEA2572-1	U George	YE68
CEA2573-1	Sihamba Nawe Kelina	YE68
CEA2574-1	Intliziyo Yam	YE59
CEA2575-1	Wayenbathini	YE59

Johannesburg   *1951*
CEA2619-1	Khala Zome	YE65
CEA2620-1	Emajikeni	YE65

MOUNTAIN SIDE TUGELA FERRY

1982

IGH1010

(IGH1010 entitled *Mountain Side Tugela Ferry.* No information on individual track titles.)

MSHENGU WHITE MAMBAZO

VOCALS: Nkosinathi Shabalala (first part), Myekeni Bhengu (alto), Thokonzani Dludla (bass), Themba Hadebe (bass), Zenzeleni Mlangeni (bass), Msizi Shabalala (tenor), Phumlani Shabalala (bass), Sibongiseni Shabalala (bass), Thamsanqa Shabalala (alto), Thulani Shabalala (bass), Bheki Shange (bass)

Johannesburg   *23 Oct 1987*

GRC259	Siyahamba Kulomhlaba	
	Elethu Basha	
	Ingunaphakade	
	Ubuguquguqu	
	Limnandi Ujulile	BL646
	Hhaye Mafini	
	Woza Sambe	
GRC260	Ithemba Usenkosini	
	Zangiqhwebela Enkosini	
	Obaba Bandiza Ngebhanoyi	

(All titles released on BL646, *Okumhlophe. . . .*)

Durban   *Jan 1990*

GRC427	Umkhumbi Ka-Nowa	
	Sukuma Sambe	
	Uzovuna Okutshalile	
	Alikho Ithemba	
	Devil Will Do Me No Harm	BL691
	Emahlathini	
	Uyeza Masinyane	
GRC428	Zonk'Zono Maziphele	
	We-Malindi	
	Kuhl'Ukuthandaza	

(All titles released on BL691, *Umkhumbi Ka-Nowa.*)

PHILLIP MSIMANGA'S SHOOTING STARS (see SHOOTING STARS)

PHILLIP MSIMANGA'S ZULU CHOIR (see SHOOTING STARS)

M . T . A . Mbube Group
VOCALS: Enoch Mtambo, others unknown
Johannesburg   *21 April 1976*

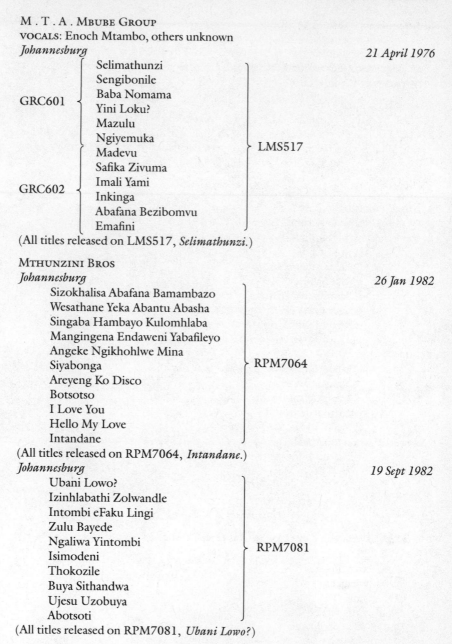

GRC601 {
    Selimathunzi
    Sengibonile
    Baba Nomama
    Yini Loku?
    Mazulu
    Ngiyemuka
}   LMS517

GRC602 {
    Madevu
    Safika Zivuma
    Imali Yami
    Inkinga
    Abafana Bezibomvu
    Emafini
}

(All titles released on LMS517, *Selimathunzi*.)

Mthunzini Bros
Johannesburg   *26 Jan 1982*

Sizokhalisa Abafana Bamambazo
Wesathane Yeka Abantu Abasha
Singaba Hambayo Kulomhlaba
Mangingena Endaweni Yabafileyo
Angeke Ngikhohlwe Mina
Siyabonga   RPM7064
Areyeng Ko Disco
Botsotso
I Love You
Hello My Love
Intandane

(All titles released on RPM7064, *Intandane*.)
Johannesburg   *19 Sept 1982*

Ubani Lowo?
Izinhlabathi Zolwandle
Intombi eFaku Lingi
Zulu Bayede
Ngaliwa Yintombi
Isimodeni   RPM7081
Thokozile
Buya Sithandwa
Ujesu Uzobuya
Abotsoti

(All titles released on RPM7081, *Ubani Lowo?*)

Johannesburg   *1987*
 Wozani Siyezulwini
 Nang'Usathane
 Jesu Wafa Ngenxa Yethu
 Sengathi Ngingavuma
 In The Evening
 Ngikhokhele   CEL539
 Usuku Lwephasika
 Jerusalema
 Zilungiseleni
 Old Time Religion
(All titles released on CEL539, *Wozani Siyezulwini.*)

MTUBATUBA BROS
VOCALS: E. Mathe, N. Mathe, T. Mathe, B. Mthiyane, H. Ndlovu, J. Ntabane,
others unknown
Johannesburg   *15 Aug 1978*

      Singa Bafana Bomculo
      Sesikhulile
ABC8102 Intombi Zakudala
      Silihambile Lonke Ilizwe
      Kumnandi Ukuphila
      Khulekani Zinsizwa   BL159
      Ubani?
      Uxolo Zinsizwa
      Ngasala Ngedwa
ABC8103 Umfazi Ongemama
      Nkosi Ngiyabonga
      Salani Kahle
(All titles released on BL159, *Kumnandi Ukuphila.*)

MTUSENI NEZI NKONKONI
VOCALS: S. Khoza, M. Sibiya, others unknown
Johannesburg   *1984*
 Isitimela
 Ukhozi
 Thembekile
 Wankamfula
 Angisenamali
 Izinkomozami   JML7013
 Intandane
 Hlukana Nendaba Zabantu
 George Uyisigebengu
 Udade Ungowami
(All titles released on JML7013, *Isitimela Esisha.*)

MTWALUME YOUNG AGES
Durban   *18 Nov 1984*
      Hamba Hamba   Rounder 5023
(Rounder 5023 entitled *Mbube!*)

MZOLO MBUBE GROUP
Johannesburg   *1974*
      Sasiyavalelisa
      Izimbadada Zikafalaza   }   LT14313
      Khawuleza
VOCALS: Zephaniah Mzolo (leader), Zeblon Mzolo, others unknown

                                                                                  1974
ABC33115, ABC5800   Umlimela Omuhle   MO514 ⎤
ABC33116, ABC5801   Umoya Omkhulu   MO514 ⎥
ABC33117, ABC5800   Wawushisiumlilo   MO515 ⎥
ABC33118, ABC5801   Khawuleza Mfana   MO515 ⎬ DLPL291/2
ABC33119, ABC5800   Indoda Yelembe   MO516 ⎥
ABC33120, ABC5801   Ngicebiseni Bakithi   MO516 ⎦
ABC33121   Angizwanga   MO517
ABC33122   Ngiyankashela Egoli   MO517
(DLPL291/2 entitled *Cothoza Mfana.*)

                                                                                  1974
ABC33267   Umama Kabuhle   MO563
ABC33268   Ngibongubaba   MO563
ABC33269   Lindiwe Wami   MO564
ABC33270   Angisoze Ngikhohlwe   MO564
ABC33271   Inj'Emnyama   MO565
ABC33272   Phelelani Zinsizwa   MO565
ABC33273   Wemfana Wembube   MO566
ABC33274   Ntandane Kababa   MO566
ABC33275   Akasalaleli Ubaba   MO567
ABC33276   Ikhubalo   MO567
ABC33277   Lobola Soka Lam   MO568
ABC33278   Sekusehlule   MO568
VOCALS: Z. Mzolo, others unknown
Johannesburg   *1983*
      Isomiso Sika 1983   ⎤
      Indodemnyama   ⎥
      Mfokababa   ⎥
      Sambamba   ⎥
      Wena Xam Lahoshoza   ⎬ RPM7088
      Yakhal'Ekusenj Imbongolo   ⎥
      Aphelile Mame   ⎥
      Itaba Iyakhuluma   ⎥
      Ubodlamasi Mntanami   ⎦
(All titles released on RPM7088, *Isomiso Sika 1983.*)
VOCALS: Z. Mzolo, others unknown

Johannesburg *1986*

    Amabulandlela
    Ubongilinda Mfana
    Amaviyo
    Inqubeko
    Umlimelomuhle
    Umuthiwenyanga   ABRL1002
    Wawushimlilo
    Ngephulimiyalo Kababa
    Aphamagoso
    Izimbamgi

(All titles released on ABRL1002, *Aphamagoso*.)

Johannesburg *1988*

    Unyaka Wezimanga U 1987
    Wawuhluphabazali
    Wemfana Wembube
    Ngibonga Ubaba
    Izinkomo Zamabheka
    Imisebenzi Yabalele   CRS191
    Yehlula Abazali Beyifundisa
    Sangishiyisitimela
    Jesus Give The Weary Calm
    Umama Ka Buhle

(All titles released on CRS191, *Unyaka Wezimanga U 1987*.)
VOCALS: Z. Mzolo, others unknown

Johannesburg

    Ngiyashweleza
    Kodwa Yini Kuwe
    Siyakhuleka
    Nampa Bengibiza
    Jabulani Nonke
    Hobhu Mawulele   CRS203
    Baba Ngobese
    Izinsizwe Ezimbili
    Why Should You Hate Liquor
    Walibamba Umfana
    My Beautiful Woman

(All titles released on CRS203, *Ngiyashweleza*.)

NATAL AB
Johannesburg *1974*

    Sinyathela Kancane
    Wejuba Lami   LT14335
    Wena Ntombi
    Amakhehla Avehleli

NATAL CHAMPIONS (see DUNDEE WANDERING SINGERS)

NATAL CHAMPIONS
VOCALS: David Zikhole, others unknown
Durban   *1967*
16165   Izintaba Zase Goli   NV3526
16166   U Dumazile   NV3526
Durban   *8 Aug 1971*
    Johan Umbabadisi   ⎫
    Angikathali   ⎬   Trutone Unissued
    Wentaba   ⎪
    Sishole   ⎭
Johannesburg   *18 Aug 1971*
    Ngambona   RPM876
    Wemallime   RPM876

NATAL JUNIOR CHAMPIONS
Johannesburg   *June 1960*
    Nesizwa Zonke   T5727
    Vukani Bandhla   T5727
    Kuko Indawo   T5728

NATAL TRY SINGERS
Johannesburg   *1979*
    Siyophola Emgababa   ⎫
    Ulwandle   ⎪
    Wakhal 'Umama   ⎪
    Ngibambe Sdudla   ⎪
    Giya Dlamini   ⎪
    Buyelekhaya   ⎪
    Mfokankozi, Kudi   ⎬   WZLP503
    Phuma Emgodini   ⎪
    Idla Amagama Ami   ⎪
    Zihusisiwe   ⎪
    Ikhalaphi   ⎪
    Simon Ka Petro   ⎭
(All titles released on WZLP503, *Cothoza Mfana*.)

NATAL WANDERING SINGERS
VOCALS: unknown
Durban(?)   *1954*
ABC12560   Sehle Ntabeni   GB2084
ABC12561   Ngaboni Mfene   GB2084
ABC12567   Shushu   GB2086
ABC12569   Uyotin Ubaba   GB2086
VOCALS: L. Ngcobo, others unknown
Durban(?)   *1957*
ABC16230   Sakubona We Mama   GB2694
ABC16231   Isangoma   GB2694

Durban *1959*
ABC17649 Wami Ongawesibi Ulilo GB2948
ABC17650 Obaba GB2948
ABC17651 Ngangi Semncane GB3005
ABC17652 Ubani Longqongqozayo GB3005
VOCALS: R. Mboyisa, others unknown
Durban(?) *March 1961*
ABC19982 Ifakabile GB3207
ABC19983 Izinsizwa GB3207

NAUGHTY BOYS
VOCALS: Enoch Mbanjwa, others unknown
Johannesburg *8 Nov 1973*
ABC32779 Kukhon'Indaba MO445
ABC32780 Wen'Uyankhohlisa MO445
ABC32781 Thembitshe MO446
ABC32782 Wothi Wabonani? MO446

NAUGHTY BOYS CHOIR
VOCALS: Amos Hlatshwayo, Alfred Khuzwayo (leader), Elias Makhanya, Albert
Mathebula, George Mkhaliphi, Mbijana Shembe
Johannesburg *1939*
1562 Umkomasi Unissued
1563 Kala Zome DC15
1564 Sani Bona DC47
1565 Aka Sabala Unissued
1566 Intandi Upuma DC47
1567 Uduma Lwama Naughty Boys DC15
(1568 untraced.)
Johannesburg *c 1953*
ABC10061 Mkhonto Ka Chaka DC707
ABC10063 Sodla Ngoluda La DC707

NBA CHAMPIONS
VOCALS: N. Mbatha, P. Khumalo, H. Mbatha, others unknown
Johannesburg *c 1971*
17711 Balekani Zinsizwa
17712 Amabeshu Ami
17713 Masambeni Zinsizwa
17714 Nathinta Thina
17715 Usobhuzo
17716 Lindiwe
17717 Wangilamla Ubaba PKLP705
17718 Umlazi Omsha
17719 Qhaphela
17720 Usizi Nanto
17721 Usizi Lona
17722 Ubaba
(All titles released on PKLP705, *Iqhawe Lethu.*)

Johannesburg   *c 1971*
18057   Ngiyolala Emasimini   PK3055
18058   Wangilaya Umama   PK3055
18059   Avuthiwe Amabele   PK3054
18060   Ngikhala Njenge Ndoda   PK3054

NEWCASTLE FIVE ROSES
Johannesburg   *1975*
　　　Sambamb'Utikoloshe
　　　Ngadibana Nomama
　　　Bamb'Izinja Zakho Mfoka Lavuno   ⎬   LT15099
　　　Ulithemba Lami
　　　Jumaima
Durban
　　　Kwakhala Insingizi
　　　Nangu Umthakathi
　　　Hambani Niyocela Amasiko
　　　Bhukulani Izidwaba
　　　Sizombamba Usathane   ⎬   RL116
　　　Ntombi Yakwamkhize
　　　Uyayibona Lendoda
　　　Vumelani Abantwana Beze
　　　Kudala Ngangihamba
(All titles released on RL116, *Kwakhala Insingizi.*)
VOCALS: N. V. Makhaza, others unknown
Johannesburg
　　　Izwe Elikude
　　　Bambizinja Zakho
　　　Kwakhal'Insingizi
　　　Wemfana Omncane
　　　Sizombam Bu'Sathane
　　　Ngidedelani Ngigite   ⎬   OSA100
　　　Bantu Bakithi
　　　Ngake Ngahamba Mina
　　　Uqondeni Kodwa Ndoda
　　　Yeka Okwami Okwezandla
　　　Nisithand'Uma Nisibona
　　　Wemaqola Hlanganani
(All titles released on OSA100, *Izwe Elikude.*)
VOCALS: Wilson Khumalo, Victor Makhaza, others unknown

Johannesburg *1981*

    Ungabomthemba Umuntu
    Wemfana Yekela
    Usathane Uxakile
    Kwelama Xhosa
    Thina Sibadala
    Sesihambile   RPM7055
    Anibobhasobha
    Sibongile
    Kwakhala Isikhova
    Thinasizinyoni
    Kwaphinda Kwenzeka
(All titles released on RPM7055, *Newcastle Five Roses.*)

Johannesburg *22 May 1982*

    Mubi Umakhelwane
    Kade Besibuza
    Thinta Thina Nje
    Asambeni Sothandaza
    Intombi Ingalile
    Caroliner   RPM7079
    Vimbani Amaphekula
    Lizwe Elikude
    Sobhe Kaphi Na Thixo
    Susa Zonke Izoho Zami
    Hambani Kancane
    Jerusalema Ikhaya Lami
(All titles released on RPM7079, *Mubi Umakhelwane.*)
VOCALS: V. Makhaza, others unknown

Johannesburg *1986*

    Ithemba Alibulali
    Gijimani Maqola
    Asishayi Ingoma Yomuntu
    Emafini "Nango Eza"
    Sesiyahamba Ilanga Lishonile
    Xwayani Abantu   JUL204
    Ungabongala Ntombi
    Kukude Egoli
    Sihamba No Makhaza
    Uphi Irene Wami
(All titles released on JUL204, *Ithemba Alibulali.*)
VOCALS: V. Makhaza, others unknown

Johannesburg   *1987*
    Hayi Mazulu
    Letha Ikhubalo
    Wemadoda Asegoli
    Ngikhumbula Leyomini
    Mapetla
    Xwayani Nina Bakithi   JUL220
    Ungahlehleli Emuva
    Ngidebana Nomama
    Morrina
    Bayasazi
(All titles released on JUL220, *Hayi Mazulu.*)
VOCALS: V. Makhaza, others unknown

Johannesburg   *1988*
    Waze Wangilayandoda
    Bamba Izinja Zakho
    Dudla Ntombi
    Mtakwethu Mina
    Ungabondlala Ngomama
    Sikhulekela Indawo   JUL259
    Ubogiya Ngezakho
    Wobethela Umuzi
    Bayothini Obaba
    Ezinsukwini Zaku Dala
(All titles released on JUL259, *Waze Wangilayandoda.*)

NEWCASTLE NALA BOYS

                                                                               1975

VOCALS: Bhekithemba M. Ntombela, others unknown

ABC33297	Amakwaitosi	MO551
ABC33298	Senkhalel'Inkomo Zami	MO551
ABC33299	Sangena Thina	MO552
ABC33300	Yibo Labafana	MO552
ABC33301	Yakhal'Inkomo	MO553
ABC33302	Ninabakwantshangase	MO553
ABC33303	Umakoti Akahloniphi	MO554
ABC33304	Seng'Khathele	MO554
ABC33305	Intandane	MO555
ABC33306	Khula Mfana Wami	MO555
ABC33307	Qiniselani	MO556
ABC33308	Abakhongi	MO556

                                                                               1975

ABC33611	Sibezwile Lababantu	MO616
ABC33612	Yibambeni Bafana	MO616
ABC33613	Kukhona Umlilo	MO617
ABC33614	Khawulani Ukudakwa	MO617

ABC33615   Wentombi Emhlophe   MO618
ABC33616   Kudala Sihamba   MO618
ABC33617   Uphi Ozelweyo   MO619
ABC33618   Kosanini Ngihambe   MO619
ABC33619   Ma Ufuna Ukusibona   MO620
ABC33620   Lalelani Madoda   MO620
ABC33621   Ubongisiza   MO621
ABC33622   Wentombi   MO621

NEWCASTLE STAR ROSES
Johannesburg   1970
      Emadadeni   LT12087
      Yiyo Lentombi Ebengiyithanda   LT12087

NEW CROCODILE ROVERS
VOCALS: Wilmot Masondo, others unknown
Durban   1963
13144   Mendi   OK480
13145   Khethintikazi   OK480

NEW CROCO STARS
VOCALS: R. Mchunu, others unknown
Johannesburg   1962
J279 Ejimolo   KA56
J280 E Nazareth   KA56

NEW HEAVY STARS
VOCALS: Moses Mbonambi, others unknown
Durban   1983
      Thina Siyakulela
      Hlakanipha Nhliziyo Yami
      Udumo
      Umusa Kajehova
      Sondela Nkosi
      Baba Wethu   RPM7085
      Nganglyo Sebenz'Imali
      Bambisanini
      Sesiwuhambile Lomhlaba
      Vukani Zingilosi
(All titles released on RPM7085, *Baba Wethu*.)

NEW LUCKY BOYS
VOCALS: Simon Ngubane (leader), Senzakuphi Mchunu, Wilson Ngcobo, others
unknown
Johannesburg   *14 May 1974*
ABC32987   Manje Dali   MO465
ABC32988   Ulizzie Wami   MO465
ABC32989   Bayakhal'Emsinga   MO466

ABC32990   Ubani
            Ongashel'Isangoma   MO466
ABC32991,
ABC5410   Dudu Madlamini   MO467, DLPL291/2
ABC32992,   Imali Yimpande Yesono   MO467, DLPL291/2
ABC5411
(DLPL291/2 entitled *Cothoza Mfana*.)

Johannesburg   1974
    Sidedeleni   ⎤
    Unomathemba   ⎥
    Igugu   ⎬ LT14315
    Obabamkhulu   ⎦

Johannesburg   2 May 1975
ABC33455   Izinxane Lembube   MO594
ABC33456   Ngemuka Kudala   MO594
ABC33458   Angina Bhulukhwe   MO595
ABC33459   Nansi Lendoda   MO596
ABC33460   Naso Isitimela   MO596

Johannesburg   c 5 March 1976
ABC33780, ABC6442   Okwami Okwezandla   ⎤
ABC33781, ABC6442   Gubha Amagagasi   ⎥
ABC33782, ABC6443   Intombi Enamadevu   ⎥
ABC33783, ABC6442   Dudu Nomathemba   ⎥
ABC33784, ABC6443   Shwele Siyakhuleka   ⎥
ABC33785, ABC6442   Ngangi Ngazi   ⎥
ABC33786, ABC6442   Sayibamb'Ekuseni   ⎬ BL70
ABC33787, ABC6443   Uyingcwele   ⎥
ABC33788, ABC6443   Osezulwini   ⎥
ABC33789, ABC6442   Emhlabeni   ⎥
ABC33790, ABC6443   Intsha Yonakele   ⎥
ABC33791, ABC6442   Ithemba Labazazi   ⎦

Johannesburg   20 Mar 1982
            ⎧ Kuhle Ukukholwa   ⎫
            ⎥ Ngangingazi   ⎥
            ⎥ Iqili   ⎥
ABC10684   ⎨ Ukufa   ⎥
            ⎥ Siyakhuleka   ⎥
            ⎩ Bayozisola   ⎬ BL357
            ⎧ Mathand 'Ukwenzelwa ⎥
            ⎥ Akenibheke   ⎥
            ⎥ Kukhon 'Intombi   ⎥
ABC10685   ⎨ Hlala Kahle   ⎥
            ⎥ Thandiwe   ⎥
            ⎩ Ziyadula   ⎭
(All titles released on BL357, *Kuhle Ukukholwa*.)

Johannesburg   *29 Apr 1983*

ABC11241 { Zidedeleni
Bekhuluma Ngathi
Izingelosi
Isonto
Isalukazi

ABC11242 { Namhla Silapha
Ushobane
Umhlengi Wami
Ngithethelele
My Dreams

BL432

(All titles released on BL432, *Zidedeleni.*)

Johannesburg   *29 Apr 1983*

Isonto
Umhlengi Wami
Thula Ungakhali
Dumisani

SMC5010

(All titles released on SMC5010, *Isonto.*)

Johannesburg(?)

Indoda   YMA014
Jane   YMA014

NEW MORNING STARS
VOCALS: unknown
Johannesburg(?)   *c early 1960s*
NA10136   Byakhala Bo   ZZ74
NA10137   Nyakanyaka   ZZ74

NEW MOUNTAIN
VOCALS: Daviyana Sibisi (leader), others unknown
Johannesburg   *1976*
Omama Bayakhala   LT15858
Emalonjeni   LT15858

NGCOLOSI MIGHTY BOYS
VOCALS: Aaron T. Luthuli, others unknown
Johannesburg   *25 May 1987*

GRC10062 { Kholwa Izwi
How Sweet Is the Song
Ngiyacabanga
Baba Wethu
Okhetho'Wakho
Nkosi Baba Usibheke

GRC10063 { Batsheleni
Vukani Baholi
Kuthokoza Izinyoni
Ngikhangele
I Don't Mind

BL592

(All titles released on BL592, *Kholwa Izwi.*)

Herzon Ngobese Choir and Concertina Orchestra (see Morning Light Choir)

Herzon Ngobese with Morning Light Choir (see Morning Light Choir)

NHL Home Defenders
VOCALS: Jeremiah Buthelezi (leader), others unknown
Durban   *21 May 1974*

ABC33003, ABC5410	Uyizwil'Indaba	MO471, DLPL29½
ABC33004, ABC5411	Makoti Asambe	MO471, DLPL29½
ABC33005, ABC5410	Shosholoza S'Timela	MO472, DLPL29½
ABC33006, ABC5411	Zimb'Indaba	MO472, DLPL29½
ABC33007	Bonke Bayamazi	MO473
ABC33008	Nang'Uthekwane	MO473

(DLPL29½ entitled *Cothoza Mfana*.)
Durban   *May 1974*

ABC33037	Umfokankosi	MO487
ABC33038	Umfokamfeka	MO487
ABC33039	Carolina	MO488
ABC33040	Ngethelekise Na	MO488
ABC33041	Asikhulume	MO489
ABC33042	We Deliwe	MO489

Nkandla Bros
VOCALS: Ewert Mncube, Russiel Mncube, Lucas Manyathi, others unknown
Johannesburg   *21 Jan 1982*

ABC10620	Umpande	
	Sakhenawe Thina	
	Hlabangani	
	Inhlangla Mayibenani	
	Kwakhe Kwangenza	
	Cishe Safa	BL346
ABC10621	Udingaan	
	Umadlokovu	
	Ngizwile Bekhuluma	
	Sake Sahlaka Zeka	
	Oh Ekhaya	
	Ngcondo Mayi Hambe	

(All titles released on BL346, *Amakhosi Akithi*.)

N.K.A. Special
Durban   *18 Nov 1984*

| Hamba Njalo | Rounder 5023 |

(Rounder 5023 entitled *Mbube!*)

NONGOMA JUMPING BOYS

1982

VOCALS: Enoch Mnguni, others unknown

Uthando Luka Jesu Luy Amangalisa	
Ngiyamthanda U Jesu	
Nkosi Khanyisa Isibane	
Tshala Ekuseni Nasemini	
Jerusalem Ikhaya Lami	
Kuyinsindiso Inye	
Ngiyamthanda	IAL3050
Ngikhululiwe	
Bonke Bawele I Jordan	
Vuthelani Icilongo	
Siyokumshumayela U Jesu	
Hamba Nathi Mkhululi Wethu	

(All titles appear on IAL3050, *Ukukholwa Ku Jesu.*)

NONGOMA 100% BROTHERS
VOCALS: Mcnazelem Dlamini, others unknown
Johannesburg

1983

Dr. Khis'Inja	
Intonjana Emnyama	
Ngisese Mhlabeni	
Zindala Zombili	
Sanibona	
Makhelwane Wani	GAL110
Amnandi Amazwi	
Usenzekile	
Ecacela	
Baningi	

(All titles released on GAL110, *Usenzekile.*)

N. Q. HOME DIVISION
Johannesburg

Feb 1956

Ubani Ozosithinta	T2488
Iyangithanda Intombi	T2488
Zimbambe Ndoda	T2489
Khuluma Nentsimbi	T2489

OCEAN BLUES: ESTCOURT
Johannesburg

1970

Wosiza Ubuye	
Mahlathi Amnyama	
Inamawala Lendoda	LT11907
Yasho Ingqungqulu	
Nozizwe	

ORLANDO FLYING BIRDS
VOCALS: ———Mchunu (conductor), others unknown
Johannesburg   *c 1938*
XYZX85   Wangi Shaya U Baba   GE830
XYZX86   Talaza A Ngimbone   GE830
(XYZX71–106 untraced.)
Johannesburg   *c 1940*
1692   Abazali
1693   E-Gemara
1694   Ayi Hlasete   } Unissued
1695   Nkosi Sikelela
1696   Bayi
(1697 untraced. 1695 is listed in the ILAM catalogue as by Awa Evening Birds. As
it is unlikely that a different group would have made a single side in the middle of
another's session, this designation may turn out to be a listing error in the catalogue or on the label of the test pressing.)

ORLANDO NAUGHTY BOYS
VOCALS: G. Ngwenya, others unknown
Johannesburg
       Bowulelephi Izolo
       Siyabhula Isangoma
       Basho Labafana Base Soweto
       Wawuthini Wenandoda
       Yamemeza Indoda
       Laze Lashona Ilanga
       Nangu Umagwegwe Eza   } SK80153
       Balekani Makwedini
       Khethi Wozakimi
       Galela Uze Udinwe
       Wawuthini Kimi
       Nampa Bengibiza
(All titles released on SK80153, *Bowulelephi Izolo*.)

ORLANDO TRAINED SINGERS
VOCALS: unknown; BANJO: unknown; PIANO: unknown
Johannesburg
1788 Hard Nut   DC33
1789 Nlele Zindudumeni   Unissued
1790 Natal   DC33
1792 Adam No Eva   Unissued
(1786–87, 1791, 1793–94 untraced.)

PIMVILLE YOUNG STARS
Johannesburg   *1983*
    Wonke Amehlo
    Ujesu!
    U Ya Phila
    Yakahaza Intsimbi
    Nkosi E No Musa
    Masi Hambe
    Sise Busweni Bakho   SEH4004
    Baphi O'Shampheni
    Bale Kani
    Siya Bonga
    Gabi Gabi
    Ukhula
(All titles released on SEH4004, *Gabi Gabi*.)

PRETORIA ROLLING STARS
Johannesburg   *9 Feb 1981*
    Sambamba
    Hambani
    Wena We Nhliziyo
    Bengine Ntombi
    Ngiboniseleni
    Vuma Balambile
    We Ntombazane   CYL1053
    We Makholwa
    Lizi Mntanami
    Impi Mayigwaza
    Uyaphi Na Nomthwalo?
    Woza Sambe
(All titles released on CYL1053, *Sambamba Utikoloshe*.)

QOLI AND HIS NEW EVENING BIRDS
VOCALS: unknown; GUITAR (1): unknown
Johannesburg   *1958*
ABC17093   Izintombi Zingibizile   GB2867
ABC17094   Isitimela (1)   GB2867

RAYMA ZULU BOYS MALE VOICE CHOIR
VOCALS: unknown; PIANO: unknown
Johannesburg   *c 1945*
    Ngobathina   RB6
    Mnguni   RB6

ROVERS
Durban   *18 Nov 1984*
    Wathintha Thina   Rounder 5023
(Rounder 5023 entitled *Mbube!*)

ROYAL BLUES
VOCALS: Ephraim Zwane, others unknown
Johannesburg   *8 Nov 1973*
ABC32795, ABC5016   Seliyana   SJM142, BSLP22, BL22
ABC32796, ABC5017   Irene   SJM142, BSLP22, BL22
ABC32797   Indod'Enamawala   SJM143
ABC32798   Lomnumzane   SJM143
(BSLP22, BL22 entitled *Ufakazi Yibheshu* featuring Empangeni Home Tigers.)
Durban   *21 May 1974*
ABC33009   Uqam Kavinjelwa   MO474
ABC33010   Indod'Emnyama   MO474
ABC33011   Sofika Kusasa   MO475
ABC33012   Ngishel 'Emabaceni   MO475

ROYAL CROWN STARS
VOCALS: Samson Khuboni (leader), others unknown
Johannesburg   *1961*
OAS1617   Nanguya   JP674
OAS1618   Minya   JP674

THE ROYALS
VOCALS: unknown
Johannesburg   *c late 1951*
ABC3931   Mziyoni Baleka   DC126
ABC3935   Usizi Ejabavu   DC126
ABC3936   Izintombi Lezi   DC127
ABC3937   Wena We Ndoda   DC127
(ABC3926 – 30, ABC3932 – 34, ABC3938 – 39 untraced.)

ROYAL STAR
Johannesburg   *5 Nov 1976*
          Umkhulu Umade Vu
          Siceli Ntokozo
          Baphi Lababantu
          Ihawu Lakhe
          Ethekwini
          Ngizogiya   } MAL7006
          Ntsizwa
          Lendoda
          Ubaba No-Mama
          Okunga Pheli
(All titles released on MAL7006, *Royal Star*. This may be the same group as the
Durban Royal Stars.)

SCORPIONS
VOCALS: Gershon Mcanyana (leader), others unknown
Johannesburg   *1966*
          Yewu Yewu   LT6765
          Cothoza Mfana   LT6765, Rounder 5025

Sithandwa Sami
eNatali
Kuhle Kumnandi
Heyi Wentombi } LT6766
Ngifuna Ukukhuluma Nawe
Isitimela
(Rounder 5025 entitled *Mbube Roots*.)

Johannesburg   *1968*

Bayajabula
Kwaswayaimani
Ikhaya Lami
Ulimbambe Lingashoni } LT10247
Baba Nomame
Heyi Wemfana

Johannesburg   *1975*

Yise Kamfana
Ngikhumbula Umama } LT15646
Ngibonga Inkosi
Hamba Phepha Lami

Sea Waves Choir
Johannesburg   *c early 1942*
1923 Pra Dikeleoi
1924 Nma Motlalepule
1925 Nabina
1926 Nfaziwe Dolo } Unissued
1927 Ama Banana
1928 Pra Bontlen
(1929–34 untraced. This may not be an *mbube* choir.)

Sesela Smiling Boys
VOCALS: Absalom Mlambo (leader), others unknown

1976

Umanutu   LT15684

Shining Stars Male Voice Choir
VOCALS: unknown; CONCERTINA: unknown; GUITAR: unknown
Johannesburg   *c 1942*
Intombi Ya Kala   XU56
Abafana   XU56
Balekani   XU57
Abancane   XU57

Shooting Stars
VOCALS: Phillip Msimanga (leader), others unknown; PIANO: unknown
Johannesburg   *1938*
OAS239-1 Si Fikile Izolo   JP23
OAS240-1 Yek'Emarabini   JP23, Rounder 5025
(OAS241–44 untraced. Rounder 5025 entitled *Mbube Roots*.)

Johannesburg   *1938*
OAS269-1   We 'Mahlalela Hamba 'O   JP27
               Sebenza
(JP27 issued as Shooting Stars Zulu Choir with Kuzwayo's Band. OAS265-8
untraced.)
Johannesburg   *1938*
CEA2321-1   Molo'Mathaba   YE48
CEA2325-1   Yi Wo Ama Shooting Stars   YE52
CEA2338-1   Sa Dhl'Isambhane   YE40
CEA2339-1   Wo! Sashothina Ama   YE40
               Shooting Stars
CEA2340-1   Wo Lala Wo Lala   YE48
CEA2341-1   Si Na Bona Ni   YE52
(YE40, 48 issued as Phillip Msimanga's Zulu Choir. YE52 issued as Phillip
Msimanga's Shooting Stars.)

SITHOLE BROTHERS
VOCALS: Agrippa Sithole (leader), Samuel Hadebe (tenor), David Ngema (tenor),
Christopher Sithole (bass), Henry Sithole (tenor), Moses Sithole (bass)
Johannesburg   *1980*
      Ntombi Ngalile
      Mendi Ungowami
      Egibiba
      Nkosi Yami
      Esikolweni
      Thula Musukukhala
      Abafokazana   BOL100
      Nangu Dudwami
      Uzunga Khali
      Balele Labantu
      Ujesu
      Sizubenami
(All titles released on BOL100, *Nkosi Yami*.)

SIYAUM M.V. CHOIR
VOCALS: unknown
Johannesburg   *c 1955*
AD479   Qoma Njalo   BZ1211
AD480   Mfo Ka Luthuli   BZ1211

SUMMER ROSES
VOCALS: unknown
Durban   *10 Dec 1960*
10841   Konakele   TJ883
10842   Ukuthula   Unissued
10843   Lezomini   Unissued
10844   Bambulele   TJ883

SWAZILAND SINGING SEVEN
Johannesburg   *1936*

1247	Singa Hamble Busuko	⎫	
1248	Ilele Intsizwa	⎬	Unissued
1249	Ikubalo	⎭	
1250-1	Mase E Goli		GE153
1251-1	Ngilileleni		GE153

(1252 untraced. 1248 is listed in the ILAM catalogue as by Eight Hot Sparks. As it is unlikely that a different group would have made a single side in the middle of another's session, this designation may turn out to be a listing error in the catalogue or on the label of the test pressing.)

SWAZI MALE VOICE CHOIR
VOCALS: unknown; PIANO: Mark S. Radebe
Johannesburg   *1933*

WEA1396-1	Belumbi	AE30

(WEA1397–1405 untraced.)
Johannesburg   *1933*

WEA1526-1	Singani Sami	AE30
	Nkosi U-Sobhuza	AE29
	Noma Sihamba	AE29

(AE29, 30 issued as Swazi Male Voice Choir, accompanied by Jazz Revellers Band. No copy of AE29 has been found; titles are listed in the Columbia catalogue. These may have been recorded at this session or the one following. WEA1516–25, 1527–64 untraced.)
VOCALS: unknown; PIANO(1): W. P. Zikali
Johannesburg   *1933*

WEA1573-1	Imali Iyembiwa	AE109
WEA1574-1	Kuze Singazi Soli (1)	AE109

(AE109/WEA1573-1 issued as Swazi Male Voice Choir, accompanied by Jazz Revellers Band. AE109/WEA1574-1 issued as Swazi Male Voice Choir; piano accompaniment, W. P. Zikali. WEA1568–72, 1575–93 untraced.)

THULISA CHOIR
VOCALS: R. Ndima, others unknown
Johannesburg

Wayedaliwe	⎫	
Imbali Yezwa		
Imali		
Inhlambamasoka		
Wawuyaphi	⎬	SONOR022
Zimiselenj		
Icilongo		
I Love the Music		
Inhliziyo		
Umswazi	⎭	

(All titles released on SONOR022, *Wayedaliwe*.)

THULA SIZWE
Salisbury   *1974*
VOCALS: Lutu Moyo, Masala Moyo, Jatu Ncube, others unknown
ABC33157   Ekuhle Makhwaya   MO524
ABC33158   Sake Sahamba   MO524
ABC33162   Isimanga Esikhulu   MO526

TIMOTE DLAMINI AND THE TRY SINGERS
Swaziland   *1958*
Maqumbo Mano Mhlaba
Uyadela Try Singers   } TR71
Pinda Zimshaya

TINY BOY'S CHOIR
Johannesburg   *1942*
1989 Paulina Wase Turfontein
1990 Incwadi
1991 Darlie Yimi Isiponeno
1992 Sabela Mfana
1993 Ngase Goli   } Unissued
1994 Into Yami
1995 Vuma Sigonane
(1988 untraced.)

TRANSVAAL BLACK MAMBAZO
Johannesburg   *12 Aug 1975*
Ukuzi Jabulisa
Umbono Wamambazo
Buya Ndingindaba
Ngi 'Khaza Ngiyabaze Ka
Ayilaze
Indaba Yabafana Bamambazo   } SML7002
Ezimnyana
Hamb Ntomba Zana
Madoda Silapha
Izintombi
(All titles released on SML7002, *The Black Axe*.)
Johannesburg   *3 Feb 1977*
Indodana
Nkosi
Sifo Somtu
Ebusweni Bakho
Simoni Ka John
Ekufeni Kwakhe
Izulu   } SML7005
Morena Rethuse
Singaba Hambayo
Haleluya
Inkosi Yamabandla
Phumani Emahlathini
(All titles released on SML7005, *Lala Ngokuthula*.)

TRY SINGERS
VOCALS: unknown

Johannesburg (?)		*c 1960*
TD113 Mfokamgadi	BZ1683	
TD114 Cwayanani	BZ1683	
Durban (?)		*c 1962*
Vulamasango	BRM021	
Olwandle	BRM021	
Durban(?)		*c 1966*
Imbazo Yami	B13	
Inyako Musha	B13	

(B13 issued as A Natal Try Singers.)
VOCALS: Petros Mngadi, others unknown

Durban		*13 Aug 1967*
ABC30871 Zibusisiwe Izintombi	AB3001	
ABC30872 Bheke Zanzi	AB3001	
ABC30873 Inkomo Azibuye	AB3003	
ABC30874 Isipampam	AB3003	
ABC30875 Ikhalaphi	AB3004	
ABC30876 Uzodela	AB3004	

(AB3001, AB3003, AB3004 issued as A Natal Try Singers.)

Durban(?)		*June 1968*
ABC27604 Enkunzini	AB3022	
ABC27605 Ithenisi	AB3022	
ABC27606 Emthini	AB3023	
ABC27607 Lezonkomo	AB3023	
ABC27608,		
ABC28032 Amantombazane	AB3024	
ABC27609,		
ABC28033 Umakoti Wabaleka	AB3024	
ABC27626 Walila Umtwana	AB3026	
ABC27627 Hebe	AB3026	

(AB3022, AB3023, AB3024, AB3026 issued as A Natal Try Singers.)

TUGELA FERRY HOME SINGERS
VOCALS: Dan Sithole, others unknown

Johannesburg		*1978*
Phalizwe	BFM136	
Umfazi Omdala	BFM136	
Johannesburg		*27 Mar 1980*
GRC4145 I Am So Happy	AB473	
GRC4146 My Darling	AB473	
GRC4147 Matsidiso	AB474	
GRC4148 Ditulo	AB474	
GRC4149 Ngiyathandwa Bo	AB475	
GRC4150 Intsha Yanamhlanje	AB475	

VOCALS: Dan Sithole, Israel Makhunga, Robert Makhunga, Samson Makhunga, Michael Mdletshe, Alson Mntungwa, Enoch Mntungwa, Victor Ngubane, William Ngubane, Robert Nyandeni, John Shungula, Ishmael Sokhela

Johannesburg   *26 Feb 1983*

GRC8179 ⎰ Ungabomthemb' Umuntu
        ⎱ Musani Ukwenzenje
          Bayaifuna
          Bathini Lababantu
          Wozani Nonke   NZL97
          Uphalizwe
          Yekani Imikhuba
GRC8180 ⎰ Sikhulume Saqeda
        ⎱ Intombi Emhlophe
          Emhlabeni

(All titles released on NZL97, *Ungabomthemb' Umuntu.*)

Ubuka King Stars
Durban   *1983*

Wemadoda Yini Lena
Safika Besonta
Thulu Lalele
Jabulani Zingilosi
Izintombi Ezilishumi
Thula Nhliziyo Yami   RPM7084
Wemafulela
Khulekani
Nkosi Yami
Wema-Mkhize

(All titles released on RPM7084, *Wemadoda Yini Lena.*)

Umlazi Male Voice Choir
Johannesburg   *Aug 1959*

Isishimeyana   T5051
Ngivela Ehaudini   T5051

Johannesburg   *Oct 1959*

EMalvern   T5192
Kukhalwa Ngezintombi   T5192
Sakubona Usaphila   T5193
Angiqonywa   T5193

Johannesburg(?)   *c early 1960s*

NA10126   Nganka Kudala   ZZ60
NA10127   Zasho Engnai   ZZ60

(ZZ60 issued as the Umlaza Male Voice Choir.)

Umtwalume Flying Swallows
VOCALS: unknown
Johannesburg   *c 1961*

ADB492   Imboza   BZ1649
ADB493   Umsunduzi   BZ1649

UNHLANHLA NEZIMBALI
VOCALS: W. N. Zwane, Lolo Mkhize, H. P. Zwane, others unknown
Johannesburg   *6 June 1982*

    Uzubekhona Emngcwabeni Wami
    Isina Muva Liyabukwa
    Izolo Ngimbonile Ehamba Naye
    Sasithunywe Abazali
    Bayokhala Omama
    Kwalaphi Ungiqome
    Ikhaya Lami   } Shine 1
    Kudala Ngikuncenga
    Wenzani Umakoti
    Koze Kubenini
    Ngisababhale Awuphenduli
    Asesabi Lutho

(All titles released on Shine 1, *Uzubekhona Emngcwabeni Wami.*)

UNION EXPRESS COMPANY
VOCALS: A. Mwelase (conductor), others unknown; BANJO: unknown; PIANO:
unknown
Johannesburg   *1940*

ABC348	Sikalela	DC20
ABC349	Amatambo	GE886
ABC350	Buya	DC20
ABC351	Dilika	GE886
ABC352	Shorty	GE885
ABC353	Mgijimi	GE885
ABC354	Kusile	GE884
ABC355	Ngagonywa	GE884

(DC20 issued as Decca Wandering Minstrels.)

UNKNOWN
Durban   *1958*

ABC16885	Unknown	Unknown
ABC16886	Unknown	Unknown

UTRECHT CHAMPIONS
VOCALS: unknown

T3149	Uyawatenga Amafufunyane	XU407
T3150	eT. J. Bayakala	XU407

(XU407 is a dubbed reissue circa late 1940s of an earlier untraced XU issue using
new masters T3149/50.)

VOLKSRUST TRY SINGERS
VOCALS: George Ngwenya, others unknown
Johannesburg

Mashihambeni	RPM879
Yethi-Yethi	RPM879

| | Mntakwethu | RPM880 |
| | Ungabo Mashaya Umfazi | RPM880 |

Johannesburg   *14 Jan 1981*
    Ngeke Ngishade   HB654
    Uyangidumaza   HB654
    Bavimbile   HB655
    Ikhaya Lami   HB655

VOCALS: George Ngwenya, Samuel Zwane, others unknown

Johannesburg   *14 May 1982*
    Ngiyamzonda
    Ngekengishade
    Mbambeni
    Selikude Ikhaya
    Ntombi Uyangidumaza
    Bavimbeni   ⎫
    Ngiyofike Ngithini   ⎬ RPM7073
    Yibolabafana
    Ngiyozingela
    Hambani Magoduka
    Iyahlaba   ⎭
    Sobhekaphina

(All titles released on album RPM7073, *Ngiyozingela*.)

VUKA SIZWE

VOCALS: Naphtali Nkosi, others unknown

Durban   *10 Nov 1974*

ABC33281	Intombi Yensizwa	MO570
ABC33282	Sebeyababaza	MO570
ABC33283	Uyamazubaba	MO571
ABC33284	Sawubona Fakazile	MO571

VULTURES

VOCALS: Elias Dhlamini (leader), others unknown

Johannesburg(?)   *c 1952*

| AD91 | Zinyane Le Isilo | BZ69 |
| AD92 | Lindiwe | BZ69 |

Durban   *c 1954*

ABC12131	Jabula Ntombi	GB2065
ABC12136	Sokwenze Njani	GB2065
	Woza Lapha Sitandwa	
	Sami	GB2064
	Siwuhambile Umhlaba	GB2064

(GB2064, GB2065 issued as Vultures Choir.)

WANDERING BOYS

VOCALS: unknown

Johannesburg(?)   *c early 1960s*

| NA10097 | Sithilele Utshwala | ZZ46 |
| NA10098 | Selimathunsi | ZZ46 |

WATERKLOOF CHOIR
VOCALS: Paulos Mtombela, others unknown; PIANO: Emily Motsieloa
Johannesburg   *c 1939*
ABC99-2   Ubongilinda Emasangweni   DC38
ABC100   Nomazanana   Unissued
ABC101   Studebaker   DC38
ABC102   Tilala   Unissued
(ABC90–98, ABC103–105 untraced.)

WATERSMEET MORNING STARS
VOCALS: Ephraim Nkosi, others unknown
Johannesburg   *c Dec 1977*
ABC34342   Ujesu Wabathelwa   MO695
ABC34343   Usozabile   MO695
ABC34344   Azikho Izinkomo   MO696
ABC34345   Sihambile   MO696

WELKOM MORNING STARS
Johannesburg   *1974*
   Ntombi Kangikhathali   ⎫
   Ziphi Izinsizwa   ⎪
   Ngeke Salungelwa Lutho   ⎬ LT14417
   Ngabona Amadoda   ⎪
   Ngambona Lomnumzane   ⎭

WHITE MOUNTAINS
Johannesburg   *1942*
1996 Kanjani   ⎫
1997 Izono Emhlabeni   ⎪
1998 U Dali   ⎬ Unissued
1999 Emahlatini   ⎪
2000 Ntombi Yami   ⎭

WINTER ROSES
VOCALS: Stanley Ndlela, others unknown
Johannesburg   *1958*
OAS1064   Ngikhathele   JP2096
OAS1065   Uthando   JP2096
Johannesburg   *April 1960*
   Ngozula No Thandi   T5633
   Umhla Woupela   T5633
   Sanibonani Nonke   T5634
   Umubi Ntombi   T5634
(T5633, T5634 issued as Winter Roses Male Voice Choir.)

Johannesburg   *1970*
   Jemima Wami
   Akenivuke Kusile
   Inkomo Zami   LT12607
   Sahamba Sa Fika
   Sambamba Utikoloshe
   Ithendele
   Kulezontaba   LT12608
   Nqo, Nqo, Nqo

WORCESTER BLACK TIGERS
VOCALS: D. Gumada, C. Ntsomi, others unknown
Johannesburg   *1987*
          Lonyaka
          Intaba Yetafile
  GRC83 Wonderful Son
          Nank' uJesu
          Somebody Is Calling Your Name
          Who Is Fooling Who   BL607
          Sihamba Ngezimoto
  GRC84 Hoza Baba
          Homeless
          Ukuhlabelela
(All titles released on BL607, *Intaba Yetafile.*)

XOLO HOME BOYS
Durban   *21 Feb 1982*
   Buya Afrika   Heritage HT313
(Heritage HT313 entitled *Iscathamiya.*)

YOUNG STAR BROTHERS
                                  1979
   Banaamagwala   BS101
   Safikeswazini   BS101
   Sizwile Mfokamzimande   BS102

ZULU CHAMPIONS (see DUNDEE WANDERING SINGERS)

ZULU CHOIR
Johannesburg   *early 1942*
1957 We Mdubane   Unissued
1958 Siyangena   Unissued

ZULU VULTURES
VOCALS: Silwayiphi Mkhize (leader), others unknown
Johannesburg   *1976*
   Asambeni Zinsizwa Siye
      Kwa-Khetha   LT15858
   Akesiyoshela Wethu   LT15858

ZULU WANDERING SINGERS (see DUNDEE WANDERING SINGERS)

Glossary

abakhaya: Lit., "home people." A term designating migrants originating from the same rural district.

amahubo: (Sing., *ihubo*) A genre of collective song and dance often symbolizing the unity and identity of a patrilineage.

ifolosi: Derived from Afrikaans, lit., "the lead ox," the leader in an *ingoma* dance team.

igoso: The leader of an *ingoma* dance team.

ikhetho: A dance performed at weddings.

indiki: A type of malevolent spirit possession.

ingoma: Lit., "song," but more commonly used as a term designating a wide range of dances performed by migrant workers.

isicathulo: Lit., "shoe." A dance commonly danced with rubber boots.

isiChunu: A style of song and dance performed by the Chunu people.

isigekle: A dance performed at weddings.

isigodi: Districtlike political and territorial divisions in the precolonial Zulu kingdom.

isikambula: Derived from English "gambling," this term was widely used in the 1940s as a synonym of *isikhwela Jo.*

isikhunzi: Derived from "coons," this term refers to one of the earliest protostyles of isicathamiya based on vaudeville music.

isikhwela Jo: Lit., "go for it, Jo." The prevalent style of isicathamiya, 1940s–1960s, characterized by high-pitched, almost yelling singing.

isithululu: Derived from *thula,* "to be quiet." Often used as a synonym for the low-key isicathamiya pioneered by the King Star Brothers and Ladysmith Black Mambazo.

izibongo: Heroic poetry created in performance.

izingoma zomtshado: Wedding songs. Often applied to more Christianized, hymn-influenced songs.

kompithi: Competition.

makwaya: Derived from the English word "choir." A choral music influenced by Western four-part.

maskanda: From Afrikaans "musikant." A strolling musician playing guitar or concertina. Maskanda music is at the root of much contemporary *mbaqanga.*

mbaqanga: A type of neotraditional music popular among all sectors of society.

'mbombing: From English "bomb" or isiZulu *mbomba,* "to take by surprise." A synonym for *isikhwela Jo.*

mbube: Lit., "lion." Named after Solomon Linda's hit song "Mbube" of 1939, the term is often used as a synonym for isicathamiya.

stokvel: Derived from "stock fair." Voluntary associations based on a rotating credit principle.

ubugagu: Excellence in performance and music making.

ubuqhawe: Heroism, bravery, leadership.

umgqashiyo: A variety of *mbaqanga* pioneered by the female group Mahotella Queens.

umuzi: The rural homestead with its layout of dwellings and cattle enclosure.

References

Abrahams, Peter. 1946. *Mine boy.* London: Heinemann.

Adams, Charles. 1974. Ethnography of Basotho evaluative expression in the cognitive domain "Lipapali" (games). Ph.D. diss., Indiana University.

Adorno, Theodor W. 1993. *Beethoven: Philosophie der Musik.* Frankfurt: Suhrkamp.

Allingham, Rob. 1989. *Singing in an open space: Zulu rhythm and harmony, 1962–1982.* Johannesburg: Gallo (Africa). Album liner notes.

Alverson, Hoyt. 1978. *Mind in the heart of darkness: Value and self-identity among the Tswana of southern Africa.* New Haven: Yale University Press.

Andersson, Muff. 1981. *Music in the mix: The story of South African popular music.* Johannesburg: Ravan Press.

Appadurai, Arjun. 1990. Disjuncture and difference in the global cultural economy. In *Global culture: Nationalism, globalisation, and modernity,* ed. Mike Featherstone. London: Sage Publications.

Arendt, Hannah. 1958. *The human condition.* Chicago: University of Chicago Press.

Asad, Talal. 1986. The concept of cultural translation in British social anthropology. In *Writing culture: The poetics and politics of ethnography,* ed. James Clifford and George E. Marcus. Berkeley and Los Angeles: University of California Press.

Atkins, Keletso E. 1988. "Kafir time." Pre-industrial temporal concepts and labour discipline in nineteenth-century colonial Natal. *Journal of African History* 29, no. 2:229–44.

Bakhtin, Mikhail M. 1986. From notes made in 1970–71. In *Speech genres and other late essays.* Austin: University of Texas Press.

Ballantine, Christopher. 1993. *Marabi nights: Early South African jazz and vaudeville.* Johannesburg: Ravan Press.

Banton, Michael. 1957. *West African city: A study of tribal life in Freetown.* Oxford: Oxford University Press.

Barber, Karin. 1987. Popular arts in Africa. *African Studies Review* 30, no. 3: 1–78.

Bataille, Georges. 1988. *The accursed share.* New York: Zone Books.

Baudrillard, Jean. 1993. *The transparency of evil: Essays on extreme phenomena.* London: Verso.

Bauman, Richard. 1984. *Verbal art as performance.* 2d ed. Prospect Heights, Ill.: Waveland Press.

Bauman, Richard, and Charles L. Briggs. 1990. Poetics and performance as critical perspectives on language and social life. *Annual Review of Anthropology* 19: 59–88.

Becker, Judith, and Alton Becker. 1981. A musical icon: Power and meaning in Javanese gamelan music. In *The sign in music and literature,* ed. Wendy Steiner. Austin: University of Texas Press.

Beidelman, T. O. 1986. *Moral imagination in Kaguru modes of thought.* Bloomington: Indiana University Press.

Beinart, William. 1987. Worker consciousness, ethnic particularism and nationalism: The experiences of a South African migrant, 1930–1960. In *The politics of race, class, and nationalism in twentieth-century South Africa,* ed. Shula Marks and Stanley Trapido. London: Longman.

———. 1991. The origins of the Indlavini: Male associations and migrant labour in the Transkei. *African Studies* 50, nos. 1–2:103–28.

Beinart, William, and Colin Bundy. 1986. *Hidden struggles: Rural politics and popular consciousness in South Africa.* London: James Currey.

Benjamin, Walter. 1968. *Illuminations.* Edited by Hannah Arendt, and translated by Harry Zohn. New York: Harcourt, Brace & World.

———. 1973. *Charles Baudelaire: A lyric poet in the era of high capitalism.* London: New Left Books.

Berglund, Axel-Ivar. 1975. Heaven-herds: A study in Zulu symbolism. In *Religion and social change in southern Africa,* ed. Michael G. Whisson and Martin West. Cape Town: David Philip.

———. 1976. *Zulu thought-patterns and symbolism.* Bloomington: Indiana University Press.

Bhabha, Homi. 1992. The world and the home. *Social Text* 31–32: 141–53.

Blacking, John. 1955. Some notes on a theory of African rhythm advanced by Erich von Hornbostel. *African Music* 1, no. 2: 12–20.

———. 1973. *How musical is man?* Seattle: University of Washington Press.

———. 1980a. Political and musical freedom in the music of some black South African churches. In *The structure of folk models,* ed. Ladislav Holy and Milan Stuchlik. ASA Monograph no. 20. London: Academic Press.

———. 1980b. Trends in the black music of South Africa, 1959–1969. In *Musics of many cultures,* ed. E. May. Berkeley and Los Angeles: University of California Press.

———. 1985. Movement, dance, music, and the Venda girls' initiation cycle. In *Society and the dance,* ed. Paul Spencer. Cambridge: Cambridge University Press.

———. 1987. Intention and change in the performance of European hymns by some black South African churches. In *Transplanted European music cultures,* ed. Geoffrey Moon. Miscellanea Musicologica: Adelaide Studies in Musicology, vol. 12. Adelaide, South Australia: University of Adelaide.

Blum, Stephen. 1991. Ethnomusicologists and modern music history. Prologue to *Ethnomusicology and modern music history,* ed. Stephen Blum, Philip V. Bohlman, and Daniel M. Neuman. Urbana: University of Illinois Press.

———. 1992. Analysis of musical style. In *Ethnomusicology: An introduction,* ed. Helen Myers. New York: W. W. Norton.

Bohlman, Philip V. 1988. *The study of folk music in the modern world.* Bloomington: Indiana University Press.

Bonner, Philip L. 1990. "Desirable or undesirable Sotho women?" Liquor, prostitution, and the migration of the Basotho women to the Rand, 1920–1945. In *Women and gender in southern Africa to 1945,* ed. Cherryl Walker. Cape Town: David Philip.

Bonner, Philip, Isabel Hofmeyr, Deborah James, and Tom Lodge, eds. 1989. *Holding their ground: Class, locality, and culture in nineteenth and twentieth century South Africa.* Johannesburg: Ravan Press and Witwatersrand University Press.

Bourdieu, Pierre. 1977. *Outline of a theory of practice.* Cambridge: Cambridge University Press.

———. 1987. The biographical illusion. Working papers and proceedings of the Center for Psychosocial Studies, no. 14, Chicago.

Bourdieu, Pierre, and Loïc Wacquant. 1992. *Résponses: Pour une anthropologie réflexive.* Paris: Seuil.

Bozzoli, Belinda. 1987. Class, community, and ideology in the evolution of South African Society. In *Class, community, and conflict: South African perspectives,* ed. Belinda Bozzoli. Johannesburg: Ravan Press.

Bozzoli, Belinda, and Peter Delius. 1990. Radical history and South African society. *Radical History Review* 46–47: 13–46.

Bradford, Helen. 1987. *A taste of freedom: The ICU in rural South Africa, 1924–1930.* New Haven: Yale University Press.

———. 1990. Highways, byways and culs-de-sacs: The transition to agrarian capitalism in revisionist South African history. *Radical History Review* 46–47: 59–88.

Breckenbridge, Keith. 1990. Migrancy, crime and faction fighting: The role of the Isitshozi in the development of ethnic organisations in the compounds. *Journal of Southern African Studies* 16, no. 1:55–78.

Burke, Kenneth. 1966. *Language as symbolic action.* Berkeley: University of California Press.

Campbell, James. 1989. Our fathers, our children: The African Methodist Episcopal Church in the United States and South Africa. Ph.D. diss., Stanford University.

Campschreur, W., and J. Divendal, eds. 1989. *Culture in another South Africa.* New York: Olive Branch Press.

Caraveli, Anna. 1982. The song beyond the song: Aesthetics and social interaction in Greek folksong. *Journal of American Folklore* 95, no. 376: 129–58.

———. 1985. The symbolic village: Community born in performance. *Journal of American Folklore* 98, no. 389. 259–86.

Charsley, Simon. 1992. Dreams in African churches. In *Dreaming, religion, and society in Africa,* ed. M. Charles Jedrej and Rosalind Shaw. Leiden: E. J. Brill.

Chernoff, John Miller. 1979. *African rhythm and African sensibility: Aesthetics and social action in African musical idioms.* Chicago: University of Chicago Press.

———. 1984. The pilgrimage to Mecca: An excerpt from a drummer's testament. *Chicago Review* 34, no. 3:68–93.

Clegg, Jonathan. 1981a. The music of Zulu immigrant workers in Johannesburg—a focus on concertina and guitar. Paper presented at the Symposium
on Ethnomusicology, ed. Andrew Tracey. International Library of African
Music, Grahamstown, South Africa.

———. 1981b. Ukubuyisa isidumbu—bringing back the body: An examination
into the ideology of vengeance in the Msinga and Mpofana rural locations,
1982–1944. Vol. 2 of Working Papers in Southern African Studies, ed.
Philip Bonner. Johannesburg: Ravan Press.

———. 1982. Towards an understanding of African dance: The Zulu isishameni
style. Paper presented at the 2d Symposium on Ethnomusicology, ed. Andrew Tracey. International Library of African Music, Grahamstown, South
Africa.

———. 1984. An Examination of the Umzansi Dance Style. Paper presented at
the 3d Symposium on Ethnomusicology, ed. Andrew Tracey. International
Library of African Music, Grahamstown, South Africa.

Clifford, James. 1986. On ethnographic allegory. In *Writing culture: The poetics
and politics of ethnography*, ed. James Clifford and George E. Marcus. Berkeley and Los Angeles: University of California Press.

———. 1988. *The predicament of culture: Twentieth-century ethnography, literature, and art.* Cambridge, Mass.: Harvard University Press.

Cockrell, Dale. 1987. Of gospel hymns, minstrel shows, and jubilee singers: Toward some black South African musics. *American Music* 5, no. 4:417–32.

Coka, Gilbert. 1936. The story of Gilbert Coka of the Zulu tribe of Natal, South
Africa, written by himself. In *Ten Africans*, ed. Margery Perham. London:
Faber & Faber.

Comaroff, Jean. 1985. *Body of power, spirit of resistance: The culture and history of
a South African people.* Chicago: University of Chicago Press.

———. 1993. The empire's clothes: Dress and fashion in the consciousness of a
South African people. Unpublished manuscript.

Comaroff, Jean, and John Comaroff. 1991. *Of revelation and revolution: Christianity, colonialism, and consciousness in South Africa.* Vol. 1. Chicago: University of Chicago Press.

Comaroff, John, and Jean Comaroff. 1987. The madman and the migrant: Work
and labor in the historical consciousness of a South African people. *American Ethnologist* 14, no. 2:191–209.

———. 1992. *Ethnography and the historical imagination.* Boulder, Colo.: West-
view Press.

Cope, Nicholas. 1990. The Zulu petit bourgeoisie and Zulu nationalism in the
1920s: Origins of Inkatha. *Journal of Southern African Studies* 16, no. 3.

Coplan, David. 1979. The African musician and the development of the Johannesburg entertainment industry, 1900–1960. *Journal of Southern African
Studies* 5, no. 2:135–64.

———. 1982. The urbanisation of African music: Some theoretical observations.
Popular Music 2:113–30.

———. 1985. *In township tonight! South Africa's black city music and theatre.* Johannesburg: Ravan Press.

————. 1986. Performance, self-definition, and social experience in the oral poetry of Sotho migrant mineworkers. *African Studies Review* 29, no. 1:29–40.

————. 1987a. Eloquent knowledge: Lesotho migrants' songs and the anthropology of experience. *American Ethnologist* 14, no. 3:413–33.

————. 1987b. The power of oral poetry: Narrative songs of the Basotho migrants. *Research in African Literatures* 18, no. 1:1–35.

————. 1988. Musical understanding: The ethnoaesthetics of migrant workers' poetic song in Lesotho. *Ethnomusicology* 32, no. 3:337–68.

————. 1991. Fictions that save: Migrants' performance and Basotho national culture. *Cultural Anthropology* 6, no. 2:164–92.

————. 1993. A terrible commitment: Balancing the tribes in South African national culture. In *Perilous states: Conversations on culture and nation,* ed. George E. Marcus. Chicago: University of Chicago Press.

Couzens, Tim. 1993. The courtship of Regina and Dan Twala. Paper read at conference, Transregional Culture and Local Practice in Southern Africa, Berlin.

Cowan, Jane K. 1990. *Dance and the body politic in northern Greece.* Princeton, N.J.: Princeton University Press.

Crapanzano, Vincent. 1980. *Tuhami: Portrait of a Moroccan.* Chicago: University of Chicago Press.

————. 1986. Hermes' dilemma: The masking of subversion in ethnographic description. In *Writing culture: The poetics and politics of ethnography,* ed. James Clifford and George E. Marcus. Berkeley and Los Angeles: University of California Press.

Crush, Jonathan, and Charles Ambler, eds. 1992. *Liquor and labor in southern Africa.* Athens: Ohio University Press.

Dargie, David. 1987. *Xhosa Zionist church music.* Bergvlei, South Africa: Hodder & Stoughton Educational.

de Certeau, Michel. 1984. *The practice of everyday life.* Berkeley and Los Angeles: University of California Press.

————. 1988. *The writing of history.* New York: Columbia University Press.

Dehoux, Vincent. 1986. *Chants à penser Gbaya (Centrafrique).* Paris: Editions SELAF.

Denselow, Robin. 1989. *When the music's over: The story of political pop.* London: Faber & Faber.

Doke, Clement M. and Benedict W. Vilakazi. 1972. *Zulu-English dictionary.* 2d ed. rev. Johannesburg: Witwatersrand University Press.

Drewel, Margaret Thompson. 1991. The state of research on performance in Africa. *African Studies Review* 34, no. 3:1–64.

————. 1992. *Yoruba ritual: Performers, play, agency.* Bloomington: Indiana University Press.

Du Toit, Brian M. 1969. Co-operative institutions and culture change in South Africa. *Journal of Asian and African Studies* 4:275–99.

Durham, Deborah, and James W. Fernandez. 1991. Tropical dominions: The figurative struggle over domains of belonging and apartness in Africa. In *Beyond metaphor: The theory of tropes in anthropology,* ed. James W. Fernandez. Stanford, Calif.: Stanford University Press.

Edgar, Robert R., ed. 1992. *An African American in South Africa: The travel notes of Ralph J. Bunche, 28 September 1937–1 January 1938*. Athens: Ohio University Press.

Engard, Ronald K. 1989. Dance and power in Bafut (Cameroon). In *Creativity of power: Cosmology and action in African societies,* ed. W. Arens and Ivan Karp. Washington: Smithsonian Institution Press.

Epstein, A. L. 1958. *Politics in an urban African community*. Manchester: Manchester University Press.

Erlmann, Veit. 1985. Black political song in South Africa—some research perspectives. *Popular Music Perspectives* 2:187–209.

———. 1989. "Horses in the race course": The domestication of ingoma dancing in South Africa. *Popular Music* 8, no. 3:259–74.

———. 1991. *African stars: Studies in black South African performance*. Chicago: University of Chicago Press.

———. 1993. The politics and aesthetics of transnational musics. *World of Music* 2:3–15.

Fabian, Johannes. 1990. *Power and performance: Ethnographic explorations through proverbial wisdom and theater in Shaba, Zaïre*. Madison: University of Wisconsin Press.

Fardon, Richard. 1990. *Localizing strategies: Regional traditions of ethnographic writing*. Edinburgh: Scottish Academic Press; Washington: Smithsonian Institution Press.

Feld, Steven. 1982. *Sound and sentiment: Birds, weeping, poetics, and song in Kaluli expression*. Philadelphia: University of Pennsylvania Press.

———. 1984. Sound structure as social structure. *Ethnomusicology* 28, no. 3: 383–409.

Ferguson, James. 1992. *The country and the city on the copperbelt*. Cultural Anthropology 7, no. 1:80–92.

Fernandez, James W. 1974–75. Dance exchange in western Equatorial Africa. *CORD Dance Research Journal* 8, no. 1:1–6.

———. 1984. Emergence and convergence in some African sacred places. *Geoscience and Man* 24:31–42.

———. 1986. *Persuasions and performances: The play of tropes in culture*. Bloomington: Indiana University Press.

———. 1988. Andalusia on our minds: Two contrasting places in Spain as seen in a vernacular poetic duel of the late nineteenth century. *Cultural Anthropology* 3:21–35.

———. 1990. The body in Bwiti: Variations on a theme by Richard Werbner. *Journal of Religion in Africa* 20, no. 1:92–110.

Finnegan, Ruth. 1970. *Oral literature in Africa*. Oxford: Oxford University Press.

Foucault, Michel. 1972. *The archaeology of knowledge*. Translated by A. Sheridan. London: Tavistock.

———. 1980. Questions on geography. In *Power/knowledge: Selected interviews and other writings, 1972–1977,* ed. Colin Gordon. Brighton: Harvester Press.

Frank, Arthur W. 1991. For a sociology of the body: An analytical review. In *The body: Social process and cultural theory,* ed. Mike Featherstone, Mike Hepworth, and Bryan S. Turner. London: Sage Publications.

Friedrich, Paul. 1991. Polytropy. In *Beyond metaphor: The theory of tropes in anthropology,* ed. James W. Fernandez. Stanford, Calif.: Stanford University Press.

Geertz, Clifford. 1983. *Local knowledge: Further essays in interpretive anthropology.* New York: Basic Books.

———. 1986. Making experience, authoring selves. In *The anthropology of experience,* ed. Victor W. Turner and Edward M. Bruner. Urbana: University of Illinois Press.

Giddens, Anthony. 1991. *Modernity and self-identity: Self and society in the late modern age.* Cambridge: Cambridge University Press.

Grenier, Line, and Jocelyne Guilbault. 1990. "Authority" revisited: The "other" in anthropology and popular music studies. *Ethnomusicology* 34, no. 3: 381–98.

Guilbault, Jocelyne. 1993. On redefining the "local" through world music. *World of Music* 2:33–47.

Gunner, Elizabeth. 1981. The pool of metaphors: Poetic language and its use in Zulu praise poetry. In *Memory and poetic structure: Papers of the Conference on Oral Literature and Literary Theory,* ed. P. Ryan. London: Middlesex Polytechnic.

———. 1986. A dying tradition? African oral literature in a contemporary context. *Social Dynamics* 12, no. 2:31–38.

———. 1988. Power house, prison house—an oral genre and its use in Isaiah Shembe's Nazareth Baptist Church. *Journal of Southern African Studies* 14, no. 2:204–27.

Gupta, Akhil, and James Ferguson. 1992. Beyond "culture": Space, identity, and the politics of Difference. *Cultural Anthropology:* 6–23.

Guy, Jeff. 1980. Ecological factors in the rise of Shaka and the Zulu kingdom. In *Economy and society in pre-industrial South Africa,* ed. Shula Marks and Anthony Atmore. London: Longman.

Guy, Jeff, and Motlatsi Thabane. 1987. The Ma-Rashea: A participant's perspective. In *Class, community, and conflict: South African perspectives,* ed. Belinda Bozzoli. Johannesburg: Ravan Press.

———. 1988. Technology, ethnicity and ideology: Basotho miners and shaft sinking on the South African gold mines. *Journal of Southern African Studies* 14, no. 2:257–78.

Hamilton, Carolyn, and John Wright. 1993. The beginnings of Zulu identity: The image of Shaka. *Indicator SA* 10, no. 3:43–46.

Hamm, Charles. 1989. Graceland revisited. *Popular Music* 8, no. 3:299–304.

———. 1991. "The constant companion of man": Separate development, Radio Bantu, and music. *Popular Music* 10, no. 2:147–74.

Hammond-Tooke, W. D. 1970. Urbanisation and the interpretation of misfortune. *Africa* 40:25–38.

Hanna, Judith Lynne. 1983. *The performer-audience connection: Emotion to metaphor in dance and society.* Austin: University of Texas Press.

Harries, Patrick. 1987. Songs, stories, rhymes, and riddles: African folklore and people's history. University of the Witwatersrand History Workshop, Johannesburg.

Harries-Jones, P. 1969. "Home-boy" ties and political organization in a copperbelt township. In *Social networks in urban situations,* ed. J. Clyde Mitchell. Manchester, England: Manchester University Press.

Harris, Verne. 1985. White farmers, African tenants and changing forms of agricultural labour on white-owned farms in northern Natal, 1910–1936. Conference on the History of Natal and Zululand, University of Natal, July 1985. Durban: University of Natal Press.

Hayman, Graham, and Ruth Tomaselli. 1989. Ideology and technology in the growth of South African broadcasting, 1924–1971. In *Broadcasting in South Africa,* ed. Ruth Tomaselli, Keyan Tomaselli, and Johann Muller. New York: St. Martin's Press; London: James Currey.

Hebdige, Dick. 1979. *Subculture: The meaning of style.* London: Routledge.

Hemson, David. 1979. Class consciousness and migrant labour: Dockworkers in Durban. Ph.D. diss., University of Warwick.

Herzfeld, Michael. 1985. *The poetics of manhood: Contest and identity in a Cretan mountain village.* Princeton, N.J.: Princeton University Press.

Hobsbawm, Eric. 1983. Inventing traditions. Introduction to *The invention of tradition,* ed. E. Hobsbawm and T. Ranger. Cambridge: Cambridge University Press.

Hollander, J. 1959. *Versions, interpretations, and performances,* ed. R. A. Brower. Cambridge, Mass.: Harvard University Press.

Humphries, Patrick. 1989. *Paul Simon: Still crazy after all these years.* New York: Doubleday.

Huskisson, Yvonne. 1968. *The Bantu composers of southern Africa.* Johannesburg: South African Broadcasting Corporation.

Jameson, Fredric. 1991. *Postmodernism or, the cultural logic of late capitalism.* Durham, N.C.: Duke University Press.

Jones, Schuyler. 1980. Institutions of violence. In *Not work alone: A cross-cultural view of activities superfluous to survival,* ed. Jeremy Cherfas and Roger Lewin. London: Temple Smith.

Joseph, Rosemary. 1987. Zulu women's bow songs: Ruminations on love. *Bulletin of the School of Oriental and African Studies* 50, no. 1:90–119.

Keali'inohomoku, Joann W. 1979. You dance what you wear, and you wear your cultural values. In *The fabrics of culture: The anthropology of clothing and adornment,* ed. Justine M. Cordwell and Ronald A. Schwarz. The Hague: Mouton.

Keegan, Tim. 1988. *Facing the storm: Portraits of black lives in rural South Africa.* London: Zed Books; Athens: Ohio University Press.

Keil, Charles. 1979. *Tiv song.* Chicago: University of Chicago Press.

———. 1985. People's music comparatively: Style and stereotype, class and hegemony. *Dialectical Anthropology* 10, nos. 1–2:119–30.

———. 1987. Participatory discrepancies and the power of music. *Cultural Anthropology* 2, no. 3:275–83.

Kiernan, J. 1974. Where Zionists draw the line: A study of religious exclusiveness in an African township. *African Studies* 33, no. 2:79–90.

———. 1976. Prophet and preacher: An essential partnership in the work of Zion. *Man,* n.s., 3:356–66.

———. 1977. Poor and Puritan: An attempt to view Zionism as a collective response to urban poverty. *African Studies* 36, no. 1:31–41.

———. 1985. The social stuff of revelation: Pattern and purpose in Zionist dreams and visions. *Africa* 55:304–18.

———. 1990. The canticles of Zion: Song as word and action in Zulu Zionist discourse. *Journal of Religion in Africa* 20, no. 2:188–203.

Kivnick, Helen Q. 1990. *Where is the way? Song and struggle in South Africa.* New York: Penguin Books.

Klopper, Sandra. 1989. Mobilizing cultural symbols in twentieth century Zululand. Africa Seminar. University of Cape Town, Centre for African Studies.

———. 1991. You need only one bull to cover fifty cows: Zulu women and "traditional" dress. In *Regions and repertoires: Topics in South African politics and culture,* ed. Stephen Clingman. Johannesburg: Ravan Press.

Koetting, James T. 1975. The effects of urbanization: The music of the Kasena people of Ghana. *World of Music* 17, no. 4:23–31.

Koskoff, Elen, ed. 1987. *Women and music in cross-cultural perspective.* New York: Greenwood Press.

Krige, Eileen. 1950. *The social system of the Zulus.* Pietermaritzburg, South Africa: Shuter & Shooter.

Kristeva, Julia. 1978. Gesture: Practice or communication? In *Social Aspects of the Human Body,* ed. Ted Polhemus. Harmondsworth, England: Penguin Books.

Kuckertz, Heinz. 1990. *Creating order: The image of the homestead in Mpondo social life.* Johannesburg: Witwatersrand University Press.

Kuper, Hilda, and S. Kaplan. 1944. Voluntary associations in an urban township. *African Studies* 3:178–86.

La Hausse, Paul. 1987. The dispersal of the regiments: African popular protest in Durban, 1930. *Journal of Natal and Zulu History* 10:77–102.

———. 1989. The message of the warriors: The ICU, the labouring poor, and the making of a popular political culture in Durban, 1925–1930. In *Holding their ground: Class, locality, and culture in nineteenth- and twentieth-century South Africa,* ed. Philip Bonner, Isabel Hofmeyr, Deborah James, and Tom Lodge. Johannesburg: Witwatersrand University Press and Ravan Press.

———. 1990. The cows of Nongoloza: Youth, crime, and Amalaita gangs in Durban, 1900–1936. *Journal of Southern African Studies* 16, no. 1:79–111.

Langer, Suzanne K. 1953. *Feeling and form: A theory of art.* New York: Charles Scribner's Sons.

Larlham, Peter. 1981. Isicathamia competition in South Africa. *Drama Review* 25, no. 1:108–12.

Lefebvre, Henri. 1991. *The production of space.* Oxford: Basil Blackwell.

Legassick, Martin. 1974. South Africa: Capital accumulation and violence. *Economy and Society* 3.

Lestrade, G. P. 1937. Traditional literature. In *The Bantu-speaking tribes of South Africa: An ethnographical survey,* ed. I. Shapera. London: Routledge & Kegan Paul.

Little, Kenneth. 1957. The role of voluntary associations in West African urbanization. *American Anthropologist* 59 : 579–96.

Lortat-Jacob, Bernard. 1990a. Savoir les chanter, pouvoir en parler: Chants de la passion en Sardaigne. *Cahiers de musiques traditionnelles* 3 : 5–22.

———. 1990b. *Chroniques sardes.* Paris: Julliard.

Lukhele, Andrew Khehla. 1990. *Stokvels in South Africa: Informal savings schemes by blacks for the black community.* Johannesburg: Amagi Books.

Magubane, Bernard Makhosezwe. 1979. *The political economy of race and class in South Africa.* New York: Monthly Review Press.

Malan, Jacques P. 1982. *South African music encyclopedia.* Vol. 2. Cape Town: Oxford University Press.

Malan, Rian. 1990. *My traitor's heart.* London: Bodley Head.

Marcus, George E., ed. 1993. A terrible commitment: Balancing the tribes in South African national culture. In *Perilous states: Conversations on culture, politics, and nation.* Chicago: University of Chicago Press.

Maré, Gerhard. 1992. *Brothers born of warrior blood: Politics and ethnicity in South Africa.* Johannesburg: Ravan Press.

Maré, Gerhard, and Georgina Hamilton. 1987. *An appetite for power: Buthelezi's Inkatha and the politics of "loyal resistance."* Johannesburg: Ravan Press.

Marks, Shula. 1986a. The historiography of South Africa. In *African historiographies,* ed. Bogumil Jewsiewicki and David Newbury. Beverly Hills, Calif.: Sage.

———. 1986b. *The ambiguities of dependence in South Africa: Class, nationalism, and the state in twentieth century Natal.* Johannesburg: Ravan Press.

———. 1989a. Cultures of subordination and subversion. *Social History* 14 : 225–31.

———. 1989b. Patriotism, patriarchy and purity: Natal and the politics of Zulu ethnic consciousness. In *The creation of tribalism in Southern Africa,* ed. Leroy Vail. London: James Currey; Berkeley and Los Angeles: University of California Press.

Marks, Shula, and Richard Rathbone, eds. 1982. Introduction to *Industrialisation and social change in South Africa: African class formation, culture, and consciousness, 1870–1930.* London: Longman.

Martin, Randy. 1990. *Performance as political act: The embodied self.* New York: Bergin & Garvey.

Mayer, Philip, ed. 1980. *Black villagers in an industrial society: anthropological perspectives on labour migration in South Africa.* Cape Town: Oxford University Press.

Mayer, Philip, and Iona Mayer. 1961. Townsmen or tribesmen. Cape Town: Oxford University Press.

Mbatha, Mphiwa B. 1960. Migrant labour and its effects on tribal and family life among the Nyuswa of Botha's Hill. Master's thesis, University of Natal.

McAllister, P. A. 1981. Umsindleko: A Gcaleka ritual of incorporation. Institute of Social and Economic Research Occasional Paper no. 26, Grahamstown.

McCracken, Grant David. 1988. *Culture and consumption.* Bloomington: Indiana University Press.

McNamara, J. K. 1980. Brothers and work mates: Home friend networks in the social life of black migrant workers in a gold mine hostel. In *Black villagers in an industrial society: Anthropological perspectives on labour migration in South Africa,* ed. P. Mayer. Cape Town: Oxford University Press.

Meintjes, Louise. 1990. Paul Simon's *Graceland,* South Africa, and the mediation of musical meaning. *Ethnomusicology* 34, no. 1:37–74.

Merriam, Alan P. 1982. African musical rhythm and concepts of time-reckoning. In *African music in perspective.* New York: Garland Publishing.

Mitchell, J. Clyde. 1956. *The Kalela dance: Aspects of social relationships among urban Africans in Northern Rhodesia.* Rhodes-Livingstone Papers no. 27. Manchester, England: Manchester University Press.

Møller, Valerie. 1985. *Quality of life in retirement. A survey evaluation of return migration to KwaZulu.* Centre for Applied Social Sciences Monograph no. 10. Durban: University of Natal.

———. 1991. *Lost generation found: Black youth at leisure.* Durban: Indicator Project South Africa.

Møller, Valerie, and Lawrence Schlemmer. 1982. Migrant workers: A profile of their rural resources. Centre for Applied Social Sciences Fact Paper no. 5, University of Natal, Durban.

Møller, Valerie, and G. J. Welch. 1985. *Polygamy and well-being among Zulu migrants.* Centre for Applied Social Sciences. Durban: University of Natal.

Moodie, Dunbar. 1988. Migrancy and male sexuality on the South African gold mines. *Journal of Southern African Studies* 14, no. 2:228–56.

———. 1991. Social existence and the practice of personal integrity—narratives of resistance on the South African gold mines. *African Studies* 50, nos. 1–2: 39–64.

Moore, Henrietta L. 1986. *Space, text, and gender: An anthropological study of the Marakwet of Kenya.* Cambridge: Cambridge University Press.

Mthethwa, Bongani N. 1986. Shembe's religious dances: Can African Christianity survive without dance? Paper given at the NERMIC Conference, 3–4 July at University of the Witwatersrand, Johannesburg.

Murray, Colin. 1980. Migrant labour and changing family structure in the rural periphery of Southern Africa. *Journal of Southern African Studies* 6, no. 2: 139–56.

———. 1988. Displaced urbanization: The rural slums. In *South Africa in question,* ed. J. Lonsdale. Cambridge: University of Cambridge African Studies Centre in association with James Currey and Heinemann Educational Books.

———. 1992. *Black mountain: Land, class, and power in the Eastern Orange Free State, 1880s–1980s.* Edinburgh: Edinburgh University Press.

Nettl, Bruno. 1983. *The study of ethnomusicology: Twenty-nine issues and concepts.* Urbana: University of Illinois Press.

Ngubane, Harriet. 1977. *Body and mind in Zulu medicine: An ethnography of health and disease in Nyuswa-Zulu thought and practice.* London: Academic Press.

Ntuli, D. B. 1990. Remarks on Maskandi poetry. *South African Journal of African Languages* 10, no. 4:302–6.

Nyembezi, Cyril Sibusiso. 1963. *Zulu proverbs.* Rev. ed. Johannesburg: Witwatersrand University Press.

Okely, Judith. 1992. Anthropology and autobiography: Participatory experience and embodied knowledge. In *Anthropology and autobiography,* ed. Judith Okely and Helen Callaway. London: Routledge.

Olney, James. 1972. *Metaphors of self: The meaning of autobiography.* Princeton, N.J.: Princeton University Press.

Penfield, Joyce. 1983. *Communicating with quotes: The Igbo case.* Westport, Conn.: Greenwood Press.

Pewa, Eliot S. 1984. The chorus—a re-Africanisation of hymn singing in schools and churches. Bachelor's honors thesis, University of Natal.

Phimister, Ian R., and Charles van Onselen. 1979. The political economy of tribal animosity. A case study of the 1929 Bulawayo location "faction fights." *Journal of Southern African Studies* 6, no. 1:1–43.

Pratt, Mary Louise. 1990. Fieldwork in common places. In *Writing culture: The poetics and politics of ethnography,* ed. James Clifford and George E. Marcus. Berkeley and Los Angeles: University of California Press.

Ramphele, Mamphela. 1993. *A bed called home: Life in the migrant labour hostels of Cape Town.* Cape Town: David Philip.

Ranger, Terence. 1975. *Dance and society in Eastern Africa 1890–1970: The Beni Ngoma.* London: Heinemann.

———. 1993. The invention of tradition revisited: The case of colonial Africa. In *Legitimation and the state in twentieth-century Africa,* ed. Terence Range and Ofumeli Vaughan. Oxford: Macmillan.

Robbins, David. 1984. What's the matter with Msinga? University of Cape Town Carnegie Conference Paper no. 55, Cape Town.

Rosaldo, Renato. 1976. The story of Tubkaw. In *The biographical process: Studies in the history and psychology of religion,* ed. F. E. Reynolds and D. Capps. The Hague: Mouton.

Rycroft, David. 1971. Stylistic evidence in Nguni song. In *Essays on music and history in Africa,* ed. K. P. Wachsmann. Evanston: Northwestern University Press.

———. 1957. Zulu male traditional singing. *African Music* 1, no. 4:33–35.

———. 1977. Evidence of stylistic continuity in Zulu "town" music. In *Essays for a humanist.* Spring Valley, N.Y.: Town House Press.

———. 1985. Zulu melodic and non-melodic vocal styles. Papers presented at the 5th Symposium on Ethnomusicology, ed. Andrew Tracey. International Library of African Music, Grahamstown.

Sack, Steven. 1989. "Garden of Eden or political landscape?": Street art in Mamelodi and other townships. In *African art in Southern Africa: From tradition to township,* ed. Anitra Nettleton and David Hammond-Tooke. Johannesburg: Ad. Donker.

Sarkissian, Margaret. 1992. Gender and music. In *Ethnomusicology: An introduction,* ed. Helen Myers. New York: W. W. Norton.

Schlemmer, Lawrence, and Valerie Møller. 1985. Constraint, stress, and reaction: The responses of migrant contract workers to their situation. In *Up against the fences: Poverty, passes, and privilege in South Africa,* ed. Hermann Giliomee and Lawrence Schlemmer. Cape Town: David Philip.

Schneider, Elizabeth Anne. 1989. Art and communication: Ndzundza Ndebele wall decorations in the Transvaal. In *African art in southern Africa: From tradition to township,* ed. Anitra Nettleton and David Hammond-Tooke. Johannesburg: Ad. Donker.

Schutte, A. G. 1974. Dual religious orientation in an urban African church. *African Studies* 33, no. 2 : 113–20.

Scotch, N. A. 1970. Magic, sorcery, and football among urban Zulu: A case of reinterpretation under acculturation. In *Black Africa: Its peoples and their cultures today,* ed. John Middleton. London: Collier-Macmillan.

Scott, James. 1990. *Domination and the arts of resistance: Hidden transcripts.* New Haven: Yale University Press.

Seeger, Anthony. 1987. *Why Suyá sing: A musical anthropology of an Amazonian people.* Cambridge Studies in Ethnomusicology. Cambridge: Cambridge University Press.

Shostak, Marjorie. 1981. *Nisa. The life and words of a !Kung woman.* Cambridge, Mass.: Harvard University Press.

Simmel, Georg. 1903. Soziologie der Konkurrenz. *Neue Deutsche Rundschau* 14 : 1009–23.

———. 1908. *Soziologie. Untersuchungen über die Formen der Vergesellschaftung.* Leipzig: Duncker & Humblot.

———. 1965. How is society possible? In *Essays on sociology, philosophy, and aesthetics,* ed. and trans. by K. H. Wolff. New York: Harper & Row.

Soja, Edward W. 1989. *Postmodern geographies: The reassertion of space in critical social theory.* London: Verso.

Sitas, Ari. n.d. The flight of the gwala-gwala bird: Ethnicity, populism, and worker culture in Natal's labour movement. Unpublished manuscript.

Sithole, Elkin. 1979. Ngoma music among the Zulu. In *The performing arts: Music and dance,* ed. John Blacking and J. Keali'inohomoku. The Hague: Mouton.

Smith, David M., ed. 1992. *The apartheid city and beyond: Urbanization and social change in South Africa.* London: Routledge.

Spencer, Paul, ed. 1985. *Society and the dance: The social anthropology of process and performance.* Cambridge: Cambridge University Press.

Stadler, Alf. 1987. *The political economy of modern South Africa.* London: Croom Helm; Johannesburg: David Philip.

Stichter, Sharon. 1985. *Migrant laborers.* Cambridge: Cambridge University Press.

Stoller, Paul. 1989. *The taste of ethnographic things: The senses in anthropology.* Philadelphia: University of Pennsylvania Press.

Stone, Ruth. 1982. *Let the inside be sweet: The interpretation of music event among the Kpelle of Liberia.* Bloomington: Indiana University Press.

———. 1985. In search of time in African music. *Music Theory Spectrum* 7 : 139–48.

Sundkler, Bengt G. M. 1961. *Bantu prophets in South Africa.* 2d ed. London: Oxford University Press.

———. 1976. *Zulu Zion and some Swazi Zionists.* London: Oxford University Press.

Tedlock, Barbara, ed. 1987. *Dreaming: Anthropological and psychological interpretations.* Cambridge: Cambridge University Press.

Thomas, Harold J. 1988. Ingoma dancers and their response to town: A study of ingoma dance troupes among Zulu migrant workers in Durban. Bachelor's honors thesis, University of Natal.

Tomaselli, Keyan, and Ruth Tomaselli. 1989. Between policy and practice in the SABC. In *Broadcasting in South Africa,* ed. Keyan Tomaselli, Ruth Tomaselli, and Johan Muller. New York: St. Martin's Press; London: James Currey.

Tomaselli, Keyan, Graham Hayman, Abner Jack, Nofikile Nxumalo, Ruth Tomaselli, Nhlanhla Ngcabo. 1989. Square vision in colour: How TV2/3 negotiates consent. In *Broadcasting in South Africa,* ed. Keyan Tomaselli, Ruth Tomaselli, and Johan Muller. New York: St. Martin's Press; London: James Currey.

Tomaselli, Ruth, Keyan Tomaselli, and Johan Muller. 1989. *Broadcasting in South Africa.* New York: St. Martin's Press; London: James Currey.

Tracey, Hugh. 1948. *Lalela Zulu: One hundred Zulu lyrics.* Johannesburg: African Music Society.

Turino, Thomas. 1989. The coherence of social style and musical creation among the Aymara in southern Peru. *Ethnomusicology* 33, no. 1 : 1–30.

———. 1993. *Moving away from silence: Music of the Peruvian altiplano and the experience of urban migration.* Chicago: University of Chicago Press.

Turner, Terence S. 1980. The social skin. In *Not work alone: A cross-cultural view of activities superfluous to survival,* ed. Jeremy Cherfas and Roger Lewin. London: Temple Smith.

Turner, Victor. 1982. *From ritual to theatre: The human seriousness of play.* New York: PAJ Publications.

———. 1985. *On the edge of the bush: Anthropology as experience.* Ed. Edith Turner. Tucson: University of Arizona Press.

Tyler, Stephen A. 1986. Post-modern ethnography: From document of the occult to occult document. In *Writing culture: The poetics and politics of ethnography.* Berkeley and Los Angeles: University of California Press.

Vail, Leroy, ed. 1989. *The creation of tribalism in southern Africa.* London: James Currey; Berkeley and Los Angeles: University of California Press.

Vail, Leroy, and Landeg White. 1991. *Power and the praise poem: Southern African voices in history.* Charlottesville: University Press of Virginia; London: James Currey.

van Onselen, Charles. 1982. *Studies in the social and economic history of the Witwatersrand, 1886–1914.* Vol. 1, *New Babylon.* Vol. 2, *New Nineveh.* Johannesburg: Ravan Press.

———. 1988. Race and class in the South African countryside: Cultural osmosis and social relations in the sharecropping economy of the South-Western Transvaal, 1900–1950. African Studies Seminar Paper no. 237. Johannesburg, African Studies Institute, University of the Witwatersrand.

Vilakazi, Absolom. 1965. *Zulu transformations: A study of the dynamics of social change*. Pietermaritzburg, South Africa: University of Natal Press.

Wachsmann, Klaus Peter. 1961. Criteria for acculturation. Report of the Eighth Congress of the International Musicological Society.

Walker, Cherryl. 1990. Gender and the development of the migrant labour system, c. 1850–1930: An overview. In *Women and gender in Southern Africa to 1945,* ed. Cherryl Walker. Cape Town: David Philip.

Wallis, Roger, and Krister Malm. 1984. *Big sounds from small peoples: The music industry in small countries*. New York: Pendragon.

Walser, Robert. 1993. *Running with the devil: Power, gender, and madness in heavy metal music*. Hanover, N.H.: Wesleyan University Press.

Waterman, Christopher. 1990. *Jùjú: A social history and ethnography of an African popular music*. Chicago: University of Chicago Press.

———. 1991a. Yoruba MTV: Fuji style as a map of transnational networks. Unpublished MS.

1991b. Jùjú history: Toward a theory of sociomusical practice. In *Ethnomusicology and modern music history,* ed. Stephen Blum, Philip V. Bohlman, and Daniel M. Neuman. Urbana: University of Illinois Press.

Weintraub, Karl J. 1975. Autobiography and historical consciousness. *Critical Inquiry* 1, no 4:821–48.

Werbner, Richard P. 1990. Bwiti in reflection: On the fugue of gender. *Journal of Religion in Africa* 20, no. 1:63–91.

West, Martin. 1975. *Bishops and prophets in a black city: African independent churches in Soweto, Johannesburg*. Cape Town: David Philip.

White, Hayden. 1973. *Metahistory: The historical imagination in nineteenth-century Europe*. Baltimore: Johns Hopkins University Press.

Willan, Brian P. 1978. The South African native labour contingent, 1916–1918. *Journal of African History* 14, no. 1.

Wilson, Francis. 1972. *Migrant labour*. Johannesburg: South African Council of Churches and Spro-Cas.

Wilson, Monica, and Archie Mafeje. 1963. *Langa: A study of social groups in an African township*. Cape Town: Oxford University Press.

Wolpe, Harold. 1972. Capitalism and cheap labour power: From segregation to apartheid. *Economy and Society* 1:425–56.

Wright, John. 1986. Politics, ideology, and the invention of "Nguni." Vol. 4 of *Southern African Studies,* ed. T. Lodge. Johannesburg: Ravan Press.

Xulu, Musa K. 1992. The re-emergence of Amahubo song styles and ideas in some modern Zulu musical styles. Ph.D. diss., University of Natal, Durban.

Yotamu, Moses. 1979. My two weeks fieldwork in Ivory Coast. *Review of Ethnology* 6, nos. 21–24:161–92.

Index

437